The Future of
Interreligious Dialogue

The Future of Interreligious Dialogue

A Multireligious Conversation on Nostra Aetate

Edited by

Charles L. Cohen

Paul F. Knitter

Ulrich Rosenhagen

ORBIS BOOKS

Maryknoll, New York 10545

ORBIS BOOKS
Maryknoll, New York 10545

Fathers and Brothers
MARYKNOLL™

Founded in 1970, Orbis Books endeavors to publish works that enlighten the mind, nourish the spirit, and challenge the conscience. The publishing arm of the Maryknoll Fathers and Brothers, Orbis seeks to explore the global dimensions of the Christian faith and mission, to invite dialogue with diverse cultures and religious traditions, and to serve the cause of reconciliation and peace. The books published reflect the views of their authors and do not represent the official position of the Maryknoll Society. To learn more about Maryknoll and Orbis Books, please visit our website at www.maryknollsociety.org.

This book was published with the support of the Lubar Institute for the Study of the Abrahamic Religions at the University of Wisconsin-Madison.

Lubar Institute
for the Study of the Abrahamic Religions
University of Wisconsin–Madison

Published by Orbis Books, Maryknoll, New York 10545-0302.
Manufactured in the United States of America.

Library of Congress Cataloging-in-Publication Data

Names: Cohen, Charles Lloyd, editor.
Title: The future of interreligious dialogue : a multi-religious conversation
    on Nostra aetate / edited by Charles L. Cohen, Paul Knitter, and Ulrich Rosenhagen.
Description: Maryknol : Orbis Books, 2017. | Includes bibliographical references
    and index.
    Identifiers: LCCN 2017005160 (print) | LCCN 2017026376 (ebook) |
    ISBN 9781608337101 (e-book) | ISBN 9781626982451 (pbk.)
Subjects: LCSH: Catholic Church—Relations. | Christianity and other religions. |
    Vatican Council (2nd : 1962–1965 : Basilica di San Pietro in Vaticano).
    Declaratio de ecclesiae habitudine ad religiones non-Christianas.
Classification: LCC BX1787 (ebook) | LCC BX1787 .F88 2017 (print) |
    DDC 201/.5—dc23
LC record available at https://lccn.loc.gov/2017005160

In Memory of Rita M. Gross

Participant in Our Two-Day Conference

Scholar, Advocate, and Friend for a Lifetime

CONTENTS

Introduction: Some Declarations on the Relation of the Non-Christian
     Religions to the Church 1
Charles L. Cohen

Part I. *Nostra Aetate*: Origins and Challenges

1. *Nostra Aetate*: Origin, History, and Vatican II Context 23
 John Borelli

2. *Nostra Aetate*: A Milestone in the History of Religions?
 From Competition to Cooperation 45
 Paul F. Knitter

Part II. Roman Catholic Perspectives

3. Foreign to the Mind of Christ: *Nostra Aetate* in America's
 Religio-Racial Project 61
 Jeannine Hill Fletcher

4. Toward a Renewed Theology of Christianity's Bond with Judaism 77
 John T. Pawlikowski, OSM

5. The Christian Spiritual Vision from the Perspective of
 Nostra Aetate 93
 Roger Haight, SJ

Part III. Protestant and Orthodox Christian Perspectives

6. Fullness of Truth in Christ Alone: Early Protestant Responses
 to *Nostra Aetate* 107
 Ulrich Rosenhagen

7. Social Justice in *Nostra Aetate* and in Black Liberation Theology 127
 Dwight N. Hopkins

8. *Nostra Aetate*: Views from a Sibling on Inclusivism and Pluralism 143
 Peter C. Bouteneff

Part IV. Jewish Perspectives

9. "Who Do You Say That I Am?" Jewish Responses to *Nostra Aetate*
    and Post-Holocaust Christianity 159
    Rabbi David Fox Sandmel

10. Lot's Wife: On the Dangers of Looking Back......................... 179
    Rabbi Shira L. Lander

Part V. Islamic Perspectives

11. Beyond the Rays of Truth? *Nostra Aetate*, Islam, and the
    Value of Difference... 203
    Jerusha Tanner Lamptey

12. A Muslim Woman's Perspective on Interreligious Dialogue
    in the Light of *Nostra Aetate* 219
    Riffat Hassan

Part VI. Buddhist and Hindu Perspectives

13. A Buddhist Response to *Nostra Aetate* 237
    Rita M. Gross

14. The Eternal Veda and the "Truth which Enlightens All":
    Correspondences and Disjunctures between Nostra Aetate and
    Swami Vivekananda's Vedantic Inclusivism 249
    Jeffery D. Long

Part VII. Moving with and beyond *Nostra Aetate*

15. In Our Time: Coformation as a Modality for Interreligious
    Teaching and Learning 265
    Jennifer Howe Peace

16. Buddhism and Christianity in a Globalizing and
    Supplementing World... 275
    Sallie B. King

17. Learning from (and Not Just about) Our Religious Neighbors:
    Comparative Theology and the Future of *Nostra Aetate* 289
    John J. Thatamanil

List of Contributors... 303

Index 309

Introduction:
Some Declarations on the Relation of the Non-Christian Religions to the Church

Charles L. Cohen

The Second Vatican Council (1962–65), popularly known as Vatican II, was arguably one of the most transformative religious events of the twentieth century.[1] The first ecumenical council convened in nearly a century, it initiated far-reaching changes in how the Roman Catholic Church understands itself and wants to present itself to the rest of the world. In an effort to lead the faithful to "fully conscious, and active participation" in the liturgy, the council introduced such reforms as celebrating the Mass in the vernacular rather than in Latin and rotating the officiant's posture so that he showed the congregation his face rather than his back.[2] Perhaps even more dramatically, the council—cognizant of the "serious difficulties" that a "new stage of history" had imposed on human life—positioned the church to accommodate rather than rebuke modernity; as announced in *Gaudium et Spes*, one of four constitutions the conclave proclaimed, the church "sincerely professes that all men [*sic*], believers and unbelievers alike, ought to work for the rightful betterment of this world in which all alike live," an ideal that requires "sincere and prudent dialogue."[3] In this vein, the council took major, perhaps unprecedented, steps to open and refresh the church's conversations with other religious bodies. Lamenting the division among Christians that "scandalizes the world," it recognized the "movement toward unity . . . called 'ecumenical'"—among Trinitarians, at least—and set out the ways in which Catholics too could respond to this

---

[1] For a brief introduction to the council in the context of Christian history, see Diarmaid MacCulloch, *Christianity: The First Three Thousand Years* (New York: Viking, 2009), 967–75.

[2] *Constitution on the Sacred Liturgy—Sacrosanctum Concilium*, promulgated by Pope Paul VI (Vatican City, 1963), sec. 14, http://www.vatican.va/archive/hist_councils/ii_vatican_council/documents/vat-ii_const_19631204_sacrosanctum-concilium_en.html.

[3] *Pastoral Constitution on the Church in the Modern World—Gaudium et Spes*, promulgated by Pope Paul VI (Vatican City, 1965), secs. 4, 21, http://www.vatican.va/archive/hist_councils/ii_vatican_council/documents/vat-ii_cons_19651207_gaudium-et-spes_en.html. Pope Pius IX's "Syllabus of Errors" (1864) represents a less generous view of modernity in its generation.

"grace" and "divine call."[4] Even more strikingly, having "consider[ed] what men [*sic*] have in common," it "exhort[ed]" the faithful to "dialogue and collaboration with the followers of other religions." The main text for this unilateral approach to non-Christians was the declaration *Nostra Aetate*—"In Our Time."[5]

Nostra Aetate emerged as the church sought to resituate itself in a world that war and decolonization had convulsed. As the council convened, concerns generated by Hitler's "Final Solution" and political upheavals in the Third World converged to fix attention on the church's relationship with other religions. The Holocaust had implicated Christianity in endorsing genocide. To what degree might nearly two millennia of supersessionist theology and preached contempt against Jews and Judaism have underwritten the death camps? Pope John XXIII and the German Cardinal Augustin Bea, SJ, took special pains to place the church's troubled relationship with the Jews on the council's agenda. Tackling that issue did not, however, necessitate a wholesale reappraisal of the church's stance toward other faiths. *Nostra Aetate*'s broader overtures grew from interests voiced by loosely connected groups of scholars, missionaries, and clergy, many of whom served in areas recently freed from European hegemony. As John Borelli demonstrates, one set, working in Muslim lands, urged a "more positive assessment" of Islam; another, primarily bishops from Africa and Asia, warned of pressures menacing Catholic minorities. Support for creating closer ties with non-Christian believers swelled as the council progressed, yet, as Borelli relates, no one at the time could have guaranteed that it would deliver a statement even about Judaism, let alone any other religion. Steering successive drafts through political maelstroms required extensive shepherding, notably by Pope Paul VI, who ascended to Saint Peter's throne after John XXIII died in June 1963.[6] In the end, those voices supporting open conversations with other faiths won out. The document that the council promulgated on October 28, 1965, muted traditional Christian triumphalism. It overturned the theological basis for antisemitism, insisting that "the Jews should not be presented as rejected or accursed by God, as if this followed from the Holy Scriptures," encouraged Catholics to "recognize, preserve and promote the good things, spiritual and moral, as well as the socio-cultural values found" among non-Christians, and climaxed by reproving "any discrimination against men [*sic*] or harassment of them because of their race, color, condition of life, or religion."[7] Borelli deems the proclamation "one of the council's greatest achievements."[8] By comparison, argues

---

[4] *Decree on Ecumenism—Unitatis Redintegratio*, promulgated by Pope Paul VI (Vatican City, 1964), sec. 1, http://www.vatican.va.

[5] *Declaration on the Relation of the Church to Non-Christian Religions—Nostra Aetate*, proclaimed by Pope Paul VI (Vatican City, 1965), sec. 2, http://www.vatican.va/archive/hist_councils/ii_vatican_council/documents/vat-ii_decl_19651028_nostra-aetate_en.html.

[6] John Borelli, "*Nostra Aetate*: Origin, History, and Vatican II Context," chapter 1 of this volume.

[7] *Nostra Aetate*, secs. 4, 2, 5.

[8] Borelli, "*Nostra Aetate*: Origin, History, and Vatican II Context."

Ulrich Rosenhagen, a Lutheran clergyman, Protestants have "failed to produce a text of their own of equal reach and significance," certainly nothing as comprehensively welcoming to interreligious dialogue as what *Nostra Aetate* essayed.[9]

Small wonder, then, that *Nostra Aetate*'s golden anniversary in 2015 occasioned widespread commemorations. Addressing an interreligious general audience fifty years to the day after its pronouncement, Pope Francis extolled its "always timely" message, noted the past half-century's multitude of "events, initiatives, institutional or personal relationships with the non-Christian religions," and urged both believers and nonbelievers to cooperate in tackling such global problems as war, hunger, poverty, the environmental crisis, and violence, "especially that [violence] committed in the name of religion."[10] During a three-day conference hosted by the Pontifical Gregorian University that drew more than 350 delegates from around the world, the audience was scheduled to attend panels with titles such as "Violence and the Engagement of Religions for Peace," whose two round tables paired a Muslim with a Jew, and a Catholic with a Buddhist.[11] Among the many celebrations of *Nostra Aetate*'s fiftieth anniversary, a few had political overtones,[12] but more emphasized religious, cultural, or festive themes.[13] Strictly academic proceedings were relatively infrequent, although three leading US Catholic universities hosted major scholarly gatherings.[14] A complete survey of all the commemorative conferences

---

[9] Ulrich Rosenhagen, "Fullness of Truth in Christ Alone: Early Protestant Responses to *Nostra Aetate*," chapter 6 of this volume.

[10] Pope Francis, "Interreligious General Audience on the Occasion of the 50th Anniversary of the Promulgation of the Conciliar Declaration 'Nostra Aetate,'" October 28, 2015, 1, 3, https://w2.vatican.va/content/francesco/en/audiences/2015/documents/papa-francesco_20151028_udienza-generale.html.

[11] See the conference program, "50th Anniversary of '*Nostra Aetate*': The Declaration of the Second Vatican Council on the Relations of the Catholic Church with Non-Christian Religions," http://www.unigre.it/Univ/eventi/documenti_15_16/151026_28_PUG_Nosta_Aetate_programma_v4_en.pdf; Rabbi Gilbert S. Rosenthal, "A Conference Marking the Fiftieth Anniversary of *Nostra Aetate* at the Gregorian Pontifical University in Rome October 26–28, 2015," http://nationalcouncilofsynagogues.org/wp-content/uploads/docs/CONFERENCE%20AT%20THE%20GREGORIAN%20OCT%2026-282015.pdf.

[12] The Israeli Embassy to the Holy See and the Pontifical Urbaniana University organized a conference during which Ambassador Zion Evrony stated that the Vatican's "'recognition of the State of Israel" would "not have been possible" without *Nostra Aetate*. See "Conference—50th Anniversary of Nostra Aetate," on the Embassy's website, http://embassies.gov.il/holysee-en/NewsAndEvents/Pages/conference-to-commemorate-the-50th-anniversary-of-the-Conciliar-Declaration-Nostra-Aetate.aspx.

[13] See, for example, the "Jubilee" put on by the Roman Catholic Archdiocese of Atlanta and the American Jewish Committee Atlanta, which culminated in "a celebration of art, music and religion," "A New Era in Catholic-Jewish Relations," http://archatl.com/events/nostra-aetate.

[14] Catholic University of America: "*Nostra Aetate:* Celebrating Fifty Years of the Catholic Church's Dialogue with Jews and Muslims," http://www.cuatoday.com/s/817/

is impossible, but a quick search of the internet reveals some predictable patterns: the hosting organizations were predominantly Roman Catholic; the occasions usually included Catholic clergy (with the more prestigious ones featuring the weightiest churchmen); the dominant perspective tended to emanate from the church rather than from outside it; and programming leaned toward celebration rather than analysis. Many events targeted the church's relationship with a specific religious group—Jews most usually, Muslims occasionally, and adherents of non-Abrahamic religions almost never.[15] Given *Nostra Aetate*'s signal reinterpretation of Judaism and the contemporary tensions caused by certain Islamist movements, these inclinations are hardly surprising. Nevertheless, *Nostra Aetate*'s more universalistic implications—its inclusion of Hindus and Buddhists, its call for ending discrimination—seem to have been overlooked.[16]

This book distills reflections on *Nostra Aetate* prompted by a conference that departed from the norm in several ways. It took place at a public university—the University of Wisconsin–Madison—neutral ground that favored no religious tradition as a host. The meeting was sponsored by an academic center, the Lubar

---

internal.aspx?sid=817&gid=1&pgid=2904&crid=0&calpgid=61&calcid=3803; Georgetown University: "Vatican II—Remembering the Future: Ecumenical, Interfaith and Secular Perspectives on the Council's Impact and Promise," http://dc2015.ei-research.net/program/; http://dc2015.ei-research.net/wp-content/uploads/2014/06/DC2015-Main-Program.pdf; University of Notre Dame: "Church and Synagogue: Conceptions of Community in Jewish and Christian Thought," http://theology.nd.edu/events/special-events/upcoming-special-events/nostra-aetate-conference.

[15] For Catholic-Jewish events, see, for instance, "Symposium Marking the 50th Anniversary of the Second Vatican Council" at Tel-Aviv, University, which included the deputy-president of Israel's Supreme Court, the president of the Pontifical Commission for Religious Relations with the Jews, and the Latin Patriarch of Jerusalem, https://networks.h-net.org/node/2645/discussions/101101/symposium-marking-50th-anniversary-second-vatican-council-%E2%80%9Cnostra; and "Jewish, Catholic Leaders Mark Historic Anniversary," a celebration in Miami Gardens, Florida, presented by the American Jewish Committee, the Archdiocese of Miami, and Saint Thomas University. For a Catholic-Muslim event, see "Catholics, Muslims Seek Common Ground at Troy Interfaith Gathering," *Michigan Catholic*, October 30, 2015, http://www.themichigancatholic.org/2015/10/catholics-muslims-seek-common-ground-at-troy-interfaith-gathering. For an event that did go beyond the Abrahamic religions (initiated, interestingly, by the Islamic Networks Group in San Jose, California), see "Fiftieth Anniversary of Nostra Aetate: Hindu Reflection," https://ing.org/events/fiftieth-anniversary-of-nostra-aetate-hindu-reflection.

[16] Though see the Anniversary Reflections by the Australian Catholic Bishops Conference 2015, which, besides showing pictures of Buddhists and Hindus, counsels Catholics wanting to build dialogue to, among other things, "offer greetings on major feast days, such as *Deepavali* (Hindu) . . . and *Vesach* (Buddhist)," "Nostra Aetate: Declaration on the Relation of the Church to Non-Christian Religions," https://www.catholic.org.au/about/bishops/statements/1726-nostra-aetate-declaration-on-the-relation-of-the-church-to-non-christian-religions-50th-anniversary.

Institute for the Study of the Abrahamic Religions, whose mission—"to create better understanding of the Abrahamic traditions and their interrelationships by encouraging ongoing discussion of these traditions among scholars, members of those traditions, and the general public"—highlighted its dedication to researching and promoting interreligious exchanges.[17] Although focused primarily on Judaism, Christianity, and Islam, the institute extended its programming beyond those borders when appropriate, which was certainly the case for exploring *Nostra Aetate* thoroughly. In accordance with the institute's priorities, the organizers cum editors from the outset conceived of a conference in which participants would examine *Nostra Aetate* from different religious, theological, and cultural vantage points, privileging no faith's doctrines. We instructed invitees to evaluate its historical significance, offer a critique of its content, assess where it may have brought interreligious dialogue in the present, and suggest ways of improving such efforts in the future. Intent on publishing the conference's deliberations, we sought to maximize the perspectives brought to bear on each essay, designing the event as a workshop more than a formal conference. Authors submitted their papers beforehand so that everyone could read them prior to the event. During each session, presenters quickly summarized their arguments, leaving the majority of time for discussion. We returned these papers with initial comments, reviewed subsequent drafts, and selected the strongest articles for publication. Another round of comments and revision followed.

As the chapters below attest, the contributors have reached a consensus in assessing *Nostra Aetate*: it constituted a milestone in interreligious dialogue. Milestones, however, do not move; they only demarcate a point left behind en route. Now, these essays urge, people of faith must not merely appreciate that other traditions reflect a "ray of that Truth which enlightens all men [*sic*]"; they must risk suspending their own beliefs at least long enough to entertain the ways in which those rays might enlighten themselves.[18] How to foster such collaborative dialogue is no easy task, however, a challenge reflected in the variety of suggestions for moving ahead; on this subject, the participants reached greater accord about ends than means. By any accounting, though, the contributors have ably fulfilled their brief by assessing *Nostra Aetate* and its influence candidly, and the editors hope

---

[17] See http://lubar.wisc.edu/welcome/mission.html. As a unit within an American public university, the Lubar Institute had no denominational ties; needless to say, the University of Wisconsin–Madison does not offer formal courses in theology. For an example of an academic conference that did occur in such a context, see "Conference Report: Kirchliche Zeitgeschichte Meeting, 2015," which reports on a conference held at Carl von Ossietzky University, "'Ein neues Klima': Rezeptionsgeschichte des Zweiten Vatikanischen Konzils in Ost- und Mitteleuropa," hosted by the Institut für Evangelische Theologie at Oldenburg, https://contemporarychurchhistory.org/2016/03/conference-report-kirchliche-zeitge-schichte-meeting-2015.

[18] *Nostra Aetate*, sec. 2.

that their labors have produced a collective exegesis worthy of the document. We also acknowledge an ironic gap in this volume's coverage. No speaker considered any of the "world religions"—e.g., Confucianism, Jainism, or the Baha'i Faith—that *Nostra Aetate* overlooked, let alone the indigenous traditions whose spiritual insights, however profound they may be, the proclamation backhandedly compared to the "more refined concepts" and "developed language" of faiths associated with "an advanced culture."[19] Committed to examining what *Nostra Aetate* actually inscribed, this book has replicated its structural logic, thereby failing to fully take heed of everyone whom the church—and all of us who tread in *Nostra Aetate's* steps—might want to engage.[20]

Nostra Aetate in History, History in *Nostra Aetate*

Academic conferences are not always noteworthy for producing agreements, but, as these essays demonstrate, in this instance participants across the religious spectrum concur with Borelli's claim that *Nostra Aetate* is historically momentous. Writing as a Catholic, Paul Knitter deems the declaration "monumental" and "revolutionary" because it "calls Christians to an attitude toward other religions that they had simply never held before." Its invitation to dialogue was so transformative that one might regard it as auguring a new "axial age," a "quantum evolution in religious consciousness." Mirroring this sentiment from a Muslim perspective, Riffat Hassan acknowledges that *Nostra Aetate* likewise holds "profound historic significance" for non-Christians, especially those specifically mentioned. Sallie King echoes that judgment, calling it a "visionary and courageous declaration" from whose openness to other religions "Buddhists have particularly benefited."[21] The profundity of its accomplishment can be gleaned by comparing its opening to non-Christians with the lack of effort undertaken by Christianity's other major branches. Despite efforts by groups like the World Council of Churches to achieve a more positive relationship with other believers, Protestant churches have, as Rosenhagen points out, "often rejected outright *Nostra Aetate's* dialogical engagement with other religions." For the most part they have been unable (or unwilling) to consider "interfaith dialogue" as a "legitimate way of communicating the Christian gospel" without regarding conversation partners as targets for conversion.[22] The Orthodox have done even less.

---

[19] Ibid.

[20] Nor does it mention atheists, who are excluded for the obvious reason that *Nostra Aetate* does not regard them as conversation partners, but whose interest in matters of ethics, justice, and discrimination raised by *Nostra Aetate* might warrant rethinking their dismissal.

[21] Paul Knitter, "*Nostra Aetate*: A Milestone in the History of Religions? From Competition to Cooperation," chapter 2 of this volume; Riffat Hassan, "A Muslim Woman's Perspective on Interreligious Dialogue in the Light of *Nostra Aetate*," chapter 12 of this volume; and Sallie B. King, "Buddhism and Christianity in a Globalizing and Supplementing World," chapter 16 of this volume.

[22] Rosenhagen, "Fullness of Truth in Christ Alone."

Perhaps the strongest appreciation of *Nostra Aetate*'s capacity to inspire religious change comes from Dwight Hopkins, a Baptist, who credits it for pioneering the link between interreligious dialogue and social justice that would subsequently be elaborated by black liberation theology, a line of thought that he espouses. Originally voiced by such figures as Martin Luther King Jr. and James Cone, this hermeneutic emerged not so coincidentally in the immediate aftermath of Vatican II, insisting that any reflections valuing human dignity "must deal with the social and economic conditions that oppress the health of individuals and communities." Hopkins asserts that black liberation theology has magnified the implications of *Nostra Aetate*'s final section, which reproved discrimination on the basis of "race, color, condition of life, or religion," as "foreign to the mind of Christ,"[23] especially as they pertain to race and class. Black liberation theology and other forms of liberation theology argue that fully realizing every person's worth means giving oppressed communities more power and resources, a position affirmed by both the teachings of Jesus and the biblical doctrine that we are created in God's image. *Nostra Aetate*'s call for sustained interreligious dialogue was "prescient" because, according to Hopkins, it linked interfaith comity to broader concerns about social justice that black liberation theology has since emphasized.[24]

As transformative as *Nostra Aetate* may have been, however, the contributors also agree that it constitutes a rickety platform for launching further progress in interreligious dialogue because it does not treat non-Christian interlocutors as equals. Knitter laments that it poses "serious and threatening obstacles" for the future because it inscribes a tension "between affirming the value of other religions and the need for dialogue, on the one hand, and asserting the supremacy of Christianity—Catholic Christianity—over all other religions, on the other." Jerusha Lamptey details how this dynamic works in the specific case of Catholic–Muslim relations. *Nostra Aetate* is novel in acknowledging that it can find worth in some Muslim beliefs and practice, but this statement is not the same thing as esteeming other traditions "holistically" or accepting the possibility that they may have something "unfamiliar yet valuable" to offer the church. "In *Nostra Aetate*," she charges, "the 'rays' found outside of the church must always emanate from and reflect the familiar contours of the 'sun' that is Christ." Islam, consequently, becomes a "distant other" requiring no "deep theological engagement" or self-reappraisal. Restating Lamptey's critique in general terms, Rita Gross faults *Nostra Aetate* for regarding religious diversity as problematic rather than normative and for refusing to concede that "teachings that may be unknown to or quite different from Catholic or Christian teachings might be workable and worthwhile." John Thatamanil caps off this appraisal by calling the declaration captive to "an ethos of religious self-sufficiency," the unexamined postulate that the church "possesses all it needs to know about religious truth," thus implying that Christians have no need to learn anything about the

---

[23] Dwight N. Hopkins, "Social Justice in *Nostra Aetate* and in Black Liberation Theology," chapter 7 of this volume (emphasis in original); *Nostra Aetate*, sec. 5.

[24] Hopkins, "Social Justice in *Nostra Aetate*."

divine life from their neighbors.[25] In *Nostra Aetate*, the chorus declaims, the church speaks of reverencing non-Christians' truths while its own voice drifts into one ear and out the other.

Jeannine Hill Fletcher deepens the analysis of *Nostra Aetate*'s limitations by demonstrating how social and ideological factors heightened the theological contradictions already noted. She agrees that its departure from the long-standing assertion that no one is saved outside the church was "groundbreaking," but its potential for encouraging open conversations between Catholics and members of other religions was muted, at least in the United States, by its submersion in the US church's religio-racial project. A racial project, Hill Fletcher explains, assigns people to categories on the basis of constructed races and apportions material benefits accordingly. These categories influence how religion—like any cultural formation—is lived out, and sometimes the boundaries between racial and religious identification elide. *Nostra Aetate* was released at a moment when the conjunction of the civil rights movement and the Immigration Act of 1965 positioned the United States "on the horizon of greater racial justice and increased religious diversity," and its internal logic created the possibility for imagining a religio-racial project "grounded in justice and mutuality," one that would welcome both "nonwhite[s] and non-Christian[s]." This possibility was stunted, however, because the majority of US Catholics (like other US Christians) understood Jesus and their church as white, thereby subordinating the interests of co-religionists who are black and frustrating approaches to nonwhite newcomers importing their own faiths. Not only did *Nostra Aetate* assert Christian supremacy, its tacit complicity in the religio-racial project of whiteness, coupled with its manifest argument about the cultural superiority of certain world religions, "would have allowed US Catholics in 1965 to value the Other only insofar as the Other may have reflected truths Catholics themselves already held." Whatever its intentions, Hill Fletcher concludes, *Nostra Aetate*'s rhetorical force, confined by its insistence on Christian supremacy, was perhaps insufficient to overcome "the notion of the United States as a white Christian nation" and to generate the interfaith (and, necessarily, interracial) dialogue to which it aspired. Reading Hill Fletcher in tandem with Hopkins suggests why the most robust articulation of *Nostra Aetate*'s antidiscrimination clauses came from African American Protestants rather than Caucasian Catholics.[26]

Although most chapters are less avowedly immersed in history than Hill Fletcher's or Borelli's, an awareness that *Nostra Aetate* both embeds and is embedded in the past threads through the book. History and memory substantially influence

---

[25] Knitter, "*Nostra Aetate*: A Milestone"; Jerusha Tanner Lamptey, "Beyond the Rays of Truth? *Nostra Aetate*, Islam, and the Value of Difference," chapter 11 of this volume; Rita M. Gross, "A Buddhist Response to *Nostra Aetate*," chapter 13 of this volume; and John J. Thatamanil, "Learning from (and not just about) Our Religious Neighbors: Comparative Theology and the Future of *Nostra Aetate*," chapter 17 of this volume.

[26] Jeannine Hill Fletcher, "Foreign to the Mind of Christ: *Nostra Aetate* in America's Religio-Racial Project," chapter 3 of this volume.

non-Christians' reception of it. Jeffery Long's discussion of Swami Vivekananda, the nineteenth-century Indian monk and religious thinker who popularized Vedanta in the West, provides one example. Vivekananda's understanding of the Hindu tradition as accepting all religions as true while upholding the *Vedas* as the ultimate repository of sacred wisdom parallels *Nostra Aetate*'s respect for other faiths while nevertheless witnessing to the "fullness of religious life" found in Christ. Some Hindus follow his lead, Long notes, and identify Christ as "the very eternal truth proclaimed by the *Vedas*," but others demur—not on theological grounds, but because they resent Christianity's "predatory" proselytizing and "demonization" of Hinduism, behaviors rooted in the "historical realities" of imperial conquest and evangelization. The longer, bloodier conflict between Christianity and Islam underlies why, Hassan comments, major messages of goodwill between the confessions encode a selective amnesia. *Nostra Aetate* recognizes that "many quarrels and hostilities" have divided Christians and Muslims but studiously refuses to discuss them, urging instead that the two parties simply "forget the past." A similar tack surfaces in "A Common Word between Us and You"—the reply by Muslim clerics, scholars, and politicians to Pope Benedict's 2006 Regensburg speech accusing Muhammad of condoning violence to spread Islam. "A Common Word" has become the most important recent Muslim statement promoting interfaith reconciliation. Seeking to correct what it regarded as the pope's inaccuracies, the open letter avoided religious differences while emphasizing the twin "*'golden' commandments*" to love God and one's neighbor—the titular "common word" that Christians and Muslims share. Well aware of theological differences as well as "the long history of conflict and confrontation," the authors in each case chose to avoid them because unpacking them, Hassan presumes, would not have conduced to building the positive relationship both documents envision.[27]

Strategic forgetfulness is not an option in the case of Jewish-Catholic relations. As we have seen, the desire for the church to grapple with this "troubled relationship" was central to the concerns that eventuated in *Nostra Aetate*. Rather than alluding generically to a few "quarrels and hostilities," as it did in addressing Islam, *Nostra Aetate* deliberately invokes the seminal events of church history and Christianity's sibling rivalry with Judaism—the implication of Jews in the execution of Jesus, their rejection of Jesus as the Messiah, and the opposition of "not a few" Jews to the gospel's spread.[28] After enduring nearly two millennia of taunts and terrors actuated by Christian vengefulness, Jews' suspicion of—indeed, aversion to—Christians and Christianity has cemented itself into their historical consciousness. Collective nightmares about antisemites explain why the two essays on Jewish responses are less concerned than any other set of essays with imagining specific ways to move beyond interreligious relationships as set out in *Nostra Aetate*, and

---

[27] Jeffery D. Long, "The Eternal Veda and the 'Truth Which Enlightens All': Correspondences and Disjunctures between *Nostra Aetate* and Swami Vivekananda's Vedantic Inclusivism," chapter 14 of this volume; Hassan, "Muslim Woman's Perspective."

[28] Borelli, "*Nostra Aetate*: Origin, History, and Vatican II Context"; *Nostra Aetate*, sec. 4.

more focused on assessing Jews' capacity to believe that the church's change of heart toward them and their religion evidenced in Vatican II can be trusted. Reviewing six diverse Jewish responses—most issuing from private parties, and none of which claims to be authoritative—Rabbi David Sandmel concludes that they all both presume that Protestant as well as Catholic teachings about Jews and Judaism have "changed for the better" and that they manifest the positive "sea change" in Jewish-Christian relations that *Nostra Aetate* initiated. Nevertheless, he observes that "official pronouncements" alone do not necessarily betoken the "complete elimination of anti-Jewish thinking or attitudes," and that, since the "new era of Jewish-Christian relations is in its infancy," celebrating it "might be premature." Rabbi Shira Lander is even more forceful in rehearsing Jewish trepidation, noting that Jews have been "slow to respond to Catholic gestures," hesitance she attributes to Jews' historical memory and long experience of subjection. Less optimistic than Sandmel about how much Jews may have shrugged off their doubts, she contends that understanding the roles collective remembrance plays in the present may help Jews move beyond a "lachrymose recitation of history" to chart a new relationship "built on mutual understanding and respect." Forging strong interfaith relationships in the future, numerous contributors make clear, will require facing the past with more than good faith alone.[29]

Framing the Future

Nostra Aetate postulated a universe of interreligious relationships centered on the unquestioned salvific superiority of the Roman Catholic Church. To employ a comparative taxonomy that scholars and theologians frequently use to evaluate religions, this position belongs within the category of inclusivism, which can be defined, per Long, as the stance that one's own religion possesses a "final, definitive truth" available to others "only imperfectly," and that this truth provides the

---

[29] David Fox Sandmel, "'Who Do You Say That I Am?' Jewish Responses to *Nostra Aetate* and Post-Holocaust Christianity," chapter 9 of this volume; Shira L. Lander, "Lot's Wife: On the Dangers of Looking Back," chapter 10 of this volume. The profound shadow that history has cast over Jewish-Christian relations can be gauged by how tenaciously Jewish distrust of Christian intentions persists even though *Nostra Aetate* arguably privileges Judaism above all other religions as being closest to Christianity theologically and spiritually (and hence truer than any other non-Christian faith). Contending that *Nostra Aetate* "resolutely" grades non-Christian religions, Thatamanil notes how it accords Judaism far greater attention than any other tradition, suggesting that it stands closest to the Christian "center." See Thatamanil, "Learning from . . . Our Religious Neighbors." Jerusha Lamptey asserts that *Nostra Aetate* treats Judaism as having an especially "proximate" relationship to Christianity. This "self-understanding," she intimates, enjoins Christians to engage Judaism with deep "self-reflection and theological contemplation," such as biblical study and "'fraternal [*sic*] dialogues'" [*Nostra Aetate*, sec. 4], that they need not tender to more "'distant others'"—like Islam. See Lamptey, "Beyond the Rays of Truth?"

standard for measuring all claims. Contributors to this volume agree unanimously that *Nostra Aetate* took a salutary step beyond exclusivism, the claim that limits saving truth to "one's own tradition alone" and casts all competing claims as "false or delusory."[30] But, as indicated previously, most of the essayists reject its particular brand of inclusivism, which John Thatamanil calls "graded"—because it ranks religions as having more or less salvific potency—and "hierarchical"—because it holds that the Catholic Church alone possesses the fullness of truth. Such a stance, he charges, fails to "rupture religious self-sufficiency" and stunts the "reality of interreligious learning" toward which *Nostra Aetate* otherwise gestures.[31] The declaration has "often been scolded for its limited inclusive approach to comprehend[ing] religious otherness," Rosenhagen agrees, though he offers some mitigating context: when *Nostra Aetate* was promulgated, "theological models of pluralism were not yet available."[32]

Critics like Thatamanil prefer to structure interreligious relationships along lines usually denominated as pluralism, which, put simply, "sees the world's religions as more or less equal in terms of their ability to express and embody truth and salvation."[33] Denying that any religion enjoys theological superiority is, it would appear at first glance, the position best calibrated to encourage the most frank and productive interchanges between adherents of different faiths. Yet even some who most strongly avow this agenda as the preeminent way to advance beyond *Nostra Aetate* doubt that pluralism—at least in those forms that essentially consider different religions' truth claims to be equal—has the capacity to achieve it. Thatamanil would jettison "parity pluralism"—which deems religions to be "of equal merit"—because making any meaningful judgment about the intrinsic worth of religions as wholes is simply unsustainable. For similar reasons, Gross would scrap the entire taxonomic project as irrelevant. The germane questions for her concern not whether religions may at some deep level be congruent but why the existence of religious diversity troubles so many and how traditions can flourish in the midst of diversity.[34]

The most detailed critique of pluralism, along with an ardent defense of *Nostra Aetate*'s inclusivism, issues from Peter Bouteneff, who affirms that Orthodox Christianity is "theologically close" to Catholicism and united with it on the "essential question of what the church is: the Body of Christ." Casting pluralism

---

30 Long, "Eternal Veda."
31 Thatamanil, "Learning from . . . Our Religious Neighbors."
32 Rosenhagen, "Fullness of Truth in Christ Alone."
33 Long, "Eternal Veda." For positive valuations of pluralism, see Knitter, "*Nostra Aetate*: A Milestone"; Roger Haight, "The Christian Spiritual Vision from the Perspective of *Nostra Aetate*," chapter 5 of this volume; and Thatamanil, "Learning from . . . Our Religious Neighbors," where he prefers the term "mutuality" because it "names and recognizes the need for mutual learning and transformation between traditions."
34 Thatamanil, "Learning from . . . Our Religious Neighbors"; Gross, "Buddhist Response."

as maintaining that all great religious traditions access truth equally and differentiating it categorically from both inclusivism and exclusivism because of its epistemologically radical denial that absolute truth—if it exists—can be known, he repudiates pluralism on several counts.[35] Philosophically, pluralism presents itself as an "evident reality" when in fact it harbors "its own ontological presuppositions" and warrants no greater claim to authority than any other philosophical stance. Theologically, it requires "substantial realignments" that require traditions to sacrifice "fundamental principles"—such as de-literalizing the Incarnation or equating the Hindu pantheon with the Trinity—in a way that renders faiths "all but unrecognizable to their main adherents." Morally, it can lay no greater claim to promoting tolerance and opposing religious violence than some species of inclusivism—witness *Nostra Aetate*'s condemnation of antisemitism while proclaiming Jesus' "unique divine identity." Had *Nostra Aetate* pushed into a pluralist position, the move would have constituted a "revolution" that would have "distance[d] the text from conciliar Roman Catholicism."[36]

Add Bouteneff's analysis to the doubts about pluralism's coherence, voiced above, as well as Long's assertion that inclusivism avoids relativism's "trap," and it is evident that the conference participants file no unalloyed brief for pluralism. If one accepts the whole taxonomy as a convenient but admittedly flawed heuristic, they array themselves in the conceptual borderlands between a relatively open kind of inclusivism and a staunch strain of pluralism.[37] From one vista, Lamptey, who applauds Pope Francis's "affirmation of religious difference" as a "marked departure" from *Nostra Aetate*'s inclusivism, nonetheless credits it for stepping "headlong into the divine mystery" and generating a viewpoint "that transcends the somewhat superficial or one-dimensional depictions of religious others" reified by taxonomies. From another, Bouteneff states that inclusivism "encompasses a range of positions," some of them quite open-minded, though he also recognizes that it can produce "its share of condescending and intolerant expressions."[38] The participants dispute the degree to which claims to theological superiority corrode the possibility of meaningful interreligious exchange; but, by whatever name they designate the optimum conditions, they aver that acknowledging at least a quantum of divine truth in every religion, together with a readiness to learn from that truth, is the sine qua non for fruitful interreligious relations.

Navigating between respect for other traditions and commitment to one's own religious convictions is tricky, however, for theological claims do matter. Perhaps

---

[35] Peter Bouteneff, "*Nostra Aetate*: Views from a Sibling on Inclusivism and Pluralism," chapter 8 of this volume.

[36] Ibid.

[37] Long, "Eternal Veda." Cf. his location of Vivekananda's views "as occupying a position on the boundary between inclusivism and pluralism." See also Thatamanil's characterization that his "new pluralism" for a "new *Nostra Aetate*" walks a "fine line between . . . 'open inclusivism,' and an explicit affirmation of pluralism" ("Learning from . . . Our Religious Neighbors").

[38] Lamptey, "Beyond the Rays of Truth?"; Bouteneff, "*Nostra Aetate*: Views from a Sibling."

none poses a greater conundrum for future progress in interreligious dialogue than the church's declaration of "Christ crucified," a "stumbling block" and "foolishness" to non-Christians since Paul's day (1 Cor 1:23, NRSV). *Nostra Aetate* pronounced that the church "proclaims, and ever must proclaim Christ 'the way, the truth, and the life'" (Jn 14:6), in whom God "has reconciled all things."[39] Non-Christians herein unanimously counter that such testimony will not do, at least in its absolutist or triumphalist forms. The visceral disagreement over Jesus' identity can render public exchanges between Jews and Christians especially edgy. Prudence and politics, no less than theology, explain why Jesus barely figures in the six Jewish responses to *Nostra Aetate* that Sandmel analyzes. Examining Christian claims would necessarily involve rejecting Jesus' divinity, a "self-defeating" posture in efforts meant to "move beyond a contentious past." Pondering a statement by some Catholic bishops that God's promises to Israel are found only in Jesus Christ, Lander wonders how Jews and Catholics can possibly form a meaningful relationship "if each thinks the other's claim to Israelite patrimony is unwarranted and illegitimate."[40]

Muslims have similar difficulties, despite the "exceptional dignity that the Qur'an accords 'Isa ibn Maryam'" and the love they bear him. In Hassan's experience, Christology is for "the vast majority of Christians" a "nonnegotiable proposition" that has brought "interreligious dialogue to a bitter impasse." After closely reading Pope John Paul II's statements to Muslims, Lamptey discerns a tension—born from his conclusion that Christianity and Islam manifest significantly different theological anthropologies—in his struggle to balance *Nostra Aetate*'s "affirmation of rays of truth and goodness [in other religions] with his unequivocal assertion that perfect and complete truth is found only in Christ." This view impedes his fully engaging with Islamic theology, though Lamptey credits Pope Francis with holding a "new vision of religious difference" that regards Muslims as serious theological interlocutors.[41] From a Buddhist perspective, Gross sounds equally forthright, although her problems with proclaiming Jesus the only universal savior have less to do with the proposition's content per se and more with how Christians flaunt it with dogmatic fervor. Sallie King makes the same point more gently, urging Christians to "please show us the Jesus whom you love," bring his parables "to life for us," and show us "the Christ spirit that lives in you and in other Christians," but ditch the "barriers for non-Christians" like "insist[ing] on Jesus as the 'one and only' way." Long proposes a Hindu resolution: the parallel between the "doctrine of rebirth" and the possibility envisaged by some theologians of a "posthumous encounter with Christ" may mitigate the need to "convert others to one's own path."[42]

The strongest avowal that Christology poses a stumbling block to dialogue proceeds, however, from some Christian commentators. "The fundamental question"

---

[39] *Nostra Aetate*, sec. 2.
[40] Sandmel, "Who Do You Say That I Am?"; Lander, "Lot's Wife."
[41] Hassan, "Muslim Woman's Perspective"; Lamptey, "Beyond the Rays of Truth?"
[42] Gross, "Buddhist Response"; King, "Buddhism and Christianity"; Long, "Eternal Veda."

that *Nostra Aetate* poses for Christians, Knitter stresses, "is how to understand Jesus' uniqueness" so that they can simultaneously be "fully committed to him and his message" and also "fully open" to dialogue with members of other religions. Some theologians, he regrets, prefer to close debate; the "issue of Jesus' uniqueness is just too complex, too threatening, too neuralgic."[43] Two contributors, however, rise to his challenge.

Like Knitter, John Pawlikowski thinks that Christian theologians have ignored *Nostra Aetate*'s most profound implications. A student of the Holocaust, he is particularly concerned with Christian-Jewish relations, where the "Christological question" towers "above all" other theological matters. He refers to both contemporary biblical scholarship, which has emphasized Jesus' Jewishness and early Christianity's intimate ties to Judaism, and the last three popes, who have insisted that "Judaism is implanted" in Christianity's "very heart," in order to advocate a theology "devoid of supersessionism"—devoid of the Christian claim that the church has supplanted the Jews as God's people and that its new covenant has extinguished their old one.[44] Pawlikowski proposes an Incarnational Christology as the best approach to understanding the Christ Event in a way that both "leaves legitimate theological space for Judaism" and retains a continuing role for the Jewish people in human redemption. He does so on the basis of his claim that the Christian doctrine of incarnation in Jesus implies that every person "somehow shares in divinity"; God has always had a human dimension, and humanity has eternally been "an integral part of the Godhead." The Christ Event was a singular insight that gave this phenomenon extraordinary transparency, without which humanity could never have fully comprehended its ultimate link with God. Nevertheless, this revelation "should not be taken as a full and complete vision of human salvation by itself."[45] Pawlikowski thinks that some elements within Jewish tradition, notably Hasidism, share a similar incarnational vision. Moreover, he cites no less an authority than the Pontifical Biblical Commission to affirm that "Jewish messianic expectations are not in vain," from which basis he opines that Jewish perspectives may better expose some messianic traits that Jesus may not have made visible. Thus, Pawlikowski argues, Judaism inscribes both a presumption of God's immanence and a messianic hope that are legitimate, albeit different from Christianity's equally valid visions. In Pawlikowski's view the two communities' paths may be distinctive now, but they will ultimately coalesce—though only God knows how and when.[46]

If Pawlikowski shows Christians how they can fulfill *Nostra Aetate*'s promise of reconciliation by acknowledging Christological insights within Judaism, Roger Haight suggests how adopting a version of Christian spirituality premised on *Nostra Aetate* can foster Christians' appreciation for "what is true and holy" in non-Chris-

---

[43] Knitter, "*Nostra Aetate*: A Milestone."

[44] John T. Pawlikowski, "Toward a Renewed Theology of Christianity's Bond with Judaism," chapter 4 of this volume.

[45] Ibid.

[46] Ibid.

tian religions. By spirituality, Haight means the logic that shapes a person's identity according to a "value or ultimately important idea or thing"; Christian forms of spirituality center on the formula "following Jesus Christ." Elaborating on *Nostra Aetate*'s premises, Haight "reimagine[s] the Christian narrative" so that it retains the significance of Jesus' message but focuses on God the Creator rather than Jesus the Son as the origin of the divine love for humanity that the message conveys. Haight intends thereby to avoid christocentrism and the "somewhat exclusivist version of the Christian story" that it encourages. This reconfiguration, he proposes, "stays faithful to the tradition and at the same time inspires a way of life that responds positively to a religiously pluralistic world according to the intimations of *Nostra Aetate*."[47]

Haight's complex construction of Christian spirituality may be best summarized in his own words:

> Human beings are a self-conscious part of the universe whose very existence depends at every moment on the active creative power of God. . . . On the basis of Jesus' person and ministry, Christians relate to God as personal lover of what God created. . . . Building on these foundations, the Christian understands reality as a dynamic grace-filled natural world. . . . The personal self-gift of God to all, more than ancestry or genetic codes, makes us brothers and sisters to each other and, as such, responsible to God. . . . As a human race, together, we are not able to rank in value the different manifestations of God's actual presence to human beings. But we can compare them and discuss them.[48]

The phrase "grace-filled natural world" describes a universe suffused with God's creating, one in which nature and grace are inseparable.[49] By envisioning God as "the ground of being and not as a single or specific finite agent," it is also consonant with a scientific worldview. The energy that grounds life can be signified religiously by the Spirit of God and naturalistically as the postulated source for evolution. "Grace-filled natural world" is also meant to explicate the mechanism by which what is true and holy exists in other religions, a condition that *Nostra Aetate* asserts but does not explain. Haight's account of Christian spirituality does so, he maintains, by linking the doctrine of God's sustaining presence and power in the whole finite order with the realization that it extends to all people and thus manifests itself in other traditions. Throughout history, all human beings have turned "toward absolute mystery," although it is fruitless to ponder which may do so with greater truth.[50] The love that Christ taught, when understood fundamentally as God's

---

47 Ibid.; *Nostra Aetate*, sec. 2; Haight, "Christian Spiritual Vision."

48 Haight, "Christian Spiritual Vision."

49 In a note in "Christian Spiritual Vision" Haight describes this position as "panentheism," holding that "all things subsist within the power of God and that God, as creator and as inseparable from God's power, is within all finite reality."

50 Ibid. Eschewing relativism, Haight insists that there must be some basis for

creating power suffusing the world rather than as limited to Christ's incarnation, removes the necessity of insisting that other religions recognize a superior truth in Christ while affirming for Christians the true divinity of Christ's message.

Convincing Christians that they can decenter their appraisal of Christ while upholding their devotion to Jesus' message and person—all in the name of advancing interreligious comity—will not be easy. The Vatican, it is said, thinks in centuries, and, as is well known, the Congregation for the Doctrine of the Faith barred Haight in 2009 from teaching and writing about theological subjects on account of his Christological speculations.[51] But improving interreligious relationships involves more than just religious elites disputing formal propositions. As Pawlikowski himself appreciates, discussion about the theological relationship between Jews and Christians must "embrace the growing number of people who have important spiritual links to either religious community without formal ties to their institutional structures," and incorporate itself "into the wider interreligious conversation."[52] Haight wrestles with how to reach these disparate audiences. Though couched in highly philosophical tones, his argument is ultimately less about metaphysics than about connecting different faith communities. Our mere belonging to the same species, he trenchantly observes, "does not make us affectively brothers and sisters." His proposed spirituality views people as belonging to a unity composed of plural religious communities "moving through history together in dialogue with absolute mystery and with each other." A Christian telling of God's grace can generate reciprocating non-Christian responses. One might suggest that Haight answers King's request for Christians to "show us the Jesus whom you love" without insisting on his salvific primacy.[53]

Hassan goes a step further, flatly rejecting theology and the "wonderland/wasteland of interreligious dialogue" as a means for bridging religious differences. Despite the public successes achieved by *Nostra Aetate* and "A Common Word between Us and You," she questions whether the vast majority of devout Christians and Muslims will be able to transcend their attachment to the "nonne-

---

determining whether or not something is true and holy. He identifies such a criterion as arising from humanity's existential predicament: "What is transcendently true and holy must respond to the fundamental human questions about moral weakness, sickness and death, and the ultimate meaning of human existence." He does not, however, think that determining which religions might do so more effectively is possible, a disinclination that echoes Thatamanil's.

[51] John L. Allen, "Rome Orders Roger Haight to Stop Teaching, Publishing," *National Catholic Reporter*, January 5, 2009, https://www.ncronline.org/news/rome-orders-roger-haight-stop-teaching-publishing.

[52] Pawlikowski, "Toward a Renewed Theology."

[53] Haight, "Christian Spiritual Vision." In an abstract accompanying an earlier draft of his chapter, Haight underlined the affective dimension to sparking interreligious dialogue: a "Christian spiritual vision of the interrelation between the world's faiths . . . generates gratitude for other religions and encourages them [to contribute] to a larger experience of our common ultimate ground of being."

gotiable theological beliefs" that form the "bedrock of their religions." The answer, she holds, lies "not in further academic or intellectual exploration, but in the realm of the spirit." Parsing the Qur'an, she finds that all human beings receive God's grace "irrespective of religious identity," an Islamic analogue to Haight's "grace-filled natural world." The firmest bonds between those who profess different faiths occur when they internalize this revelation as completely as did the Trappist monk Thomas Merton and the Sufi poet Jalal ad-Din Rumi, two mystics who realized "the essential unity of human beings despite everything that separated them." For Hassan, the truest way to achieve spiritual kinship is to meditate on God as *Rahman* and *Rahim* ["Most Gracious, Most Compassionate"] and to accept Rumi's invitation: "Out beyond ideas of wrongdoing and rightdoing, / there is a field. I'll meet you there."[54]

Hassan channels a broader malaise with much contemporary interreligious dialogue: it is overly intellective, too top-heavy with religious leaders, and theologically sclerotic. On the first two points, Jennifer Peace concurs that interfaith engagement has overemphasized "formal dialogues and interfaith panels," inspiring an excess of "priest-, rabbi-, and imam-styled" sessions that "do not do justice to the diversity of perspectives and practices encompassed by any living tradition." On the third, Knitter notes that *Nostra Aetate* left behind "a lot of complex theological baggage," but he recommends that we clear it away by adopting an ancient Christian formula: belief follows practice. Doing (i.e., dialogue) will clarify knowing (i.e., theology).[55] But, one may ask, for what goals should properly construed interfaith encounters strive? Adamant that too much dialogue has wasted itself on matters of no consequence, Gross underlines what it should accomplish. The question we need to address, she insists, is not if religions are true (or "more true") but "Do they work? Are their believers kind to women, animals, the unfortunate, and nature?" How "effective [are they] as skillful means for relevant ethical transformation?" King amplifies the Mahayana principle of skillful means: "whatever ameliorates" *duhkha* (suffering) and "nurtures wisdom and compassion" moves us "in the right direction as sentient beings, and thus is good."[56] Although several authors urge that interfaith engagement should contribute, in *Nostra Aetate*'s words, to "social justice and moral welfare, as well as peace and freedom,"[57] that dialogue should become more oriented to achieving practical results represents in this volume a particularly Buddhist emphasis.

---

[54] Hassan, "Muslim Woman's Perspective."

[55] Jennifer Howe Peace, "In Our Time: Coformation as a Modality for Interreligious Teaching and Learning," chapter 15 of this volume; Knitter, "*Nostra Aetate*: A Milestone."

[56] Gross, "Buddhist Response"; King, "Buddhism and Christianity."

[57] Notably Hopkins, "Social Justice in *Nostra Aetate*." See also Hill Fletcher's use of quotations from Gross's essay to support her profession that Catholic Christians might need to hold "our" truths "lightly in order that they might do the work of salvation and healing rather than the work of discrimination and destruction" ("Foreign to the Mind of Christ"). *Nostra Aetate*, sec. 3.

So if, as claimed, interfaith dialogue has remained too much the province of religious elites, how can laypeople from different traditions become more involved? To some degree, this process is already happening spontaneously, as individuals throughout the world selectively cull beliefs and practices from various sources without consulting (and sometimes directly defying) their own tradition's authorities. King warns about the dangers inherent in such "bricolage," notably its tendencies toward rendering religious life egotistical and superficial, but she also observes that religions have borrowed from each other throughout history, and that, in any case, individuals cannot be stopped from stitching up spiritual patchworks in "the age of [the] internet and globalization."[58] Nevertheless, bricolage threatens the survival of the institutions that carry most of humankind's religious heritage. The continuing "vitality and integrity" of those legacies concern her because she values how a tradition's masters ensure its integrity, which "carries what is most precious from the past into the future." Personalized spirituality without institutional anchors, in contrast, cannot be self-sustaining. One way in which traditions might adapt, she surmises, would be to intervene in the process of bricolage, not to control or stem it but to provide "spiritual guidance" for those who might want it. The church, for instance, has, since Vatican II, taken Buddhist spirituality very much to heart and sanctioned the study of Buddhist meditation by Catholic monastics. Why, King asks, could the church not give its blessing to the laity, offering "guidance, support, and a context for understanding" what they might find? Such direction, she avers, could counter "egotism and superficiality." In King's thought experiment, the impetus for dialogue comes from ordinary adherents, who, motivated by their own spiritual impulses, seek out other religions' wisdom with instruction, not constraint, from their own traditions.[59]

Peace lays out a more deliberate model, which she helped develop for religious leaders as co-director of the Center for Interreligious and Communal Leadership Education at Andover Newton Theological School. The core concept involves "learning *with* the religious other" as opposed to "*about*" them, a process that Peace denominates "coformation." Cognizant that "students are not formed in isolation but in connection to a dynamic web of relationships," coformational pedagogy operates on the presumption to which a Muslim PhD student, reflecting on how immersion in America's religious pluralism was transforming her, powerfully witnessed: "Our experiences change who we are." It seeks to create a variety of spaces—physical, virtual, and professional—to encourage the "interfaith friendships and co-learning opportunities" vital for dismissing "deadly stereotypes and hateful caricatures." Practice with this mode of interreligious education has redefined Peace's priorities for the goals of interfaith work, whose "central quest," she

---

[58] King, "Buddhism and Christianity." She takes the term "bricolage" from religious sociologist Peter Beyer.

[59] Ibid. Besides providing spiritual direction, religious institutions faced with bricolage will also, King postulates, need to continue offering spaces for community and loci for group social action ("Buddhism and Christianity").

concludes "is not to promote unity but rather to create and sustain healthier and more collaborative relationships" with everyone—believers and nonbelievers, human beings, and "the rest of creation." Coformation makes experiential learning a critical part of interfaith dialogue. How to extend this model beyond the confines of seminaries, so that larger populations might be involved, warrants further sustained consideration.[60]

By every account, *Nostra Aetate* deserved its fiftieth-anniversary laudations, for it transformed the church's relationship with non-Christian religions. But if our remembrances are only celebratory, they will mummify it. For *Nostra Aetate* to remain a living document requires recognizing to what extent it belongs to a certain historical era and determining how to elaborate its call to improve inter-religious relationships for subsequent generations. Specific suggestions made here include: continuing theological exploration and evolution; broadening contact and discussion among all members of religious communities, not just elites; taking more flexible views of doctrine and official teachings that allow for (and even approve) incorporating religious beliefs and disciplines from other traditions into one's own practice; encouraging dialogue that aims not simply to instruct audiences in each other's beliefs but urges religious communities to work together for common goods; and implementing outreach programs, professional and otherwise, to teach people of different faiths how to study together. This collection may be scattershot rather than systematic, but it reflects two common axioms. For one thing, effectu-ating *Nostra Aetate*'s call for "dialogue and collaboration with the followers of other religions" will require a willingness to listen to each other without feeling impelled to defend one's own faith commitments. This mutualism presupposes that every religion has wisdom to share with every other, and that trying to determine who has the most superior truth is folly. In addition, the foremost goal of dialogue is not to learn *about* each other but *from* and *with* each other in order to improve human life.[61] Accentuating commonalities and tolerating differences may be good in them-selves, but they serve a greater end.

---

[60] Peace, "In Our Time." The Lubar Institute for the Study of the Abrahamic Reli-gions presented one such approach. Its civic (as opposed to academic) programming brought together Jews, Christians, and Muslims in the community forum (held for adults unaffiliated with the University of Wisconsin–Madison), the student interfaith forum (which gathered students monthly during the academic year), and the student interfaith fellowship, whose members met weekly. All of these groups, particularly the fellows, were designed along lines similar to those Peace describes, as was the "Courage Project," which for two years brought together local high school students for four months. Their programs culminated in variety shows in which they performed what they had learned about each other. These projects had results comparable to those Peace reports, but the number of participants was also finite, never exceeding about two dozen in any one instance.

[61] And, if one follows Knitter, enter into a "green interfaith dialogue" determined to "heal the earth" (*"Nostra Aetate*: A Milestone").

Nostra Aetate graciously renounced the church's ancient habit of menacing non-Christian religions from its fortress of Christian supremacy. How to further demilitarize relationships between all religions and create not merely a truce among them but an alliance to promote human well-being and spiritual growth is the challenge for interreligious dialogue in our time. Surmounting it will not be easy. We will have done quite well if anyone remembers our efforts fifty years on.

Part I

Nostra Aetate: Origins and Challenges

1

NOSTRA AETATE:
ORIGIN, HISTORY, AND VATICAN II CONTEXT

John Borelli

"Until that day it had not occurred to John XXIII that the Council had to deal also with the Jewish question and antisemitism. But from that day on he was completely taken by it."[1]

These words by then-Monsignor Loris Capovilla come from a brief memorandum, dated March 14, 1966, barely three months after the close of the Second Vatican Ecumenical Council, or Vatican II, its more widely used name. Capovilla, who had served as private secretary to Pope John XXIII, was recalling some important details for Father Stjepan Schmidt, SJ, secretary to Cardinal Augustin Bea. Cardinal Bea was the person most responsible for the successful promulgation of *Nostra Aetate*, the Second Vatican Council's *Declaration on the Relation of the Church to Non-Christian Religions*. Capovilla's recollections pertain to a meeting on June 13, 1960, between Pope John and the Holocaust survivor and scholar Dr. Jules Isaac. So significant was that June 1960 event to *Nostra Aetate* that, without it, there would have been no such declaration. Monsignor Loris Capovilla, made a cardinal by Pope Francis at age ninety-eight and in May 2016 passed away at one hundred, testified in his memorandum fifty years ago that Isaac's audience with Pope John planted an idea that the pope never forgot: "I remember very well that the pope remained extremely impressed by that meeting, and he talked about it with me for a long time."[2]

No account of the Second Vatican Ecumenical Council, or of *Nostra Aetate*, the shortest of its sixteen documents and, by many accounts, its most controversial, can begin without reference to Pope John XXIII.[3] Just three months after his

---

[1] The memorandum rests in the Vatican Secret Archives, as they are called, in the Vatican II files of the Secretariat for the Promotion of Christian Unity: Archivio Segreto Vaticano, *Concilio Vaticano II*, Secretariatus ad Christianorum Unitatem Fovendam, Box 1452. Hereafter cited as ASV, *Conc. Vat. II*.

[2] Capovilla, "Memorandum to Father Stjepan Schmidt," March 14, 1966, ASV, *Conc. Vat. II*, Box 1452.

[3] One of the first on staff for the council to work on the initiative leading to *Nostra Aetate*, Thomas F. Stransky, CSP, begins his recollections of the declaration by drawing

election, Pope John surprised the world by announcing his intention to convoke a universal council of the church. He first announced it in private to those cardinals who had joined him for a service of prayer on January 25, 1959—the close of the annual Church Unity Octave on the feast of the Conversion of Saint Paul. His words were met with stunned silence. The next day, the Vatican newspaper, *L'Osservatore Romano*, announced the coming council with these three vaguely worded purposes: a means of spiritual renewal, reconciliation of the church to the modern world, and service to the unity of Christians.[4] That last purpose, the unity of Christians, explains the appropriateness of announcing the council on January 25—the Feast of the Conversion of Saint Paul—the close of eight days of prayer for Christian unity and, as we will see, for Jewish relations too, though no one, even Pope John, could anticipate in early 1959 such an implication. Saint Paul, like the other apostles, was a Jew.[5]

Two months later, on Good Friday, March 28, 1959, Pope John XXIII did something else quite surprising. Prior to the beginning of the usual services, he took a pen and scratched out the derogatory Latin words describing Jews as "perfidious" and marked by their "perfidy" from the great prayer for the Jews in the Roman Missal. That act, occurring more than a year before Isaac's visit, signaled to the world and especially to Jews that the new pope was sensitive to the effects of centuries of negative teachings about the Jews.

Pope John made good on his goal to make the council a truly ecumenical one. When he appointed preparatory commissions, he also announced a Secretariat for Promoting Christian Unity (SPCU) and appointed the elderly Jesuit biblical scholar Augustin Bea as its president. The central role of Bea in the months prior

---

attention to its size and the amount of turbulence that this smallest of texts caused. He cites one of the most astute council fathers, the Viennese Cardinal Franz König, *Offen für Gott—Offen für die Welt*, ed. Christa Pongratz-Lippitt (Freiburg: Herder, 2005), 107, and *Unterwegs mit den Menschen*, ed. Anne Marie Frenzl (Kevelaer: Topos Plus, 2004), 235. From 2006 on, the present author has worked with Father Stransky directly on publishing his recollections and analysis of the genesis and development of *Nostra Aetate*. On more than one occasion, Stransky noted how, among the council's documents, *Nostra Aetate* was the least debated inside the council's hall and the most debated outside.

[4] "Bollettino," *L'Osservatore Romano* (January 26/27, 1959). See also "Sollemnis Allocutio," *Acta Apostolicae Sedis* 51 (1959): 68–69, hereafter cited as *AAS*; and commented on by Thomas F. Stransky, "The Foundation of the Secretariat for Promoting Christian Unity," in *Vatican II Revisited by Those Who Were There*, ed. Alberic Stacpoole (Minneapolis: Winston Press, 1986), 62. It was unusual, if not historic, that a pope would personally close the Church Unity Octave, as Pope John did in 1959; surprised by the invitation to join him, not all the cardinals living in Rome chose to attend and thus did not hear the announcement of his intention to call a council that he made privately in the sacristy after the service.

[5] The final text of *Nostra Aetate*, according to Stransky's translation, has this sentence, which educated many at the time of the obvious: "[The church] also recalls that the Apostles, the church's foundation stones and pillars, as well as most of the early disciples who proclaimed the Gospel of Christ to the world, sprang from the Jewish people."

to June 1960 and in the establishment of the secretariat is a well-researched topic and explains his appointment.[6] Both Pope John and Bea were born in 1881. In late 1959, the pope had made Father Bea a cardinal. Bea, already actively developing the ecumenical goal for the council, and Pope John seemed to understand each other from their first conversation. Both turned seventy-nine in 1960, the year of Dr. Isaac's visit. A week after the June 5 announcement of the SPCU, the eighty-three-year-old Isaac arrived in Rome for a papal audience.

Isaac testified to Pope John's comment that, at the moment he saw Isaac walking into the room, he realized that he ought to have Cardinal Bea and his new secretariat look into questions about the Jews.[7] Capovilla tells us in his memorandum that Pope John "directed Isaac to Cardinal Bea, 'in whom he trusted and had confidence.'" They met two days later, on June 15, 1960. Cardinal Bea, cheerfully surprised that the pope had referred Isaac to him, reflected on the file of materials that Isaac had brought with him, and, on September 18, three months later, when he met in audience with Pope John, suggested that, in addition to handling the ecumenical dimensions of the upcoming council, his secretariat could also—and I choose these words carefully—facilitate relations with Jews in the preparations for the council.[8]

Such were the tenuous developments that led to *Nostra Aetate*. In September 1960, it was not even clear whether the SPCU would have authority, beyond inviting non-Catholic Christian observers, to prepare its own drafts for the council's agenda.[9] Three years and two months later, on November 18, 1963, as Cardinal Bea presented the first draft of *Nostra Aetate* to the 2,500 council fathers gathered in Saint Peter's Basilica, he would be the only one of these three eighty-year-old men still alive.[10] This is how fragile the origins of this historic document were.

---

[6] Stransky, "Foundation of the Secretariat," 64–67; Mauro Velati, "La proposta ecumenica del segretatiato per l'unità dei cristiani," in *Verso il Concilio Vaticano II (1960–1962): Passagi e problemi della preparazione conciliare*, ed. Giuseppe Alberigo and Alberto Melloni (Genoa: Marietti, 1993), 273–76, and retold by Mauro Velati, "Introduzione," *Dialogo e Rinnovamento: Verbali e testi del segretariato per l'unità dei cristiani nella preparazione del concilio Vaticano II (1960–1962)* (Bologna: il Mulino, 2011), 18–20.

[7] Isaac's account is all that we have. It first appeared in *Le Service international de documentation judéo-chrétienne* (SIDIC), 3 (1968): 10–11; it was republished as "La Réception de Jules Isaac par Jean XXIII," *La Documentation Catholique* 65, no. 1528 (November 17, 1968): 2015–16.

[8] Stjepan Schmidt, *Augustin Bea, Cardinal of Unity* (New Rochelle, NY: New City Press, 1992), 336–37.

[9] Contrary to popular understanding, the assignment that Cardinal Bea received at this important first audience with Pope John on September 18, 1960, to make the council ecumenical did not include a papal mandate to write a document on the Jews. Rather, he was told to facilitate relations with Jews in the preparations for the council.

[10] This first draft to make it to the council floor bore this title translated into English: "On the Relation of Catholics to Non-Christians, above all, to the Jews," *Acta Synodalia Sacrosancti Oecuemici Concilii Vaticani II* (Vatican City: Typis Polyglottis Vaticanis, 1970–99), II/5, 431–32, hereafter cited as *AS*.

Thus, *Nostra Aetate* originated in an effort to address the troubled relationship of the church to Jews. But I would like to suggest that there were two other efforts, independent of this one and not as obvious, which folded into the making of the declaration. While a small but growing cadre of scholars, theologians, and church and Jewish leaders were at work for three decades prior to Vatican II addressing, reassessing, and attempting to reverse centuries of negative anti-Jewish attitudes and theological reflections among Christians, an even smaller and less organized group of scholars, missionaries, and church leaders was at work seeking to present a positive assessment of Muslims and the Islamic faith.[11] You would find them among Missionaries of Africa (Pères Blancs, or White Fathers), Dominicans, and Jesuits active in the Middle East, Africa, and India, and among those in the orbit of Louis Massignon, the most renowned Catholic scholar of Islam at that time. Massignon passed away in October 1962, just as the council was getting under way, but he had influenced some at the council, especially Cardinal Giovanni Battista Montini, Archbishop of Milan. On the death of Pope John in June 1963, the College of Cardinals elected Montini, who, as Pope Paul VI, would steer the council to a successful conclusion in 1965.[12]

And there was a third effort, which became more pronounced after the council got under way, represented by Europeans serving as missionary bishops and indigenous bishops from Africa and Asia, where Christians lived as minority communities among large populations of Muslims, Hindus, Buddhists, and the followers of other religious traditions. These missionary and indigenous bishops clamored for the council to respond to their interreligious situations by creating, as a first step, a new secretariat relating to the followers of all these other religions. From this group of bishops, Cardinal Thomas Tien Ken-sin, Archbishop of Peking but resident in Taipei, sent an official proposal to the newly elected Pope Paul VI in July 1963.[13]

On September 12, 1963, Paul VI outlined certain changes that he was instituting for the council in a letter to Cardinal Eugène Tisserant, dean of the College of Cardinals. In one sentence, he declared that, because of concerns expressed to him, he would in due time create a secretariat like the one already created, but

---

[11] The best account of the preconciliar history of efforts among Christians and Jews leading to *Nostra Aetate* is given by John Connelly, *From Enemy to Brother* (Cambridge, MA: Harvard University Press, 2012).

[12] The story of preconciliar influences on incorporating a more positive understanding of Muslims in the work of Vatican II has yet to be written. Elements of it can be found in the following works: John Borelli, "Vatican II: Preparing the Catholic Church for Dialogue," *Origins: CNS Documentary Service* 42, no. 11 (August 2, 2012): 168–70; Robert Caspar, "La vision de l'Islam chez L. Massignon et son influence sure l'Eglise," in *Louis Massignon*, ed. J.-F. Six (Paris: L'Herne, 1962), 126–47; and Georges C. Anawati, OPOP, "L'Islam à l'heure du Concile: Prolégomènes à un dialogue islamo-chrétien," *Angelicum* 41 (1964): 145–68.

[13] Ralph M. Wiltgen, SVD, gives the details of these developments in *The Rhine Flows into the Tiber: The Unknown Council* (New York: Hawthorne Books, 1967), 73–78.

that it would relate to those who are non-Christians.[14] This expression of commitment to interreligious relations in broad terms by the newly elected Pope Paul was extraordinary when we consider that no draft on the topic had yet been presented to the council fathers and that few of them were aware of any developments in that direction. Officials of the SPCU responded that there were no plans to include "non-Christian observers" at the council.[15] Paul VI eventually established a distinct Secretariat for Non-Christians (SNC) on Pentecost Sunday 1964 (May 19), roughly halfway through the council.[16]

The Effort Begins

Cardinal Augustin Bea's proposal to Pope John to address "Questions on the Jews" was a bold gesture. His tiny staff at the SPCU began preparations for the first plenary meeting of bishop members and scholarly consultors scheduled for November 14–15, 1960. The last of the ten items on the agenda was "Questions on the Jews."[17] Though the topic was *sub secreto*, "confidential," word had already gotten out.

Is it more than a coincidence that two months later, on January 25, 1961, the chief officer of the Congregation for the Oriental Church, one of the Vatican's main agencies, began discussions with the Missionaries of Africa to find a specialist on Islam to fill a new position at the Congregation? There is only the briefest mention of this event in the five-volume *History of Vatican II*, but its significance is evident in the archives of the Missionaries of Africa in Rome. Josef Cuoq, a Missionary of Africa and specialist on Islam, began service on September 5, 1961, at the Congregation for the Oriental Church, one year before the council would begin.[18]

---

[14] The wording in the Apostolic Letter "Quod Apostolici" is vague and awkward but still clear enough that efforts would in due time be extended to non-Christians. *AS* II/1, 12.

[15] "Provisions Are Yet to Be Made for Non-Christian Representatives at Council's Second Session," National Catholic Welfare Conference News Service, September 23, 1963, Archives of the Catholic News Service, USCCB, Washington, DC. There was some initial confusion as to whether the existing Secretariat for Promoting Christian Unity would include interreligious efforts or whether the pope would create a new secretariat. A note in French in the files of the Secretariat for Promoting Christian Unity, prepared by its secretary, Monsignor Johannes Willebrands, on September 21, 1963, indicates that he interpreted the words of Paul VI to mean that a new secretariat would be established. He goes on to indicate how different relations with Jews to the church are in comparison to those with Muslims and Buddhists. A pen note at the end says that this note was transmitted by Cardinal Bea to Pope Paul on September 23. ASV, *Conc. Vat. II*, Box 1453.

[16] Recall that Pope John had announced the Secretariat for Promoting Christian Unity on Pentecost Sunday, 1960.

[17] Velati, *Dialogo e Rinnovamento*, 173–74. Note the plural, not "the Jewish Question," which carries so many negative overtones.

[18] John Borelli, "The Origins and Development of Interreligious Relations during the Century of the Church (1910–2010)," *U. S. Catholic Historian* 28, no. 2 (Spring 2010): 34;

As Cuoq's archives indicate, he began almost immediately networking with other missionaries and scholars interested in improving interreligious relations and reassessing missionary work. Eventually, he would shift over to the new Secretariat for Non-Christians in 1964 as its first undersecretary.[19]

Dominican Georges Anawati teamed up with Cuoq to promote a positive understanding of Islam. Anawati arrived in Rome for the second period of the council (1963) as a consultor on relations with Eastern Christians for the SPCU. Yet on November 29, 1963, while the secretariat's initial public draft on the Jews was under discussion in the hall of the council, he gave a lecture at the Angelicum, the Dominican university in Rome, titled "Islam at the Time of the Council."[20] The first public draft of *Nostra Aetate*, titled "On the Relation of Catholics to Non-Christians, above all, to the Jews," offered only a vague reference to "those who are not Christians, who nevertheless worship God, or at least with goodwill, strive to follow their conscience in carrying out the moral law which is innate in human nature." Anawati's detailed lecture on Islam, presented while the draft was under discussion as an instruction for the council fathers who attended, seems more than coincidental.[21]

Nostra Aetate would not have happened without the initial seed planted in the mind of Pope John by Jules Isaac in June 1960 that the church needed to address its relationship with Jews in order to correct church teachings and to address antisemitism. That thread continued through the council until the promulgation of *Nostra Aetate* on October 28, 1965, whose centerpiece is its fourth section on relations with Jews. Yet there were two other threads—specific concerns for better relations with Muslims and promotion of broader interreligious relations—both of which were bolstered by the personal interests of Paul VI. These other factors, by themselves and without the primary resolve to overhaul Catholic teachings on Jews, were not strong enough to have initiated a separate document. What allowed these other threads and factors to have influence was the council's process itself.[22]

History of Vatican II, 5 vols., ed. Giuseppe Alberigo and Joseph A. Komonchak (Maryknoll, NY: Orbis Books; Leuven: Peeters, 1995–2006), 5:215.

[19] Cuoq's archives, held at the Generalate of the Missionaries of Africa on Via Aurelia, 269, in Rome, are a virtual treasure of information on Cuoq's activities behind the scenes while with the Congregation for the Oriental Church and during his later tenure with the Secretariat for Non-Christians.

[20] The lecture was later published as "L'Islam à l'heure du Concile: Prolégomènes à un dialogue islamo-chrétien," *Angelicum* 41 (1964): 145–68.

[21] Father Stransky told me that he attended hoping to meet Father Anawati, who had not yet shown up for a meeting of the secretariat, and described the lecture as his first class on Islam.

[22] By late 1963, the suggestion might have been entertained by council leaders that an eventual conciliar document on missions might take up interreligious relations, but the Commission on Missions was largely ineffective and unproductive for three-quarters of the council. See Alberigo and Komonchak, eds., *History of Vatican II*, 4:331–45; 5:427–51. See also Wiltgen, *Rhine Flows into the Tiber*, 192–98; E. Louchez, "La Commission De

Four Major Crises

The First Crisis: Overcoming Initial Opposition and Disinterest

The genesis and development of *Nostra Aetate* is truly a window on how tortuously the Second Vatican Council's stand on the church's relationship with non-Christian religions came together. Of the more than 100,000 words in the council's sixteen documents, only 1,141, in forty-one sentences and in five sections, are in *Nostra Aetate*.[23] There had been no previous solemn statements of the Catholic Church regarding other religions. Similar to the other texts belonging exclusively to the Secretariat for Promoting Christian Unity—the *Decree on Ecumenism* and the *Declaration on Religious Liberty*—this *Declaration on the Relation of the Church to Non-Christian Religions* promoted dialogue but was itself "pre-dialogical" in that these texts preceded formal programs of dialogue for the church. *Nostra Aetate* represents a major shift within the Catholic Church toward dialogue, and its composition was fraught with complications and contingencies.[24]

One way to understand the historical progress of drafting *Nostra Aetate* is to follow the four crises that the document survived. My major source for this story is ten years of collaboration with Thomas F. Stransky, CSP, more than five decades after he was invited to serve on the newly formed Secretariat for Promoting Christian Unity.

As already noted, the tenth item on the secretariat's agenda for its first plenary in November 1960 dealt with "Questions on the Jews," but no one initially volunteered to work on these questions. During a break, consultor Gregory Baum, an Augustinian friar at the time, approached Cardinal Bea, indicating that he had undertaken some research on Jewish-Christians relations and could prepare an initial report.[25] Baum's report first pointed out that the relationship of the church

---

Missionibus," in *Les Commissions Conciliares à Vatican II*, ed. Mathijs Lamberigts, Claude Soetens, and Jan Grootaers (Leuven: Bibliotheek van de Faculteit Godgeleerdheid, 1996), 262–69.

[23] The only authoritative text is the Latin in *Constitutiones, Decreta, Declarationes* (Rome: Vatican Polyglot Press, 1966), 1:365–71. Translations are not official; for example, the English version of *Nostra Aetate* on the Vatican website: http://www.vatican.va/archive/hist_councils/ii_vatican_council/documents/vat-ii_decl_19651028_nostra-aetate_en.html. For citations from *Nostra Aetate* throughout this essay, this author is using the translation of Thomas F. Stransky, currently in manuscript but intended for publication in a volume on the document's genesis and development.

[24] See John W. O'Malley, SJ, "Dialogue and the Identity of Vatican II," *Origins* 42, no. 25 (November 22, 2012): 398–403.

[25] Baum might have been referring to a book he would publish in 1961, *The Jews and the Gospel* (London: Newman Press, 1961). By Baum's own admission, and according to the archives of Monsignor John M. Oesterreicher (who later joined Baum as a consultor to the secretariat) at Seton Hall University, Baum consulted with Oesterreicher in preparing this initial report. Stransky commented to this author that Oesterreicher worked the hardest of

to the Jews is a theological matter, and that certain ancient and medieval views are incompatible with that theology. It then made three points aimed at clarifying what St. Paul says about the Jews in his Letter to the Romans in order to enable Christians to better appreciate Jews and so to stem the tide of antisemitism:

1. In speaking of the genesis and nature of the church of Christ, the intimate connection between the church and Israel of old should clearly be spelled out, showing how the New Covenant ratifies, renews, and transcends the Old Covenant but does not invalidate the Old Testament.
2. It should be stated that Jesus Christ was welcomed and received by a holy remnant of the Jewish people, so that it is untrue and unscriptural to regard the Jews as an accursed race or a rejected people.
3. It should be proclaimed that the church cherishes the never-waning hope for Israel's ultimate reconciliation and that, until then, the Christian's attitude toward his or her Jewish neighbor must be one of love, respect, and final expectation. Antisemitism must be condemned.[26]

After discussions in three more plenaries, Bea and the secretariat realized that a whole text addressing the church's relationship to the Jews was needed, not only because of the topic's urgency, but also because the Theological Commission[27] was refusing to hear the recommendations that the secretariat was already producing. On February 1, 1962, Pope John gave Cardinal Bea further authorization for the SPCU to prepare its own drafts on the Jews and on religious liberty. By then, the Second Vatican Council was set to open on October 11, 1962.[28] After it got under

---

anyone on *Nostra Aetate*, likely because of his Jewish heritage. He fled Vienna in 1938 after the *Anschluss*, moving first to Paris, then to Lisbon, before coming to the United States.

[26] ASV, *Conc. Vat. II*, Box 1452. Contrary to Velati's arrangement, *Dialogo e Rinnovamento*, 488–91, which places Baum's report at the third plenary in April 1961 (the first plenary that John Oesterreicher attended), Stransky recalled that Baum's report was handed out at the second plenary in February 1961, and discussed informally after the given business of the day had concluded. Velati's mistake might have happened because Baum's report was filed in the folder for the third plenary in the Archivio Segreto Vaticano. Having already studied copies found in other archives, this author was surprised to discover it in that folder.

[27] The Theological Commission was one of eleven commissions and three secretariats established by Pope John XXIII as preparatory bodies for the council. The SPCU, with Cardinal Augustin Bea as president, was one of those three secretariats. The Theological Commission, listed first among the commissions, had the task of investigating questions concerning sacred scripture, sacred tradition, faith, and morals. Once Vatican II convened, this commission became the Commission on Doctrine of the Faith and Morals. Cardinal Alfredo Ottaviani served as president of both phases of this commission, see the apostolic letter, *Superno Dei nutu* 7 (June 5, 1960), http://w2.vatican.va/content/john-xxiii/la/apost_letters/1960/documents/hf_j-xxiii_apl_19600605_superno-dei.html. For its first eighteen months of preparatory work, the SPCU drafted recommendations for the commissions.

[28] On the special permission for the secretariat to prepare its own drafts, see Velati,

way, Pope John intervened again and declared that the Secretariat for Promoting Christian Unity was now a permanent commission of the council, with the authority to prepare its own drafts.[29]

Dealing with the Theological Commission was a minor problem compared with the first real crisis. Just a few days before the Central Preparatory Commission[30]—the body charged with sorting through the stacks of drafts submitted for the council's agenda—met in June 1962, the World Jewish Congress (WJC) announced that Chaim Wardi, Israel's Minister for Christian Affairs, would serve as the observer to Vatican II for the WJC. There were several unfortunate aspects to this announcement, the worst being that it put a major strain on diplomatic relations. Representatives of Arab and of other Islamic governments linked a draft on relations with Jews to steps by the Vatican toward establishing diplomatic relations with the State of Israel. Thus when the Central Preparatory Commission convened and looked at the draft "On the Jews," prepared by the secretariat, Cardinal Amleto Cicognani, the Vatican Secretary of State and acting chair of the Central Preparatory Commission, made clear that such a draft could not be considered for the council's agenda. He observed that the text did not mention Muslims, who were also descendants of Abraham, and had raised suspicions that the Vatican was using a putatively religious issue to mask developing diplomacy toward Israel.[31]

No references to Jewish relations or interreligious relations are recorded in the proceedings of the council's first period (October–December 1962). Only after the bishops had left Rome in December 1962 did Cardinal Bea ask Pope John to restore a theological statement on the relationship of Jews to the church to the council's agenda. Bea sent him a two-and-one-half-page memorandum retracing the history of the draft and arguing for its need despite understandable political objections. Bea urged that a draft be prepared apart from any political questions. He emphasized the need for a statement to offset the monstrous crimes of antisemitism and the continuing false charges of deicide. He insisted that, without such a statement, the pope's efforts to renew the church would be inadequate. Pope John

---

Dialogo e Rinnovamento, 818–19. One might now say that this permission, given to Bea in audience with Pope John XXIII on February 1, 1961, represents the "mandate" to Bea to write a statement on the Jews.

[29] *AS* I/1, 78; VI/1, 193–94.

[30] Among the preparatory commissions and secretariats established by Pope John XXIII was a Central Preparatory Commission, which he headed in name, though Cardinal Amleto Cicognani, the Vatican Secretary of State, served as de facto chair, with Archbishop Pericle Felici serving as secretary. Felici would continue serving as secretary of the council and secretary for the coordinating commission once the council began, with Cardinal Cicognani serving as that commission's president. For a full account of the preparatory commissions and commissions serving the council, see *Il Concilio Vaticano II, Annunzio e Preparazione*, vol. 2, parts 1 and 2, ed. Giovanni Caprile, SJ (Rome: La Civiltà Cattolica, 1966) 1:185–211; 2:597–607.

[31] *Acta et Documenta Concilio Oecuemico Vaticano II apparando: Series secunda (Praeparatoria)* (Vatican: Typis Polyglottis Vaticanis, 1964–69), II/4, 22–23.

once again intervened, and, in a personal note written on Bea's letter to him, stated that action must be taken.[32]

Pope John's death in June 1963 might have derailed that initiative, had his successor chosen to discourage it, but Pope Paul VI instead pushed it even further. At the beginning of September, he announced that a secretariat for interreligious relations would be established in due time. Then, in his opening address for the council's second period on September 29, 1963, the pope urged a fourth goal for the council: developing a vision of the church for the modern era. This concern was to complement the three goals originally set by Pope John: spiritual renewal, reconciliation to the modern world, and service to Christian unity. In the final paragraphs of that opening speech, which articulated a new, more outward-looking understanding of the church, Pope Paul asked the council fathers to look beyond their own sphere and take notice of other religions.[33]

In the council's final public session of 1963, Pope Paul made another surprising announcement: he would undertake a pilgrimage to the Holy Land. The visit took place in early January 1964. In Bethlehem on the Feast of the Epiphany, he greeted "those who profess monotheism and direct their religious worship to the one true God," the first time a pope had publicly invited Jews and Muslims into a dialogical relationship.[34]

Also contributing to the context that influenced the council was Pope Paul VI's first encyclical, *Ecclesiam Suam,* released in August 1964. In it, he used the term "dialogue" more than seventy times, applying it not only to relations with other Christians but also to relations with Jews, Muslims, all religious believers, and all people of goodwill. Paul VI used "dialogue" as a theological term to describe relationships within God, God's relationships with humanity, and relationships among all people—all of which formed the overarching concept of the dialogue of salvation.

Meanwhile, the SPCU's members and staff were acting to prevent the council from ignoring issues about the Jews and religious liberty by writing these concerns into chapters 4 and 5, respectively, of the draft decree *On Ecumenism.* They formally presented a five-chapter first draft to the council in November 1963. The fourth chapter's title was no longer simply "On the Jews" but "On the Relation of Catho-

---

[32] ASV, *Conc. Vat. II*, Box 1452. Accounts of the incident can be found in Alberigo and Komonchak, eds., *History of Vatican II*, vol. 1, 396–98 and Thomas Stransky, "The Genesis of *Nostra Aetate*: An Insider's Story," in *Nostra Aetate: Origins, Promulgation, Impact on Jewish–Catholic Relations*, ed. Neville Lamdan and Alberto Melloni (Berlin: Lit Verlag, 2007), 41–44.

[33] *AAS* 55:856. A translation appears in *Interreligious Dialogue: The Official Teaching of the Catholic Church from the Second Vatican Council to John Paul II (1963–2005)*, ed. Francesco Gioia (Boston: Pauline Books and Media, 2006), 157.

[34] Pope Paul's original text was in French: http://w2.vatican.va/content/paul-vi/fr/speeches/1964/documents/hf_p-vi_spe_19640106_epiphanie.html. An English translation can be found in Gioia, ed., *Interreligious Dialogue*, 157–59.

lics to Non-Christians, above all, to the Jews." It differed from the language that the Central Preparatory Commission had refused to place on the council's agenda the previous year primarily by including two sentences:

> After we have treated the principles of Catholic ecumenism, we do not wish to pass over in silence the fact that, taking account of diverse conditions, these same principles ought to be applied to the way of conversing and collaborating with those who are not Christians, who nevertheless worship God, or at least with goodwill, strive to follow their conscience in carrying out the moral law which is innate in human nature. Above all, this holds for the Jews, for they are linked with the church of Christ in a special way.[35]

This fourth chapter essentially repeated the three points that Father Baum had originally introduced (see discussion earlier).

When Cardinal Bea presented this chapter on November 18, 1963, he outlined the text's history and cautioned: "The decree is very brief, but the material treated in it is not easy. . . . There is no national or political question here. In particular, there is no question of recognition of the State of Israel by the Holy See."[36] After two days of general discussion on all five chapters, with several interventions calling for chapter 4 to be retained, the council fathers spent the rest of November discussing the first three chapters on ecumenism. On December 3, 1963, Bea took the microphone to calm the fears of those who would worry that chapters 4 and 5 might be dropped from the draft because they had not been discussed in detail. He assured the council fathers and all interested parties that, though they had not been discussed, they were not off the agenda.[37]

By the end of 1963, then, the first crisis regarding the promulgation of *Nostra Aetate*—that various forces opposed to addressing the church's position vis-à-vis other religions, especially Judaism—had passed. Neither diplomatic tensions over the State of Israel, the death of Pope John XXIII, nor lack of concern with issues of interreligious relationships had sufficed to bury the subject. Nevertheless, the germ of *Nostra Aetate* remained on the council's agenda primarily because of the efforts of Cardinal Bea, without whose ministrations the council might never have proceeded to frame the document that it did. At this point, no one could have predicted what position Vatican II might ultimately take.

---

[35] The translation is that of Thomas F. Stransky. The Latin text is available in *AS* II/5, 431–32.

[36] *AS* II/5, 481. English translations of Bea's introductions (*relationes*) are in Augustin Cardinal Bea, SJ, *The Church and the Jewish People: A Commentary on the Second Vatican Council's Declaration on the Relation of the Church to Non-Christian Religions*, trans. Philip Loretz, SJ (London: Geoffrey Chapman, 1966), 154–72.

[37] *AS* II/6, 364–66.

Second Crisis: Mixed Messages about the Church and the Jews

Sentiment for the council to take a strong position on the Jews and on religious liberty continued to mount. After Pope Paul VI returned from his pilgrimage to the Holy Land, he received a message from Cardinal Albert Meyer of Chicago. If the last two chapters of the draft *On Ecumenism* "are rejected and not acted upon favorably," Meyer worried, "I fear very much for the cause of the whole ecumenical movement, and indeed of anything that comes out of the council." Furthermore, he predicted: "Without these two chapters, the cause of the Catholic Church in the United States, I am afraid, will suffer greatly." Meyer was not alone in linking the credibility of Vatican II in the United States to these two chapters.[38] Cardinal Ritter (St. Louis) sent a similar letter, as did others.[39] Nevertheless, crafting appropriate language to define a new relationship with the Jews, much less other non-Christian religions, proved difficult and eventually produced a firestorm of anger among Jews, even those most inclined to promote a rapprochement.

The secretariat met in March 1964 and made a few modest changes in the text on the Jews. With the help of Fathers Anawati and Cuoq, they also attempted a paragraph on Muslims, but the SPCU bishop members hesitated to approve it. They argued that they had neither sufficient expertise in Islam nor a mandate to expand the text. A new draft, once again titled "On the Jews," was forwarded to the Coordinating Commission, which had replaced the Central Preparatory Commission as the chief administrative body once the council was under way. At this point, the statement was no longer a chapter of the draft decree on ecumenism but its second appendix.[40]

---

[38] Peter Hebblethwaite first mentions two letters (January 25 from Meyer and Pope Paul's reply on February 1) in his *Paul VI: The First Modern Pope* (New York: Paulist, 1993), 375. A letter from Meyer, received on January 29, 1964, making similar points to Cardinal Bea is in the archives of Father Thomas F. Stransky, Box 10, File 5, Catholic University of America, Washington, DC, and also of Father John Long (Woodstock Library, Georgetown University), now being catalogued. At the time, *Nostra Aetate* was still chapter 4 of the draft *On Ecumenism*. Edward Kaplan, *Spiritual Radical: Abraham Joshua Heschel in America, 1940–1972* (New Haven, CT: Yale University Press, 2007), 254, reports that, on the night of January 2, 1964, Rabbi Heschel and American Jesuit Gustave Weigel, a consultor to the Secretariat for Promoting Christian Unity, discussed the need for supporting the chapter on the Jews in the current draft of *On Ecumenism* and decided that they would contact Cardinals Spellman, Meyer, and Ritter to send supportive messages to Cardinal Bea. Weigel died of a heart attack the next day.

[39] *AS* VI/3, 107–8. See also Alberigo and Komonchak, eds., *History of Vatican II*, 3:381–82. Additional letters from US bishops are in the Vatican archives.

[40] The narrative is based on Thomas F. Stransky's remarks to the author. Together they consulted drafts and minutes in Stransky's papers and those of John F. Long, SJ, another former member of the SPCU during the council. Long's archives are being catalogued for the Woodstock Theological Library, Georgetown University. Stransky's archives have now moved to the Vatican II archives of the Catholic University of America.

In response to the religious and political concerns that Cardinal Cicognani had voiced in 1962 when the original draft, "On the Jews," was deleted from the council's agenda, the Coordinating Commission formally recommended including material on Muslims. It also recommended including an extended paragraph against all forms of discrimination and retitling the draft "On the Relation of Christians to Jews and to the Universal Human Family." Paul VI sent notes and further suggestions. Three more drafts were floated back and forth, resulting in another new title: "On Jews and on Non-Christians." Bea, cognizant that these exchanges were occurring outside the SPCU's plenary, wrote to the bishop members on July 17 explaining why the text now on the agenda was different from the one they had approved in March, and wondering if his colleagues now wanted to retain any responsibility for the new draft, since it "neither reproduces completely our revision nor has it been voted upon in a subsequent session of the secretariat."[41] Bea invited their emendations and admitted that the draft would likely be leaked to the press.

The Coordinating Commission also decided that the contents of the appendices "On Religious Liberty" and "On the Jews and Non-Christians" were so distinct that they should become separate declarations. The decision to distinguish "declarations" from "decrees" may seem completely arbitrary, but it was based on practical considerations and was ultimately of little import. As the council progressed, the number of major pronouncements exceeded original expectations, so, to ensure that important statements each received due attention, items that had once been part of the same document were issued separately.[42] Moreover, as John O'Malley has argued, appreciating the council's general language and how it differs from the language of previous councils is more important than parsing the nomenclature of its documents and trying to determine a text's significance on the basis of the category to which it was assigned.[43]

The second draft to appear on the council floor, now titled "On Jews and on Non-Christians," was thus awkwardly worded due to insertions and rearranged sentences authored by both the Coordinating Commission and the pope. A passage recalling the Christian hope for "the union of the Jewish people with the church," together with one citing St. Paul's hope that all Israel would be saved (see Rom 11:25), appear just before an admonition that catechetical instruction, preaching,

---

[41] ASV, *Conc. Vat. II*, Box 1454, Busta #8. The extended proceedings behind the scenes are evident in the notes of Archbishop Pericle Felici, general secretary of the council, *AS* V/2, 570–79.

[42] *AS* V/2, 289–23. The members of the Coordinating Commission did not decide that the contents of declarations were less important than the contents of decrees by their agreement to separate the appendices on the Jews and on religious liberty into independent declarations. That *Nostra Aetate* is a declaration does not make it less authoritative than any of the four constitutions or nine decrees. It is the language of each text that gives clues to the importance of what is being said.

[43] John W. O'Malley, *What Happened at Vatican II* (Cambridge, MA: Harvard University Press, 2008), 43–52.

and daily conversation should be free of anti-Jewish expressions, and following a reminder that responsibility for the death of Jesus should not be attributed "to the Jews of our own time." The resulting arrangement was unfortunate. The text seemed to suggest that the hope for an eventual union of Jews with the church was a motive for improved behavior of Christians toward Jews.[44] Jews would read these lines as a Christian expectation of their conversion.

The text did advise Catholics "to pay great attention to the opinions and teachings of others, which, although they differ from our own in many ways, contain nevertheless many rays of that Truth which enlightens everyone in this world." This passage was written by SPCU staff and available consultors in their first response to the Coordinating Commission's request to expand the text, but it seems to have been inspired by Paul VI. The reworked text now contained an added sentence on Muslims, whose teachings and opinions should receive Catholics' attention because they "adore the one God, personal and judge, and they stand close to us in a religious sense and they draw near to us with many expressions of human culture set before us." No longer does the text contain the word "deicide," which Paul VI considered a despicable and foolish term; nevertheless, the text "condemns" (*damnat*) hatred and persecutions of Jews and discrimination of all kinds.[45]

On September 3, 1964, nine days in advance of the opening of the third session, an unauthorized translation of a leaked draft of "On Jews and on Non-Christians" appeared in the *New York Herald Tribune*. The *New York Times* published it the next day. Rabbi Abraham Joshua Heschel, a member of the American Jewish Committee (AJC) who had already met with Cardinal Bea and the SPCU staff on a few occasions, was particularly disturbed by what he read. He was repulsed by what seemed an expression of hope that Jews would be converted through dialogue. *Time* magazine reported Rabbi Heschel's now famous statement that he was "ready to go to Auschwitz any time, if faced with the alternative of conversion or death." He and Zachariah Shuster, the AJC's European director, were given an extraordinary private and secret meeting with Paul VI on September 14, the day that the third session opened.[46] They complained about both the implied mission to convert Jews through dialogue and the dropping of "deicide," the exact charge hurled at Jews by Christians for centuries. Both Heschel and the pope used the word "mission," but they understood it in vastly different ways. For Heschel, mission implied a negative form of proselytizing; for Paul VI, it meant an expansive and positive understanding of "evangelization," a concept that he would develop in

---

[44] This draft is found in *AS* III/2, 327–29; English translation is by Stransky.

[45] For the likely sources of Pope Paul VI's influence, see the concluding paragraphs of his opening address to the second session of the council on September 29, 1963, and passages in his first encyclical, *Ecclesiam Suam*, which he was presumably preparing in the spring and early summer 1964 while the draft of the secretariat was being tossed about.

[46] "What Catholics Think about Jews," *Time* 84, no. 11 (September 11, 1964): 78. An account of the meeting appears in Kaplan, *Spiritual Radical*, 259–68.

the decade after Vatican II.[47] The two seemed to understand neither what the other was saying nor how each was offending the other. The second crisis resulted in a draft the ambiguities of which raised Jewish concerns rather than assuaged them.

Nevertheless, the council had come some distance from the previous year, for it could no longer ignore the imperative to make a considered statement on the church's relationships with Jews and members of other religions. That "On the Jews and on Non-Christians" had achieved status as a separate declaration indicated that Cardinal Bea and the SPCU had demonstrated the importance of its subject matter. When Bea approached the podium at the council eleven days later (September 25) to present the text, he received enthusiastic applause from the bishops, a highly unusual response, indicating that he and his team were back in charge of their draft and enjoying the support of the council fathers.[48] A concerted debate on the declaration took place over the next three days. No vote was taken, but the secretariat received support for its work, the near unanimous recommendation to expand the text, and dozens of suggested changes.

Third Crisis: Splintering the Draft and Its Message

By this point, the council was considering many initiatives at once. Three drafts— a constitution on the church, the SPCU's *Decree on Ecumenism,* and another decree on Catholic eastern churches—were moving toward their final voting. By September 1964, a new Secretariat for Non-Christians was putting together its staff. Expertise was needed on religions of Asia and Africa.

A separate working group on Islam had come into existence within the SPCU, with Georges Anawati (already a consultor), Josef Cuoq (now undersecretary of the Secretariat for Non-Christians), and his fellow Missionary of Africa, Robert Caspar, now appointed a SPCU consultor to help with passages on Islam. Jean Corbon, a diocesan priest from Lebanon, joined them as a fourth consultor. They met on October 9, 1964, convened by John Long, SJ, an SPCU staff member. They wrote what essentially became section 3 of the next draft, which would be devoted entirely to relations with Muslims.

On the day before, however, Cardinal Bea received a letter from Archbishop Pericle Felici, the council's general secretary, announcing that control of the declaration on relations with Jews and followers of other religions would be taken away from the SPCU. The draft was to be broken into pieces and its contents dispersed. The statement on the Jews would be appended to the *Dogmatic Constitution on the Church,* and the one on other religions would be included in the draft on missions. The section that condemned antisemitism and all forms of discrimination would

---

[47] The literature on dialogue and mission is immense. We can say that the question of mission and dialogue, left open by *Nostra Aetate* and Vatican II, remains an unanswered question.

[48] See Alberigo and Komonchak, eds., *History of Vatican II,* 4:135.

go into the developing draft of the *Church in the Modern World*.[49] On October 9, a second letter from Felici asserted that a joint commission, composed of members from both the SPCU and the Commission on the Doctrine of the Faith and Morals (hereafter called the doctrine commission), would take control of the declaration on religious liberty.[50] Collectively, these efforts constitute the third major crisis that *Nostra Aetate* faced—the possibility that the component statements on the church's relations with the Jews and members of other religions, its condemnation of antisemitism and discrimination, and its declaration of religious liberty would be scattered and thereby lose the gravitas that a unified presentation would provide.[51] This time, however, Bea was not about to hand over control of the drafts, and he drew on the pope's support, though Bea was more adamant on keeping the draft on religious liberty under the SPCU's complete control than about determining where the contents of the declaration on the Jews and non-Christians might eventually be placed.[52]

Cardinal Franz König (Vienna), a scholar on the history of religions, rallied to Bea's side.[53] On October 19, he asked Father Stransky to deliver a message requesting four consultors—Yves Congar, OP, Charles Moeller, Paul Pfister, SJ, and Josef Neuner, SJ—to gather the next day in the sacristy of Saint Peter's Basilica. Pfister had accompanied the Japanese bishops to the council as their consultor, while Neuner had come as a consultor with the bishops of India and as adviser to the commission on mission. Congar and Moeller served as consultors to the doctrine commission. The next morning, Cardinal König informed them that their help was needed because the text on the Jews had to be expanded if it were to survive.[54]

---

[49] *AS* V/2, 754–65.

[50] Ibid., 773.

[51] Alberigo and Komonchak, eds., *History of Vatican II*, 4:166–93.

[52] As late as January 1965, Bea's biographer tells us that the cardinal was still holding onto the notion that the heart of the expanded November 1964 text of *Nostra Aetate* would somehow be appended to the *Dogmatic Constitution on the Church*, which the council had already promulgated at the end of November 1964. Bea felt that the message on the relationship of Jews to the church would be strengthened by being appended to the *Dogmatic Constitution*. See Schmidt, *Augustin Bea*, 515n79. In the end, it made little sense to append a second document to a text that had already been promulgated.

[53] König had already published *Christus und die Relgionen der Erde*, 3 vols. (Vienna: Herder, 1956), and *Religionswissenschaftliches Wörterbuch: Die Grundbegriffe* (Freiburg: Herder, 1956).

[54] Dietmar W. Wingler, *Wann Kommt die Einheit? Ökumene als Programm und Herausforderung*, Kardinal König Bibliothek 4 (Vienna: Styria, 2014), 96–99. Wingler provides a picture of a note on secretariat stationery of Stransky informing König that he had delivered the notes for the meeting the next day. See also the accounts of Congar and Neuner on this meeting and the next developments: Yves Congar, OP, *My Journal of the Council*, trans. Mary John Ronayne, OP, and Mary Cecily Boulding, OP (Collegeville, MN: Liturgical Press, 2012), 634, and Joseph Neuner, SJ, *Memories of My Life* (Pune, India: The Provincial, Pune Jesuit Society, 2003).

On the afternoon of October 21, Stransky convened Congar, Moeller, Pfister, and Neuner. Stransky had brought an ordo, or outline, composed in Latin.[55] It proposed an introduction and four sections. Together, these would become the five numbered sections of *Nostra Aetate*. In fact, this ordo contained those two exact words, "Nostra Aetate," referring to the suitableness or advantage of the declaration "in our time." They became the first two words of the next Latin draft. The introduction would recognize that the foundation for dialogue rests in the unity of humanity and in the age-old questions with which all peoples struggle. The next section would cover how various religions address these questions of ultimate concern, especially Hinduism and Buddhism. The already prepared draft on Muslims would come next, followed by the already refined text on Jews. A final section would draw logical conclusions from the universal fatherhood of God—toleration and no discrimination of any kind.

This group reconvened with others from the SPCU on October 25. This time, Monsignor Johannes Willebrands, SPCU secretary, presided. The drafts of Neuner and Pfister were adopted as a basis for the opening sections.[56] Comparing them with the final form of *Nostra Aetate* makes clear that sections 1 and 2 of the final text drew from both drafts. Neuner composed the original sentence on Hinduism, and Pfister, the one on Buddhism. The paragraphs already composed on Muslims and Jews would then become sections 3 and 4. By October 30, the new draft, beginning with the words "Nostra Aetate," was spliced and ready.[57] Thus *Nostra Aetate* is the product of three drafting groups. The original group composed much of sections 4 and 5 on Jews and on rejecting all forms of discrimination. Section 3, on Muslims, was drafted by the group of specialists on Islam. Sections 1 and 2 were composed by the group that Cardinal König had summoned and Stransky had convened. The SPCU staff, with the help of some of these consultors, combined the sections into a single text under the direction of Willebrands.

On November 12, the doctrine commission signed off on the new draft of *Nostra Aetate*. On November 20, Cardinal Bea presented the new and expanded version of the draft: "No council in the history of the church, unless I am mistaken, has ever set out so solemnly the principles concerning [non-Christian religions]."[58] The new draft exhorted Catholics to converse and collaborate with the followers of other religions to "preserve and promote those spiritual and moral goods as well as those sociocultural values found among those followers." The SPCU restored the term "deicide" to section 4 on the Jews. There was little discussion in the hall, and then three votes on the text were taken: first, on sections 1–3 (the general introduction, religions in general with special mention of Hinduism and Buddhism, and Muslims); then, on

---

[55] ASV, *Conc. Vat. II*, Box 1455.

[56] Congar, *My Journal*, 643.

[57] All these drafts are in ASV, *Conc. Vat. II*, Box 1455. Stransky told the present author in late 2015 that the questions listed in the opening section of *Nostra Aetate* were composed by Charles Moeller, an aficionado of religion and the arts.

[58] *AS* III/8, 650.

sections 4 and 5 dealing with Jews and condemning all forms of discrimination; and finally, a third vote on the whole text. The first two votes were to be "yes" or "no." The third vote could be "yes," "no," or "yes with reservations." Nearly 2,000 council fathers voted, with only 136 voting "no" on sections 1–3, and only 185 on sections 4 and 5. On the whole declaration, out of a total of 1,996 votes, 1,651 were "yes," 99 were "no," and 242 were "yes with reservations," with 4 ballots invalid.

Council rules called for two votes, and the November 1964 ballot was only the first, but it was clear to everyone that, barring unexpected developments, the new and expanded *Nostra Aetate* would pass a second vote even after modifications were considered. Nevertheless, still worried about political implications, particularly an implied recognition of Israel, Cardinal Cicognani urged Cardinal Bea to prepare an article for immediate publication in *L'Osservatore Romano* clarifying what the text did and did not say.[59] Bea noted that the document had received "an overwhelming majority vote of approval," and he emphasized the "exclusively religious character of the text": "Just as the sections of the Declaration concerning the Hinduists [*sic*], Buddhists, and Musulmans [*sic*] have nothing to do with politics—that is evident, so also does the passage on the Jews exclude any political interpretation." The document, he wrote, "clearly in complete accord with the Gospel, is inspired by truth, justice, and Christian charity."

The Fourth Crisis: Opposition from Middle East Bishops

Those voting against *Nostra Aetate* might have collectively constituted a small minority, but one group among them needed to be heard to prevent undermining the document's expansive vision. Opposition to the text concentrated essentially in two groups—a collection of very conservative bishops who came to be known as the International Group of Fathers (*Coetus Internationalis Patrum*), and nearly all bishops from the Middle East, most of whom headed Eastern Catholic jurisdictions.[60] The archconservatives could not be won over, but both Cardinal Bea and Pope Paul wanted Eastern Catholic bishops, especially those who were Arabs, to feel they could still offer suggestions for *Nostra Aetate* for the sake of Catholic unity. Melkite Patriarch Maximos IV had even suggested that he might walk out of the hall of the council in protest during the final voting on *Nostra Aetate*.[61] Paul VI did not want to see such a walkout because it would not only represent a rejection of *Nostra Aetate* but would also affront the vision of a unified and collegial church that the pope was promoting as one of the council's major themes.

---

[59] "A proposito della Dichiarzaione conciliare circa i non cristiani," *L'Osservatore Romano* (November 30, 1964).

[60] On the *Coetus Internationalis Patrum*, see Alberigo and Komonchak, eds., *History of Vatican II*, 4:66, 113, 117, 157–70, 278–89, 515–18.

[61] Alberigo and Komonchak, eds., *History of Vatican II*, 4:552. The bishops of the Middle East argued that religion and politics could not be separated as *Nostra Aetate* was attempting to do.

Cardinal Bea dispatched Monsignor Willebrands and another member of his staff, Father Pierre Duprey, a Missionary of Africa who had spent most of his career in the Middle East, to meet with leading Eastern Catholic bishops, first in Syria and Lebanon (March 18–23, 1965), and then in Jerusalem and Cairo (April 22–30). They returned with only a gloomy report of protests, rejection, and intransigence.[62] The bishops in the Middle East were adamant in their opposition. The final presentation and voting on the declaration could get ugly, despite the almost certain prospect of *Nostra Aetate* passing.

The members and consultors of the SPCU gathered at the end of May 1965 for what was probably their most difficult and stormy meeting on *Nostra Aetate*. Pope Paul had intervened again. He wanted the term "deicide" dropped and the verb regarding antisemitism and forms of discrimination changed from "*damnat*," although an overwhelming majority had already approved the use of both words. They also discussed softening the section on the Jews. Bishop Josef Stangl (Würzburg) pleaded for a strong text; otherwise, he made clear, the German church would feel that its self-examination of its role during the period of National Socialism would be impeded.[63] The secretariat ended up changing "*damnat*" to "*deplorat*" ("deplores" or "decries"), which some might consider a stronger word. They reluctantly agreed to drop "deicide." Finally, it was decided that another mission to the Middle East was needed; this time Cardinal Bea would seek papal authorization. The delegation would include the persuasive Bishop Emiel-Jozef De Smedt (Bruges), a much-appreciated orator in the council. Willebrands and Duprey joined him. They traveled to Beirut, Jerusalem, and Cairo, with Pope Paul sending letters to their host bishops in advance of their visits. The trip took place at the end of July 1965. They returned with a number of recommendations, even from Maximos IV, that the secretariat could consider along with the modifications already recorded from the previous November.[64] In the end, it seems that the Middle East bishops primarily wanted their point of view heard. For them, religion and politics could not be separated. Cardinal Bea had argued for a purely theological text, suspecting that otherwise no statement on relations with Jews would have been possible. They disagreed with that point of view, stated their opposition, but respected the desire of Pope Paul and the majority of bishops to approve the text.

The final draft of *Nostra Aetate* was mailed to the council fathers in August 1965 and presented for voting on October. A series of nine votes followed, with more or less the same pattern of negative votes as in the previous November. The votes were presented and explained on October 15. This time there was a separate vote on the section on Muslims, which received 1,910 "yes" and only 189 "no"

---

[62] Willebrands's report on the second journey appears in *AS* V/3, 313–20. Stransky commented to this author that Bea insisted Willebrands put his name on it as his private report and not that of the secretariat.

[63] The minutes of the May 1965 were carefully recorded by John F. Long, SJ, and a copy is in his archives. This account follows those minutes and Father Stransky's recollection.

[64] ASV, *Conc. Vat. II*, Box 1459.

votes. Section 4 on the Jews was broken into four thematic votes. Most of the negative votes rejected any correction to the teachings of church fathers that the Jews
were a cursed people; on this point, there were 1,821 positive and 245 negative
votes. Of the 2,023 votes cast in the final vote on the whole of *Nostra Aetate*, 1,763
were positive, 250 were negative, and 10 were invalid. Father Stransky remembers
that Pope Paul wanted no more than 400 negative votes on any single vote. When
the text was solemnly promulgated on October 28, 1965, the negative votes had
dwindled to 88, with 2,221 council fathers affirming the Declaration.

At a news conference on October 15, 1965, after the final round of voting on
Nostra Aetate, Father Stransky observed: "What is said in the declaration may seem
naïve in centuries to come, but at the present, it would be difficult for the council to
come up with any more than it has."[65] In that sense, *Nostra Aetate* is pre-dialogical
in that it exhorts Catholics to dialogue with the followers of other religions without
presenting much insight on the nature of dialogue itself. Wisdom would come from
experience.

In understanding why the text of *Nostra Aetate* is the way that it is, one should
look at the whole of Vatican II and not isolate any text or other official act, paragraph, or sentence from the whole. About the text's growth, Cardinal Bea invoked
the biblical image of the mustard seed that in the course of discussions grew into
a tree in which all the birds of the air nest.[66] The first context of *Nostra Aetate* is
the council itself and the variety of streams and developments flowing into it and
through its complicated proceedings. No single person was completely in control of
any single act or text of the council. With regard to *Nostra Aetate*, Cardinal Bea was
in control of its destiny more often than anyone else; however, at times, he had to
manage the conciliar process much like a gondolier, who must steer the craft taking
account of currents, winds, and unexpected tides.

Historian Giovanni Miccoli asserts that "it took the will of John XXIII and the
perseverance of Cardinal Bea to impose the declaration on the council."[67] Perhaps,
though, the declaration should be understood as an aspect both of Pope John's
initial wish that the council be ecumenical and of the SPCU's successful influence
on the council.[68] Some of the same hands that worked on the *Declaration on the*

---

[65] *Council Daybook: Vatican II, Session 4, Sept. 14, 1965 to Dec. 8, 1965*, ed. Floyd
Anderson (Washington, DC: National Catholic Welfare Conference, 1966), 140.

[66] *AS* III/8, 649.

[67] Alberigo and Komonchak, eds., *History of Vatican II*, 4:137.

[68] As Giuseppe Alberigo writes, "Together with the documents on ecumenism and
religious freedom this document [*Nostra Aetate*] completed the work of the Secretariat for
Christian Unity. This body had come into existence as a simple bureau supplying non-Catholics with information about the council, but by putting on the agenda subjects most central
to the *aggiornamento* [updating and reconciling the church with the times] desired by John
XXIII, it had acquired a decisive influence on the council's work." Alberigo and Komonchak, eds., *History of Vatican II*, 5:231.

Relation of the Church to Non-Christian Religions also worked on the *Decree on Ecumenism* and *The Declaration on Religious Liberty*. Section 4 of *Nostra Aetate* (the section on the Jews) manifests insights and wishes of John XXIII, and the whole text resonates with the views and commitments of Paul VI. It received the overwhelming support of the council fathers and represents one the council's greatest achievements.

2

NOSTRA AETATE:
A MILESTONE IN THE HISTORY OF RELIGIONS?

From Competition to Cooperation

Paul F. Knitter

Marking a New Axial Shift in Religious History

What makes *Nostra Aetate* so monumental, so revolutionary, is that it calls Christians to an attitude toward other religions that they had simply never held before. "Never held before" is a rather sweeping claim, but I think it accurate. Yes, individual Christians, such as Nicholas of Cusa,[1] had occasionally recognized the value of other religious traditions, but never before, as far as I know, had the official teaching body of the Roman Catholic Church—the magisterium—issued a pronouncement that was so positive, so stunningly different, in what it said about other religious traditions.

I suggest that what makes *Nostra Aetate* so revolutionary is to be found not primarily in what it, and other Vatican II documents, say *about* other religions, but, rather, in what it says about how Christians should *act* toward other religious believers. *Nostra Aetate* opens up whole new directions—not, primarily, in its *doctrine* about the meaning of other religions, but rather in its *ethics* about how Christians should interact and relate to followers of other religions.

Certainly, what Vatican II teaches about other religions is important: Christians can expect to find in other religions teachings that are "true and holy" (*Nostra Aetate*, sec. 2),[2] "precious elements of religion and humanity" (*Gaudium et Spes*, sec. 92),[3]

---

[1] See *Nicholas of Cusa's De Pace Fidei and Cribratio Alkorani: Translation and Analysis* (Minneapolis: A. J. Banning Press, 1994).

[2] *Declaration on the Relation of the Church to Non-Christian Religions—Nostra Aetate*, proclaimed by Pope Paul VI (Vatican City, 1965), http://www.vatican.va/archive/hist_councils/ii_vatican_council/documents/vat-ii_decl_19651028_nostra-aetate_en.html.

[3] *Pastoral Constitution on the Church in the Modern World—Gaudium et Spes,* promulgated by Pope Paul VI (Vatican City, 1965), http://www.vatican.va/archive/hist_councils/ii_vatican_council/documents/vat-ii_cons_19651207_gaudium-et-spes_en.html.

elements of "truth and grace" (*Ad Gentes*, sec. 9),[4] "good things, spiritual and moral" (*Nostra Aetate*, sec. 2), "seeds of the Word" (*Ad Gentes*, sec. 11), and a "ray of that Truth which enlightens all humankind"[5] (*Nostra Aetate*, sec. 2). These statements ground a wholly new theology of religions, one that recognizes—simply, powerfully, and for the first time in the history of the Roman Catholic Church—that God is alive and well and active in other religions. This proclamation is radically new.

But even more radical and transformative of the church in the long run is the gentle, but clear and commanding exhortation tucked at the end of the second section of *Nostra Aetate* declaring that Christians "through dialogue and collaboration with the followers of other religions, carried out with prudence and love . . . [should] recognize, preserve and promote the good things, spiritual and moral, as well as the socio-cultural values found among them"[6] (sec. 2).[7]

Here Christians are being exhorted to do something that they had never before counted among their Christian obligations—to engage, talk, and even collaborate with persons of other faiths. They are being called to step out of their Christian backyards and dialogue with their neighbors who don't speak their religious language. That directive means, by the very definition of dialogue, not just to get along with them, but to learn from and cooperate with people who had previously been strangers to convert, not companions to learn from! *Nostra Aetate*, I think we can say, made dialogue with persons of other religions an ethical responsibility, even an obligation. This call to dialogue, I am suggesting, did much more to transform the Catholic Church, and eventually other Christian churches as well, than the positive doctrinal teachings about "the elements of truth and good" in other faiths.

Throughout the five decades since the Second Vatican Council, more and more Catholics all over the world have started talking with, working with, learning from, and befriending persons of other religious communities. An official Vatican department, now called the Council for Interreligious Dialogue, was established during the council to support, foster, and expand these experiences. Through this practice of interreligious friendship, a growing number of Christians have been discovering that the most satisfying—and most Christian—way of relating to their neighbors is not to oppose, belittle, or try to convert them, but to engage them in every possible way, so that all could learn from each other.

---

[4] *Decree—Ad Gentes: On the Mission Activity of the Church*, promulgated by Pope Paul VI (Vatican City, 1965), http://www.vatican.va/archive/hist_councils/ii_vatican_council/documents/vat-ii_decree_19651207_ad-gentes_en.html.

[5] Out of special deference to the urgings of our recently departed colleague Rita Gross, I have changed the original text from "all men" to "humankind." Sexist language, understandable in the 1960s, is still used in Vatican II documents.

[6] The original text reads: "among these men." See preceding note.

[7] Filios suos igitur hortatur, ut cum prudentia et caritate per colloquia et collaborationem cum asseclis aliarum religionum . . . , illa bona spiritualia et moralia necnon illos valores socio-culturales, quae apud eos inveniuntur, agnoscant, servent et promoveant.

In the early 1990s, the magisterium endorsed and expanded on that little sentence calling Catholics to "dialogue and collaborate" with other religions. Both Pope John Paul II, in his encyclical *Redemptoris Missio*,[8] and the Vatican Council for Interreligious Dialogue, in its statement *Dialogue and Proclamation*,[9] officially announced that dialogue with other religions was now part of the job description of Catholic missionaries. The mission of the Christian church was newly—I would say revolutionarily—defined (better, redefined) as not only to *proclaim and teach*, but also to *listen and learn*.[10]

So it was that, by the mid-1990s, the Catholic bishops of Asia could declare that dialogue was a "new way of being church."[11] This claim was truly novel; ever since the church had become the official religion of first the Roman Empire and then of subsequent European polities, it did not seem to think that it had much to learn from other religions and cultures. Critics might say that "domination was the traditional way of being church" for much of its history. Now, the church is declaring itself committed to dialogue rather than domination. Again we see how revolutionary *Nostra Aetate* was.

The epicenter of this seismic, dialogical shift may be located in *Nostra Aetate* and the Second Vatican Council, but it also resonated with and inspired multiplying calls for interreligious dialogue among the mainline Protestant communities represented in the World Council of Churches (WCC). The General Assembly of the WCC had already used the challenging word "dialogue" in a 1961 statement issued in Delhi, and the challenge was noted even more resolutely six years later in a WCC conference in Sri Lanka. A kind of inner-Christian dialogue developed between the WCC and the Vatican, which reciprocally

---

[8] *Encyclical of Pope John Paul II—Redemptoris Missio: On the Permanent Validity of the Church's Missionary Mandate* (Vatican City, 1990), http://w2.vatican.va/content/john-paul-ii/en/encyclicals/documents/hf_jp-ii_enc_07121990_redemptoris-missio.html.

[9] Pontifical Council for Inter-religious Dialogue, *Dialogue and Proclamation: Reflection and Orientations on Interreligious Dialogue and the Proclamation of the Gospel of Jesus Christ* (Vatican City, 1991), http://www.vatican.va/roman_curia/pontifical_councils/interelg/documents/rc_pc_interelg_doc_19051991_dialogue-and-proclamatio_en.html.

[10] Both documents, in an astonishingly new and clear way, lay out the characteristics of authentic dialogue: (1) Dialogue is "a method and means of *mutual* knowledge and enrichment" in which "a witness [is] *given and received* for mutual advancement" (*Redemptoris Missio*, paras. 55, 56, emphases mine). (2) In dialogue "Christians too must allow themselves to be questioned" and corrected (*Dialogue and Proclamation*, sec. 32), since "other religions constitute a positive challenge to the church" (*Redemptoris Missio*, 56). (3) In the dialogue, all sides must be ready to change their minds and even their religious identities, for "'the decision may be made to leave one's previous spiritual or religious situation in order to direct oneself toward another'" (*Dialogue and Proclamation*, sec. 41). (For texts and commentary on the Vatican's new understanding of dialogue, see Paul Knitter, *Jesus and the Other Names: Christian Mission and Global Responsibility* [Maryknoll, NY: Orbis Books, 1996], 136–40.)

[11] Tom C. Fox, *Pentecost in Asia: A New Way of Being Church* (Maryknoll, NY: Orbis Books, 2002), 185–97.

supported this new opening toward other religions. In 1971, reflecting what the Vatican had done by setting up the Council for Interreligious Dialogue, the WCC formally established the "Sub-unit on Dialogue with People of Living Faiths and Ideologies" under the pioneering leadership of Stanley Samartha.[12] Dialogue was becoming "a new way of being church" not only for the Roman but also for the mainline Protestant Church. I believe that, over the past decade or so, one can also detect a growing awareness among the Evangelical churches that the diversity of religions is not going to go away, and that interreligious collaboration is becoming increasingly urgent.[13]

The realization that dawned with *Nostra Aetate* has become clearer and more pressing for an increasing number of Christian churches: the manyness of religions is something that churches must embrace rather than try to stamp out by making everyone Christian. More and more Christians are reaching a conclusion that before *Nostra Aetate* was simply inconceivable—the diversity of religions must be God's will. God wants there to be many religions, not just one. And in *Nostra Aetate* God is calling the religions not to compete and struggle with each other so that only the strongest and the best is left standing, but, rather, to collaborate and learn from each other so that all religions and all people can rest more securely and happily in their differences, while also standing together.

A New Axial Age

Nostra Aetate, I suggest, can also be considered a milestone not only in the history of the Catholic and other Western churches but also in the history of religions. To state this suggestion even more dramatically, I think that there are good reasons to regard *Nostra Aetate* as the harbinger of a new "axial age"—a term that some, if not all, religious scholars use to identify what they consider a quantum evolution in the religious consciousness of the human species.[14] It took shape, scholars like Karl Jaspers tell us, roughly and unevenly between 900 and 200 BCE, and can be detected in four different geographical locations, giving rise to the major religious traditions that nourish humanity today: Confucianism and Daoism in China, Hinduism and Buddhism in India, philosophical rationalism in Greece, and monotheism in Israel, the latter being carried forward by Christianity and Islam.

This shift in consciousness included the realization that, while religious experience is always transmitted communally, its roots must lie in personal experience

---

[12] For a concise history of the WCC's opening to interfaith dialogue, see the article by Wesley Ariarajah on the WCC website: http://bit.ly/1j9sV2L.

[13] Gerald R. McDermott, *Can Evangelicals Learn from World Religions? Jesus, Revelation and Religious Traditions* (Downers Grove, IL: InterVarsity Press, 2000); Wesley Wildman and Stephen Chapin Garner, *Lost in the Middle! Claiming an Inclusive Faith for Moderate Christians Who Are Both Liberal and Evangelical* (Herndon, VA: Alban Institute, 2009).

[14] The notion of an axial age was first proposed by Karl Jaspers, *The Origin and God of History*, trans. Michael Bullock (London, 1953), 1–70.

and responsibility. You have to feel it and live it, not just believe in what others say about it. Also, in the axial shift, religious convictions and practice became what John Hick terms "soteriological"—religion no longer was deployed simply to maintain the status quo but was tasked with improving the human condition, at least in a future life if not always in this one. Karen Armstrong points out that, for these axial religions, such improvement of the human condition would come about primarily through compassion, through humans moving from a self-centered to an other-centered way of living: "The only way you could encounter what they [the sages of the axial religions] called 'God,' 'Nirvana,' 'Brahman,' or the 'Way' was to live a compassionate life."[15] However one may judge the accuracy of the way scholars portray this period of religious history, I suggest that the "axial age" can serve as a metaphor for what is starting to take place in our present stage of religious history.

This proposal might stir uneasiness in some scholars of religion. They would warn me that the very notion of "religion" was a creation of Western scholars and colonizers, and should be used, if at all, only with great caution.[16] In response, I would appeal to a highly respected scholar and sociologist of religion who was aware of such caveats and who nonetheless described and predicted the growing evolution of humanity's religious awareness and practice now taking shape. Robert Bellah, at the conclusion of his magisterial final book, announces that today the religious history of humankind is on the brink of a new axial age. He identifies "the possibility . . . of understanding our deepest cultural differences, including our religious differences, in a *dramatically different way* than most humans have ever done before."[17] "Dramatically different" because, he reminds us, for most of religious history, each religion claimed to be the one true, or truest, religion:

> Each of them [the major religious figures of the first axial age] considered his own teaching to be the only truth or the highest truth, even such a figure as the Buddha, who never denounced his rivals but only subtly satirized them. Plato, Confucius, Second Isaiah, all thought that it was they and they alone who had found the final truth.[18]

But today, Bellah announces, we have begun "to see the emergence of a new point of view, one that could understand and appreciate all religions on their own

---

[15] John Hick, *An Interpretation of Religion* (New Haven, CT: Yale University Press, 1989), 22–33; Karen Armstrong, *The Great Transformation: The Beginning of Our Religious Traditions* (New York: Anchor Books, 2007), xviii (see also xv–xxiii).

[16] Russell McCutcheon, *Manufacturing Religion: The Discourse on Sui Generis Religion and the Politics of Nostalgia* (Oxford: Oxford University Press, 2003); Tomoko Masuzawa, *The Invention of World Religions* (Chicago: University of Chicago Press, 2005).

[17] Robert Bellah, *Religion in Human Evolution: From the Paleolithic to the Axial Age* (New York: Belknap Press of Harvard University Press, 2011), 602.

[18] Ibid.

terms and that was not driven to set up one as the apex, either because it was the best, or because it was the most historically progressive."[19] So he summarizes his hope for the next axial age by referencing "the increasing number of serious students of religion who can accept religious pluralism as our destiny without making a claim to the superiority of [any] one tradition."[20] *Nostra Aetate*, I have suggested, is both an expression of and a stimulus toward what Bellah calls "a new point of view," one that will affirm religious diversity not as a problem but as "our destiny" and a source of richness within the human condition.

The Roadblock of "Religious Supremacy"

At this point, however, our perspective on *Nostra Aetate* shifts sharply. The title of this volume includes not only *Nostra Aetate* but also "the future of interreligious dialogue." We have to recognize that, while *Nostra Aetate* did, as I have claimed, open up the future of interreligious dialogue in a bold and revolutionary way, it also poses serious and threatening obstacles to that future. Bellah foresaw the problem when he recognized that we can "accept religious pluralism as our destiny" only if we cease insisting on the "superiority of one tradition [over all others]." Such claims are diametrically opposed, he reminds us, to affirming the value of religious pluralism and the possibility of real interreligious dialogue.

An Abiding Tension between Practice and Theory, Ethics and Doctrine, Dialogue and Theology

To speak ill of *Nostra Aetate* is discomfiting, but it now seems to me—as it did not some fifty years ago in the euphoria of my first reading—that it and other documents of Vatican II, despite the revolutionary theological and practical transformations they called for in the Catholic Church, still endorse what can be described as *religious supremacy*.

    Nostra Aetate inscribes a tension—maybe a contradiction—between affirming the value of other religions and the need for dialogue, on the one hand, and asserting the supremacy of Christianity—Catholic Christianity—over all other religions, on the other. After avowing that there are many "spiritual and moral goods" in other religions and "exhorting" Christians to "engage in dialogue and collaboration with followers of other religions," *Nostra Aetate*, echoing other Vatican II documents, nevertheless goes on to declare that it is only in Jesus Christ that all people "may find the fullness of religious life" (sec. 2). This declaration that the fullness of religion can be found only in Jesus leads naturally and necessarily to extending that same claim to the Catholic Church. As *Decree on Ecumenism* declares: "For it is

---

[19] Ibid., 603.
[20] Ibid.

only through Christ's Catholic Church, which is 'the all-embracing means of salvation,' that they can benefit fully from the means of salvation" (sec. 3).[21]

In light of that statement, we realize that *Nostra Aetate*'s recognition of the "ray of truth" in other religions is both a tribute and a subordinating gesture: the other religions have only a "ray," while Christians, in Jesus, have the full light of the sun. This exclusive advantage is why, as *Lumen Gentium* makes utterly clear, "Whatever good or truth is found amongst them [other religions] is looked upon by the Church as a preparation for the Gospel [*praeparatio evangelica*]" (sec. 16). This claim that Christianity bears the fullness of religious truth and that other religions serve only as a preparation for it throws a sad shadow over all the revolutionary statements that *Nostra Aetate* makes about other religions. They are ultimately designated as a kind of minor league preparing players for the big time. The same shadow of suspicion is cast over the declaration's call to dialogue: is it, too, merely "preparation" for conversion to the Gospel as proclaimed by the church?

An Abiding Tension in Post–Vatican II Developments

Such tensions between calls for dialogue and assertions of supremacy can also be found in most of the magisterium's statements on religious diversity since Vatican II. Both *Redemptoris Missio* and *Dialogue and Proclamation* called for dialogue as a "new way of being church." But they also insisted that "salvation comes from Jesus Christ. . . . In him, and *only* in him, are we set free from all alienation and doubt" (*Redemptoris Missio*, paras. 5, 11, emphasis mine).[22] Therefore, if other religions truly do serve as mediations of God's truth and grace, they "acquire meaning and value *only* from Christ's own mediation, and they cannot be understood as parallel or complementary" (*Redemptoris Missio*, sec. 5, emphasis in original). Such assertions of supremacy end up subordinating the other religions to the Catholic Church, and dialogue to evangelization. Although both dialogue and proclamation are necessary components of the Christian missionary's job description, they are, we are reminded, "not on the same level," for dialogue must always "remain oriented toward proclamation" (*Dialogue and Proclamation,* paras. 77, 82). "Dialogue should be conducted and implemented with the conviction that *the Church is the ordinary means of salvation* and that *she alone* possesses the fullness of the means of salvation" (*Redemptoris Missio*, sec. 55, emphasis in original).[23]

In view of such clear assertions of the supremacy of Jesus Christ and his church over all other religious leaders and religions, liberals in the Catholic Church should not have been so surprised and chagrined at *Dominus Iesus*, the declaration issued

---

[21] *Decree on Ecumenism—Unitatis Redintegratio*, promulgated by Pope Paul VI (Vatican City, 1964), sec. 3, http://www.vatican.va/archive/hist_councils/ii_vatican_council/documents/vat-ii_decree_19641121_unitatis-redintegratio_en.html.

[22] See also *Dialogue and Proclamation*, paras. 19, 22, 28.

[23] See also *Dialogue and Proclamation*, paras. 19, 22, 58.

by Cardinal Joseph Ratzinger's Congregation for the Doctrine of the Faith in August 2000. Fearing that all the new theologies of religious diversity and dialogue inspired by *Nostra Aetate* were diluting the Catholic Church's missionary resolve, *Dominus Iesus* provided an unvarnished, theologically in-your-face reassertion—as its subtitle proclaimed—of the "Unicity and Salvific Universality of Jesus Christ and the Church."[24] It resolutely insisted that the revelation and salvation given through Jesus was "full and complete" (6), "absolute" (4), "unique and singular," "exclusive," "the goal of human history" (15). The document explicitly condemned any attempt "to consider the Church as *one way* of salvation alongside those constituted by other religions, seen as complementary to the Church" (21, emphasis in original).

For many, the most scandalous statement in *Dominus Iesus* was that other religions "are in a *gravely deficient situation* in comparison with those who, in the Church, have the fullness of the means of salvation" (22, emphasis in original). Such sentiments did not originate with the Cardinal. Addressing the Congregation for the Doctrine of the Faith seven months before issuing *Dominus Iesus*, Pope John Paul II stated clearly that, because the revelation of Christ is "definitive and complete," non-Christians live in "a deficient situation compared to those who have the fullness of the salvific means in the Church."[25] In its basic claims about the exclusive unicity of Jesus and the Catholic Church, *Dominus Iesus* is a full-blooded, unnuanced statement of the religious supremacy implicit (if more mildly) in *Nostra Aetate*, in subsequent statements of the magisterium, and, I would add, in the positions taken by the majority of Catholic theologians.[26]

I don't mean to disparage *Nostra Aetate* and my Roman Catholic Church for their claims of religious supremacy. To point out how traditional claims for the finality or supremacy of Christianity still linger in the declaration and in so much Christian theology does not in any way deny the extraordinary achievement of *Nostra Aetate* and Vatican II in recognizing the God-given value of other religions and the urgent necessity for interreligious collaboration. Ambiguous though it may be, an axial shift has begun.

And, to be fair, Christianity holds no monopoly on assertions of religious supremacy. As Bellah has noted, most of the axial founders of religions felt that their teachings contained either the only or the superior truth compared to all other

---

[24] Congregation for the Doctrine of the Faith, *Declaration—Dominus Iesus: On the Unicity and Salvific Universality of Jesus Christ and the Church* (Vatican City, 2000), available on the Vatican website: http://bit.ly/1f7QfHf.

[25] Reported and cited in *The Tablet*, February 5, 2000, 25, available at http://bit.ly/1PG325W.

[26] This is not to deny that there are other assertions in *Dominus Iesus* that seem to contradict the teachings of Vatican II and the consensus of Catholic theologians, such as its apparent distinction between supernatural "faith" in Christianity and natural "belief" in other religions (see secs. 7 and 8), or its claim that Protestant churches without bishops "are not churches in the proper sense" (sec. 17).

contestants. Although Judaism and the indigenous religions may be the exceptions, most of the world's religious movements—especially those that seek multiethnic membership—proclaim that they possess or have been given the fullest wisdom, the most secure path to Enlightenment, or the paramount prophet. There seems to be a proclivity among religious people to claim that their god is bigger, or their enlightenment fuller, than all others. Supremacy claims are not unique to the Roman Catholic Church.

Claims of Superiority: Roadblocks to Dialogue and Peace

The pressing question that all religions must face is whether such claims of religious superiority constitute a roadblock to the axial shift that *Nostra Aetate* opened up and to which so many other religious communities say they are committed—a shift in which all religious traditions, despite their breathtaking diversity, recognize each other's validity and, because of that diversity, seek to dialogue and collaborate with each other. It seems to me that you cannot pursue goals of affirming the validity of religious others and seeking dialogue with them if you engage them from the nonnegotiable religious conviction that your god or founder has provided you with the final word on all truth and therefore with the community in which God intends all others to finally find their home. When one has been granted the "fullness" of revelation, as Christians insist has happened in Jesus, there isn't much more to learn from other religions; what is full cannot be filled. At the most, one can clarify what one already has.

But religious supremacy threatens not only interreligious dialogue; it menaces multireligious civil society too. The United States is, as Diana Eck has argued, one of the most religiously diverse countries in the world.[27] Just as claims of white supremacy threaten Americans' multiracial coexistence, Christian supremacy threatens their multireligious coexistence. Indeed, convictions about one's own religious supremacy generally feed on convictions about the superiority of one's race or ethnic group. "Manifest Destiny" was all the more manifest to European Americans because it was Christian destiny.

Finally, there have recently been multiple studies on the relationship between convictions of religious supremacy and acts of religious violence.[28] Karen Armstrong

---

[27] Typical of Americans, she asserted that we are *the* most religiously diverse nation. Diana L. Eck, *A New Religious America: How a "Christian Country" Has Become the World's Most Religiously Diverse Nation* (San Francisco: HarperSanFrancisco, 2002).

[28] Previous to 9/11: Mark Juergensmeyer, *Terror in the Mind of God: The Global Rise of Religious Violence* (Berkeley: University of California Press, 2000); R. Scott Appleby, *The Ambivalence of the Sacred: Religion, Violence, and Reconciliation* (New York: Rowman & Littlefield, 2000). Post 9/11: Charles Kimball, *When Religion Becomes Evil* (San Francisco: HarperSanFrancisco, 2002); Lloyd Steffen, *The Demonic Turn: The Power of Religion to Inspire or Restrain Violence* (Cleveland: Pilgrim Press, 2003); Lee Griffith, *The War on Terrorism and the Terror of God* (Grand Rapids, MI: William B. Eerdmans, 2002); Jessica

has recently argued that there is no *necessary* link between religious adherence and violence.[29] Generally, as she argues, the reasons one group of people takes up violence against another are economic and political.[30] Nevertheless, we must ask why religion is so easily enlisted to take up, justify, or intensify violence. With others, I strongly suspect that convictions about one's own religion being God's preference play a pivotal role. As Rita Gross has put it:

> The result of exclusive truth claims is not religious agreement; it is suffering. The track record of religions that claim exclusive and universal truth for themselves is not praiseworthy or uplifting. How much empire building, how many crusades and religious wars, big and small, have gone on in the name of defending the "one true faith"? There seems to be a cause and effect link between claims of exclusive truth and suffering; or to say it more strongly, the main result of exclusive truth claims has been suffering, not salvation.[31]

Overcoming the Roadblock: *Laudato Si´*

Where do we go from here? On one hand, *Nostra Aetate* is one of the strongest voices calling for an axial shift in the history of religions. On the other, it seems burdened with a theology that hamstrings that shift. There seems to be an inherent contradiction in *Nostra Aetate* and much of Christian theology between ethics and doctrine, practice and theory, and, you might also say, between the "*sensus fidelium*"—what the faithful are doing and feeling, and what the magisterium is insisting on.

On the ethical or experiential side, more and more Christians are living with, often engaging, people of other faiths in their schools, worksites, families, and marriage beds. They are getting along, even learning from each other, without any talk or even feelings of one religion being superior to the other. On the liturgical side, however, they are singing about Jesus being the only Son of God and Savior of the whole world, and are learning in sermons or catechism that they are to win the

---

Stern, *Terror in the Name of God: Why Religious Militants Kill* (New York: HarperCollins, 2003); Charles Selengut, *Sacred Fury: Understanding Religious Violence* (New York: Alta Mira Press, 2003); Bruce Lincoln, *Holy Terrors: Thinking about Religion after September 11* (Chicago: University of Chicago Press, 2003); Oliver McTernan, *Violence in God's Name: Religion in an Age of Conflict* (Maryknoll, NY: Orbis Books, 2003).

[29] Karen Armstrong, *Fields of Blood: Religion and the History of Violence* (New York: Anchor Books, 2015).

[30] See Paul F. Knitter, "Religion, Power, Dialogue," *Swedish Missiological Themes* 93 (2005): 29–42.

[31] Rita Gross, "Excuse Me, But What's the Question? Isn't Religious Diversity Normal?" in *The Myth of Religious Superiority*, ed. Paul F. Knitter (Maryknoll, NY: Orbis Books, 2005), 75–87.

world for Christ. The dialogue that *Nostra Aetate* called Christians to embrace has moved far ahead of the traditional theology that understands Christ and Christianity as the end point of all religious history. That's why John Hick called *Nostra Aetate* "a bridge" that connects with a wholly new way of understanding other religions and Christianity in light of other religions.[32] But, he remarked, most Christians are still on the bridge. They haven't crossed it.

To reach the other side requires that theology catch up with dialogue. Efforts to revise the theological foundations of Christian supremacy have turned into a slow, delicate, and sometimes risky slog, however, because they deal with the heart of Christian belief and practice, the question with which every generation of Jesus-followers must grapple: "Who do you say I am?" (Mt 8:29). *The pivotal problem is Christological.*

The fundamental question with which *Nostra Aetate* has presented Christians is how to understand Jesus' uniqueness in such a way that his followers can be fully committed to him and his message but at the same time fully open to and ready for dialogue with followers of other religious paths. Some theologians declare that we have reached an impasse on this central Christological question.[33] The issue of Jesus' uniqueness is just too complex, too threatening, too neuralgic. And for Roman Catholic theologians who seem to be "pushing the envelope," too dangerous: many of them have had to face censures from the Vatican or local bishops—at least before Pope Francis.[34] How can we deal with this apparent impasse?

Nostra Aetate *Suggests a Path Forward: Doing before Knowing*

Nostra Aetate indicates how we can move forward. As I have already suggested, the most revolutionary, pioneering, and potentially transformative element in this short document was its "exhortation to engage in dialogue and collaboration with followers of other religions." *Nostra Aetate* left us with a lot of complex theological baggage, but it was clear on how we are to continue the journey: engage in dialogue. And it urges a sound, accepted methodology: Christian theology is to be based on and guided by the life and experience of the Christian community. As the ancient formula put it: *lex credendi* (what we believe) is to follow *lex orandi et vivendi* (the prayer and life of the church).

More generally, this formula is sound epistemology based on what is called the "hermeneutical circle": theory and practice, or knowing and doing, feed off each other. But we enter the circle and sustain it first of all by doing. In terms of our discussion: the *doing of dialogue* will help us clarify the *knowing of theology*. If we're

---

[32] John Hick, "Whatever Path Men Choose Is Mine," in *Christianity and Other Religions,* ed. John Hick and Brian Hebblethwaite (Philadelphia: Fortress, 1980), 180–81.

[33] Amos Yong, *Beyond the Impasse: Toward a Pneumatological Theology of Religions* (Eugene, OR: Wipf & Stock, 2014).

[34] I'm thinking of Roger Haight, Peter Phan, Tissa Balasuriya—and more generally, because of suspected Christological excesses, Elizabeth A. Johnson and Jon Sobrino.

at an impasse in our theology and Christology, what we need is more, and better, dialogue. So how can we develop what Len Swidler calls a truly "deep dialogue" that will not only become "a new way of being church" but might also, we hope, get us beyond our theological impasse? For help in answering that question: I turn, like a good Catholic, to my pope.

"This Changes Everything"—Laudato Si'

Heading the words that can describe the person who is Jorge Mario Bergoglio and the pope who is Francis most accurately is "dialogue." It marks his personality and papal style. He seems to have forgotten—as his predecessors did not—that his office equips him with the heavy-duty prerogatives of infallibility and what Catholic ecclesiology calls *auctoritas suprema*—"supreme authority." He doesn't issue decrees; rather, he states his case clearly and then says, "Let's talk." The word "dialogue" came up twelve times in his address to the US Congress. In the synod that Francis convened in October 2015, he encouraged the bishops to do something that no pope has encouraged them to do since Vatican II—to speak their minds honestly, even if doing so meant disagreeing with other bishops or even with him, and then to talk about their disagreements. For Francis, dialogue is both a way of being church and of being human.

It comes as no surprise that, from the early days of his papacy, Francis has recognized the importance of the dialogue between the religions.[35] In his first encyclical, *Evangelii Gaudium* ("The Joy of the Gospel"), he transformed *Nostra Aetate*'s "exhortation" into an obligation and then extended it to all religions: "Interreligious dialogue is a necessary condition for peace in the world, and so it is a duty for Christians as well as other religious communities."[36] But it is in his recent encyclical, *Laudato Si'*, that Francis tells us what needs to be the organizing principle of interreligious dialogue: our threatened earth.[37]

In *This Changes Everything*, Naomi Klein argues that the environmental crisis necessitates changing the capitalist economic system.[38] Francis expands this charge to include how religions understand themselves and their relations with each other. The pope is urging that "the cry of the earth," which he insists is also "the cry of the

---

[35] For a record, past and current, of Pope Francis's statements on interreligious dialogue, see the archive housed at the website Dialogue Interreligieux Monastique/Monastic Interreligious Dialogue: http://bit.ly/1LoMxGi.

[36] Pope Francis, *Apostolic Exhortation—Evangelii Gaudium* (Vatican City, 2013), sec. 250.

[37] Pope Francis, *Encyclical Letter—Laudato Si'* (Vatican City, 2015), http://w2.vatican.va/content/francesco/en/encyclicals/documents/papa-francesco_20150524_enciclica-laudato-si.pdf.

[38] Naomi Klein, *This Changes Everything: Capitalism vs. the Climate* (New York: Simon & Schuster, 2015). Appropriately, Klein was among the select invitees for a Vatican conference on *Laudato Si'*, April 28, 2015.

poor" (*Laudato Si'*, 49), must become the cry that calls all religious communities into a new form of dialogue and collaboration. One can feel his pathos:

> The gravity of the ecological crisis demands that we all look to the common good, embarking on a path of dialogue which requires patience, self-discipline and generosity. . . . This [crisis] should spur religions to dialogue among themselves for the sake of protecting nature, defending the poor, and building networks of respect and fraternity. (*Laudato Si'*, sec. 201)

Francis urges a *green interreligious dialogue.* In doing so, he does not intend to exclude other topics for religious conversations, but he does call for what we might term "a preferential option for the earth." For interreligious dialogue to respond to the signs of the times, it must take the needs of our suffering earth and its creatures as its primary concern.

Earth Supremacy versus Religious Supremacy

I conclude by taking up Francis's call for a green dialogue. He presents us with an obligation that can become an opportunity. I suggest that such a green dialogue can help us deal with the theological problem of religious supremacy. Simply stated, I suspect that, if we give the earth supremacy, we can keep our inclinations toward religious supremacy in check.

By "giving the earth supremacy," I mean that, in such a green interfaith dialogue, what brings us together, guides our conversation, and determines our priorities will be the cries of the earth and its suffering creatures. In a green dialogue, we are not out to establish which religion is superior or contains the greater truth. We are not even thinking about such things. The criterion for good or bad, true or false, will be whether a particular religious belief or practice can enable us to heal the earth and oppose or redirect the forces that are harming it. Our minds and hearts will be so claimed by the sufferings of the earth and the need to protect our mother that traditional teachings about my religion having the fullest revelation or possessing the only savior or the final prophet simply won't matter. We won't have the time or energy for such issues.

But there is another way in which interreligious collaboration for the sake of the earth will diminish our need or ability to claim that my religion is superior to yours. In such a green dialogue, we share with each other what we think can best respond to the complex reality of our environmental crisis. Each of us draws on the resources of her or his religious teachings. That practice means that I the Christian will share with you the Muslim what are the resources, guidelines, and motivation for healing the earth that I find in the gospel, and you will do the same for me from your resources in the Qur'an and Hadith. In other words, we will come to see that each of us has something to offer and that no one has the only or best answer. To be sure, the Buddhist notion of interconnectedness may, in some particular cases, offer a better approach than the Christian valuing of the individual. But no one will have a "full" or "final" word on how to save this life-giving planet. Talk of "fullness or finality" simply will not be relevant.

But the most effective way in which the green interreligious dialogue that Pope Francis is calling for will help dismantle past claims of religious supremacy is because such a green dialogue is itself a greenhouse for interreligious friendships. When people from different religious or cultural backgrounds come together for a common cause, struggle and anguish together, challenge the political and economic powers that feed environmental degradation, get into trouble together and maybe even go to jail together, they will become friends with each other. Shared caring for the earth brings us, necessarily, to care for each other.

And here's my point: friends don't make comparisons about who is better, or who has the greater truth. When I consider my Buddhist, Hindu, Jewish, and Muslim friends with whom I have been in a dialogue of solidarity over the years, I cannot tell them that I as a Christian have the full and final truth, and that they would be "fulfilled" by becoming a Christian. Nor have they said any such things to me. Friends don't do that—because they can't.

A half century has passed since I held one of the early drafts of *Nostra Aetate* in my hands as a twenty-five-year-old student in Rome. The dream that document embodied—the vision of a world in which religions shift from their history of competition and struggle to one of collaboration and mutuality—has ever since grown clearer and more urgent, as well as more complex and strenuous. But is this vision of interreligious cooperation an empty pipe dream or a real promise for the future? The answer to that question will depend on whether all of us, in our differing religious or ideological communities, will continue to heed *Nostra Aetate*'s call to "prudently and lovingly engage in dialogue and collaboration with followers of other religions" for the well-being and flourishing of this earth and its inhabitants. If we do that, there is hope for the earth, for humanity, for the religions.

Part II

Roman Catholic Perspectives

3

FOREIGN TO THE MIND OF CHRIST

Nostra Aetate *in America's Religio-Racial Project*

Jeannine Hill Fletcher

Nostra Aetate from an American Catholic Perspective

There is no doubt that *Nostra Aetate* was groundbreaking for its time in the Catholic Church. When, for the better part of Catholic history, the official stance has been "Outside the Church, No Salvation," *Nostra Aetate* really does seem to say something new.[1] The novelty of its teaching is reflected in the sparse footnotes. Where so many magisterial documents rely heavily on cross-references to previous cases, *Nostra Aetate* cites very few precedents in earlier church documents, relying primarily on scriptural citation for its grounding authorization. Responding to *Nostra Aetate*, Pope Paul VI saw the declaration as evidence that the church is alive, that it thinks, speaks, and grows. "*Nostra Aetate*," he said, "is the proof, here is the breath, the voice, the song, the Church lives."[2] Indeed, many commentators noted the declaration's "revolutionary" character, since—as Mary Boys has reminded us—"for the first time in history, an ecumenical council spoke positively of other

---

[1] Contrast the statement by the third-century bishop Cyprian of Carthage—"There can be no salvation to any except in the Church" (Cyprian, Bishop of Carthage, *Epistle* 61, in *The Ante-Nicene Fathers,* ed. Alexander Roberts and James Donaldson [Grand Rapids, MI: William B. Eerdmans, 1952], 5:357) —with the statement from *Nostra Aetate* that "One is also their [the community of all peoples] final goal" (*Declaration on the Relation of the Church to Non-Christian Religions—Nostra Aetate*, proclaimed by Pope Paul VI [Vatican City, 1965], sec. 1). For an overview of this shift, see Francis Sullivan, *Salvation Outside the Church? Tracing the History of the Catholic Response* (Mahwah, NJ: Paulist Press, 1994) and Jeannine Hill Fletcher, *Monopoly on Salvation? A Feminist Approach to Religious Pluralism* (New York: Continuum, 2005).

[2] Pope Paul VI, as quoted in John M. Oesterreicher, "The Declaration on Non-Christian Religions," in *Commentary on the Documents of Vatican* II, ed. Herbert Vorgrimler (New York: Herder and Herder, 1968), 3:129, cited in Kristin M. Colberg, "The Omnipresence of Grace: Revisiting the Relationship between *Ad Gentes* and *Nostra Aetate* 50 Years Later," *Missiology: An International Review* 42, no. 2 (2014): 185.

religions."[3] The strikingly new and open-armed approach of *Nostra Aetate* gives great reason for a Catholic perspective on this document to be one of celebration.

But I would like to propose a Catholic perspective on *Nostra Aetate* that is more specific than simply noting its moment in a broad trajectory of the development of doctrine. Instead, I would like to consider an American Catholic perspective from within the particular religio-racial project of its day (and ultimately our own). The concept of a "religio-racial project" is an adaptation from the work of Michael Omi and Howard Winant.[4] As sociologists, Omi and Winant use the term "racial project" to indicate that race is not a concrete or static reality, but an imaginative construct always created in particular times and places with specific material influences and impacts. In any given context, a racial project creates the categories of "the races" for that time and place, sorts people into them, and assigns material benefits on the basis of them. In expanding this concept to that of a religio-racial project, I want to draw attention to the way religion functions within racial projects. For example, in seventeenth-century European encounters with First Nations people in Florida, native peoples were named as "red" and racialized on account of the body paint worn on sacred occasions.[5] In twenty-first-century accounts of racial dynamics in the United States, the term "Muslim" often functions as if it were a racial category rather than a religious one.[6] These examples give hints of possible intersections of our conceptual categories of "race" and "religion," and thus ask us to consider the religio-racial project of any given moment.

In using the lens of a religio-racial project, we can ask how church teachings function to provide a vision and motivation for action in ways that both spring from and impact ideas about race and religion that are current in the wider society. *Nostra Aetate* seems to recognize its part in a religio-racial project when the document insists that "the Church reproves, as foreign to the mind of Christ, any discrimination against men or harassment of them because of their race, color, condition of life, or religion" (sec. 5). The statement of the text is not just about

---

[3] Mary Boys, "What *Nostra Aetate* Inaugurated: A Conversion to the 'Providential Mystery of Otherness,'" *Theological Studies* 74 (2013): 73. A similar identification of *Nostra Aetate* as a watershed moment is articulated by Ruben Mendoza, citing Jacques Dupuis, Paul Knitter, Veli-Matti Karkkainen, and Norman Tanner. See "'Ray of Truth That Enlightens All': *Nostra Aetate* and Its Reception by the FABC," *Studies in Interreligious Dialogue* 16, no. 2 (2006): 148–72.

[4] Michael Omi and Howard Winant, *Racial Formation in the United States: From the 1960s to the 1990s*, 2nd ed. (New York: Routledge, 1994).

[5] Daniel Murphree, "Race and Religion on the Periphery: Disappointment and Missionization in the Spanish Floridas, 1566–1763," in *Race, Nation, and Religion in the Americas*, ed. Henry Goldschmidt and Elizabeth McAlister (New York: Oxford University Press, 2004), 35–60.

[6] Simran Jeet Singh chronicles this contemporary religio-racial project in his essay "Muslimophobia, Racialization, and Mistaken Identity: Understanding Anti-Sikh Hate Violence in a Post-9/11 America," in *Muhammad in the Digital Age*, ed. Ruqayya Yasmine Khan (Austin: University of Texas Press, 2015), 158–73.

religious ideas or competing visions of salvation; its ideas about race and religion intersect and might call forth certain action. Christ's call in the midst of religious and racial diversity is the concern of the text.

The call to religious and racial solidarity came at a crucial moment in US history. The year 1965 in particular was remarkable in terms of the movements for racial justice and dismantling legal barriers to multireligious citizenship. Through the lens of racial justice, 1965 saw the traumatic assassination of Malcolm X on February 21, 1965, a setback for a movement under his leadership. The year 1965 also witnessed the harrowing and triumphant civil rights demonstrations of March 7, 9, and 21–25 during the march from Selma to Montgomery, which moved the country toward greater legal securities in the Voting Rights Act that was signed on August 6 of the same year. Evidence that the struggle for racial justice would be a long one was foreshadowed in the six days of rioting in August 1965 that responded to the police brutality against a black motorist and his mother in the Watts section of Los Angeles. It was into this dynamic moment that the United States would position itself to receive new immigrants with the passage of the Hart-Celler Act of immigration reforms on October 3, 1965. These new immigrants would bring with them religious traditions that had been all but absent in the North American landscape because of legal exclusions of persons in the one hundred years prior.[7] So, when *Nostra Aetate* was released on October 28, 1965, America was poised on the horizon of greater racial justice and increased religious diversity with the signing of legislation that committed the country to a new religio-racial project.[8] Although the optimism of *Nostra Aetate* invites us to think that American Catholics would have been thrilled by this new openness that insisted that no discrimination or harassment be inflicted on the basis of race or religion, historians provide a more complex picture.

American Catholicism's Religio-Racial Project

By 1965, American Catholicism had ascended in its "whiteness," as previously disparaged Irish and Italian Catholic immigrants—who formerly had been categorized as nonwhite—now had established themselves within mainstream white culture, while the growth of US Latino Catholicism had not yet taken off.[9] Having

---

[7] A portion of the Hart-Celler Act reads: "No person shall receive any preference or priority or be discriminated against in the issuance of an immigrant visa because of his race, sex, nationality, place of birth or place of residence." See *Amendment to the Immigration and Nationality Act*, Public Law 89-236—October 3, 1965, 79 *Statutes at Large* (1965), 911, http://library.uwb.edu/guides/usimmigration/79%20stat%20911.pdf.

[8] Diana Eck grounds her study of America's religious diversity in the historic moment of the Hart-Celler Act in *A New Religious America: How a "Christian Country" Has Become the World's Most Religiously Diverse Nation* (San Francisco: HarperSanFrancisco, 2001).

[9] See Noel Ignatiev, *How the Irish Became White* (London: Routledge, 2008), and David Evans, "Regenerating the Italian Race: The Italian Methodist Mission and the Ameri-

recently won their social standing, many Catholics may have been unwilling to position themselves in ways that they feared would threaten this achievement.[10] As such, the white Catholic Church sat uneasily in the broader religio-racial project of the day. White Catholic sisters may have ministered to black Catholics in the Jim Crow South as a way of responding to social inequalities, for example, but they did so within segregated parishes, hospitals, and schools which at times reinscribed social segregation even while attempting to mitigate its impact. The white Catholic Sisters of Saint Joseph lived next door to the historic Tabernacle Baptist Church, where voter registration was being mobilized in Selma, but when white Catholic Sisters from the North came for the historic marches, Selma's own white sisters could not join them because their archbishop, Thomas Joseph Toolan, would not allow them to march.[11]

While many women religious, priests, and lay Catholics did commit themselves to the cause of racial justice, many more refused to see Catholic concern beyond white protectionism. In northern cities, numerous priests in leadership positions opposed integration and enacted discrimination and harassment of African Americans, often on the basis of protecting the white Catholic "parish boundaries." White Catholics and parish priests formed associations to resist the Federal Housing Administration's efforts to support African Americans relocating to new opportunities in the 1940s.[12] It was in a majority Catholic neighborhood outside Chicago in 1951 that Henry Clark rented an apartment for his family and was met with crowds of 5,000 to 6,000 angry whites who protested his act of racial

---

canization of Italian History," *Methodist History* 40, no. 3 (April 2011): 132–46. For an overview of US Catholicism in 1960, see chap. 5 of Jay P. Dolan, *In Search of an American Catholicism: A History of Religion and Culture in Tension* (New York: Oxford University Press, 2002). The population growth in US Latinos and Latino Catholicism after 1965 is significant, with the US Latino population growing from 4 percent in 1965 to 18 percent in 2015. Seventy percent of the growth of US Catholicism since 1970 has come from the Latino population.

[10] Amy Koehlinger describes how "Caucasian Catholics achieved unprecedented levels of economic security in the 1950s and early 1960s." See Koehlinger, *The New Nuns: Racial Justice and Religious Reform in the 1960s* (Cambridge, MA: Harvard University Press, 2007), 10.

[11] Ibid., 172. See also "The Catholic Presence in Selma, Alabama, 1965," an interview with Cecilia Moore by Joseph Wakelee-Lynch, *The Magazine of Loyola University Marymount*, March 14, 2015, http://magazine.lmu.edu/archive/2015/catholic-presence-selma-alabama-1965. Refusal to allow women religious to take part in demonstrations was also the situation in the North; as Koehlinger notes, "Representatives of the Chicago Archdiocese had made it clear to the Sisters of Saint Francis . . . that they were not to engage in political activity or protest marches during their time in Chicago" (*New Nuns*, 192).

[12] John T. McGreevy, *Parish Boundaries: The Catholic Encounter with Race in the Twentieth-Century Urban North* (Chicago: University of Chicago Press, 1996), 72–76.

integration until they were dispersed by the National Guard.[13] White Catholics did not necessarily welcome the significant increases in the African American population that northern cities experienced in the 1960s.[14] White Catholic participation in civil rights councils and demonstrations did not represent the whole of the white Catholic community, and, at the height of the civil rights movement, when Martin Luther King Jr. marched through Chicago in 1966, Catholic presence in the counterdemonstrations against King was evident. One eyewitness recounted the shock of seeing fellow congregants at the march, screaming racist epithets and "throwing rocks and dirt at King." The cognitive dissonance of Christian race-hatred was evident in the spectator's further reflection that "these [were] nice people I knew all my life. I couldn't believe it."[15] The religio-racial project of many white American Catholics on the eve of *Nostra Aetate*'s call for religious and racial nondiscrimination would have suggested that racial otherness, not racial discrimination, was foreign to the mind of Christ.[16] If, on the eve of *Nostra Aetate*, the North American church remained a white Catholic institution with the interests of white Catholics taking precedence over those of black Christians—even black Catholics—this situation would not seem to have portended well for the onset of future nonwhite immigrants who would bring non-Christian religions with them.[17]

---

[13] Ibid., 97. As McGreevy recounts, "Observers described the mob as largely Catholic, with boys wearing letter sweaters from Catholic high schools and girls fingering crosses around their necks." See also "Illinois: Segregationists in Cicero (1966)," from *Eyes on the Prize: America's Civil Rights Movement 1954–1985*, http://www.pbs.org/wgbh/amex/eyesontheprize/profiles/54_il.html.

[14] The increase of African Americans in northern cities during this period includes the increase in Chicago from 22.9 percent to 32.7 percent of the population, in Cleveland from 28.6 percent to 38.3 percent, and in Detroit from 28.9 percent to 43.75 percent. Even cities with a smaller percentage of African Americans saw an increase; Boston's African American population rose from 9.1 to 16.3 percent of the population, Milwaukee's from 8.4 to 14.7 percent, and Buffalo's from 13.3 percent to 20.4 percent, McGreevy, *Parish Boundaries*, 180.

[15] McGreevy, *Parish Boundaries*, 190. McGreevy cites accounts of the Chicago demonstrations from Father James A. Bowman, SJ, letter, *Commonweal* 85 (December 16, 1966): 323; John A. McDermott, "A Chicago Catholic Asks: Where Does My Church Stand on Racial Justice?" *Look* 30 (November 1, 1966): 82ff.; William Graney, "Saddest Part of Riot: 'Catholic' Know Nothings," *New World* (August 5, 1966); Dennis Geaney, "Trouble in Chicago," *Ave Maria* 104 (October 1, 1966): 11.

[16] McGreevy, *Parish Boundaries*, 215. McGreevy writes that liberal Catholics were "inspired by both the civil rights movement and the Second Vatican Council [and] attacked not only racism but what they perceived as outdated organizations, rituals and structures." But liberal Catholics were not the whole of the story, as McGreevy continues, "Other Catholics, especially those living in neighborhoods threatened by racial transition, now perceived fellow communicants as threats to a painfully established local moral order."

[17] McGreevy also recounts how both black Catholics who moved into northern parishes and northern blacks who converted to Catholicism, experienced hateful resistance within white Catholic parishes. See McGreevy, *Parish Boundaries*, 97–100.

In the decades immediately preceding the release of *Nostra Aetate*, restrictions on immigration meant that there was very little religio-racial difference that might have shaped Catholic consciousness beyond black and white. Along with many other immigrants from around the globe, a large number of Catholics had arrived in the United States in the nineteenth century.[18] Yet subsequent legislation made it difficult for non-Christians to find refuge here. In 1882 the Buddhist, Confucian, and traditional religions that might have come with Chinese workers and their families were restricted by the Chinese Exclusion Act. Thirty-five years later, legislation barring Muslim, Hindu, Buddhist, and Confucian immigrants from the "Asiatic Zone" further diminished the possibility that American Catholics might have interreligious exchanges with members of these traditions. Although some Catholics might encounter the dynamic mix of African traditions, Islam, and American religion in congregations like the Moorish Science Temple in New York City, no new influences from the living traditions of Africa would be brought by new African immigrants after 1924. A quota system enacted that year restricted new arrivals from any country to 2 percent of current inhabitants of that country residing in the United States, but "descendants of slave immigrants" were not even to be counted as "inhabitants of the continental United States" for these calculations.[19]

From 1924 to 1965 immigration policies severely restricted and/or rejected the arrival of persons deemed "unassimilable" to the culture of the white Christian nation—including African, Asian, Southern and Eastern European immigrants.[20] Given these political and social realities, it is hard to imagine that the American Catholic community in 1965 might prove welcoming to people who were both nonwhite and non-Christian. Yet despite the shadow cast by American Catholics' resistance to racial integration and limited contact with people of non-Christian faiths, the vision of *Nostra Aetate* created the possibility for imagining a very different religio-racial project, one grounded in justice and mutuality. As we shall

---

[18] The Catholic population rose from 5 percent to 17 percent of the total US population at the turn to the twentieth century. As historian Julie Byrne describes, "Many members of other faiths—Jews, Protestants, and even some Muslims, Hindus and Buddhists—arrived in the successive waves of massive immigration to the United States between the 1840s and 1920s. But Catholics from various countries were the most numerous—and the most noticed." Julie Byrne, "Roman Catholics and Immigration in the Nineteenth Century," http://nationalhumanitiescenter.org/tserve/nineteen/nkeyinfo/nromcath.htm.

[19] See United States Congress, *Immigration Act of 1924*. 68th Cong. 1st Sess. HR 7995. The provisions establishing the quota can be found in chapter 190, sections a–g, http://www.legisworks.org/congress/68/publaw-139.pdf.

[20] As Douglas Massey and Karen Pren explain, "Countries of the Western Hemisphere had never been included in the national origins quotas, nor was the entry of their residents prohibited as that of Africans and Asians had been." Many commentators have noted the racist attitudes embedded within these laws. See Douglas S. Massey and Karen A. Pren, "Unintended Consequences of US Immigration Policy: Explaining the Post-1965 Surge from Latin America," *Population and Development Review* 38, no. 1 (March 2012): 1.

see, however, the declaration's underlying theology and rhetorical construction sent mixed messages about racial and religious supremacy, which compromise its achievements in the areas of tolerance and mutuality.[21]

Resources in *Nostra Aetate* for an
Antisupremacist Religio-Racial Project

Nostra Aetate contains the promise of an egalitarian Catholic religio-racial project, but it did not reach its full potential because of its supremacist theological commitments and internal contradictions. The theological commitments revealed in *Nostra Aetate* begin promisingly by affirming God as the origin of all peoples. The document's doctrine of God and creation brings forth a theological anthropology that asserts that "God made the whole human race,"[22] and therefore "we cannot truly call on God, the Father of all, if we refuse to treat in a brotherly way any man, created as he is in the image of God."[23] The document builds toward a *political* ecclesiology and missiology whereby the Catholic Church is tasked with "promoting unity and love among men [*sic*], indeed among nations," because "[God's] saving design extend[s] to all men [*sic*]."[24] As Kristin Colberg concludes, "Thus it is God's inexhaustible love that provides a theological impulse for affirming what is true and holy in non-Christian religions."[25] The basic logic of the text provides positive resources for a religio-racial project of justice and mutuality.

Nevertheless, although it begins promisingly, the document's theo-logic has an underlying pull toward Christian superiority by centering God's inexhaustible love in the person of Jesus Christ. Christ serves as the singular criterion for and fullness of God's love and truth made real in the world, and is seen as fulfilling God's singular plan for all humanity. Thus *Nostra Aetate* insists that the church "ever must proclaim Christ 'the way, the truth, and the life' (John 14:6)."[26] Other religions can be valued insofar as they reflect "a ray of that Truth which enlightens all men,"[27] but it is Christ who *is* the Truth and who brings *all* people to the fullness of religious life.

Although we may not usually conceive of Christology as part of a racial project, the work of Edward Blum and Paul Harvey invites us to consider how Christocentrism might have functioned in the United States of 1965 given how

---

[21] To build an antiracist church, Joseph Barndt has deemed it necessary for Christians to enact "clear lines of mutual accountability between the church and the racially oppressed people in the larger society." See Joseph Barndt, *Becoming an Anti-Racist Church: Journeying toward Wholeness* (Minneapolis: Fortress Press, 2011), 149.

[22] *Nostra Aetate*, sec. 1.

[23] Ibid., sec. 5.

[24] Ibid., sec. 1.

[25] Colberg, "Omnipresence of Grace," 184.

[26] *Nostra Aetate*, sec. 2.

[27] Ibid.

Christ's whiteness had been increasingly asserted in the nineteenth and twentieth centuries.[28] In the 1960s, Warner Sallman's *Head of Christ* still reigned as the dominant image of a white Christ, mass-produced and found in churches, seminaries, and households across the nation. A white Christ adorned black and white churches alike, and although seeking to transcend race, even Martin Luther King Jr. reinscribed Christ's whiteness when asserting that "the whiteness of his skin does not matter."[29] To be sure, Albert Cleage had preached the "Black Christ" as the heart of his ministry in Detroit in 1953, indicating the emergence of the consciousness that would become Black Theology.[30] Nevertheless, at the time of *Nostra Aetate*'s issuing and the height of the civil rights movement, a widespread project of coloring the Christ had not taken root. James Cone had not yet published his transformative theology of the Black Christ, nor had Vine Deloria proposed that *God Is Red* (1973).[31] The Christ of *Nostra Aetate*'s Christocentric theology most likely appeared in American Catholic minds as a white Christ. Although *Nostra Aetate* is not explicitly racist in that it does not assert a white Christ, it is also not actively antiracist in challenging common cultural notions in the United States in the 1960s.

Although the religio-racial project of *Nostra Aetate* may be ambiguous in light of the logic of white supremacy, the document quite clearly asserts a logic of Christian supremacy. In fact, *Nostra Aetate* declares Christ's supremacy and values the religious Other only insofar as the Other reflects the truth of Christ. Here, the logic of Christian supremacy employs a self-referential lens that constructs religious Others against the presumed perfection of the Christian model. Placed in a wider religio-racial project, this logic would have allowed US Catholics in 1965 to value the Other only insofar as the Other may have reflected truths Catholics themselves already held.

Catholics might "esteem also the Moslems" because, like them, Muslims "adore the one God, living and subsisting in Himself; merciful and all-powerful, the Creator of heaven and earth."[32] Catholics are drawn in to a religious project of sameness, seeing what is true and holy in Islam, because Muslims "revere [Jesus] as a prophet. They also honor Mary, His virgin Mother."[33] The problem is, of course, that the project of sameness presents a portrait of Muslims without Muhammad. This Catholic Christocentrism affirms what is "true and holy" in the Shahada, the

---

[28] Edward J. Blum and Paul Harvey, *The Color of Christ: The Son of God and the Saga of Race in America* (Chapel Hill: University of North Carolina Press, 2012).

[29] Ibid., 205.

[30] Ibid., 220–21.

[31] James H. Cone's first book, *Black Theology and Black Power* (Maryknoll, NY: Orbis), was published in 1969. His presentation of the Black Christ is most fully articulated in *God of the Oppressed* (New York: Seabury, 1975). Vine Deloria published *God Is Red: A Native View of Religion* (New York: Putnam) in 1973.

[32] *Nostra Aetate*, sec. 3.

[33] Ibid.

Islamic Creed, when Muslims state the belief that "there is no God but God." But a self-referential construction refuses to consider the distinctive affirmation of Muslims, erasing their faith that "Muhammad is the messenger of God."[34]

Similarly, *Nostra Aetate* appears to value Jews for what elements of their past Christians share, but not for whatever may distinguish the two traditions in the present. This stance is apparent in how the document deploys the term "New Covenant" to gesture at Jews' and Christians' common heritage as Abraham's stock while settling the term entirely on the church and disregarding Jewish understandings of it.[35] *Nostra Aetate* underlines a common ancestry that springs from the patriarchs when it declares that "God holds the Jews most dear for the sake of their Fathers," but then it distances Christians from Jews by observing that the (Christian) Apostles "sprang from the Jewish people," leaving their Jewishness behind to establish "the Church [as] the new people of God."[36] *Nostra Aetate* self-referentially transmutes a shared heritage into a claim of Christian distinctiveness that says little about how modern Jews revere the God of Abraham, Isaac, and Jacob.

Nostra Aetate is even more challenged in its dance of sameness and difference when it comes to Buddhism and Hinduism. Its Catholic Christocentrism invokes these traditions without actually making any specific positive judgments about them, except to say that whatever is true and holy within them reflects the Truth of Christ and to imply that the fullness they seek may be found preeminently in the Christian church.[37] As a religious project, the document holds that, insofar as Muslims and Jews, Buddhists and Hindus are *like* Christians, the church values their religious traditions. The logic of Catholic teaching, however, is that the fullest form of religious life is to be found in Christ. Articulated explicitly in *Lumen Gentium*, promulgated a year before *Nostra Aetate*, this claim posits that the Christian enjoys an elevated status vis-à-vis his or her religious others, although *Lumen Gentium* urges Christians to remember that their "exalted status is to be attributed not to their own merits but to the special grace of Christ."[38]

---

[34] For a compelling explanation of the Christian logic that affirms the first clause of the Shahada but not the second, see Daniel Madigan, "Jesus and Muhammad: The Sufficiency of Prophecy," in *Bearing the Word: Prophecy in Biblical and Qur'anic Perspective,* ed. Michael Ipgrave (London: Church House Publishing, 2005), 90–99. Mahmoud Ayoub's discussion of an Islamic perspective on Jesus provides important insights on the limitations of a Christian Christocentric view. See Mahmoud Ayoub, "Isa and Jesus: Christ in Islamic Christology," in *Bearing the Word*, ed. Ipgrave, 87–90.

[35] *Nostra Aetate*, sec. 4.

[36] Ibid.

[37] See ibid., sec. 2. For a fuller reception of Hindu and Buddhist traditions, see the reception of *Nostra Aetate* by the bishops of Asia in Mendoza, "Ray of Truth."

[38] *Dogmatic Constitution on the Church—Lumen Gentium*, promulgated by Pope Paul VI (Vatican City, 1964), sec. 14, http://www.vatican.va/archive/hist_councils/ii_vatican_council/documents/vat-ii_const_19641121_lumen-gentium_en.html. For a further discussion of Christian supremacy embedded in *Lumen Gentium*, see Jeannine Hill Fletcher, "Supremacy in the Sense of the Faithful," in *Learning from All the Faithful: A Contemporary*

Christianity's elevated status may be distinctly a part of its theological project, but religious projects do not emerge free from entanglements in history and culture. Thus although *Nostra Aetate* might initially appear innocent of a racial project, we might, pressing further, see one subtly embedded in the way it introduces the notion of culture. Affirmed positively, Buddhism and Hinduism are among those religions that are "bound up with an advanced culture": Hinduism is valued for its "searching philosophical inquiry," and Buddhism for its teaching a way by which people might attain "supreme illumination."[39] Both Hinduism and Buddhism are valued for their "refined concepts" and "more developed language."[40] Yet even as *Nostra Aetate* elevates religions connected with an "advanced culture," it suggests that there are also those entangled with cultures "less advanced." *Nostra Aetate* harbors what we might call a "Great World Religions" argument.[41] The traditions of Christianity, Judaism, Islam, Buddhism, and Hinduism are named (as they might be in a "World Religions" textbook), whereas the religions of the dispossessed First Nations in America, African traditional religions, and the religions of the many indigenous communities overrun by Christian empires remain unnamed.[42] Situated as it is, the statement that "the Catholic Church rejects nothing that is true and holy in *these* religions"[43] might be interpreted to affirm what has been constructed as the "Great World Religions" and to marginalize further the religions of the dispossessed.

A sliding scale of cultures with a hidden white Christocentrism is highly problematic when considered in light of how religious superiority and racial ideologies informed each other in America's history. From the sixteenth through the twentieth centuries, an inextricable link between race, culture, and religion created widespread patterns of thought whereby the culture of white Christians was deemed to be "more advanced" than those of non-white and non-Christian Others.[44] Within

---

Theology of Sensus Fidelium, ed. Bradford E. Hinze and Peter C. Phan (Eugene, OR: Wipf and Stock, 2016), 53–68.

[39] *Nostra Aetate*, sec. 2.

[40] *Ibid.*

[41] Some of the constructed nature of the categories of "religions" might be illuminated by the work of Tomoko Masuzawa, *The Invention of World Religions; or, How European Universalism Was Preserved in the Language of Pluralism* (Chicago: University of Chicago Press, 2005).

[42] Perhaps adherents of these indigenous religions are counted as the "various peoples" who exhibit a "profound religious sense," but the rhetorical distinction between peoples with a "profound religious sense" and those whose religions are "bound up with an advanced culture" (sec. 2) raises serious questions about whether the latter are the only ones to be accepted as having true and holy elements.

[43] *Nostra Aetate*, sec. 2, emphasis added.

[44] The historical pattern of the dispossession of native peoples in US law rests on claims of the superiority of Christian culture and civilization. See Steven Newcomb, *Pagans in the Promised Land* (Golden, CO: Fulcrum, 2008). See also Stephen Ray, "Contending for the Cross: Black Theology and the Ghosts of Modernity," *Black Theology: An International*

this history, Christian claims to theological supremacy served to underwrite the global dispossession of native peoples, the enslavement of Africans, and legal exclusions of persons deemed "nonwhite." The closer peoples appeared to be white and Christian, the more legal securities they were afforded, the foundational one being citizenship. In 1682, legislation in Virginia categorized as slaves virtually "all servants . . . whose parentage and native country are not [C]hristian at the time of their first purchase."[45] Subsequent Christian arguments in defense of slavery often invoked African paganism and/or Islamic inferiority as theological justification of a religio-racial project. In the Christianization of the Americas, First Nations' religious practices were forcibly suppressed in attempting to "civilize" the "uncivilized" races. The Enlightenment project of whiteness linked Christianness with superior cultures and superior races, and, in the nineteenth century, white Christians in the United States saw as their mission the civilizing project of converting new immigrants and newly emancipated persons to white Christian ways.[46]

For many decades before *Nostra Aetate*, during which the United States was perceived as a white Christian nation, citizenship was often determined on the basis of one's affiliation with Christianity. Arguments that led to the 1882 Chinese Exclusion Act (barring Chinese immigrants from citizenship) proposed that an absence of Christianness was evidence of racial inferiority; if only the Chinese would convert, they might be offered the possibility of assimilation in the white Christian nation.[47] In 1914, when a group of Syrians sought citizenship through the American courts, they were granted citizenship in part because their "membership in the Christian fold" served as marker that they were part of the Caucasian or white race.[48] Less than ten years later, Bhagat Singh Thind was recognized by the Supreme Court as "Aryan" and therefore "Caucasian" on the basis of linguistic and genealogical criteria, but the citizenship granted to him by the state of Oregon was revoked on the basis that his "Hinduness" would render him inassimilable to white

Journal 8, no. 1 (2010): 53–68. For a global perspective, see Willie James Jennings, *The Christian Imagination: Theology and the Origins of Race* (New Haven, CT: Yale University Press, 2010).

   [45] William Waller Hening, ed., *The Statutes at Large; Being a Collection of All the Laws of Virginia, from the First Session of the Legislature, in the Year 1619* (New York: Printed for the Editor, By R. & W. & G. Bartow, 1823), 2:491.

   [46] Daniel B. Lee, "A Great Racial Commission: Religion and the Construction of White America," in *Race, Nation, and Religion in the Americas*, ed. Goldschmidt and McAlister, 85–110.

   [47] For further discussion of the religious dimensions of the 1882 Chinese Exclusion Act, see, Jeannine Hill Fletcher, "Warrants for Reconstruction: Christian Hegemony, White Supremacy," *Journal of Ecumenical Studies* 51, no. 1 (2016), 54–79.

   [48] Sarah Gualtieri, "Becoming 'White': Race, Religion and the Foundations of Syrian/Lebanese Ethnicity in the United States," *Journal of American Ethnic History* 20, no. 4 (Summer 2001): 29–58. Gualtieri notes that "the sense of Christian entitlement to share in whiteness was markedly evident in the Dow case, which became a cause célèbre for the Syrian immigrant elite in 1914" (ibid., 42).

culture.[49] The religio-racial project of America has been to establish an identity as a white Christian nation and repeatedly to value those who most closely approximate this ideal.

If one assesses *Nostra Aetate* from a Catholic perspective concerned about the religio-racial project of its day, it is not clear that the document's rhetorical force was sufficient to challenge the notion of the United States as a white Christian nation. There are openings in the text's affirmation of all humanity made in the image of God and its commitment to nondiscrimination, but the Christocentric, self-referential construction of the Other and the sliding scale of cultures do not ultimately dislodge notions of Christian superiority and white supremacy. In the context of the 1960s, the document might easily find a home in the ideology of white Christian supremacy, making necessary accommodations to the new legal affirmations of the formerly dispossessed and new immigrants but not ultimately unsettling attitudes of superiority. By employing a sliding scale of cultures and proposing an elevated Christocentrism, *Nostra Aetate* does little to undo the centuries of racism and white supremacy that have characterized the United States and US Catholicism.[50] *Nostra Aetate* has been a step in the right direction of acceptance of Others, to be sure, and one much preferred to the dictum "Outside the Church, No Salvation," but in the religio-racial project of the United States as a white Christian nation, it may have not done enough in its time, and it certainly does not do enough for ours.

Holding Lightly to Christ for the Salvation of the World

Despite my skepticism regarding *Nostra Aetate*'s efficacy in disrupting the religio-racial project of US Catholics in 1965, I propose rereading the document in light of a revised project. Key to this interpretation is the notion that our theories (and theologies) about racial and religious difference are not static, but are rather informed by concrete material, social, and political realities that lead to particular practices. Our societies change, and our theories and theologies change with them.

In returning to the document with a new religio-racial project in mind, we can see that the penultimate paragraph of *Nostra Aetate* insists: "No foundation therefore remains for any theory or practice that leads to discrimination between man

---

[49] Jennifer Snow, "The Civilization of White Men: The Race of the Hindu in *United States v. Bhagat Singh Thind*," in *Race, Nation, and Religion in the Americas*, ed. Goldschmidt and McAlister, 259–80.

[50] It is telling that in 1968, only three years after *Nostra Aetate* was promulgated, the Black Catholic Clergy Caucus opened its final report with the statement, "The Catholic Church in the United States, primarily a white racist institution, has addressed itself primarily to white society and is definitely a part of that society." See "Statement of the Black Catholic Clergy Caucus" (1968), in *"Stamped with the Image of God"—African Americans as God's Image in Black*, ed. Cyprian Davis and Jamie Phelps (Maryknoll, NY: Orbis Books, 2003), 111.

and man or people and people, so far as their human dignity and the rights flowing from it are concerned."[51] It builds its case on 1 John 4:8—"He who does not love does not know God." As such, the document presents two elements in tension with each other in the church's tradition: Catholic triumphalism and the assertion that all human beings are created in God's image. Since we have seen that theories of Christian supremacy and practices of Christian exclusion have led to both religious and racial discrimination, we might in *our* time have warrant to subordinate the strain of triumphalism present in *Nostra Aetate* to the equally present call to love each other as we love God. To make good on *Nostra Aetate*'s closing directive, we might need to relinquish the Catholic claims of religious supremacy and Christo-centric self-referential constructions of our Others.

Some Christians may find my proposal to be a challenge. They hold religious supremacy to result from a firm commitment to one's beliefs and clarity about their truth. If our Christian claims are not true, this thinking posits, then, of course we would relinquish their supremacy, but, if we believe them to be true, ought we not defend them as religiously superior to other ways of being and thinking? My Buddhist colleague Rita Gross has helped me think through this regularly articulated resistance to relinquishing religious supremacy. Against the idea that relinquishing our religious beliefs as superior thereby implies that they must be false, Gross urges religious people to stop competing over their traditions' veracity because doing so both damages everyone involved and frustrates each religion's capacity to do good in the world. Gross suggests that we *all* hold our religious claims and commitments *lightly*. She returns us to the teaching of the Buddha, who cautioned against all that would get in the way of spiritual progress and proposed a wisdom that encourages us to let go of our clinging. Gross quotes the Buddha from a Theravada scripture: "'Bhikkhus, there are these four kinds of clinging. What four? Clinging to sensual pleasures, clinging to views, clinging to rules and obser-vances, and clinging to a doctrine of self.'"[52] She glosses this text to remind us that clinging to views may hold dangers for our selves and for our Others. She writes:

> The link between suffering and clinging to religious views is important to explore. Most, if not all, wars and persecutions stem from too much conviction in the rightness and correctness of one's own views, as well as self-centeredness. Few people reflect seriously on the aggression inherent in ideology, aka holding views strongly. Holding one's own views strongly often results in aggression and disrespect toward those with whom one disagrees. One also experiences the suffering of one's own anger, one of the most painful of all emotions.[53]

---

[51] *Nostra Aetate*, sec. 5.

[52] Bhikkhu Nanamoli and Bhikkhu Bodhi, *The Middle Length Discourses of the Buddha: A Translation of the Majjhima Nikaya* (Boston: Wisdom Books, 1995), 161. See Rita M. Gross's essay in this volume, "A Buddhist Response to *Nostra Aetate*."

[53] See Gross, "Buddhist Response."

Instead of religious traditions primarily constituted by their claims to truth, Gross suggests that we ask seriously for the *work* the traditions and beliefs do, holding our religious truths lightly so as to ensure that the work they are to do is being done.[54] If *Nostra Aetate* itself insists that "no foundation remains" for "any theory or practice that leads to discrimination" between "people" pertaining to their "human dignity and . . . rights," perhaps we are in need of holding our Catholic Christian truths lightly in order that they might do the work of salvation and healing rather than the work of discrimination and destruction.

In holding our views lightly, Christians are not relinquishing Christ but Christocentric supremacy. Christ can, and will, function for Christians, not as arbiter of a universal humanity, but rather as mirror and model for a Christian way of being human. Jesus Christ is my (Christian) way of being human—a way that might transform those who follow him from self-centeredness toward greater kindness and flexibility—but there are other ways of being human, other mirrors and models that achieve these ends as well.

Holding my claims to truth lightly and recognizing the way in which Christian claims have functioned in the past toward discrimination and dehumanization, I can still proclaim that the Christ who holds a mirror to our humanity is the crucified One. Here I am responding to the invitation of another Buddhist colleague, Sallie King, when she asks Christians to *share* their deepest commitments in interfaith encounter but to do so in such a way that Christ might be compatible with other commitments as well.[55] Here is the Christ to whom I am committed passionately as mediator of our salvation, but I hold him lightly to prevent further harm to Others and further harm to the crucified.

This Christ is intimately revealed in the historical person of Jesus of Nazareth, such that Christ and Jesus are not separate realities. The Christ that was revealed to Christians is flesh and blood in the life, ministry, and death of a first-century Jew. This man Jesus saw that things could be different, if people would return to the deep wisdom of Torah and abide by the dual promise of life in love of God and love of neighbor.

In the story of the Good Samaritan (Lk 10:25–37), for instance, Jesus proposes a love that does not judge the Other on a sliding scale, but one that extends across boundaries of differences and cares intimately for the religious and racial other. As Jesus tells the story, a Samaritan encounters a stranger bloodied on the side of the road, whom his religious brothers had passed by. For Jesus' audience, this Samaritan would have been seen as religiously and "racially" outside the boundaries of their community.[56] Yet pointedly, it is this religio-racial Other

---

[54] See ibid.

[55] See Sallie B. King, "Buddhism and Christianity in a Globalizing and Supplementing World," in this volume.

[56] Because racial categories are always part of a racial project, the identification of "racial" difference in the ancient world is different from our contemporary racial categories. Nevertheless, historical perspective indicates that the social grouping of "Samaritan"

who is lifted up as one whose love across boundaries forged the path to eternal life. The example Jesus gives of the kind of life that is salvific is one that loves and cares across lines of difference.

The teacher of the story of the Good Samaritan is also the Crucified One, put to death at the hands of those who felt threatened by his teachings and those who followed them. The story is reflective of the kinds of teachings that might challenge an establishment where boundaries set the parameters for order. The message to love God and neighbor across boundaries that maintained power and privilege in the first century brought many among the powerful and privileged to desire his demise. Christ comes to the believer as the teacher of an authentic way of being human that challenged those in power in his day and continues to challenge the believer today.

The person of Christ and his witness on the cross is not simply the guarantee of God's favor upon Christians. In his commentary on the Epistle to the Romans, Karl Barth insists that the crucified Christ calls out God's judgment on all humanity. For Barth, Jesus Christ is "the point at which is perceived the crimson thread which runs through all history,"[57] reflecting back to us from the cross the depths of our sinful condition and saving us from our violent mistreatment of others. In honoring the Crucified One, Christians ought to be standing at the foot of the cross being indicted for the ways that they refuse to love and the ways that they continue to crucify others. Standing at the foot of the cross, Christians ought to be following the Crucified One to undo the many crucifying practices of the church and the world.

While there are many things I may learn from my neighbors of other faiths, the Crucified One calls me in a particular way to learn how it is that I as a practicing Christian crucify others. The light shining on my tradition by people of other faiths includes illuminating those places where my devotion to Jesus is less than liberating and actually causes harm. If I am committed to Christ as a torture victim, I need to stand on the side of the tortured and to know when I am torturing others. In this sense, I cannot be committed to Christ crucified without my Others because I need to know those places where my holding too tightly to my savior brings devastation to the Other. The point of interreligious dialogue, then, is to hear those places of hurt and to move together toward healing.

The religio-racial project of the United States as a white Christian nation in 1965 still has its echoes fifty years later when the country continues to struggle toward racial justice, and religious difference remains a site for discrimination.[58]

---

in distinction to "Jew" was both a religious categorization and an ethnic categorization. See Richard J. Coggins, *Samaritans and Jews: The Origins of Samaritanism Reconsidered* (Oxford: Basil Blackwell, 1975).

[57] Karl Barth, *The Epistle to the Romans*, translated from the 6th edition by Edwyn C. Hoskyns (London: Oxford University Press, [1933], 1968), 96.

[58] Continuing violence and discrimination against nonwhite non-Christians evidences that the United States still holds onto a religio-racial project as a white Christian nation, e.g.,

Christians and people of all faiths and convictions are called to continue to enact what is "true and holy." We must seek together what is "salve-ific," that is, what has the power to bring healing to our world.[59] Holding lightly to our Christ, caring gently for his tortured body, and witnessing his specter in those who continue to be crucified, the church might continue to grow, to live, and to speak.

---

the August 5, 2012, shooting of members of the Sikh Temple of Wisconsin; the February 10, 2015, murder of three Muslim students in North Carolina; and the ongoing political pressure to refuse Syrian refugees asylum on the basis of their not being Christian.

[59] In my study of a women's interreligious dialogue group in Philadelphia, one of the women described their work together in the following way: "When we come together, we sort of put a salve on each other's wounds." I expand on this notion of our work being "salve-ific" in *Motherhood as Metaphor: Engendering Interreligious Dialogue* (New York: Fordham University Press, 2013), 199–213.

4

TOWARD A RENEWED THEOLOGY OF CHRISTIANITY'S BOND WITH JUDAISM

John T. Pawlikowski, OSM

Since the publication of *Nostra Aetate*, there have been profound changes in the relationship between Catholics and Jews. The document itself signaled these changes most strongly in section 4, which offers a significant reformulation of the classical theology of Jews and Judaism. The following reflections seek to develop a theological understanding of the church's relationship with Judaism as well as to provide a brief introduction to some recent thinking about the relationship within contemporary Jewish scholarship. I have titled these reflections "Toward a Renewed Theology of Christianity's Bond with Judaism" because biblical and historical scholarship has in the last several decades clearly established that such a bond definitely existed during the church's earliest centuries until a perspective emerged during the Patristic era that cast Jews and Judaism in a negative light. Most of the great Patristic writers made anti-Judaism integral to their understandings of the church's fundamental identity.

For Tertullian, God's wrath was directed at the Jews because of their failure to recognize Jesus as the messiah. Tertullian argued that God wanted to rid himself of the covenant with the Jews. Origen depicted Jews as "hardhearted" because of their failure to see Jesus as Savior, something he attributed to Jewish unwillingness to understand the spiritual sense of the scriptures. Irenaeus proclaimed that God had destined the Gentiles to replace the unresponsive Jews in the kingdom. Justin saw Jewish suffering and their expulsion from Jerusalem as God's justified punishment for Jewish complicity in the death of Jesus. Finally, Eusebius and Augustine saw the Jewish community as enduring perpetual suffering and political homelessness. Augustine even added that Jews were to be seen as "witness people," as a warning to what happens to those who refuse to accept Jesus as messiah.[1] By the fourth century this perspective on Jews and Judaism had become deeply embedded in Christian theology, and this situation would prevail until *Nostra Aetate*.

---

[1] For more on the development of this anti-Jewish theology, see John T. Pawlikowski, "Religion as Hatred: Antisemitism as a Case Study," *Journal of Hate Studies* 3 (December 2004): 37–48.

While *Nostra Aetate* grew out of the historic encounter between French Jewish historian Jules Isaac (who lost much of his family in the Shoah) and Pope Saint John XXIII, it effectively wiped clean the classical negative view of Judaism and other religious traditions. With regard to the Jews, *Nostra Aetate* generated a substantially new template that presented Jews as largely uninvolved in the death of Christ, a people whose covenant remained intact after the coming of Christ, and a community whose perspectives and ethical values were embraced by Jesus and his original followers to a significant degree. Gone was the contemptuous language of the past directed against Jews and people of other faith traditions. A new day was indeed dawning.

There is no doubt that *Nostra Aetate* launched a wholesome reversal in Catholic attitudes toward Jews and Judaism. We should never underestimate its powerful, very positive redefinition of Catholicism's attitude toward the Jewish people, which has persisted and developed during the last half century. Although the picture is more complex in Protestantism, similar changes can be found in many Protestant churches. These changes have also given rise to a reversal of long-standing Jewish views of Christianity as inherently antisemitic and guilty of idolatrous faith statements and practices. The document "Dabru Emet," developed by four leading Jewish scholars associated with the three major branches of Judaism and signed by hundreds of rabbis, is but one example of change on the Jewish side.[2]

Not all the negative viewpoints on Judaism that predominated before the Second Vatican Council have, however, completely disappeared, especially in liturgical celebrations. Even Pope Francis, despite his long positive involvement with the Jewish community in Argentina, has on a few occasions lapsed into classical stereotypes about the Pharisees and Jewish responsibility for the death of Jesus. Moreover, despite the transformation of the basic template for Christian-Jewish relations and the positive path that Jews and Christians have walked together during the last half century, the movement of reconciliation launched by *Nostra Aetate* has not fully lived up to its promise. So as we celebrate the genuine and deep-seated accomplishments of the past fifty years, there is still work for those of us committed to further Christian-Jewish dialogue and to combat what remains of the classical stereotyping of Jews and Judaism.

Section 4 of *Nostra Aetate*, as well as many of the companion documents from other churches, built its arguments for a new vision of the church's relationship with the Jewish people on three foundational premises: (1) Jews were not collectively responsible for the murder of Jesus; (2) as a result, Jews cannot be portrayed as having been exiled from the original covenant with God; and (3) Jesus drew positively from the Jewish tradition of his time in his preaching. These three new perspectives on the

---

[2] For the text of "Dabru Emet" together with Jewish and Christian commentaries, see Tikva Frymer-Kensky, David Novak, Peter Ochs, David Fox Sandmel, and Michael A. Signer, eds., *Christianity in Jewish Terms* (Boulder, CO: Westview Press, 2000). For further discussion, see David Sandmel's contribution to this volume: " 'Who Do You Say I Am?': Jewish Responses to *Nostra Aetate* and Post-Holocaust Christianity."

Jewish-Christian relationship have certainly provided a solid building block for the development of a new theological understanding between the two faith communities. But the profound theological implications of *Nostra Aetate*, which, as Gregory Baum points out, represent Vatican II's most radical change in the ordinary magisterium of the church,[3] have not been fully integrated into Christian theology. Hence we need to examine more closely what has happened in Christian theology with this new vision of the church's relationship with the Jewish people.

New Scholarly Perspectives on Early Jewish-Christian Relations

Over the years a small circle of Christian scholars, along with a few institutional church leaders such as Cardinal Walter Kasper and the late Cardinal Joseph Bernardin of Chicago, has tried to reformulate basic Christian self-understanding in the key areas of Christology and ecclesiology. There have also been some attempts by theologians such as Johann Baptist Metz and Jürgen Moltmann to reflect on the impact of the Shoah on Christian theology.[4] The effort took on some steam in the first decade or so after the Second Vatican Council, but it has waned somewhat in more recent years. Scholars involved in this effort include the late Monika Hellwig,[5] as well as Paul van Buren,[6] who produced a trilogy outlining a fundamentally new theological vision of the church's relationship with the Jewish people in which the term "Israel" was defined as including both Jews and Christians. Others, such as Mary Boys,[7] Kendall Soulen,[8] and myself,[9] have contributed to this ongoing

---

[3] For a fuller assessment, see Gregory Baum, "The Social Context of American Catholic Theology," *Proceedings of the Catholic Theological Society of America* 41 (1980): 87.

[4] See Jürgen Moltmann, *The Crucified God: The Cross of Christ as the Foundation of Criticism of Christian Theology* (New York: Harper & Row, 1974); Johann Baptist Metz, *The Emergent Church: The Future of Christianity in a Postbourgeois World* (New York: Crossroad, 1981); and Johann Baptist Metz, "Facing the Jews: Christian Theology after Auschwitz," *Concilium* 175, no. 5 (1984): 26–33.

[5] Monika Hellwig, "Christian Theology and the Covenant of Israel," *Journal of Ecumenical Studies* 7 (Winter 1970): 37–51; idem, "From the Jesus Story to the Christ of Dogma," in *Antisemitism and the Foundations of Christianity*, ed. Alan T. Davies (New York: Paulist Press, 1979).

[6] Paul M. Van Buren, *A Theology of the Jewish-Christian Reality, Parts 1–3* (New York: Harper & Row, 1980, 1983, 1988).

[7] Mary Boys, *Redeeming Our Sacred Story: The Death of Jesus and Relations between Jews and Christians* (New York: Paulist Press, 2013).

[8] R. Kendall Soulen, *The God of Israel and Christian Theology* (Minneapolis: Fortress Press, 1996).

[9] John T. Pawlikowski, *Christ in the Light of Christian-Jewish Dialogue* (Eugene, OR: Wipf and Stock, 2011), and *Restating the Catholic Church's Relationship with the Jewish People: The Challenge of Super-Sessionary Theology,* Frontiers of Scholarly Research (Lewiston, NY: Edward Mellen Press, 2013).

theological discussion. Each has added valuable perspectives, but no one has as yet produced an interpretation that has caught the attention of a significant segment of the Christian theological community. So, with regard to theology, a new understanding of the Christian-Jewish relationship is still in its infancy. The one major change that has taken place, though, is the perspectival reversal from a theology of Jewish covenantal *exclusion* after the Christ Event to a theology of continued Jewish covenantal *inclusion*.

One of the most remarkable transformations in scholarship generated as part of the fundamental reconsideration of the early Christian-Jewish relationship has occurred in the area of biblical studies. Beginning in the 1980s, a movement often termed the "Parting of the Ways" scholarship arose. Early participants included John Gager, Robin Scroggs, and the late Anthony Saldarini. In 1986, Scroggs, a professor at Catholic Theological Seminary at the time and subsequently at Union Theological Seminary, summarized the essential components of this new vision. As he saw the situation during and immediately after the time of Jesus, certain realities shaped the relationship between the church and the synagogue: (1) The movement begun by Jesus and continued after his death in Palestine can best be described as a reform movement within the Jewish community of the time; (2) the Pauline missionary movement as understood by Paul a Jewish mission that focused on the Gentiles as the proper object of God's call to God's people; (3) prior to the end of the Jewish war with the Romans in 70 CE, there was no such reality as "Christianity." Followers of Jesus did not have a concept of themselves as a religion over and against Judaism; a distinct Christian identity began to emerge only after the Jewish-Roman war; and (4) the later portions of the Second Testament all show some signs of a movement toward separation, but they also generally retain some contact with their original Jewish matrix.[10] Saldarini added to this picture. In various essays he underlined the continuing presence of the "followers of the Way" within the wide tent that was the Jewish community of the time. He especially underscored the ongoing nexus between Christian theology and practice and Judaism in the Eastern sectors of the church—a reality that is often ignored in Western theological discussions.[11]

The initial scholarship on the first several centuries of the Common Era has been advanced by an increasing number of other scholars, both Christian and Jewish.[12] John Meier, for example, argues that, from a careful examination of New

---

[10] Robin Scroggs, "The Judaizing of the New Testament," *Chicago Theological Seminary Register* 75 (Winter 1986): 36–45.

[11] Anthony J. Saldarini, "Jews and Christians in the First Two Centuries: The Changing Paradigm," *Shofar* 10 (1992): 32–43, and "Christian Anti-Judaism: The First Century Speaks to the Twenty-First Century," The Joseph Cardinal Bernardin Jerusalem Lecture 1999 (Chicago: Archdiocese of Chicago, the American Jewish Committee, Spertus Institute of Jewish Studies, and the Jewish United Fund/Jewish Community Relations Council, 1999).

[12] See Adam H. Becker and Annette Yoshiko Reed, eds., *The Ways That Never Parted:*

Testament evidence, Jesus must be seen as presenting himself to the Jewish community of his time as an eschatological prophet and miracle worker in the likeness of Elijah. According to Meier, Jesus was not interested in creating a separatist sect or a holy remnant along the lines of the Qumran sect. But he did envision the development of a special religious community within Israel. The idea that this community "would slowly undergo a process of separation from Israel as it pursued a mission to the gentiles ... finds no place in Jesus' message or practice."[13] And David Frankfurter has insisted that within the various "clusters" of groups that included Jews and Christians there existed a "mutual influence persisting through late antiquity." There is evidence for a degree of overlap, that, all things considered, threatens every construction of a historically distinct "Christianity" before at least the mid-second century.[14] Finally, Paula Fredriksen questions the term "Parting of the Ways." For her, the term is unhelpful because it implies two solid blocks of believers when, in fact, the various groups were intertwined for several centuries.[15]

One other implication of the "Parting of the Ways" scholarship has to do with a perspective on Paul and his writings. These writings have had a pervasive influence on much of Christian theology, Christology in particular, especially within the Protestant churches. Recent scholarship has literally turned much of the traditional understanding of Paul that has served as a bedrock for Christological interpretation on its head. Paul is now seen as standing far more within the Jewish context of his day than previous Christologies had imagined. To argue that Pauline thought represents the ultimate break between the church and the synagogue is increasingly being challenged by the emerging new scholarship on Paul.[16]

The "Parting of the Ways" scholarship has certainly implanted the notion of Jesus' fundamental Jewishness in Christian consciousness. But this recognition of Jesus' Jewishness has not had much of an impact on Christian theological reflection, especially in the area of Christology. A few Christian scholars, such

---

Jews and Christians in Late Antiquity and the Early Middle Ages, Texts and Studies in Ancient Judaism 95 (Tübingen: Mohr Siebeck, 2003). Also see Matt Jackson McCabe, ed., *Jewish Christianity Reconsidered: Rethinking Ancient Groups and Texts* (Minneapolis: Augsburg/Fortress, 2007); Fabian E. Udoh, ed., *Redefining First-Century Jewish and Christian Identities: Essays in Honor of Ed Parish Sanders* (Notre Dame, IN: University of Notre Dame Press, 2008); and Hershel Shanks, ed., *Partings: How Judaism and Christianity Became Two* (Washington, DC: Biblical Archaeology Society, 2013).

[13] John P. Meier, *A Marginal Jew: Rethinking the Historical Jesus*, vol. 3: *Companions and Competitors* (New York: Doubleday, 2001), 251.

[14] David Frankfurter, "Beyond Jewish-Christianity: Contributing Religious Scholars of the Second and Third Centuries and Their Documents," in *Ways That Never Parted*, ed. Becker and Reed, 132.

[15] Paula Fredriksen, "What 'Parting of the Ways?' Jews, Gentiles, and the Ancient Mediterranean City," in *Ways That Never Parted,* ed. Becker and Reeds, 35–64.

[16] On new perspectives on Paul and Judaism, see Reimund Bieringer and Didier Pollefeyt, eds., *Paul and Judaism: Crosscurrents in Pauline Exegesis and the Study of Jewish-Christian Relations* (London: T&T Clark International, 2012).

as Wesley Ariarajah, have even called the efforts to return Jesus to his original Jewish context a "futile attempt" that has little relevance for Christians in a non-Western context. Although Ariarajah does not deny Jesus' Jewish roots, he argues that they carry no significance for theological statements in Asian and other non-Western contexts. For him it is far more important to relate Jesus to Buddhist thought.[17]

The argument advanced by Ariarajah, however, is incomplete. I agree that we need to inculturate the teachings of Jesus, and we ultimately have to present his mission in a language that relates to the particular culture of an area. This includes relating our teachings about Christ to other religious perspectives. This must remain a priority for the contemporary church. But I profoundly disagree with his idea that we can present the authentic meaning of Jesus' teachings and the early theological tradition about his person and ministry without situating him in his deeply Jewish context. The process of reinserting Jesus into his actual setting, including the theological implications of this process, is still in an embryonic state.[18]

Papal Reflections

If recent scholarship on early Christianity has suggested closer ties between Christians and Jews than traditional histories have supposed, some recent papal statements have begun to urge more positive approaches from a theological standpoint. On a number of occasions, Pope Saint John Paul II spoke of an inherent bond between Jews and Christians:

> The Church of Christ discovers her "bond" with Judaism by "searching into her mystery" (*Nostra Aetate*, sec. 4). The Jewish religion is not "extrinsic" to us, but in a certain way "intrinsic" to our own religion. With Judaism, therefore, we have a relationship which we do not have with any other religion.[19]

---

[17] Wesley Ariarajah, "Towards a Fourth Phase in Jewish-Christian Relations: An Asian Perspective," unpublished paper, Conference on Christian-Jewish Dialogue, Temple Emmanuel, New York, co-sponsored by the Center for Interreligious Understanding and the Office of Interreligious Affairs of the World Council of Churches, November 2003. For a somewhat different Asian perspective, see Peter C. Phan, "Jews and Judaism in Asian Theology: Historical and Theological Perspectives," *Gregorianum* 86 (2005): 806–36.

[18] On Jesus as a Jew, see Hans Hermann Henrix, "The Son of God Became Human as a Jew: Implications of the Jewishness of Jesus for Christology," in *Christ Jesus and the Jewish People Today*, ed. Philip A. Cunningham et al. (Grand Rapids, MI: Wm. B. Eerdmans, 2011), 114–43; and Barbara Meyer, "The Dogmatic Significance of Christ Being Jewish," in *Christ Jesus and the Jewish People Today,* ed. Cunningham et al., 144–63.

[19] See Eugene J. Fisher and Leon Klenicki, eds., *Spiritual Pilgrimage: Texts on Jews and Judaism 1979–1995, Pope John Paul II* (New York: Crossroad and ADL, 1995).

And, in his acclaimed Apostolic Exhortation, *Evangelii Gaudium* ("The Joy of the Gospel"), Pope Francis says much the same:

> We hold the Jewish people in special regard because their covenant with God has never been revoked, for "the gifts and the call of God are irrevocable" (Rom 11:29). The Church, which shares with Jews an important part of the sacred Scriptures, looks upon the people of the covenant and their faith as one of the sacred roots of her Christian identity (cf. Rom 11:16–18). As Christians, we cannot consider Judaism as a foreign religion; nor do we include Jews among those called to turn from idols and to serve the true God (cf. 1 Thes 1:9).[20]

These theological affirmations by Pope Saint John Paul II and Pope Francis raise for Christians today the question as to whether Jewish texts and traditions need to be seen as "in-house" resources for the expression of Christian belief. Put another way, how much do we need to "re-Judaize" Christianity to bring it into conformity with these papal perspectives? A few theologians, such as Johann Baptist Metz, have argued for the necessity of such integration into Christian faith today.[21] And Pope Benedict XVI, in his address at the Rome synagogue in 2010, spoke of the usefulness of certain postbiblical Jewish resources for the articulation of Christian faith. Such reflections by the heads of the Catholic Church are salutary, but they have been essentially isolated statements that the rest of the church has generally passed by. A substantive change in the church's theological reflection remains a task to be accomplished.[22]

Nonsupersessionist Christology in the Making

Although the ecclesiological question will remain central in theological discussion of the Christian-Jewish relationship, the issue above all is the Christological question—that is, how Christianity has interpreted Jesus and his ministry over the centuries. I have presented an overview of how some prominent Christian theologians have approached this challenge, most recently in *Restating the Catholic Church's Relationship with the Jewish People* (2013). Here I would like to lay out a possible approach to Christology in light of the church's new perspective on Judaism and the Jewish people.

---

[20] Pope Francis, *Apostolic Exhortation—Evangelii Gaudium* (Vatican City, 2013), sec. 247, http://w2.vatican.va/content/francesco/en/apost_exhortations/documents/papa-francesco_esortazione-ap_20131124_evangelii-gaudium.html.

[21] Metz, "Facing the Jews," 27.

[22] Pope Benedict XVI, *Visit to the Synagogue of Rome—Address of His Holiness Benedict XVI, Sunday, 17 January 2010*, https://w2.vatican.va/content/benedict-xvi/en/speeches/2010/january/documents/hf_ben-xvi_spe_20100117_sinagoga.html. The pope's observation notwithstanding, Christian theology has largely ignored postbiblical Jewish texts.

As a preface, let me say that I believe we live in a time when the theological discussion should remain open-ended. I sense in some Christian circles a desire to set up strict parameters for such a discussion. This boundary-marking, in my judgment, will stifle creative proposals. Pope Paul VI provided a bit of a model for an open approach. In his rewriting of the classical Good Friday prayer for the Jews in the 1970 missal that incorporates the vision of the Second Vatican Council into liturgical celebration, he affirmed the ongoing covenantal inclusion of the Jewish people while leaving open how this affirmation might be squared with the classical Christian claim of Christ's universal redemptive work. The latter issue is something for theologians to continue to explore, but it is certain that any such gradual definition must emerge from robust theological discussion rather than ecclesial fiat.

Along with scholars such as Franz Mussner, who authored one of the more comprehensive volumes on Christology within the context of Christian-Jewish dialogue,[23] I believe that Incarnational Christology is the best approach to understanding the Christ Event in a way that leaves legitimate theological space for Judaism.[24] But here we encounter a difficult challenge for any attempt to forge a postsupersessionist theology within the churches. Christian leaders, both Protestant and Catholic, have generally insisted that only a single covenantal perspective on Jewish-Christian relations is valid in order to protect the traditional notion of the universality of Christ's redemptive work. If I were a Jew, I am rather sure I would not rejoice at having my religious identity defined via a covenant in Christ. Yet the option of two totally separate covenants is equally unacceptable to Christians. It fails to take into account the increasingly emphasized notion of Jesus' fundamental rootage in the Jewish community of his day and the continuing deep-seated links between the two religious communities for several centuries after his death. And it would also ignore the strong insistence—starting with Pope Saint John Paul II and continued by Pope Benedict XVI and now Pope Francis—that Judaism is implanted in the very heart of Christianity. In my view, any acceptable model will need to affirm connectedness and distinctiveness equally.

My theological perspective clearly views Incarnational theology as the only viable option for moving toward a constructive theology of the Christian-Jewish relationship. Incarnational theology focuses on the presence of God within humanity, a view which makes some positive connections with elements within the Jewish tradition. In so doing I am de-emphasizing the two other classical options for Christology in Christian history as a foundation for a post-*Nostra Aetate* theology of Jewish-Christian relations. The first, which is predominant in the synoptic

---

[23] Franz Mussner, *Tractate on the Jews: The Significance of Judaism for Christian Faith,* trans. Leonard Swidler (Philadelphia: Fortress, 1984); idem, "From Jesus the 'Prophet' to Jesus the 'Son,'" in *Three Ways to One God: The Faith Experience in Judaism, Christianity, and Islam,* ed. Abdoldjavad Falaturi, Jacob J. Petuchowski, and Walter Strolz (New York: Crossroad, 1987), 76–85.

[24] I am speaking here from the perspective of Christian theology. Jews may rightly feel they do not need theological validation from Christianity for their faith.

gospels, depicts Jesus as fulfilling all major messianic prophecies in the prophetic literature. The second, found strongly in the Pauline literature, underscores the sacrificial aspect of his ministry, especially the spilling of his blood to wash away human guilt and the stain of original sin. This Christology became central in the patristic period. Both of these viewpoints leave little or no meaningful role for Judaism after the Christ Event. If Christ has fulfilled all the messianic prophecies, then Judaism retains no redemptive meaning after his coming. And, if Jesus washed away all obstacles to human salvation, what redemptive option remains for Jews if they do not acknowledge that reality? Both Christological perspectives remove the Jewish people from any continuing role in human redemption.

I recognize that these Christological perspectives are deeply entrenched in Christian self-understanding, so they will not be easy to put aside. This difficulty is particularly pronounced for the "messianic" interpretation of Christology that so permeates the Christian liturgy. But, in light of *Nostra Aetate*, I feel that Christian theologians are mandated to produce a theology of Jewish-Christian relations devoid of supersessionism. And I fail to see how that solemn responsibility can be met in today's church through either the "messianic" or "blood" Christologies.[25] Only what I am calling an Incarnational Christology provides some pathway toward this end.[26]

My current approach to the creation of a nonsupersessionist Christology picks up much of what I have written earlier on this topic.[27] Working within an Incarnational framework and with an understanding of the gradual development of Christological consciousness in the early church, I would continue to maintain that what ultimately came to be recognized with greater clarity for the first time through the ministry and person of Jesus was how profoundly integral humanity is to divinity. This insight in turn implies that each human person somehow shares in divinity. "Christ" is the theological term that the church selected to try to express this reality. As the later strata of the New Testament stress, the humanity of Jesus existed in the Godhead from the very beginning. Thus, in a very real sense, we can

---

[25] "Messianic Christologies" insist that Jesus in his lifetime fulfilled all the major biblical prophecies in the Hebrew Scriptures about the coming of the Messiah. Since Jesus fulfilled them, all peoples, including Jews, need to accept Jesus as their lord and savior, leaving Judaism no continuing role in the redemptive process. "Blood Christologies" argue that Jesus washed away human guilt through the shedding of his blood on Calvary. People must commit themselves to this understanding to achieve salvation. Again, Judaism has no continuing role in this process. Hence, only Incarnational Christology offers some possibilities for making a positive theological connection between Judaism and Christianity.

[26] The liturgical aspects of reaching this goal are daunting, but some liturgists, such as Liam Tracey, OSM, have begun to take us on this path. See Liam Tracey, OSM, "The Affirmation of Jewish Covenantal Vitality and the Church's Liturgical Life," in *Christ and the Jewish People Today*, ed. Cunningham et al., 268–86.

[27] John T. Pawlikowski, *Jesus and the Theology of Israel* (Wilmington, DE: Michael Glazier, 1989); idem, *Christ in the Light of Christian-Jewish Dialogue* (Eugene, OR: Wipf and Stock, 2001).

say with Paul that God did not become man in Jesus. God in fact has always had a human dimension. Humanity has been an integral part of the Godhead eternally. The Christ Event was crucial, however, for the manifestation of this reality to the world. In this regard, I would be quite comfortable theologically with the term "transparent," which Paul van Buren floated in meetings of the Christian Scholars Group but which he never published. In this perspective, the Christ Event gave greater transparency to the human-divine linkage.

The above vision does not mean to equate God with the totality of humanity. Such an equation would represent a fundamental misreading of my approach. From my perspective a gulf remains between God and the human community that is forever impassable. Moreover, despite the intimate link with God revealed through the Christ Event, humankind remains equally conscious of the fact that this God is the ultimate Creator of the life that is shared with men and women as a gift. Nor does my understanding of the link between divinity and humanity mean that there was not a uniqueness in which humanity and divinity were united in Jesus. Humanity could never have come to the full awareness of the ultimate link between itself and God without the express revelation occasioned by the Christ Event. While this event will allow us to experience a new closeness with the Creator God, our humanity will never have the same intimacy with the divine that existed in the person of Jesus.

In recent years, I have made one major modification to my original vision of a nonsupersessionist Christology. I would now introduce the term "kingdom of God" or "reign of God" more centrally into the expression of my Christological vision. I have been persuaded on this point in a particular way as a result of a seminar exchange with Dr. Amy-Jill Levine, the co-editor of the *Jewish Annotated New Testament*.[28] As a Jewish New Testament scholar, Levine sees Jesus' sense of the presence of the kingdom as the most distinctive aspect of his teaching. I find her persuasive on this point. But I would go on to tie this notion very directly with my vision of Jesus as making transparent the full linkage between humanity and divinity. It is the revelation of this linkage that makes possible the proclamation that the kingdom is already in our midst, even if not yet fully realized. The presence of the kingdom can be perceived both within human consciousness and human history. Here I would underscore the importance of seeing history and human consciousness as profoundly intertwined, a reality that allows for some opening for theological dialogue between the biblical and Asian religious traditions. This is a reality, I admit, that needs further elaboration as I continue the development of my thinking on a Christology that can move beyond supersessionism.

Here we come to a key point in terms of Christian-Jewish relations. The new transparency with respect to divine presence that I regard as the core of the Christ Event's revelation should not be taken as a full and complete vision of human salvation by itself. The Protestant scholar Kendall Soulen has made an invaluable

---

[28] Amy-Jill Levine and Marc Zvi Brettler, eds., *The Jewish Annotated New Testament: New Revised Standard Version* (Oxford: Oxford University Press, 2011).

contribution to the discussion of the theological perspective I am proposing in this essay when he insists that it must include as absolutely central the Hebrew Scriptures' vision of the immersion of God in history and in creation, hallmarks of the revelatory core of the Jewish covenantal tradition. Both God active in history and God active in creation, Soulen correctly insists, are critical to an authentic path toward final human redemption. In the period prior to the end-time, however, the Jewish and the Christian communities walk distinctive paths dominated by one or the other of these two revelatory visions.[29] Their paths are parallel and sometimes intersect. Ultimately they will coalesce, though how that will occur is known only to God. Even though I am aware that he does not particularly like the term "paths," I believe that this is the theological vision left to us by Cardinal Walter Kasper in his several writings on the theological relationship between Jews and Christians.[30]

Before ending this brief overview of the challenges involved in generating a postsupersessionist theology of the Christian-Jewish relationship, I need to draw attention to *The Jewish People and Their Sacred Scripture in the Christian Bible.*[31] This important document, issued by the Pontifical Biblical Commission in 2001, carries a supportive introduction by Cardinal Joseph Ratzinger (later, of course, Pope Benedict XVI), under whose jurisdiction at the Congregation for the Doctrine of the Faith the document ultimately fell. Released with a minimum of fanfare, this statement opens up several new possibilities for expressing the significance of the Christ Event while leaving space for the ongoing validity of Judaism. Despite definite limitations in the way it portrays postbiblical Judaism, the document makes an important contribution to the development of a new constructive Christological understanding in the context of Catholic theologians' continuing reflection on how to include Jews as well as Christians in the covenant with God. Two statements in particular are significant for this discussion. Both occur in the same paragraph.[32]

The first is the affirmation that Jewish messianic expectations are not in vain. Although I wish that this pronouncement had been worded more positively and directly, it does, in my view, undercut the rather simplistic Christology based on Jesus' supposed fulfillment of Jewish messianic prophecies that so dominate Catholic liturgical expression. The commission's statement appears to recognize the

---

[29] R. Kendall Soulen, *The God of Israel and Christian Theology* (Minneapolis: Fortress Press, 1996).

[30] See Cardinal Walter Kasper, "The Good Olive Tree," in *America* 185, no. 7 (September 17, 2001): 12–14; "Christians, Jews, and the Thorny Question of Mission," *Origins* 32, no. 28 (December 19, 2004): 464; and Foreword to *Christ Jesus and the Jewish People Today*, ed. Cunningham et al., x–xvii.

[31] Pontifical Biblical Commission, *The Jewish People and Their Sacred Scripture in the Christian Bible* (Vatican City: Liberia Editrice Vaticana, 2002). For a discussion of the document, including my own reflections, see the special issue of *The Bible Today* 41, no. 3 (May/June 2003).

[32] Pontifical Biblical Commission, *Jewish People and Their Sacred Scripture*, 60 [Part II.A.5.21].

continuing validity of these messianic prophecies as distinctly understood within Judaism, thereby ruling out the church's traditional claim that Christ fulfilled all of the prophecies and thus is the expected Jewish messiah, whom the Jewish people have nevertheless refused to accept. Such a claim has been at the core of supersessionist theology within Christianity. But this document seems to be arguing that the Jewish messianic texts found in the Hebrew Scriptures represent an authentic insight into final eschatological fulfillment. They remain an integral part of genuine religious hope. Accordingly, we have the seeds of a recognition by Christian biblical scholarship of a distinctive path to the end-time for the Jews, something that, as I have already mentioned, has been proposed by Cardinal Walter Kasper when he wrote that "if they [i.e., the Jews] follow their own conscience and believe in God's promises as they understand them in their religious tradition they are in line with God's plan."[33]

The second statement from the Pontifical Biblical Commission's document is somewhat more oblique but has potential for being developed into an important theological statement.[34] This key text in the Pontifical Biblical Commission's document reads as follows: "Like them [i.e., the Jews], we too live in expectation. The difference is that for us the One who is to come will have the traits of the Jesus who has already come and is already present and active among us."[35] While this statement certainly claims messianic fulfillment in and through Jesus, it seems to imply that this fulfillment is not yet complete. Might we say that the Jewish eschatological vision adds something critical to complete messianic understanding? A critical "trait" visible in and through Jesus might in fact be the enhanced transparency in our understanding of the divine-human linkage that stands at the heart of Incarnational Christology. This statement also opens up the possibility that not all messianic traits have been made visible in and through Jesus but in fact have been better exposed within Jewish messianic perspectives. Finally, the statement seems to legitimate a discussion whether the "traits" seen by Christians in and through Jesus might be expressed in a different set of theological categories.

Recent Jewish Responses

Let me conclude with a few additional observations about where the theological discussion on the Christian-Jewish relationship needs to move. First of all, I want to underscore my belief that Christian theologians must make an essential decision

---

[33] Cardinal Walter Kasper, ""The Commission for Religious Relations with the Jews: A Crucial Endeavour of the Catholic Church," address delivered at Boston College, November 6, 2002, sec. 3, https://www.bc.edu/content/dam/files/research_sites/cjl/texts/cjrelations/resources/articles/Kasper_6Nov02.htm.

[34] The Pontifical Biblical Commission does not have theological formulation as part of its mandate. That responsibility falls upon the Pontifical Theological Commission, which has never formally addressed the theological implications of the Pontifical Biblical Commission's statement.

[35] Pontifical Biblical Commission, *Jewish People and Their Sacred Scripture*, 60.

at the outset as to which of the Christological traditions within Christianity is the most appropriate for building a constructive approach to the covenantal continuity of the Jewish people. I have made clear my decided preference for Incarnational Christology. But I recognize that this is not an easy choice, since the two other major Christological perspectives, found in the synoptic gospels and in the Pauline literature, have played a central role in defining Christianity over the centuries and influencing its liturgical expression. Christology stands at the nerve center of Christian identity, so we must go slowly and with appropriate caution in proposing any major adjustment to our Christological outlook.

My Incarnational approach is written from within and for the Christian community. But I believe there is also a task for Jewish religious scholars as well. Christianity does have theological implications for Jewish theological self-expression that cannot go unrecognized by Jewish theologians when Christian leaders such as the last three popes speak of the church's bondedness with Judaism. Connectivity cannot be a one-way street. I raised this challenge in an essay some twenty-five years ago. In a brief response to that piece, the Jewish scholar Irving Greenberg acknowledged the validity of such two-sided bondedness but went on to say that few Jews have thought of other religions, or of their positive significance for Judaism. In his mind, this lack of reflection remains an unfulfilled goal in Jewish theology.[36] I suspect that the issue of theological bondedness and a mutually explored understanding of the continuing link between Judaism and Christianity will need to focus on whether the two traditions are intertwined within a single covenantal framework that makes their relationship quite different from the relationship either has with other religious communities, or whether they exist today as two quite separate religions. In other words, are the findings of the "Parting of the Ways" scholarship referenced above permanently significant for an understanding of the Jewish-Christian relationship?

Hence, the process of reconnecting the church with its Jewish roots will also require exploration of some of the recent writings on Jesus, and even on Christology, from the Jewish side. Although Jewish scholars are hardly rushing to embrace the investigation of the Jewish context of Jesus' teaching and the theological tradition that grew up around his person, we are beginning to see a new interest in this subject among a handful of scholars. The works of people such as Daniel Boyarin,[37] Elliot Wolfson,[38] Benjamin Sommer,[39] and the various contributors to the volume *Teaching the Historical Jesus*,

---

[36] John T. Pawlikowski, "Rethinking Christianity: A Challenge to Jewish Attitudes," *Moment* 15, no. 3 (August 1990): 36–39. See the "Response" by Irving Greenberg, "Jews Have Thought Little about the Spiritual Dignity of Other Faiths," 39.

[37] Daniel Boyarin, *The Jewish Gospel: The Story of the Jewish Christ* (New York: New Press, 2012).

[38] Elliot Wolfson, "Gazing Beneath the Veil: Apocalyptic Envisioning the End," in *Reinterpreting Revelation and Tradition: Jews and Christians in Conversation*, ed. John Pawlikowski and Hayim G. Perelmuter (Franklin, WI: Sheed & Ward, 1997), 77–103.

[39] Benjamin D. Sommer, *The Bodies of God and the World of Ancient Israel* (Cambridge: Cambridge University Press, 2009).

edited by Zev Garber,[40] represent an important breakthrough, given the virtual taboo on this subject even a few years ago. When Daniel Boyarin argues that what Christian theologians term "Christology" was not created especially for application to Jesus but already existed within the Judaism of the time, he is obviously challenging long-held views in both Christianity and Judaism that Christology constitutes a wall of separation between the two faith communities. Although Boyarin would never say that the expression of Christology in Greek-based philosophical terms has a basis in Judaism, he does insist that the basic notion behind this Christian belief, that is, that the divine can penetrate humanity, has definite roots in Second Temple Judaism. Even though such a view sits on the cutting edge of contemporary Jewish thought and will be rejected by many Jewish scholars, Boyarin has laid seeds for a new discussion of such a perspective within Jewish circles, boring holes in a taboo that has existed for centuries.

The discussion has recently taken a new and important step with the publication of a volume by Shaul Magid.[41] In *Hasidism Incarnate*, Magid presents Hasidism as a perspective on Judaism in which the divine/human boundary is permeable and sometimes even crossed. In examining the Hasidic tradition anew, we discover a resurgence of the very Incarnational theology that more mainstream forms of Judaism have basically rejected, in large part clearly to distinguish the Jewish tradition from Christianity. Yet within Hasidic writings, Magid argues, God and humanity have been reintegrated.

For Magid, the key sources for his argument about the incarnational nature of Hasidism are the writings of noted rabbis such as Nachman of Bratzlav and Levi Yitzhak of Berdichev. Their portrayal of the *tsaddik*, the ultimate spiritual leader in the Hasidic tradition, as the person who intercedes between God and humanity, rekindles Incarnational theology within Judaism even though Magid himself is careful to assert that Hasidic Incarnationalism differs substantially from notions of Christology in the Christian tradition. Magid attempts to delineate the difference between Hasidic views of the *tsaddik* and Christian understandings of Jesus as the Christ. Christian theology has argued that in Jesus the word became flesh. But in Hasidic Judaism, people such as Rabbi Nachman envisioned themselves as "fleshy beings" who have chosen to speak the word of God. Such language suggests, according to Magid, a certain penetration of the classical boundary between the divine and the human that can be labeled "Incarnationalism." Such an understanding is not found in traditional rabbinic literature nor even in non-Hasidic forms of Jewish mysticism.

Magid acknowledges some kabbalistic influence on this Hasidic "Incarnationalism." But, generally speaking, non-Hasidic forms of Judaism have been reluctant to acknowledge such hints of God's immanence, lest they blur the distinction between the Jewish community and Christianity, especially in regions of Europe

---

[40] Zev Garber, ed., *Teaching the Historical Jesus: Issues and Exegesis* (New York: Routledge, 2015).

[41] Shaul Magid, *Hasidism Incarnate: Hasidism, Christianity, and the Construction of Modern Judaism* (Palo Alto, CA: Stanford University Press, 2015).

where Jewish leaders were struggling to preserve a clear sense of Jewish identity in the face of Christian political and social domination. Hasidism, as a movement that stood far more beyond the eyes of Christianity than did mainstream Rabbinic Judaism, had an easier time embracing and promoting the seeds of Incarnationalism already present in the Kabbalah. Because of its relatively greater insulation from non-Jews, Hasidism had a greater freedom to endow its image of the *tsaddik* with quasi-divine status, an image that may have appeared as too Christian in streams of Jewish thought that intersected far more readily with Christian society.

Magid's contention has received some pushback. Incarnationalist notions were not the Hasids' invention; they were, as he himself notes, already present in, for instance, the *Zohar*, the classic kabbalistic text, which presented its chief protagonist, Rabbi Shimon Bar Yochai, as a messianic hero.[42] Magid's view has received criticism from scholars of Jewish mysticism such as Moshe Idel,[43] who has also criticized the works of Elliot Wolfson in similar terms. Idel believes that "Incarnationalism" is a bad term to describe the relating of divinity and humanity in various streams of Judaism. Its use tends to stamp a univocal Christian notion upon a plurality of Jewish views. My own comment here would be that Idel is somewhat straitjacketing the notion of Christology in the Christian tradition. Christology is far more pluralistic in nature than he would allow.

Although I will not pass judgment on whether "Incarnationalism" is an apt term for explaining key elements of the Hasidic tradition, a certain sense of divine immanence in humanity does seem present in Judaism in light of the research of Magid, Wolfson, Boyarin, and Sommer. For the Christian theologian, this subject becomes an important area of continuing study in the context of the Jewishness of Jesus. It has potential impact for Christianity's Christological assertions and can affect what Christological affirmation assumes primacy among the options of Messianic Christology, Incarnational Christology, and Atonement Christology. In my judgment, the case for the primacy of Incarnational Christology is very strong. It appears to be the only Christological option that does not automatically undercut the notion of continued Jewish covenantal inclusion. It also suggests that the early Christological proclamations, which, according to Raymond Brown, emerged in a liturgical setting,[44] did not automatically rule out the continued participation of certain Jews who joined the early Christian movement. In other words, the so-called impenetrable wall between Judaism and

---

[42] See Jay Michaelson, "How Hasidism Bridges Boundary between Christianity and Judaism," *Forward.com* (February 4, 2015), http://forward.com/culture/213732/how-hasidism-bridges-boundary-between-christianity.

[43] Moshe Idel, *Ben: Sonship and Jewish Mysticism* (New York: Continuum, 2002). For a positive evaluation of Magid's thesis, see Arthur Green's review, *Studies in Christian-Jewish Relations* 10, no. 1 (2015), https://ejournals.bc.edu/ojs/index.php/scjr/article/viewFile/9120/8220.

[44] Raymond Brown, "Does the New Testament Call Jesus God?" *Theological Studies* 26, no. 4 (December 1965): 545–73.

Christianity on the Christological question was in fact more porous at the outset than we have traditionally imagined.

The discussion about the theological relationship between Jews and Christians must move beyond institutional theological circles to embrace the growing number of people who have important spiritual links to either religious community without formal ties to their institutional structures. The dialogue will also have to increasingly incorporate the Christian-Jewish theological discussion into the wider interreligious conversation, particularly with Islam. And the Christian-Jewish dialogue has important theological consequences for the church's discussions with all other religious traditions.

There are those in Jewish and Christian circles who may be apprehensive about the theological challenges I have raised. These challenges may appear to undermine necessary boundaries among religious traditions, between Christianity and Judaism in particular. But, for me, fear is the enemy of conviction and commitment. As the Pontifical Biblical Commission has underscored, Christians and Jews equally live in eschatological hope. Let that be the prevailing context as we face the theological challenges in our Jewish-Christian relationship.

5

The Christian Spiritual Vision from the Perspective of *Nostra Aetate*

Roger Haight, SJ

This essay is an effort to understand the Christian spiritual vision of reality in such a way that it allows Christians to "acknowledge, preserve and encourage the spiritual and moral truths found among non-Christians, together with their social life and culture."[1] The essay works on the supposition that an internalization of this proposition from *Nostra Aetate* requires a retelling of the christocentric and somewhat exclusivist version of the Christian story of reality.

To accomplish this, I take several key passages from *Nostra Aetate* and use them as thematic guides for constructively reimagining the Christian narrative. The still dominant Christian story begins with creation and is followed by what came to be seen as a fall of the human race. In the West, the significance of Jesus Christ focuses not exclusively but primarily on humanity's fallen condition, and the salvation Jesus accomplished is understood as an objective atonement and forgiveness of sin.[2] *Nostra Aetate*, however, pushes our spiritual imagination in the direction of a new paradigm. This essay suggests an outline for a theocentric understanding of Christian spirituality that stays faithful to the tradition and at the same time inspires a way of life that responds positively to a religiously pluralistic world according to the intimations of *Nostra Aetate*.

Why should one attempt this reimagining from the perspective of spirituality and not through a new parsing of the classical doctrines or beliefs of Christian tradition? A response to this question requires a brief explanation of what the term "spirituality" refers to. Spirituality in this writing means the way persons or groups live their lives in the face of ultimate reality. It refers to the logic of a person's whole life according to the value or ultimately important idea or thing that actually centers a person and shapes his or her identity. As a way of life, spirituality cannot be reduced to words or propositions or other formulas. But the phrase "following Jesus

---

[1] *Declaration on the Relation of the Church to Non-Christian Religions—Nostra Aetate*, proclaimed by Pope Paul VI (Vatican City, 1965), sec. 2, http://www.vatican.va/archive/hist_councils/ii_vatican_council/documents/vat-ii_decl 19651028_nostra-aetate_en.html.

[2] See Anselm of Canterbury, "Why God Became Man," in *A Scholastic Miscellany: Anselm to Ockham*, ed. and trans. Eugene R. Fairweather (New York: Macmillan, 1970), 100–183.

Christ" refers to and recapitulates Christian spirituality. On that premise, people continually have to find the words and values that formulate the existential or lived reality and its implications. Spirituality keeps the discussion of Christian beliefs and values, which should correlate with the spiritual practice, close to the ground of people's experience of Christian symbols in actual life. If one is speaking about the vital meaning of doctrines, spirituality is where a constructive interpretation of them has to begin.[3] It opens up the place where the doctrines can communicate affective contact with transcendent reality.

I develop this outline of a revised form of the Christian story in five points, each of which is guided by a text from *Nostra Aetate*. The five parts engage the following themes: (a) spiritual implications of the doctrine of creation, (b) the impact of Jesus Christ on spirituality, (c) a conception of a "grace-filled natural world." These three ideas point to (d) the conviction that all people are brothers and sisters because of our common relationship to God. And this leads to the conclusion, (e) that religions should not compete with each other and that Christians should encourage practitioners of other religious traditions. All people should be spiritually open toward each other because of God's friendship with all human beings and the assurance of God's effective love for each person and their cultures. What is being formulated here is not a common interreligious spirituality or view of reality, but a Christian spirituality that respects and promotes pluralism.

Belief in One Creator God

> One is the community of all peoples, one their origin, for God made the whole human race to live over the face of the earth. One also is their final goal, God.[4]

The doctrine of creation is underrated. Protology (Creation) and eschatology (on the End-time) form the bookends of the Christian understanding of all reality: all things (the world, human beings, history, Jesus Christ, and church) are situated within this framework.[5]

Creation, more than other doctrines, offers an entrée into a universal perspective and in so doing has the potential to define a connection with other religions. As *Nostra Aetate* says, other religions, too, ask, "What is the ultimate mystery, beyond human explanation, which embraces our entire existence, from which we take our origin and towards which we tend."[6]

---

[3] I am distinguishing "vital meaning" here from "conceptual meaning." Conceptual meaning is reconstructed by historical examination of the genesis of the doctrine and the debate that usually surrounded it.

[4] *Nostra Aetate*, sec. 1.

[5] Edward Schillebeeckx, *Christ: The Experience of Jesus as Lord* (New York: Crossroad, 1980), 638–44.

[6] *Nostra Aetate*, sec. 1.

Even without developing an entire theology of creation, we should pay attention to the significance of the idea of "creation out of nothing." "God creating" does not point to something that God did in the beginning of time. Rather, "creating" indicates the permanent relationship of God to all that exists: God is continually creating finite reality, so that all things, actually in each moment, depend on God creating.[7] Moreover, the idea that God creates out of nothing entails the proposition that God-causing-things-to-be is intrinsic to every element of finite being. God constitutes the inner power of the being of all finite beings, their actions, and their continuous becoming. This claim means that God should be understood as the interior active dynamism of all reality. God is not out there/up there; all that is subsists in the energy that is God. Called "panentheism," this view means that all things are in God and God is the "within" of all that is.[8]

This "panentheism" sets up a situation that at first may seem paradoxical: God is most readily accessible to all and yet impossible to imagine or conceive adequately. Because God is the "within" of all that is, people encounter God within their subjectivity, usually with the help of external stimuli. Many are the testimonies to such experiences. Yet because God is transcendent and infinite, precisely other than any finite thing, no earthly concept can adequately encompass God's inner reality. This inability to articulate God fully puts all religions in the same position of modesty before the *mysterium tremendum* of ultimate reality.

Monotheism affirms that there is only one God, and hence that all finite reality comes from a single source and has a common ground of being. This affirmation correlates with a sense of the oneness and integrity of all reality. And when the Christian scriptures record Peter's insight that this one "God shows no partiality" (Acts 10:34), this feeds an understanding that the creator God of all loves all that God creates; nothing that God creates escapes the embrace of God's love. This common love of all on the part of God serves as a framework that protects the small and weak members of the human family from the larger and more powerful who naturally dominate. In this way the idea of creation carries one deeply into the transcendent ground and source of all ethics, spirituality, and religion.

A Christomorphic Construal of God

[The Church] proclaims and ever must proclaim Christ "the way, the truth, and the life" (John 14:6).[9]

Religions have a great influence on how persons raised within them understand the ultimate reality to which they are related. In Christianity, people relate to the object

---

[7] The classical term for this absolute dependency on God's free action of creation is "contingency." The mystery of why anything at all exists is hidden within God's freedom.

[8] The term "panentheism" is used here to say that all things subsist within the power of God, and that God, as creator and as inseparable from God's power, is within all finite reality.

[9] *Nostra Aetate*, sec. 2.

of their faith, God, in the way that the church represents God. The church in turn draws its message about God from Jesus of Nazareth. The basic idea that flows from the text affirming that Christ "is the way, the truth, and the life" is that Christian faith understands God christomorphically. This fairly straightforward idea needs some explanation, because the word is intimidating.

All religions have some idea of ultimate reality that has been adopted from some this-worldly experience, image, or analogue. Since ultimate reality is not empirically available to us, the ideas that we apply to God have to be drawn from this-worldly experience, however inadequate that might be. There may be many sources for an experience of transcendent reality, but when we envision what ultimate reality is, when the imagination tries to give that abstract idea some specific content, it is shaped by a finite source. In terms of this theory of human understanding of ultimate reality, Jesus lies at the foundation of the particularly Christian understanding of God. When that is not the case, the normativity of scripture calls us back to the character of Jesus represented in the Bible as the source of faith's understanding of God. Specifically Christian faith in God entails allowing Jesus to shape our understanding of the character of God. The Christian idea of God is the one whom Jesus called Father.

Jesus preached in Galilee in ancient Israel and formed a group of disciples who continued his ministry after his death. Their faith was shaped by Jesus' preaching of the rule of God and by their Easter experience that Jesus was raised from death by God. Gradually this Jesus movement grew into a Christian church, and Jesus, the revealer of a particular view of God and God's rule, shaped the faith of the movement. This, too, was the birth of what is known as Christology, the theological interpretation of Jesus Christ, and much more has to be said about that subject than can be said here. But without going into Christology, by remaining within the limited perspective of spirituality, we can affirm that Jesus shapes or molds specifically Christian faith in God. On a fundamental historical, functional, and spiritual level, Jesus provides the Christian way, truth, and life.

Based on Jesus' preaching about God and God's rule "on earth as it is in heaven,"[10] Christians relate to God as personal and loving. God is not a neutral energy suffusing the universe. God is personal without being an individual person, that is, in a way that cannot be adequately imagined. God loves and cares in a transcendent way. Jesus' teaching and his broader ministry provide the concrete media that fix these basic characteristics of God within the Christian imagination.

Belief in a Grace-Filled Natural World

The Catholic Church rejects nothing that is true and holy in these religions.[11]

---

[10] Mt 6:10.

[11] *Nostra Aetate*, sec. 2.

Nostra Aetate urges Christians to affirm and defend the spiritual and moral truth that is found outside the Christian sphere. But for a church that used to maintain that there was no salvation outside the Christian sphere,[12] it does not explain how this spiritual and moral truth found its way into these other religions and cultures of the world. The phrase "a grace-filled natural world" is meant to offer that rationale by merging aspects of the doctrine of creation with the conviction that God is personal and loving.

But before taking up the question of how God's grace is universally available, we need some background. For centuries Augustine's doctrine of original sin blocked Christian vision from seeing the world as suffused with grace. Augustine understood the sin of Adam and Eve as a catastrophic historical event that influenced human nature itself. This condition was passed on to all the descendants of the first couple, setting up a human state or condition of being with a darkened mind and a weakened will. This premodern view set up a background for Western theology up to the modern period.[13]

Following the Enlightenment, two developments have broadened the Christian view. The first followed the recognition that the story of Adam and Eve was a mythical symbol and not a historical narrative. Its point was to confess a sense of guilt and to show that God the creator was not the source of sin.[14] The story called attention to an existential proclivity of human beings rather than to a fallen state of being. The post-Enlightenment theologian Friedrich Schleiermacher did not attribute this condition to a mythical Adam and Eve: "We have no reason for explaining universal sinfulness as due to an alteration in human nature brought about in their person by the first sin."[15] A historical original sin of a first couple altering human nature is not compatible with evolution. Thereafter, modern theology has tended to interpret original sin as a deep tendency within human existence.

The second breakthrough in Western theology has been to insist on the inseparability of the orders of nature and grace. Karl Rahner and other theologians have insisted on the universal offer of God's grace so that no one can be separated from the offer.[16] Since God wills the salvation of all people, and this requires the grace of

---

[12] This language goes back to Cyprian of Carthage, who, in a controversy with the Novatian schismatics, wrote that "there is no salvation out of the Church." See his letter to Jubaianus, Epistle 72, para. 21 (http://www.newadvent.org/fathers/050672.htm).

[13] Paul Ricoeur, "'Original Sin': A Study in Meaning," in *The Conflict of Interpretations: Essays in Hermeneutics*, ed. Don Ihde (Evanston, IL: Northwestern University Press, 1974), 269–86, gives an incisive account of the story of Adam and Eve, Augustine's interpretation of it, and a hermeneutical method for retrieving its meaning for our context.

[14] See Paul Ricoeur, *The Symbolism of Evil* (New York: Harper & Row, 1967).

[15] Friedrich Schleiermacher, *The Christian Faith* (New York: Harper & Row, 1963), #72, 291.

[16] See, for example, Karl Rahner, "The Order of Redemption within the Order of Creation," in *The Christian Commitment: Essays in Pastoral Theology* (New York: Sheed and Ward, 1963), 38–74; Karl Rahner, "Nature and Grace," *Theological Investigations*, IV (Baltimore: Helicon Press, 1966), 165–88.

God, the effectiveness of God's salvific intent requires us to imagine that through one means or another God's grace is available to all persons. Thus, in Rahner's theology of grace, the gratuity of grace does not convert into its scarcity. Rahner's view of grace allows people to interpret the world as a world of grace as in the title of the book: *A World of Grace*.[17]

How, then, should the universality of grace be imagined? We have seen how the doctrine of creation out of nothing entails the immediate presence of God to all that God creates. In the scriptures, this active, sustaining presence and power of God in the finite order of history is called "the Spirit of God." Also, in the theological tradition, God's grace in many but not all theological languages correlates neatly with this same "Spirit of God." The New Testament especially bears witness to an experience of God working in individual persons and in communities that construe the Spirit as the energy of the love and forgiveness of God, a power that binds the community together in love and urges it on. *From the perspective of creation theology*, the Spirit of God can be equated with the creator's presence and power within all reality. "God as Spirit" names God's creating energy and effectiveness that is internal to each created thing and its activity. God's "Spirit" correlates with, in the terms of Thomas Aquinas, God's primary creating causality as distinct from the whole system of finite secondary causes that operate in the created order.[18] *From the perspective of the New Testament witness*, God creates out of love for what God creates. Love is a motive and a quality of God's creating activity. The Spirit of God thus actualizes God's love and is present to each person and to the community as a whole. In short, God's entwined creating and loving cannot be separated or even imagined as really distinguishable within God. God's primary creating causal power is never anything but loving. And this is experienced and construed as the Spirit of God at work in persons and community. Panentheism means that in God's love "we live and move and have our being" (Acts 17:28).

The dialogue between Christian faith and science also pushes us in the direction of an imaginative framework characterized as a "grace-filled naturalism." Scientists who are Christians and Christians who want to understand their faith in

---

[17] Subtitled *An Introduction to the Themes and Foundations of Karl Rahner's Theology*, ed. Leo J. O'Donovan (New York: Crossroad, 1984).

[18] "Primary causality" refers to God's causing or communicating "being" in the absolute sense of contrast with nonbeing. All things that exist are on the basis of the creating power of God that sustains them in being. This mode of causality is proper to God alone, and distinct from all other forms of influence or causality that finite beings have on one another. This latter kind of causality is called "secondary." See Thomas Aquinas, *Summa Theologica*, I, 45, 5 in *Basic Writings of Saint Thomas Aquinas*, ed. Anton C. Pegis (New York: Random House, 1945) for a discussion that defines the point of the distinction. There Aquinas writes: "Now to produce being absolutely, and not merely as this or that being, belongs to the nature of creation. Hence it is manifest that creation is the proper act of God alone." God's creating causality is a completely different kind of causality than the web of finite causality.

a way that is coherent with a scientific imagination are not inclined to construe God as an individual actor outside the created order intermittently intervening in the finite network of causality. Rather, God is present to the whole of the finite order in a way that is appropriate to God creating and sustaining, as the ground of being and not as a single or specific finite agent. From a Christian perspective it makes perfect sense to correlate the metaphysically conceived primary or creating causality of God with the loving power and the divine energy that are symbolized by the religious language of "the Spirit of God." This correlation is not an appeal to a proof text, as in a theology "from above" and based only on a traditional authority. It is, rather, an insight into how two distinct languages, of faith and of philosophical reasoning, can be seen to apply to the same reality.[19]

The use of this kind of language is even more striking when used by a philosopher of science. The creative thinking that follows comes from the Gifford Lectures of 1997, delivered by Holmes Rolston.[20] Appreciation of the value of life, of dynamic fecundity, he writes, leads to reverence and a sense of sacrality. "So the secular—this present, empirical epoch, this phenomenal world, studied by science—does not eliminate the sacred after all; to the contrary, the secular evolves into the sacred. If there is any holy ground, any land of promise, this promising Earth is it" (362). But if humans can experience the awesome sacredness of life itself, "then why not say that here, if anywhere, is the brooding Spirit of God? One needs an adequate explanation for generating the sacred out of the secular. Indeed, why not even go on to say that the genesis of value is the genesis of grace" (362).

The experience of sacrality and grace or giftedness leads to an idea of God. In an evolutionary world, the idea of God becomes a postulated source for the genetic information that stabilizes identity, for generativity, and for support. The power of God undergirds natural selection. Rolston writes:

> Here one can posit God as a countercurrent to entropy, a sort of biogravity that lures life upward. God would not do anything in particular but be the background, autopoietic force energizing all the particulars. The particulars would be the discoveries of the autonomous individuals. God

---

[19] Referring to the church, Schillebeeckx notes that "this one reality, because of its riches, is fully accessible (and then still in a limited human way) only from two (or more) different perspectives, questions and language games." Edward Schillebeeckx, *Church: The Human Story of God* (New York: Crossroad, 1990), 212. The grounds for this structure of language about what amounts to a dual perception of a this-worldly reality lies in how faith's experience is mediated through deeper questions about what is manifest on a historical empirical level. See Edward Schillebeeckx, *The Understanding of Faith: Interpretation and Criticism* (New York: Seabury Press, 1974), 91–101.

[20] Holmes Rolston III, *Genes, Genesis and God: Values and Their Origins in Natural and Human History*, The Gifford Lectures, University of Edinburgh, 1997–1998 (Cambridge: Cambridge University Press, 1999). In what follows, the references to this work appear in the text.

would be the lift-up (more than the setup) that elevates the creatures along their paths of cybernetic and storied achievement. God introduces new possibility spaces all along the way. What theologians once termed an established order of creation is rather an order that dynamically creates, an order for creating. (364–65)

This kind of language from a scientific imagination recognizes the awesome creative power that sustains all reality and is most obvious in the generativity within the sphere of life. Rolston senses an analogous experience behind the ancient religious imagination: "The Hebrew metaphor was that one needs 'wind' as well as 'dirt.' The current metaphor is that one needs 'information' as well as 'matter' and 'energy'" (365). Rolston adds to the agency of God an intention "to optimize the integrity, autonomy, and self-creativity of the creatures—letting them do their thing, generating and testing, discarding what does not work and keeping what does" (368). Overall this image or idea of God responds to the question of an ultimate and constant source for fecundity and novelty across billions of years and the quantum transitions of increased levels of life. In the creation narratives the point is not design but empowerment. "There is divine fiat, divine doing, but the mode is an empowering permission that places productive autonomy in the creation" (370).

Let me recapitulate here. *Nostra Aetate* tells Christians that they should reject nothing of "what is true and holy" in other religious traditions, but it does not explain how this truth and holiness come to be there. This invites a theological reflection in a contemporary idiom on the implicit, expansive grounds of God's saving grace, which are at the same time the basis for a Christian theology of religions. The constructive position offered here begins with a theology of creation that conceives of God as the inner power of being and action of all finite reality. This philosophically generated theological conception is conflated with the biblical symbol of the Spirit of God that points to the power and energy of God at work in the world. But the Spirit of God also represents God's personal self-communication and love in a theology of grace. The constructive reach of this conception of the single power and love of God means that God's loving presence is available to all people; this is not a distant possibility but the inner power of their own being. Its effectiveness cannot be absent from the many religious traditions. Moreover, this conception has resonance in the scientific framework of evolutionary biology; the nonduality must be felt even there. Thus the slide from reflection on the majesty of nature into the realm of transcendent mystery is not forced but spontaneous. The integrated language of the scientist illustrates a new expansive context for religious thought that is receptive to an immanent creator God who loves (grace) what God creates and is personally present within it. In sum, the reason why Christians reject "nothing of what is true and holy in [other] religions" lies in the conviction that God is a loving and creating presence to and a dynamic power within all people and finite reality itself. God is the immanent power of being, goodness, and love that constantly invites and stimulates spiritual and moral truth among all human beings.

All Are Our Brothers and Sisters

We cannot truly call on God, the Father of all, if we refuse to treat in a
brotherly way any man, created as he is in the image of God.[21]

This statement from *Nostra Aetate* can easily sound like a sentimental, counterintuitive and vapid aspiration. On the basis of the previous reflections, it is logical and
coherent. But it so contradicts historical reality and the workings of human nature
that it must seem to be a useless if not a delusory observation. It is inoperative, irrelevant, and so off the mark that it may have negative effects on people who hear it.

Nostra Aetate's statement provides a good example of a religious and metaphysical statement that goes below the surface of the empirical and transcends the
boundaries of the world of matter-of-fact: it is a statement of faith. It serves as a
ground for moral convictions: Why should we have a deep respect for our enemy?
What is the basis of the value of human life? What does it mean to affirm human
equality? From the perspective of life in history, the love of God is the guarantor of
the value of each person and the equalizer: to be loved by God as an individual gives
every person a position and a standing. It points to the ultimate source of human
existence and the destiny of all human beings. Our being of the same species in the
end does not make us affectively brothers and sisters. There are genuine hatreds
within biological families. Rather, the affirmation of a cosmic order of morality and
justice depends on God or the functional equivalent of God. Without God, one
can still affirm a unity of the species, a pragmatic rationale for justice, and even a set
of norms that protect individual rights. But a life of virtue and service to a larger
community will have no solid basis without a metaphysics that guarantees the value
of the individual on deeper grounds and invites service to our common human existence as a community.

This saying of *Nostra Aetate* reminds believers of their social responsibility and
its connection with their relation with God. But that dual human relationship to
God and to fellow human beings undergirds an ethical responsibility that is also
entailed in human community and society.

Encouraging Other Religions

The Church . . . exhorts her sons, that . . . they recognize, preserve and
promote the good things, spiritual and moral . . . found among [the
followers of other religions].[22]

If the text cited in the third section above, titled "Belief in a Grace-Filled Natural
World," were interpreted as passive toleration of other religions contrary to its

---

[21] *Nostra Aetate*, sec. 5.
[22] *Nostra Aetate*, sec. 2.

intention, that is, recognizing that religious pluralism is inevitable, this text of
Nostra Aetate positively encourages other religions. Implicitly, if taken at face value,
this text seems to imply the autonomous validity of other religions, for that is how
they conceive themselves. In other words, the statement implicitly transcends
notions of "anonymous" or "latent" Christianity as the reason for "encouraging"
other religions.[23] It would surely be an anachronism to claim that this reading
describes the motives of the authors of these texts or the meaning intended by the
bishops that approved the documents. The pluralistic implications of this text arise
from today's context in which they are being interpreted. To "encourage the spiritual and moral truths found among non-Christians" implies religious pluralism,
that is, the legitimate autonomy of other religions. As explained earlier, the reason
for this from a Christian perspective is implied in God's intrinsic presence to religious communities.

But *Nostra Aetate* does not explain the mechanism by which Christianity can
reject nothing that is true and holy within other religions and can even encourage
other religions. How is it able to say this in the face of so many differences among
the religions? How does a Christian know whether something in another religion
is true and holy? Should what is holy in other religions be judged from the point
of view of Christianity? Is any religion able to affirm another religion's authenticity
against the grain of its own vision of reality?

The problem that *Nostra Aetate* seems to run into at this point is relativism,
at least in the eyes of those within every religion who take their vision of reality
as the absolute norm for what is true and holy. Relativism means that human
beings cannot affirm the absolute truth about anything transcendent. This point
is obvious, because what is transcendent cannot be adequately comprehended, and
because the perspective of a particular time and place limits all perception. Therefore, one cannot say that all sets of belief and practice are true and holy. And one
cannot step outside one's own convictions to find a universal perspective that will
allow a judgment that discerns ultimate truth against ultimate error.

The idea of "pluralism," as distinct from a sheer plurality of differences, helps to
address this issue. Pluralism refers to differences that coexist within a larger sphere
of unity, or a fundamental unity that holds together within itself differences that
are acceptable within the whole. But this does not provide the criterion by which
to judge that something is not true or holy; and such a criterion is necessary for a
credible judgment. Is there a criterion for truth that crosses the borders of many
religions?

One such criterion arises out of the fundamental condition of human existence. What is transcendently true and holy must respond to the fundamental

---

[23] The phrase "anonymous Christian" is invariably associated with Karl Rahner. See
Karl Rahner, "Anonymous Christians," *Theological Investigations, VI* (Baltimore: Helicon
Press, 1969), 390–98; Paul Tillich used the phrase "the latent church" in an analogous way.
See Paul Tillich, *Systematic Theology*, III (Chicago: University of Chicago Press, 1963),
152–54.

human questions about moral weakness, sickness and death, and the ultimate meaning of human existence.[24] These basic human questions seem to be universal; they define the human quest for wholeness, integrity, and comprehensive meaning. At the same time they look for a transcendent response. The true and the holy respond to the ultimate questions of human existence itself.[25] In this view, something is true and holy when it corresponds with and promotes the comprehensive integrity of humanity in its personal and social dimensions. From a Christian point of view this correlates fairly closely with what Jesus meant by the rule of God[26] and what Christians mean by "salvation": a situation of communion between human beings and God and among themselves.[27]

Nostra Aetate was an extraordinary document for its time, and it provided warrant for creative thinking that branched out in several directions: interfaith dialogues, theology of religions, comparative theologies, and interreligious spiritual practices and cooperation. We have come a long way since its publication. Relying on developments since then, let me conclude with an outline of a holistic Christian vision of the human race as a single community, which is by nature pluralistic in its religious communities, which are in turn moving through history together in dialogue with absolute mystery and with each other.

Human beings are a self-conscious part of the universe whose very existence depends at every moment on the active creative power of God. The symbol "Spirit of God" refers to the immanent sustaining presence of God within all things. On the basis of Jesus' person and ministry, Christians relate to God as personal lover of what God created. The God who loves and who promises an eternal life of meaningful fulfillment guarantees the value of each human being within a comprehensive framework of love and justice.

Built on these foundations, the Christian understands reality as a dynamic grace-filled natural world. God does not "intervene" into the finite world because God is its sustaining and suffusing ground of being.[28] This means that the world is

---

[24] These three negative anthropological constants are drawn from Paul Tillich, *The Courage to Be* (New Haven, CT: Yale University Press, 1952), 46–57. They are negative qualities of estranged human existence from which Christianity offers salvation.

[25] These questions of guilt, of the significance of death, and of comprehensive meaning are not exclusively religious in nature; they are asked in the most secular and pragmatic of cultures. They are better described as prereligious, spiritual, and universally relevant.

[26] The phrase "the rule of God" is another way of saying "the kingdom of God," which expresses both the central concern of Jesus' ministry and the framework for understanding what he said and did. A direct route into the meaning of "the rule of God" is to see the following phrase as a strict parallelism to it or in apposition to it: "Thy will be done on earth as it is in heaven" (Mt 6:10). It shows that the "kingdom" is not a place but the present and the final situation in which God's intent for creation is harmoniously accomplished.

[27] Gustavo Gutiérrez, *A Theology of Liberation* (Maryknoll, NY: Orbis Books, 1973), 151.

[28] In the thematic heading of the third section of this essay, I referred to a grace-filled natural world, in effect a grace-filled naturalism. God does not intervene in this world,

evolving through time and is empowered ontologically from within by the presence and power of God, who is at the same time personal and loving. The personal
self-gift of God to all, more than ancestry or genetic codes, makes us brothers and
sisters to each other and, as such, responsible to God. In their movement through
history, all human beings together are turned toward absolute mystery. As a human
race, together, we are not able to rank in value the different manifestations of God's
actual presence to human beings. But we can compare them and discuss them. This
discussion thus forms an integral part of the historical existence and evolution of
the species.

The notion of a grace-filled (sacred) naturalism describes what is going on in
the created sphere that is suffused with God's love. This grace is not a second sphere,
not an add-on as in a response to a fall; it is not rooted in a second motivation of
God, and not a supernatural existential or a "second gratuity."[29] It is precisely the
love of God for what God creates that is intrinsic to the action of creating itself.
This formulation cuts through any distinction between the natural and supernatural
orders, or nature and grace, a distinction that has occasioned too many misconcep-
tions to be useful. The economy of creation and salvation is one; it is rooted in
God's love, which, in the Christian view of things, is the motive of creation itself.
Grace is not rare; it is coterminous with creation. In a panentheistic worldview, all
things subsist within the love of God. Grace or God's empowering self-gift is the
personal and loving character of God's primary causality.[30]

This conclusion is not the direct teaching of *Nostra Aetate*. But looking back
at that document from our present situation, this is a Christian spiritual vision to
which the text and the implicit intent of *Nostra Aetate* give rise.

---

because God is already present within it; there is no place outside the world that God can
intervene from. Moreover, God is God and does not act as a secondary cause in the finite
world; such action is appropriate only to finite beings. God's creation and human freedom
within it are semiautonomous; that is, God sustains in being and accompanies an unfolding
universe, planet, and history that are not strictly regulated by God but are sustained by being
within the power of God. Hence the scientific notion of contingency, meaning randomness,
which is so different from the theological. There is obviously more to be said here but not
within the limits of an essay that has its own goal.

[29] This is a reference to Karl Rahner, who preserves the distinction between the natural
and the supernatural orders as a sign that grace is truly gratuitous. But it is not "more"
gratuitous than creation itself. This is precisely the distinction that Edward Schillebeeckx
overcomes with his creation theology. See Roger Haight, "Catholic Pluralism on Religious
Pluralism: Rahner and Schillebeeckx," in Roger Haight, *The Future of Christology* (New
York: Continuum, 2005), 103–22.

[30] There is, of course, more to be said here. The world is filled with violence; human
beings implicitly reject God's grace; human sin mars our lives and does so in horrific
measure. These are things that the religions have to talk about with each other.

Part III

Protestant and

Orthodox Christian Perspectives

6

FULLNESS OF TRUTH IN CHRIST ALONE

Early Protestant Responses to Nostra Aetate

Ulrich Rosenhagen

Immediately following the end of the Second Vatican Council, *Time* magazine published a long essay titled "How Vatican II Turned the Church toward the World." Written for a broad and general audience in the United States, the essay succinctly summarized the elated zeitgeist of December 1965. It attempted to grasp the unprecedented "spirit that brought the Council together and inspired its discussions." According to the essay, something beyond human comprehension had been at work in Rome. It quoted Otto Dibelius, the presiding bishop of the Evangelical Church in Germany, who marveled: "If the Roman Catholic Church had looked 450 years ago as it looks today, there would never have been a Reformation." By way of the council, the Catholic Church had abandoned its triumphalist stand and had finally adjusted to the modern world and its religious pluralism. With a sense of astonishment and clear appreciation, the article's anonymous author observed, "Without denying its own belief that [the church] has a special divine mission, Catholicism now acknowledges that it is but one of many spiritual voices with something to tell perplexed modern man."[1]

Some of those diverse spiritual voices were of course present throughout the four sessions of the council between October 1962 and December 1965. In the ecumenical spirit of the time, the Secretariat for Promoting Christian Unity, under the presidency of Cardinal Augustin Bea, invited non-Catholic Christian observers and guests to Rome to join in the conversations. Such a move had been unheard of in the history of the Catholic Church. At the second session from September 29 to December 4, 1963, the number of non-Catholic observers grew to sixty-three representatives from a great variety of Christian branches and traditions.[2] Along

---

[1] "How Vatican II Turned the Church toward the World," *Time*, December 17, 1965, 36–41.

[2] Fifty-four ecumenical observers attended the first session of the council, from October 11, 1962, to December 8, 1962. Twenty-eight came from Protestant churches. At the fourth session, from September 14, 1965, to December 8, 1965, 106 ecumenical observers attended; 47 came from Protestant churches. See Bernd Jochen Hilberath,

with clergy representing Syrian Orthodox Christians, Coptic Egyptians, and Apostolic Armenians, there was a large spread of Protestants—Anglicans, Lutherans, Presbyterians, Methodists, Congregationalists, as well as Quaker and Unitarian representatives—who had been invited as official observers of the council. Despite this astonishing denominational spread, though, "almost all [of] the observers" came from Europe and North America.[3]

Steeped in their own traditions, these non-Catholic observers were uniquely positioned to move as mediators between the council and their own theological homelands. In Rome, they mixed freely with the young Joseph Ratzinger and Hans Küng, Karl Rahner, and the other four hundred *periti* who excelled in debating by night the theological drafts and footnotes on which the cardinals had to vote by day.[4] According to George Lindbeck, who represented the Lutheran World Federation while on leave from Yale University, the Secretariat for Promoting Christian Unity consulted with these mediators and briefed them regularly "beyond protocol." While moving between the roles of representing a tradition at the council and reporting on the council's doings to their own denominations, the non-Catholic observers soon attained "ambassadorial status" at the council.[5]

"Theologischer Kommentar zum Dekret über den Ökumenismus," in *Herders Theologischer Kommentar zum Zweiten Vatikanischen Konzil*, ed. Bernd Jochen Hilberath and Peter Hünermann (Freiburg i.Br.: Herder, 2005), 3:87. Observers officially represented denominations, national churches, national ecumenical bodies, and the World Council of Churches. The number of selected non-Catholic guests that had been invited by the Secretariat for Promoting Christian Unity grew from eight at the first session to sixteen at the fourth session. Among the guests were such renowned theologians as Oscar Cullmann and Roger Schutz, prior of the community of Taizé in France. See Christopher Thomas Washington, *The Participation of Non-Catholic Christian Observers, Guests, and Fraternal Delegates at the Second Vatican Council and the Synods of Bishops: A Theological Analysis* (Rome: Gregorian and Biblical Press, 2015), 92, and Hilari Raguer, "An Initial Profile of the Assembly," in *History of Vatican II*, ed. Giuseppe Alberigo and Joseph A. Komonchak (Maryknoll, NY: Orbis Books; Leuven: Peeters, 1997), 2:179, 182.

[3] Lukas Vischer, "The Council as an Event in the Ecumenical Movement," in *History of Vatican II*, ed. Giuseppe Alberigo and Joseph A. Komonchak (Maryknoll, NY: Orbis Books; Leuven: Peeters, 2006), 5:492.

[4] Though it is not really possible to assess the influence of the non-Catholic observers and guests on the council, there is some anecdotal evidence that the bishops highly valued their contributions. In his *Memoirs*, the secretary general of the World Council of Churches, Willem A. Visser't Hooft, shared his conversation with a *periti* who pointed out to him that "if an edition of the council documents could be issued in which all the passages that had been changed in the light of the remarks of the observers were printed in red, the result would be a most colorful production" (Willem A. Visser't Hooft, *Memoirs* [London: SCM; Philadelphia: Westminster, 1973], 330).

[5] George A. Lindbeck, "Reminiscences of Vatican II," in *The Church in a Postliberal Age*, ed. George Buckley (Grand Rapids, MI: Eerdmans, 2002), 12. According to French Dominican Yves Congar, the ecumenical observers were "active and influential," and their presence had a lasting and impressive religious dimension. See Yves Congar, "Die Rolle der

The Protestant observers' assessment of the council was filled mostly with praise and enthusiasm. For a great many of them, the council had been a transformative event that affected not only Rome but the whole Christian church. Even the neo-orthodox theologian Karl Barth—arguably the most influential Protestant theologian of the twentieth century—praised many of the council's outcomes and noted hopefully after its ending that he "would be happy to see the words 'Protestant' and 'Protestantism' disappear from our vocabulary."[6]

The seismic waves that the council had generated carried over into the Protestant realm. Following the Catholic Church, Protestants too began to reassess their faith and traditions. "[So] what about us non-Romans in the aftermath of Vatican II?" Albert Outler, Methodist observer and professor of theology at Southern Methodist University, asked in 1966 in *Mid-Stream*, the ecumenical journal of the Churches of Christ. Concerned that mainline Protestants might fall too far behind, Outler wanted to shake up his readers. It is the "blunt truth," he wrote, that, with Vatican II, "the Roman Catholic Church has leap-frogged the rest of us [in matters of] church renewal and ecumenical action." Hence, the Methodist minister readily added, "There is finally no evading the challenge of Vatican II that we [non-Catholics] go and do likewise."[7]

When, however, it came to *Nostra Aetate*—the council's "Declaration on the Relation of the Church to Non-Christian Religions"—Protestant commentators weren't so sure about their excitement and the call to reform their own houses. The majority of Protestant theologians in Europe and the United States clearly tried to dodge the declaration, likely because Karl Barth was disturbed by aspects of it. Indeed, for the first twenty years after the council, no official Protestant church statement explicitly mentioned it. Protestant historiography seemed to ignore it.[8]

'Beobachter' in der Entwicklung der Ökumene," in Ökumene: Möglichkeiten und Grenzen heute, ed. Karlfried Froehlich (Tübingen: Mohr, 1982), 50–62. However, the observers and guests were not allowed to intervene in the discussions of the bishops, nor did they attend the meetings of the commissions of the council. See Washington, *Participation of Non-Catholic Christian Observers*, 97 and Vischer, "Council as an Event," 491.

[6] Karl Barth, *Ad Limina Apostolorum: An Appraisal of Vatican II*, trans. Keith R. Crim (Richmond, VA: John Knox Press, 1968), 17. Barth had been invited by Cardinal Bea to attend the last two sessions of the council in 1964 and 1965 as special guest. Because of an illness, Barth could not follow up on the invitation. In September 1966, however, Barth made up for it. He traveled to Rome to meet with Bea and with several theologians serving as *periti*, and was granted an audience with Pope Paul VI. Though Barth seemed to be somewhat disappointed in Cardinal Bea, who, Barth reported, "represented a rather conventional theology," he hopefully noted in his travel diary: "I would be happy to see the words "Protestant" and "Protestantism" disappear from our vocabulary. . . . The pope is not the Antichrist!" See Barth, *Ad Limina Apostolorum*, 13, 17, and Eberhard Busch, *Karl Barth: His Life from Letters and Autobiographical Texts*, trans. John Bowden (Philadelphia: Fortress Press, 1976), 478–85.

[7] Albert C. Outler, "Vatican II—Charter for Change," *Mid-Stream* 5, no. 4 (1966): 68.

[8] As, for instance, did Gottfried Maron, who did not even mention the declaration

When Protestant theologians began to study *Nostra Aetate*'s fourth section, on the relation between the Christian church and the Jewish people, they largely neglected its three preceding sections.[9] Moreover, Protestants failed to produce a text of their own of equal reach and significance. "There is no Protestant impulse that compares to *Nostra Aetate*," wrote Rolf Rendtorff, longtime chairman of the study commission titled Church and Judaism of the Evangelical Church of Germany and an expert on interfaith matters, in 1988.[10] To be sure, the Synod of the Evangelical Church of the Rhineland in 1980 issued an influential declaration in which a Protestant church body for the first time publicly confessed its guilt for the past and rejected the old theology of supersessionism.[11] Nevertheless, Protestants never wrote a Barmen Declaration on Jewish-Christian and interfaith issues. They never drafted an Augsburg Confession for interreligious relations.[12]

---

in his quick summary of the fourth session of the council during which *Nostra Aetate* was promulgated. Instead, Maron bluntly stated that "this last session produced much editorial work and the voting on texts that had not been finalized. Among the debates only the *Pastoral Constitution on the Church in the Modern World* is worth mentioning." See Gottfried Maron, *Die Römisch-Katholische Kirche von 1870 bis 1970* (Göttingen: Vandenhoeck & Ruprecht, 1972), 240. It is indicative that Graham A. Duncan, in his short but richly resourced article "A Protestant Perspective on Vatican II & 50 Years: An Engagement with Dissent," *HTS Teologiese Studies/Theological Studies* 69, no. 1 (2013): 1–11, does not mention interreligious dialogue as a topic of significance for the Protestant reception of the council.

  [9] *Nostra Aetate* was certainly a spark for the Jewish-Christian conversations in Europe and the United States that took place in the 1970s and '80s. See Franklin Sherman, "*Nostra Aetate* at 40: A Protestant Perspective," *Midstream: A Bi-Monthly Jewish Review* 51, no. 5 (September/October 2005), available at http://www.jcrelations.net/I_Nostra_Aetate__I__at_40__A_Protestant_Perspective.2951.0.html?page=7. Though, as Petra Heldt has made clear in her critique of Sherman, the declaration did not have much of a reception among Protestants and Protestant churches. For Protestants, *Nostra Aetate* was clearly not as epochmaking as Sherman claimed. See Petra Heldt, "Protestant Perspectives after 40 Years: A Critical Assessment of *Nostra Aetate*," in *Nostra Aetate: Origins, Promulgation, Impact on Jewish-Catholic Relations*, ed. Neville Lamdan and Alberto Melloni (Berlin: Lit Verlag, 2007), 163–74. Sherman has elaborated on his thesis in "Protestant Parallels to *Nostra Aetate*," *Studies in Christian-Jewish Relations* 10, no. 2 (2015): 1–13. See also Reinhold Bernhardt, "Dialog und Theologie der Religionen: Zur evangelischen Rezeption der Religionstheologie von Nostra Aetate," *Berliner Theologische Zeitschrift* 31 (2014): 323–41.

  [10] Rolf Rendtorff and Hans Hermann Henrix, eds., *Die Kirchen und das Judentum: Dokumente von 1945–1985*, 2nd ed. (Paderborn: Bonifatius, 1989), 323.

  [11] Synod of the Protestant Church of the Rhineland, "Toward Renovation of the Relationship of Christians and Jews," trans. Franklin H. Littell, *Journal of Ecumenical Studies* 17 (1980): 211–12.

  [12] The Theological Declaration of Barmen of 1934 is a statement of faith with which the confessing church movement in Germany rejected encroachments from the nationalsocialistic government. The Augsburg Confession of 1530 is a central confession of faith in the Lutheran tradition. See John H. Leith, ed., *Creeds of the Churches: A Reader in Chris-*

How could a text so significant in the history of Catholicism prove to be so insignificant in Protestant thought and practice? Why was there such curious silence when it came to the reception of *Nostra Aetate* among Protestant contemporaries? One way to make sense of such silence is to review the ways in which Protestant theologians who were in Rome between 1962 and 1965 as ecumenical observers and guests, as well as the eminent Barth, who traveled to Rome after the council, assessed and commented on the declaration.[13] Observers and guests were the most informed about the events during the council.[14] In their early comments,

---

tian Doctrine from the Bible to the Present, 3rd ed. (Louisville, KY: Westminster John Knox Press, 1982).

[13] The Swiss Reformed theologian Karl Barth was perhaps the single most influential commentator in twentieth-century Protestantism, as Rudy Koshar has recently argued, "Where Is Karl Barth in Modern European History?" *Modern Intellectual History* 5, no. 2 (2008): 333–62. Barth's assessment of the council's outcomes, *Ad Limina Apostolorum*, was published just one year before he died. Reformed theologians in his orbit were key players at the World Council of Churches (WCC). Swiss Lukas Vischer became the director of the Faith and Order Commission of the WCC shortly after the council. Dutch Willem A. Visser't Hooft was the WCC's secretary general from 1948 to 1966. Barth's long reach was church-political as well as theological. He had hoped that Visser't Hooft as secretary general would be among the delegates representing the WCC in Rome (*Memoirs*, 335). When Barth inquired about the WCC's choices for delegates in 1963, his friend Visser't Hooft defended those choices to Barth in a letter from May 17, 1963. See Karl Barth, *Karl Barth —Willem Adolf Visser't Hooft Briefwechsel 1916–1966* (*Gesamtausgabe*, vol. 43) (Zürich: Theologischer Verlag, 2006), 316–19. A more conservative Reformed voice was the Dutch theologian and guest of the secretariat, Gerrit Cornelius Berkouwer, who published his own account of the council before it had ended—*The Second Vatican Council and the New Catholicism* (Grand Rapids, MI: Eerdmans, 1965). German theologians at the council were mostly Lutherans (like the ecumenically minded Edmund Schlink and his deputy Wolfgang Dietzfelbinger). Some conservative Lutheran commentators (Ulrich Kühn and Gottfried Maron) had considerable influence in the German-speaking Protestant world, although they did not attend the council in any official capacity. Among the Scandinavian and American Lutherans who were in Rome during the council, George Lindbeck of Yale University briefly discussed *Nostra Aetate* in his *The Future of Roman Catholic Theology* (Philadelphia: Fortress, 1970), 37–38. The Alsatian Professor of Biblical Studies Oscar Cullmann, who held a chair in New Testament studies at the University of Basel, was personally close to Barth and Vischer, but identified as Lutheran as well.

[14] A number of Protestant observers and contemporaries from Europe and North America wrote about their thoughts and experiences during the council, or commented on its outcomes shortly after it ended. Anglicans included the American William A. Norgren, who was a guest of the secretariat representing the Faith and Order Commission of the National Council of Churches; Howard E. Root, from Cambridge University; Canon Bernard Pawley of Ely Cathedral, England; and Bishop John R. H. Moorman of Ripon, England. The Baptist World Alliance turned down the invitation by the Secretariat for Promoting Christian Unity to send a representative to the council (Raguer, "Initial Profile of the Assembly," 181). However, a few Baptists were present in Rome as journalists (Walter

we can already find the concerns that would define the Protestant reception (or explain the lack thereof) in the years to come. In these early Protestant commentaries, one can find two very different modes of engagement with *Nostra Aetate*. The first mode follows the spirit of the declaration's passages that challenge the anti-Judaic theology of the Christian church and lead to the renewal of Jewish-Christian relationships. In their second mode, though, Protestant theologians who attended the council as observers approached non-Judeo-Christian religions only as objects of conversion to the Christian faith. Hence, in the new area of interreligious dialogue, the Catholic faithful soon walked at least one step ahead of their Protestant kin.

Supporting the Renewal of Jewish-Christian Relations

The "Declaration on the Relation of the Church to Non-Christian Religions" had a contested history. It is well known that *Nostra Aetate* went through many different drafts.[15] The statement was first planned as a separate declaration on the Jewish people, but later the bishops considered placing it in the *Decree on Ecumenism*. The declaration was pushed from committee to committee, with many parties, including Pope Paul, making interventions. In its final form, *Nostra Aetate* mentions Buddhism, Hinduism, and Islam, as well as Judaism, and maintained that all these religions reflected aspects of God's truth in Christ. So what had begun as a novel statement about the Jews became a bold statement about the church's relationship with non-Christian religions.

Harrelson), or as guests of the secretariat (Stanley I. Stuber). The towering Methodist voice among the observers was Albert C. Outler, who stayed in Rome throughout all four sessions. The American Methodist pastor Claud D. Nelson regularly reported from Rome as an accredited journalist. Liberal Protestants included Robert McAfee Brown, representative of the World Presbyterian Alliance; William Barnett Blakemore, minister in the Christian Church (Disciples of Christ) and professor in the Divinity School of the University of Chicago, who represented the World Convention of Churches of Christ (Disciples) during the council; and Unitarian church historian George Huntston Williams of Harvard Divinity School, who represented the International Association for Liberal Christianity and Religious Freedom. Congregationalists included Douglas Horton, former dean of Harvard Divinity School and former moderator of the International Congregational Council, who observed the council throughout, and George B. Caird, from Oxford University, who commented on its proceedings a few years later.

[15] For a short history of the text of *Nostra Aetate*, see Karl Rahner and Herbert Vorgrimler, *Kleines Konzilskompendium*, 3rd ed. (Freiburg i.Br.: Herder, 1967), 349–53; Mauro Velati, "Completing the Conciliar Agenda," in *History of Vatican II*, ed. Giuseppe Alberigo and Joseph A. Komonchak (Maryknoll, NY: Orbis Books; Leuven: Peeters, 2006), 5:185–274; esp. 211–21; and John M. Oesterreicher, "Declaration on the Relationship of the Church to Non-Christian Religions," in *Commentary on the Documents of Vatican II*, ed. Herbert Vorgrimler (Freiburg i. Br.: Herder, 1969), 3:1–138. See also John Borelli's contribution to this volume, "*Nostra Aetate*: Origin, History, and Vatican II Context."

Yet the biggest challenge for the declaration was how to reshape the relationship between the church and the Jewish people. The bishops had to overcome Christianity's contempt for Judaism without forfeiting Christianity's believed superiority over all religions. And they had to reverse attitudes about Judaism as a religion without seeming to approve of the political legitimacy of the State of Israel. Hence, openly and behind the scenes, the bishops struggled to find appropriate language for Judaism as a religion, and battled to recognize the continued holiness of the Jewish people. Those from the Middle East were especially reluctant to show sympathy for the Jewish people. In the Arab world, they feared, doing so would look like a political endorsement of Israel.

With the declaration the Catholic Church underwent a radical theological reform of its approach to Jews and Judaism. For centuries, the church had taught that the Jewish people as a whole were responsible for the death of Christ. During the council's proceedings, though, a group of bishops successfully pressed for radical theological changes that included the removal of the deicide charge in the declaration.[16] The bishops also sought to address concerns about calls to convert Jews after a draft by the Roman Curia that included a reference to convert Jews, but did not have corresponding references for Muslims and practitioners of other religions to become Christians, had become public. Following the publication of the draft, Polish American Rabbi Abraham Joshua Heschel was so shocked that he famously declared in 1964 that he was "ready to go to Auschwitz any time, if faced with the alternative of conversion or death."[17]

Liberal Protestants across the board, though, did not struggle with the council's efforts to renew the Jewish-Christian relationship and welcomed the declaration's new approach toward Jews. When a draft of the declaration in November 1964 finally clarified that neither Jews of the past as a whole nor modern Jews may rightly be accused of having been guilty for Christ's death, Congregationalist Douglas Horton of Harvard Divinity School commented with great satisfaction in his *Vatican Diary* that "another milestone is past."[18] Following the bishops' vote on *Nostra Aetate* on October 15, 1965, Horton shared his conviction that "church historians will regard it as an enlightened piece of legislation."[19] For Methodist Albert Outler, writing in January 1966, *Nostra Aetate* was a "happy outcome" of a bitter conflict between the bishops at the council. Outler greatly valued the fact that its final version "unequivocally condemned anti-Semitism" and represented "real change" for Jewish-Christian relations.[20] Baptist

---

[16] Rahner and Vorgrimler, *Kleines Konzilskompendium*, 352–53, and Velati, "Completing the Conciliar Agenda," 220.

[17] "What Catholics Think about Jews," *Time* 84, no. 11 (September 11, 1964): 78.

[18] Douglas Horton, *Vatican Diary 1964: A Protestant Observes the Third Session of Vatican Council II* (Philadelphia: United Church Press, 1965), 193. The entry is from November 20, 1964.

[19] Douglas Horton, *Vatican Diary 1965: A Protestant Observes the Fourth Session of Vatican Council II* (Philadelphia: United Church Press, 1966), 109.

[20] Albert Cook Outler, *Methodist Observer at Vatican II* (Westminster, MD: Newman Press, 1967), 181.

historian W. Morgan Patterson, also writing in 1966, considered *Nostra Aetate* of "special importance" because of its "references to the Jews." He cherished section 4 of the declaration as a "long stride in the right direction."[21] And Stanley I. Stuber and Claud D. Nelson in their 1967 Baptist/Methodist coproduction, *Implementing Vatican II in Your Community*, cheered on the very fact that the council had promulgated *Nostra Aetate*.[22] "The intention can scarcely be doubted," they wrote enthusiastically, "no longer threats, anathemas, defense against all that is not Roman Catholic. The weather shows signs of changing from cold and windy to warm and sunny."[23]

Although there was general enthusiasm among liberal Protestants, it was particularly the observers and guests under the influence of Karl Barth, as well as Barth himself, who provided the rationale for a renewed Protestant approach to Jews. New Testament scholar Oscar Cullmann—Barth's colleague at the University of Basel and one of the most influential Protestant observers at the council—was one of the first who openly took issue with the fact that *Nostra Aetate* had fused the relationship between the church and the Jewish people with a statement on other religions.[24] Although Cullmann was extremely appreciative of section 4, which dealt with the spiritual bond between the Jewish people and the church, he could barely hold back his disapproval of *Nostra Aetate*'s final format.

For Cullmann, *Nostra Aetate* conflated the originally planned declaration on the Jewish people with dissimilar matters. Judaism now appeared to be like any other religion. The declaration had approached the issues the wrong way in his estimation. "Israel's relation to the Christian church is something entirely different from its relation to other religions," Cullmann argued. And moreover, Israel was not just any other religion but "the common root for Judaism and Christianity." Hence, *Nostra Aetate* no longer recognized the particular and ongoing role of the biblical as well as the existing (theological) Israel in the events of salvation. Cullmann very much agreed with those sections of *Nostra Aetate* that firmly connected

---

[21] W. Morgan Patterson, "A Baptist Historian Views Vatican II," *Baptist History and Heritage* 1, no. 2 (1966): 58–59.

[22] Stanley I. Stuber and Claud D. Nelson, *Implementing Vatican II in Your Community: Dialogue and Action Manual Based on the Sixteen Documents of the Second Vatican Council* (New York: Guild Press, 1967). The Baptist Stuber had been in Rome throughout the council as special guest of the Secretariat for Promoting Christian Unity. He was previously the editor of the *Daily Bulletin* of the World Council of Churches. Nelson, a Methodist minister, had been in Rome as a reporter for the Religion News Service. Stuber and Nelson dedicated their book to Pope Paul VI. It is probably the only Baptist/Methodist coproduction in the history of Christianity dedicated to a pope.

[23] Stuber and Nelson, *Implementing Vatican II,* 176.

[24] For an assessment of Oscar Cullmann and his ecumenical legacy, see Martin Sallmann and Karlfried Froehlich, *Zehn Jahre nach Oscar Cullmanns Tod: Rückblick und Ausblick* (Zürich: Theologischer Verlag, 2012), and Thomas K. Kuhn, "Oscar Cullmann und das Zweite Vatikanische Konzil," *Schweizerische Zeitschrift für Religions- und Kulturgeschichte* 104 (2010): 251–74.

Christians and Jews by a mutual history of salvation. This mutual salvation history, however, excluded all nonbiblical religions.[25]

Barth shared Cullmann's harsh critique. Barth was dismayed that the declaration spoke of "the past and present history of Israel in the same breath with Hinduism, Buddhism, and Islam as a 'non-Christian' religion." Like Cullmann, Barth connected Christians and Jews by a mutual history of salvation that excluded nonbiblical religions. For him, the Christian Old Testament did not present a religion but "the original form of the one revelation of God."[26]

Likewise, Lukas Vischer, a Swiss Reformed theologian who had been one of the World Council of Churches' observers at the council, criticized the decision to combine the declaration on the Jews with the declaration on non-Christian religions, which had originally been a separate document. "God's Chosen People is thus drawn into the context of the 'religions,'" he objected. For theologians like Vischer, the biblical Israel did not present a distinct religion per se but the *original form* of God's revelation, and he subsequently questioned if "the revelation of the God of Abraham, Isaac and Jacob can be correctly understood in this context [of religions] at all."[27]

Yet Protestant theologians such as Cullmann, Barth, and Vischer greatly welcomed those sections of *Nostra Aetate* that reformed the relationship between the Christian church and the Jewish people. Because the declaration spoke of the "spiritual bond" between Christians and Jews, rebuffed the idea that Jews are rejected by God, and even invoked Saint Paul's image of the olive tree whose root supported the younger branches, the Catholic Church acknowledged that the beginnings of its election are deeply connected with its older Jewish sibling. Liberal Protestants especially, as well as theologians close to Barth and his theology, considered this new recognition of Israel's meaning for the church one of the council's groundbreaking insights. Although a number of Protestant theologians of the 1960s still clung to ideas about evangelizing Jews, observers like Vischer expressed their explicit hope that these parts of *Nostra Aetate* would also inspire a new theology of Israel at the World Council of Churches.[28]

---

[25] Cullman developed a theology of salvation that tended to emphasize God's action as narrated in the Bible. He dedicated his *Salvation in History* (New York: Harper & Row, 1967) to the Secretariat for Promoting Christian Unity.

[26] Barth, *Ad Limina Apostolorum*, 36. For Barth's theology of Israel, see Berthold Klappert, *Israel und die Kirche: Erwägungen zur Israellehre Karl Barths* (Munich: Kaiser, 1980).

[27] Lukas Vischer, "After the Fourth Session of the Second Vatican Council," *Ecumenical Review* 18, no. 2 (1966): 176. For the many facets of the work of Lukas Vischer, see the Festschrift by Karin Bredull Gerschwiler et al., eds., *Ökumenische Theologie in den Herausforderungen der Gegenwart: Lukas Vischer zum 65. Geburtstag* (Göttingen: Vandenhoeck & Ruprecht, 1991).

[28] Vischer, "After the Fourth Session," 176. Vischer's hopes began to slowly materialize with the issuing of the Bristol Declaration in 1967 by the Commission on Faith and Order of the World Council of Churches. The Bristol Declaration rejects any missionary

A Statement of Guilt

Protestant contemporaries also embraced *Nostra Aetate*'s rejection of antisemitism and discussed the declaration's omission of a statement of guilt.[29] Though the World Council of Churches had yet to produce such a confession of the churches' guilt for sins committed against the Jewish people—the World Council had publicly condemned antisemitism at its first assembly in Amsterdam in 1948, but could do so only clouded in ideas of a Christian mission to the Jews—the possibility of such a confession resonated with many ecumenically minded Protestants.[30] Not a few of them believed that a new Jewish-Christian beginning depended on a prior confession of guilt of the Christian church.

Stuber and Nelson's *Implementing Vatican II in Your Community*, for example, criticized the declaration for omitting such a confession: "What about past guilt?" they asked. The Americans minced no words: "For centuries Christians have put Jews on the cross, [and now] some degree of Christian repentance is required."[31] Barth, too, echoed the deep longing for an official Christian confession of guilt, when he wrote in his travel diary: "Would it not be more appropriate, in view of the antisemitism of the ancient, the medieval, and to a large degree modern church, to set forth an explicit confession of guilt here?"[32]

---

outreach to the Jewish community and replaces it by a call for service to it. This declaration, however, is not well known and has never really received the attention it deserved. See Franklin Sherman, ed., *Bridges: Documents of the Christian-Jewish Dialogue*, vol. 1: *The Road to Reconciliation (1845–1985)* (Mahwah, NJ: Paulist Press, 2011), doc. 46; Allan Brockway et al., eds., *Theology of the Churches and the Jewish People* (Geneva: World Council of Churches, 1988), 81; and Mauro Velati, "The Debate on *De Judaeis* and Ecumenical Dialogue," in *Nostra Aetate: Origins, Promulgation, Impact on Jewish-Catholic Relations*, ed. Neville Lamdan and Alberto Melloni (Berlin: LIT Verlag, 2007), 145–62, esp. 159–60. Willem A. Visser't Hooft also prominently welcomed the renewal of the Jewish-Christian relationship in the declaration, publicly lauding *Nostra Aetate* for expressing "the biblical truth . . . that it is through the Jewish people that divine revelation first came to men and that the profound bond which exists between Christians and Jews should be not merely a memory but a reality." See Henri Fesquet, *The Drama of Vatican II* (New York: Random House, 1967), 713.

[29] In his commentary, Vischer lamented that the declaration would have been a good opportunity for such a statement. See Vischer, "After the Fourth Session," 177.

[30] Velati, "Debate on *De Judaeis* and Ecumenical Dialogue," 145–62. Though the assembly in Amsterdam rejected antisemitism as "absolutely irreconcilable with the profession and practice of the Christian faith" and as "sin against God and man," it also insisted that the eschatological hopes of the Jewish people had been fulfilled in the coming of Christ, and that Christians were still called to "proclaim to the Jews, 'The Messiah for Whom you wait has come.'" See Helga Croner, ed., *Stepping Stones to Further Jewish-Christian Relations* (London: Stimulus, 1977), 69–72.

[31] Stuber and Nelson, *Implementing Vatican II*, 176.

[32] Barth, *Ad Limina Apostolorum*, 36.

But contrary to those who contended that the declaration did not go far enough on this issue of Christian guilt, there were still a number of conservative observers and commentators who strongly disagreed. The conservative mainstream theologians held on to deep-seated notions about the purpose of the Jewish people in God's design of universal salvation. Mainline Protestant discourse in the 1960s was still shot through with traditional religious anti-Judaisms that had provided the basis for modern antisemitism. The conservative Protestant mainstream was yet far removed from the radical revisions of the church's teachings about Jews that *Nostra Aetate* had marked for the Catholic realm.

For instance, the Scottish Presbyterian scholar of liturgy and former military chaplain Allan MacArthur, who was sent to Rome as an observer for the World Alliance of Reformed Churches during the third session of the council, was ready to defend this traditional Protestant approach. "Sacred history . . . does not continue in Judaism," he declared at a Protestant observers' meeting with the Secretariat for Promoting Christian Unity. And in explicit contrast to the views of the World Council of Churches that Lukas Vischer had explained at the same meeting, he coolly stated that "it is the Christian church into which the Lord now desires to gather his people."[33]

Especially conservative Lutherans from Germany approached their critique of section 4 of *Nostra Aetate* in a variety of ways. The usually forthcoming Heidelberg theologian Edmund Schlink, member of the confessing church movement opposing the Nazis after 1933 and special envoy of the Evangelical Church of Germany at the council, purposefully failed to address the question of Christian guilt. Although Schlink did appreciate the "biblically well-based stance and directive" of the declaration, he avoided analyzing any specific aspects of section 4 of *Nostra Aetate* and simply restated the whole section in his commentary without further interpretation.[34]

For the Bavarian Wolfgang Dietzfelbinger, though, *Nostra Aetate* was at risk of coming too close to "Phariseeism" and to being an "embarrassing self-accusation [of the church]." Dietzfelbinger took issue with the document's lack of discussion of Jewish involvement in the death of Christ and criticized "the distinction between the Jewish authorities and the present generation of Jews" as being "based on a purely juridical concept of guilt." Though the conservative Dietzfelbinger did not elaborate on the issue further, his comments implied that a juridical perspective wrongly exonerated modern Jews from the guilt assumed in Christ's day. Accordingly, Dietzfelbinger deplored the "practical attitude" of the declaration, which, in his judgment, did not allow for a "fundamental [theological] discussion of the Jewish problem."[35]

---

[33] Horton, *Vatican Diary 1964*, 3, 73.

[34] Edmund Schlink, *After the Council*, trans. Herbert J. A. Bouman (Philadelphia: Fortress, 1968), 132–33. For an introduction to Schlink's ecumenical theology, see Eugene M. Skibbe, *A Quiet Reformer: An Introduction to Edmund Schlink's Life and Ecumenical Theology* (Minneapolis: Kirk House, 1999).

[35] Wolfgang Dietzfelbinger, "Chronicle of the Fourth Session of the Vatican Council

Ulrich Kühn, an East-German ecumenist from Leipzig, went beyond even his conservative Lutheran colleagues. To him, the declaration had completely neglected the biblical critique of the Jewish people ("die judenkritische Linie der Bibel"). The council had "idealized the history of God's people" and was too afraid to disclose the final goal of the church to evangelize the Jewish people. Kühn's commentary reveals a twisted logic, reminiscent of centuries of anti-Judaic patterns and teachings. By breaking God's trust, Kühn claimed, the biblical Israel had initiated the process of universal salvation. So if one were to "reduce the guilt of the Jewish people" as well as the "necessity of their conversion to Christ," one would only reduce God's miraculous works among his people. Kühn concluded that, without the fact of the "hardening" and "disbelief" of the Jewish people, one would not be able to recognize God's grace in the world. Hence, the council had in *Nostra Aetate* failed to fully grasp God's universal salvation through Israel as his instrument.[36]

These theological voices are representative of the Lutheran branch of the Protestant Reformation. Schlink, Dietzfelbinger, and Kühn were all devoted students of Martin Luther, who stood in the epicenter of the divisions of the church in the sixteenth century. When it came to Jews and the church, Luther, like many Christian theologians before and after him, assumed that the church had replaced the people of Israel as mediator of God's grace and salvation. After the destruction of the second temple, Luther maintained, the church had superseded Israel as God's partner in the world. How these ideas have played out in Lutheran theology and culture is of course an ongoing matter of debate.[37] Not really a matter of debate, though, is the Lutheran theologians' response to *Nostra Aetate*'s new teachings on the Jews. Even twenty years after the Shoah, conservative Lutherans were not only unable to address any Christian shame and guilt, they were not even able to realize the massive anti-Judaic undertones of their own theological tradition and language.[38]

September 14 to December 8, 1965," in *Challenge and Response: A Protestant Perspective of the Vatican Council*, ed. Warren A. Quanbeck (Minneapolis: Augsburg, 1966), 7–8.

[36] Ulrich Kühn, *Die Ergebnisse des II. Vatikanischen Konzils* (Berlin: Evangelische Verlagsanstalt, 1966), 148.

[37] Eric W. Gritsch, *Martin Luther's Anti-Semitism: Against Better Judgment* (Grand Rapids, MI: Eerdmans, 2012). Gritsch pays thorough attention to the different interpretations of Martin Luther's so-called *Judenschriften*, of which *On the Jews and Their Lies* (1543) might be known best.

[38] It should be noted, though, that other Lutheran theologians of that period veered in a different direction. Harvard New Testament scholar and Swedish bishop Krister Stendahl had in 1963 already published an article in which he reassessed the theology of Paul. See Krister Stendahl, "The Apostle Paul and the Introspective Conscience of the West," *Harvard Theological Review* 56, no. 3 (1963): 199–215. In 1982, the World Council of Churches' Consultation on the Church and the Jewish People issued the "Ecumenical Considerations on Christian-Jewish Dialogue" under Stendahl's chairmanship.

Christianity's Relations with
Hinduism, Buddhism, and Islam

Nostra Aetate not only changed the church's relations to the Jewish people; it also opened new interreligious ground. Buddhism, Hinduism, and "other religions" are recognized in section 2 of the declaration. The council explicitly did not want to reject anything "that is true and holy in these religions." It asserted that all of these religions mirrored aspects of God's truth in Christ, and it acknowledged that those traditions often "reflect a ray of that Truth which enlightens all men." These lines opened the doors of the Catholic Church for interfaith conversations beyond Jewish-Christian dialogue. The first three sections of the declaration entailed the "strongest possible kind of gesture towards the great religions of the world," as one observer suggested.[39] Though truth was fully expressed only in the incarnate logos of Christ, non-Christians were endowed by their creator with reason and religion and thus not excluded from the process of divine salvation.[40] Also, the declaration dedicated two full paragraphs to Islam that sounded like an outline of a new Christian-Muslim dialogue that connected back to the Jewish people through the figure of Abraham.[41]

In the Catholic Church, *Nostra Aetate* initiated a sudden boom of theological research on other religious traditions.[42] Not so, however, in the churches of the

---

[39] *Declaration on the Relation of the Church to Non-Christian Religions—Nostra Aetate*, proclaimed by Pope Paul VI (Vatican City, 1965), sec. 2, http://www.vatican.va/archive/hist_councils/ii_vatican_council/documents/vat-ii_decl_19651028_nostra-aetate_en.html; Howard E. Root, "The Church and Non-Christian Religions," in *The Second Vatican Council: Studies by Eight Anglican Observers*, ed. Bernard C. Pawley (London: Oxford University Press, 1967), 238.

[40] In addition to natural theology, Karl Rahner's cosmic Christocentrism played a crucial role for the declaration's inclusivist approach to other religions. Instead of a radical separation of the divine and the profane, Rahner assumed an almost evolutionary consecration of the cosmos that is initiated by the incarnated logos as highest possible fulfillment of humanity. Other religions were thus included in the incarnation of God in Christ. See Karl Rahner, "Jesus Christus," *Lexikon für Theologie und Kirche*, 2nd ed. (Freiburg i. Br.: Herder, 1960), 5:953–61.

[41] On the figure of Abraham as connective tissue between Jews, Christians, and Muslims, see Karl-Josef Kuschel, *Abraham: Sign of Hope for Jews, Christians, and Muslims* (New York: Continuum, 1995). The scholarship of Louis Massignon and his interpretation of Islam as Abrahamic religion was of decisive influence for *Nostra Aetate*. See Louis Massignon, *The Three Prayers of Abraham* (1949), ed. Herbert Mason (Notre Dame, IN: University of Notre Dame Press, 1989), 3–20, and Neal Robinson, "Massignon, Vatican II, and Islam as an Abrahamic Religion," *Islam and Christian-Muslim Relations* 2, no. 2 (1991): 182–205. John Borelli notes the influence of Massignon's thought on Cardinal Giovanni Battista Montini, Archbishop of Milan, who became Pope Paul VI during the council; see in this volume Borelli, "*Nostra Aetate*: Origin, History, and Vatican II Context."

[42] Reinhard Frieling, *Der Weg des ökumenischen Gedanken: Eine Ökumenekunde*

Protestant Reformation. Although some of the early commentators considered the declaration a call for a new type of theology of religions,[43] most of them did not really make any distinctions between Buddhism, Hinduism, other religions, and Islam as the declaration had done. In their commentaries in the years following the council, no major Protestant thinker picked up on Abraham as a potentially unifying figure for Jews, Christians, and Muslims, and everything outside the Jewish-Christian realm was generically lumped together.

That said, a number of the early Protestant commentators, notably American— who had returned to a much more religiously diverse society than had most of their European counterparts—did sense that the council bishops were on to something. For William Norgren, an Episcopal priest from New York and executive director of the Faith and Order Commission of the National Council of Churches, the references to other religions paled in comparison with the section of the declaration that dealt with the Jewish-Christian relationship. Yet Norgren affirmed that the declaration was the "first official statement of the Roman Church ever [that] appreciated the values in other religions."[44] Religion News Service correspondent Claud Nelson was grateful for the inclusion of the sections on other religions in such a "respectful and cordial tone." He even predicted that, "in the very long run," those sections "may prove to be more important than the section on the Jewish religion."[45] William Barnett Blakemore, a minister in the Christian Church (Disciples of Christ) and professor in the Divinity School of the University of Chicago, considered the Catholic Church now ready to enter into dialogue with other religions. Blakemore noted that "Catholicism is more open to discussion with 'the world' at large than . . . Protestantism." A long tradition of natural theology had played out to the advantage of the Catholic Church, he suggested. If all persons are endowed with the desire for reason and religion, as natural theology taught, non-Christians could indeed participate in the divine truth revealed in Christ.[46] And for the American

---

(Göttingen: Vandenhoeck & Ruprecht, 1992), 304.

[43] According to the Congregationalist observer George B. Caird, *Nostra Aetate* "calls for the establishment of original and creative theological investigation in each major socio-cultural area, so that the dialogue between the Church and the indigenous religion and culture may be carried on." This theological research, though, "will involve not only a searching critique of the non-Christian religion, but a fresh scrutiny of the Christian tradition." See George B. Caird, *Our Dialogue with Rome* (London: Oxford University Press, 1967), 91.

[44] William A. Norgren, "The Second Vatican Council—An Appraisal," *Mid-Stream* 5, no. 4 (1966): 145.

[45] Claud Nelson, "A Response," in *The Documents of Vatican II*, ed. Walter M. Abbott, SJ (New York: Association Press, 1966), 671.

[46] William Barnett Blakemore, "Vatican II Shall Become Protestant Heritage—Also," *Mid-Stream* 5, no. 4 (1966): 123. In very similar fashion, Anglican observer Howard E. Root argued that the Catholic Church could acknowledge other religions as "proximations to the fullness revealed in Christ" because of the church's tradition of natural theology. See Root, "Church and Non-Christian Religions," 238.

Lutheran George Lindbeck, the Catholic Church had abandoned its "monopoly on true religiousness." Practitioners of non-Christian religions may now be saved, he interpreted, "not despite . . . but because these religions can truly mediate, however imperfectly, some knowledge and experience of God."[47]

But the times were not yet ripe for most Protestants to engage in respectful and cordial interfaith conversations. In 1965 the great majority of Protestants did not look at the religious other as a partner in dialogue but as an object of missionizing and conversion instead. A widely read German commentator even dismissed the approach of the declaration as "eclectic" and "purely descriptive," and complained that it had "ignored the negative elements of other religions."[48] On the stage of the World Council of Churches, it would take another twelve long years before some official guidelines were drawn up in which dialogue was no longer considered a false alternative to mission but a legitimate means of living out one's Christian faith within pluralistic communities.[49]

The call to dialogue of *Nostra Aetate* thus provoked a rigorous critique by an illustrious variety of Protestant heavyweights. Lutheran Edmund Schlink, for example, pointed out in his widely read and translated commentary on the council's documents that the relationship between the church and non-Christian religions was also dealt with in *Ad Gentes*, the "Decree on the Missionary Activity of the Church." Schlink suggested that *Nostra Aetate* had appraised God's divine grace and truth in the non-Christian religions "too optimistically" and ignored the Christian duty to proclaim Christ. In order to make sense of the declaration, Protestants first had to study the "Decree on the Missionary Activity of the Church."[50]

The approach to other religions in *Ad Gentes* was indeed quite different from that of *Nostra Aetate*, a tension that Schlink rightly noticed. Unlike *Nostra Aetate*, the decree emphasized that "every Christian's attitude toward non-Christian religions must be shaped by the missionary obligation." Hence, for the fullness of Christian truth, conversion could not be ignored. While *Nostra Aetate* welcomed interfaith engagement, Schlink considered the decree as a theologically more adequate statement that Christians ought to use as their guide when encountering

---

[47] Lindbeck, *Future of Roman Catholic Theology*, 37.

[48] Wolfgang Dietzfelbinger, "Die ersten Ergebnisse der vierten Konzilssession," *Lutherische Monatshefte* 4, no. 11 (1965): 532.

[49] These guidelines were drawn up at the theological consultation at Chiang Mai in Thailand in 1977. Ecumenist Stanley J. Samartha considers the guidelines a "landmark in the development of the dialogue debate in the ecumenical context." See Stanley J. Samartha, "Guidelines on Dialogue," *Ecumenical Review* 31, no. 2 (1979): 157. See also S. Wesley Ariarajah, "Dialogue, Interfaith," in *Dictionary of the Ecumenical Movement*, ed. Nicholas Lossky et al. (Grand Rapids, MI: Eerdmans, 1991), 281–87. Douglas Pratt, *The Church and Other Faiths* (Bern: Peter Lang, 2010), 29–166, offers a short history of the World Council of Churches' changing approach to interreligious dialogue.

[50] *Decree—Ad Gentes: On the Mission Activity of the Church*, promulgated by Pope Paul VI (Vatican City, 1965); Schlink, *After the Council*, 129, 132.

the religious other. For him, the decree overrode the declaration. Executing the missionary decree's agenda was mandatory for the individual Christian in order to stay true to the salvific purpose of the Christian church in the world. "This missionary activity among the religions grows out of the essence of the church," Schlink maintained, because, in evangelizing the religious other, "God's plan of salvation for mankind, which Jesus served, becomes a reality."[51]

Willem A. Visser't Hooft, secretary general of the World Council of Churches, criticized the declaration's paragraphs before section 4 as "very, very weak." To him, *Nostra Aetate* offered the false approach of religious dialogue. The special character of the Christian revelation was no longer the motivation for interreligious encounter. It assumed a salvific equality of religions instead of emphasizing the uniqueness of God's revelation in Christ. The declaration, in Hooft's words, only made "polite remarks about other religions."[52] Interfaith dialogue was nothing but a "temptation for syncretism" that would deny the church its basic principle "to bring all men to Christ," as Hooft had argued in another place.[53]

Lukas Vischer was equally unhappy that *Nostra Aetate* tried to level the playing field between Christianity and non-Judeo-Christian religions. To him, the declaration did not engage with "the deeper problems which are brought up . . . by the concept of religion and . . . by the question of the relationship between belief in Christ and the various religions." According to this Reformed theologian, Christianity was different from all other religions, and "the fullness of truth is to be found in Christ alone." In Vischer's view, it was impossible for Christians to enter into dialogue with other religions without announcing the distinct superiority of Christ. Despite the declaration's call in its second section for the church to always proclaim Christ, the Christological center had gone missing for Vischer.[54] He did not hide his deep disappointment with the declaration on the issue of religions beyond Judaism. He acknowledged that *Nostra Aetate* intended to create a climate for dialogue but questioned whether this could be done without "indicating the way in which the message of Christ obligates the church and determines its relationship to the world."[55]

Karl Barth's teaching of religion as a manmade attempt to comprehend God provided the material for such critique. Barth had long argued that religion as such was a *human* and not a *divine* enterprise. Therefore, he concluded that all religion

---

[51] Schlink, *After the Council*, 132–33. Very similar in his interpretation is Walther von Loewenich, *Der moderne Katholizismus vor und nach dem Konzil* (Witten: Luther-Verlag, 1970), 354–56.

[52] Robert A. Graham, SJ, "Non-Christians," in *The Documents of Vatican II*, ed. Walter M. Abbott, SJ (New York: Guild Press 1966), 658–59.

[53] Willem A. Visser't Hooft, "Pluralism—Temptation or Opportunity," in *Peace among Christians*, by Augustin Cardinal Bea and Willem A. Visser't Hooft (New York: Association Press, 1967), 226.

[54] Vischer, "After the Fourth Session," 175.

[55] Ibid.

was nothing but a form of what he called "unbelief." However, he set Christianity apart from "religion" and "unbelief," asserting that only it, of all the religions, had been transformed through the revelation of Christ. For Barth, Christian theology had to follow the one God who had revealed himself uniquely in the Christ Event. Theology had to be revealed theology that listened exclusively to God's revelation in Christ and Israel as documented in the Bible. For Barth and his students, God in Christ was thus the absolute counterpoint to all human religion. Accordingly, he was deeply troubled by the "religious" approach of *Nostra Aetate* and its lack of missionary language.[56] Instead of conducting dialogue with the religious other, he suggested proclaiming the crucified Christ. Although Barth was a key figure in the theological overhaul of Jewish-Christian relations, he vehemently rejected any attempt to regard interreligious dialogue as anything but a human and therefore ungodly endeavor.[57]

Two Types of Engagement with *Nostra Aetate*

The enthusiasm for the council as such that was generally shared by the non-Catholic Christian observers and guests in Rome translated into only halting Protestant excitement for *Nostra Aetate*. Under Karl Barth's influence, and along the lines of a traditional and conservative mainstream, some Protestants looked on the declaration with very critical eyes. The harsh assessment of several sections by Barth and other theological heavyweights left many Protestants uncertain about what to make of the new directions that had been outlined in the document.

However, one can find two very different modes of engagement with *Nostra Aetate* throughout these early Protestant commentaries. The first mode follows the passages of the declaration that challenge and revoke the traditional anti-Judaic theology of the Christian church. *Nostra Aetate* was barely acknowledged in the Protestant discourse about the meaning of Jewish people for the Christian faith that followed the council. But it was surely known among Protestants during the Jewish-Christian conversations in Europe and the United States that took place in the 1970s and '80s. With regard to the Jewish-Christian relationship, *Nostra Aetate* and the powerful Barth school complemented each other. Like *Nostra Aetate*, Barth and theologians such as Cullmann, Vischer, and Visser't Hooft recognized the role of the

---

[56] Karl Barth sharply criticized the position that the "critical and missionary task of the church in reference to the religions as such [is] only marginal to the Declaration and not central to it." See Barth, *Ad Limina Apostolorum*, 36.

[57] In his commentary on *Nostra Aetate*, Barth shrewdly asked if the "justifiable human concern of the Declaration [would not] have been expressed better by adhering to the proven methods of Paul . . . in which he proclaimed nothing to Jews and Greeks but the One who had been crucified for them . . . in order to address them as men from that point." For a succinct interpretation of Barth's theology of religions, see J. A. Di Noia, OP, "Religion and the Religions," in *The Cambridge Companion to Karl Barth*, ed. John Webster (Cambridge: Cambridge University Press, 2000), 243–57.

Jewish people as distinct partners in God's salvific plan for the world. *Nostra Aetate* offered a welcome blueprint for such new recognition that overlapped with much of what Barth and theologians close to him taught about God's revelation through Israel. Protestants quickly realized how much this declaration was "a new starting point for building brotherly spirit and practices between Christians and Jews."[58]

In the area of Jewish-Christian relations, many Protestants would soon follow the call to renewal and action. The ecumenical enthusiasm for the council carried over into a new theology of Israel. Even without the explicit mentioning of *Nostra Aetate*, theologians—in particular those of the Barth school—increasingly pondered Israel's continued chosenness and salvific meaning, and soon began to address their own shame over the teachings of their theological ancestors. Protestant churches would soon work through the issues that the Second Vatican Council had tackled in *Nostra Aetate*, begin to confess their guilt for the past, and reject the old theology of supersessionism.[59] The nearly two thousand years of anti-Judaic teaching that had paved the way for modern antisemitism were about to recede.

Beyond the profound renewal of the Jewish-Christian relationship, however, leading Protestants often rejected outright *Nostra Aetate*'s dialogical engagement with other religions. Many influential Protestant theologians of the 1960s, '70s, and '80s, made a categorical distinction between human religious practices on one side and God's revelation in Christ and Israel on the other. Many of the Protestant voices at the time of the council, who were under the influence of Karl Barth and his theology, did not follow the natural theology of the declaration that complemented its Christological inclusivism.

Drawing on natural and incarnational theology, *Nostra Aetate* reflected on the interconnections between Christianity, Islam, and other religious traditions. The declaration has often been scolded for its limited inclusive approach to comprehend religious otherness. But when *Nostra Aetate* was promulgated in 1965, theological models of pluralism were not yet available. The alternative to *Nostra Aetate* was offered by the theologians in the context of Karl Barth and his school. They called on Christianity to confront other religions while insisting on the superiority of Christianity as the one true and revealed religion. They as well as the more conservative Protestant mainstream theologians reminded the faithful of their missionary obligations. The great majority of Protestants were yet unable to follow the dialogical approach that *Nostra Aetate* had sketched out for the Catholic Church. Open interfaith dialogue was not yet considered a legitimate way of

---

[58]   Nelson, "Response," 671.

[59]   Statements of different churches are collected in *Stepping Stones to Further Jewish-Christian Relations*, ed. Helga Croner (London: Stimulus Books, 1977), and *More Stepping Stones to Jewish-Christian Relations*, ed. Helga Croner (Mahwah, NJ: Paulist Press, 1985). For recent Protestant church declarations that acknowledge the changes in the teachings on Jews as well as Christian guilt for actions in the past, see Ulrich Rosenhagen, "God Is Faithful to God's People: The New Theology of Israel in Contemporary German Protestantism," *Journal of Ecumenical Studies* 46, no. 4 (2011): 621–38.

communicating the Christian gospel. Protestants could not see the "ray of truth" in other religions of which the declaration spoke and that many Catholics began to explore after the council.[60]

"The glaciers are melting, the Alps remain," the Scottish Presbyterian observer Allan MacArthur once remarked.[61] Though MacArthur meant to summarize relations between the Catholic Church and its Protestant kin, his quip also serves as *a précis* of the early Protestant reception of *Nostra Aetate*: although the glaciers between Jews and Christians began to slowly melt for Protestants as well, mountains remained between missionizing the religious other and the beginnings of authentic interfaith dialogue south of the Alps.

---

[60] With only a few exceptions, there has been a long and frightening silence in the Protestant scholarship on interreligious dialogue in the years after the council. In the German-speaking Protestant world, Paul Knitter's Marburg dissertation, *Towards a Protestant Theology of Religion* (Marburg: Elwert, 1974) is one of those exceptions. It was written in English, though it contained a summary in German. For many years it was the lone monograph on these issues that was not written with a condescending attitude. It took another sixteen years before Reinhold Bernhardt published his dissertation, *Der Absolutheitsanspruch des Christentums: Von der Aufklärung bis zur Pluralistischen Religionstheologie* (Gütersloh: Gütersloher Verlagshaus, 1990). These two lone titles, as well as the chronological gap between them, may indicate that in the (German-speaking) Protestant world, interreligious dialogue was a different ball game than it was in the Catholic domain. For the English-speaking Protestant world, the situation was slightly better, because of the work of the World Council of Churches' theologian Stanley J. Samartha and the British Presbyterian John Hick. See Stanley J. Samartha, *Courage for Dialogue: Ecumenical Issues in Interreligious Relationships* (Maryknoll, NY: Orbis Books, 1982) and John Hick, *God Has Many Names* (Philadelphia: Westminster, 1982).

[61] "How Vatican II Turned the Church toward the World."

7

SOCIAL JUSTICE IN *NOSTRA AETATE* AND IN BLACK LIBERATION THEOLOGY

Dwight N. Hopkins

Released on October 28, 1965, the Second Vatican Council document *Nostra Aetate* remains an important and relevant statement. Especially given the twenty-first century's global cultural daily contact,[1] *Nostra Aetate* was quite farsighted in its call for positive sustained interreligious dialogue.[2] This prescient posture is remarkable because the publication touches on perennial concerns of global healthy human communities and a healthy individual in communities. Specifically, by trying to open up dialogue between the Catholic Church and members of other faith traditions, *Nostra Aetate* touched on fundamental concerns about how increasing interconnectedness might benefit the health of both human communities (in the aggregate) and individuals within those communities.

Indeed, a key theological thread interweaving concerns about the global, the interreligious, and healthy communities with a healthy individual within communities is found by focusing on social justice. To that end, this essay draws on the concluding statements of *Nostra Aetate* and how they suggest commonalities with a black theology of liberation. What is the relation between the social justice assertions in *Nostra Aetate* and black liberation theology?

Paragraphs 2 and 3 of section 5 in the document state the following:

> No foundation therefore remains for any theory or practice that leads to discrimination between man and man [*sic*] or between people and

---

[1] The impact of global cross-cultural daily contact touches on all segments of society, including business: "Ninety percent of leading executives from sixty-eight countries identified cross-cultural leadership as the top management challenge for the next century. Most contemporary leaders encounter dozens of different cultures daily." David Livermore, *Leading with Cultural Intelligence: The Real Secret to Success*, 2nd ed. (New York: American Management Association, 2015), 13.

[2] I would argue that the document has lessons for other global interreligious and ecumenical organizations such as the World Council of Churches, global Christian Protestant denominational organizations, the Council for a Parliament of the World's Religions, and the Ecumenical Association of Third World Theologians.

people, so far as their human dignity and the rights flowing from it are concerned.

The Church reproves, as foreign to the mind of Christ, any discrimination against men [*sic*] or harassment of them because of their race, color, condition of life, or religion.[3]

In its final section, *Nostra Aetate* moves from considering the "rays of Truth" in other religions to the assertion that we cannot call on God if we refuse to treat all people as equals, born as we are in God's image. This passage has been less remarked on than the document's overture toward other religions, but it contains an important implication: interreligious community is inseparable from—indeed, depends on—a theology of social justice that brings out the fullest teachings of Jesus Christ contesting discrimination in any form. *Nostra Aetate* did not elaborate these implications, but they are basic to black liberation theology, which has emphasized that the principle of antidiscrimination in matters theological—the recognition of truths in other religions—must and does also apply in matters pertaining to class, race, gender, and social condition. Developing in the aftermath of Vatican II, black liberation theology argues that any theological reflection valorizing human dignity must deal with the social and economic conditions that oppress the health of individuals and communities. In this sense, black liberation theology theologizes the case for social justice (i.e., antidiscrimination, human dignity, and living out the preaching and practice of Jesus), which *Nostra Aetate* voiced primarily in the religious realm, to all facets of human existence.

Antidiscrimination

Concerning antidiscrimination, *Nostra Aetate* and black liberation theology concur: "No foundation therefore remains for any theory or practice that leads to discrimination between man and man [*sic*] and between people and people." Antidiscrimination, moreover, includes the important task of unmasking social wrong. In fact, just as the Second Vatican Council applied this bold and pioneering antidiscrimination theological principle to its global churches, black liberation theology (in 1966, one year after the close of the council) implemented a similar theological claim in North American churches and society. However, black liberation theology accented the notion of racial and class power distribution explicitly.

By black liberation theology, I refer to an indigenous liberation theology created by the ad hoc National Committee of Negro Churchmen when they published their July 31, 1966, statement on Black Power in the *New York*

---

[3] *Declaration on the Relation of the Church to Non-Christian Religions—Nostra Aetate,* proclaimed by Pope Paul VI (Vatican City, 1965), sec. 5, http://www.vatican.va/archive/hist_councils/ii_vatican_council/documents/vat-ii_decl_19651028_nostra-aetate_en.html.

Times.[4] The document was signed by forty-seven black men and one black woman clergy and represented one of the most comprehensive ecumenical statements written in North American history. Only the National Council of Churches USA might have had a broader support in some of its pronouncements throughout its existence. These forty-eight signers were pastors, not professors. Thus, black liberation theology might be the only indigenous North American theology emerging from pastors in churches rather than from academics in higher education.

This National Committee echoed *Nostra Aetate's* warnings about discrimination and its implicit call for justice. When the black church leaders published their statement, they were asking and answering the following question: What should churches and theology have to say about poor and working-class blacks needing economic, political, and cultural power? The authors wrote: "What we see shining through the variety of rhetoric [of white Americans attacking black power] is not anything new but the same old problem of power and race which has faced our beloved country since 1619 [when the first group of Africans were brought as slaves to Jamestown]."[5]

In this concise way, the National Committee gave flesh to the bones of a general call against discrimination. These black Christian leaders wrote about jobs, educational systems, equal opportunity, income disparities, de facto segregation, the fact that only a small group of middle-class Negroes have made progress in America, the need to rebuild the urban areas, and the need for America to stop its wars of destruction abroad. They called on Negro churches to recognize the power they have and to use that power for the poor on earth instead of mainly pointing to life after death. They advised these churches to recognize that Jesus was already working for social change among black communities that were struggling for justice now.[6] Jesus was already with the working class and the poor.

---

[4] The document can be found in Gayraud S. Wilmore and James H. Cone, eds., *Black Theology: A Documentary History, 1966–1979* (Maryknoll, NY: Orbis Books, 1979), 23–30. The first single-authored text on liberation theology in a black American context was written by James H. Cone, *Black Theology and Black Power* (Maryknoll, NY: Orbis Books, 1979; originally published by Harper and Row, 1969). On the origin of black liberation theology, see James H. Cone, *For My People: Black Theology and the Black Church: Where Have We Been and Where Are We Going?* (Maryknoll, NY: Orbis Books, 1984), and Dwight N. Hopkins, *Introducing Black Theology of Liberation* (Maryknoll, NY: Orbis Books, 1999). For a global comparison of the origins, commonalities, and differences between black liberation theologies, see Dwight N. Hopkins, *Black Theology USA and South Africa: Politics, Culture, and Liberation* (Eugene, OR: Wipf & Stock, 2005).

[5] Wilmore and Cone, *Black Theology*, 23. Also see Albert J. Raboteau, *Slave Religion: The "Invisible Institution" in the Antebellum South* (Oxford: Oxford University Press, 2004), and Dwight N. Hopkins, *Down, Up & Over: Slave Religion and Black Theology* (Minneapolis: Fortress Press, 1999).

[6] Wilmore and Cone, *Black Theology*, 27. Theological claims from the 1966 document were developed in "Black Theology: Statement by the National Committee of Black Churchmen, June 13, 1969," in Wilmore and Cone, *Black Theology*, 37–39.

Furthermore, the statement saw the United States as black citizens' beloved homeland. But because the United States had not used its abundant resources to help the poor and the oppressed both at home and around the world, God's judgment was being pronounced on it. In this divine judgment, the statement claimed, we find Jesus working with the poor and the oppressed. To be Christian, all churches needed to go where Jesus was. And the role of theology was to reflect on this liberation reality as a way to enhance the full humanity of oppressed black workers and the poor. The black churchmen and woman wrote: "From the Christian faith, there is nothing necessarily wrong with concern for power."[7]

The theological content for Christian churches in the United States, argued the black church leaders, is liberation. Jesus was born, lived, died, and lived again for the liberation of the poor, the oppressed, and the working people. The role of churches is to structure its rituals and institutions to serve the poor. The calling of a Christian is to witness to the Word of Jesus' liberation from inside the church out to the streets. The long-term goal or hope of the Christian faith is to be led by the Holy Spirit to build up God's kingdom on earth. Theologically, the founders of black liberation theology observed the prevailing discriminatory imbalance of black-white race relations in the United States when they wrote:

> The fundamental distortion facing us in the controversy about "black power" is rooted in a gross imbalance of power and conscience between Negroes and white Americans. . . . The power of white men is corrupted because it meets little meaningful resistance from Negroes to temper it and keep white men from aping God. The conscience of black men is corrupted because, having no power to implement the demands of conscience, the concern for justice is transmuted into a distorted form of love, which, in the absence of justice, becomes chaotic self-surrender.[8]

Between 1966 and 1969, liberation theology emerged in the United States through the theological statements of the ad hoc National Committee of Negro Churchmen. In the 1968 St. Louis convocation of the National Committee of Black Churchmen ("Black" had replaced "Negro"), the committee began to use the phrase *black theology* to describe what they saw as the encounter of God with the black experience. An article in the November 15, 1968, issue of *Time* magazine reported on the gathering and described how "a number of speakers suggested that a major goal should be the creation of a fully developed black theology."[9] In fact, the first fully developed book on liberation theology was penned in March 1969 by an African Methodist Episcopal clergyman, James H. Cone, who was quickly joined by J. Deotis Roberts, a Baptist clergyman. With these two men, who were professors as well as ministers, we begin to see the gap between academia and the church closing,

---

[7] Wilmore and Cone, *Black Theology*, 24.

[8] Ibid., 23.

[9] "Churches: Is God Black?" *Time* 92, no. 20 (November 15, 1968): 106.

as well as the intentional theological beginnings of antidiscrimination as essential to social justice.[10] The National Committee of Negro Churchmen, James H. Cone, and J. Deotis Roberts all agreed. Resolving any kind of discrimination in human communities, they insisted, required articulating a Christian gospel of liberation.

In the movement to eliminate discrimination in the United States, one of the fundamental sources for the black liberation theology of Cone and Roberts was Martin Luther King Jr.'s emerging opposition to any "discrimination" or "harassment" based on, as *Nostra Aetate* states, "race, color, condition of life, or religion." The theology of Martin Luther King Jr., particularly his insights during the last two years of his life, further advanced what we might surmise as the document's antidiscrimination direction. We must remember that, by 1966, King, a Baptist with a PhD in systematic theology, had come a long way from the Montgomery Bus Boycott in the mid-1950s and his "I Have a Dream" speech of 1963. More than ten years of struggle by the civil rights movement had made him a rather sober North American theologian.[11] More specifically, in his mature understanding of harassment and discrimination against men and women, King tightly wedded race and class. *Nostra Aetate* is keen on unmasking social wrongs in society. Similarly, late in his life, King increasingly offered trenchant critiques grounded in racial and political economic analysis. Addressing the Southern Christian Leadership Conference in 1967, he observed:

> Another basic challenge is to discover how to organize our strength in terms of economic and political power. . . . Indeed, one of the great problems that the Negro confronts is his lack of power. . . . Stripped of the right to make decisions concerning his life and destiny he has been subject to the authoritarian and sometimes whimsical decisions of this white power structure.[12]

Intentionally or not, King had begun to parallel the theology of the National Committee of Negro Churchmen. In this instance, we could argue that both he and they were on the same antidiscrimination and antiharassment journey. That same year, he likewise proclaimed:

---

[10] Cone's first liberation theology book is titled *Black Theology and Black Power* (1969); he wrote the second book a year later: *A Black Theology of Liberation* (Philadelphia: Lippincott, 1970). In 1971, J. Deotis Roberts wrote the third book: *Liberation and Reconciliation: A Black Theology* (Louisville, KY: Westminster John Knox Press, 2005; originally published by Westminster Press, 1971).

[11] See David J. Garrow, *Bearing the Cross: Martin Luther King, Jr., and the Southern Christian Leadership Conference* (New York: HarperCollins, 1986), especially chapters 8–11.

[12] "The President's Address to the Tenth Anniversary Convention of the Southern Christian Leadership Conference, Atlanta, Georgia, August 16, 1967," in *The Rhetoric of Black Power*, ed. Robert L. Scott and Wayne Brockriede (New York: Harper and Row, 1969), 156.

There is nothing essentially wrong with power. The problem is that in America power is unequally distributed. This has led Negro Americans in the past to seek their goals through love and moral suasion devoid of power and white Americans to seek their goals through power devoid of love and conscience.[13]

We are suggesting here that black liberation theology and the theology of the older King agree with antidiscrimination and antiharassment as dimensions of social justice found in the concluding statements of *Nostra Aetate*. Yet at the same time, the apparently more radical direction taken by black liberation theology and by King differs from the stated positions in *Nostra Aetate*, because the former had begun to question the viability of the capitalist system.[14]

Human Dignity

The last part of *Nostra Aetate* underscores the lack of Christian theological foundation for any theory or practice that derogates human dignity. Black liberation theology likewise holds dear such universal Christian claims. The effective pursuit of social justice entails not only opposition to discrimination but also the affirmation of human dignity. Indeed, as a theological value, human dignity anchors black liberation theology and points to the positive relation of God to humanity.

From a Christian perspective, all human beings reflect the image of God,[15] a God of love, justice, peace, and compassion for oneself and for one's family, community, country, and the world. For black liberation theology, this belief enhances self-affirmation and community-building. It teaches our yellow, red, brown, white, and black youth—the world's future leaders— about a vocation of service to the lowest rung in society. It focuses the vision and horizons of our young people on something bigger than just themselves; as a common African saying puts it, "I am because we are."[16]

---

[13]   Martin Luther King Jr., *Where Do We Go from Here: Chaos or Community?* (Boston: Beacon Press, 1968), 37.

[14]   When Gustavo Gutiérrez published the first liberation theology book, which addressed conditions in Latin America, he indicated that the meeting of Latin American bishops in Medellín, Colombia, in 1968 concluded that the gospel of Jesus Christ had a "preferential option for the poor." These bishops were furthering the great wind of change coming out of the Second Vatican Council. One can claim that the radical emphasis of Gutiérrez is derived from the council. If so, then the radical direction of King and the National Committee of Black Churchmen is parallel to that of the council. See Gutiérrez, *A Theology of Liberation: History, Politics, and Salvation* (Maryknoll, NY: Orbis Books, 1988; originally published as *Teología de la Liberación: Perspectivas* (Lima, Peru: CEP, 1971).

[15]   Genesis 1:26–27 speaks about the "image of God" (Hebrew: *tzelem elohim*; Greek: *imago dei*). See John F. Kilner, *Dignity and Destiny: Humanity in the Image of God* (Grand Rapids, MI: William B. Eerdmans, 2015).

[16]   This African phrase is equivalent to Ubuntu philosophy or aesthetic. See Michael

Each human being is inextricably interwoven with the humanity of others. Each human being is connected to everyone else's humanity. Fundamentally, to be human is to embrace our human dignity,[17] which is both our natural-born right and our sacred right.

A major value of global religions, spiritualities, and self-cultivation practices embraces collective and individual human dignity. The necessity to have human dignity stands at the center of what it means to be a human being. Having one's basic human dignity recognized is essential for every person's identity, especially people who have little else materially and politically to sustain them. And individual human dignity takes place within the context of communal human dignity. Human dignity may appear to be identical to human rights, but the conferral of rights actually presupposes acknowledgment of one's dignity. To have human rights assumes that an oppressed community or a materially poor individual already enjoys social justice and dignity. Rights are granted to a recognized human person with recognized dignity. So, human dignity comes before human rights.

What is human dignity?[18] It is made up of at least three parts—*self-love, self-esteem,* and *self-confidence.*

Self-love means that a people love their own identity—how the Spirit and their ancestors have created them, and how they are born beautiful, healthy, and sacred as a people. Love of self accepts the self without wanting to be someone else. Self-love in different communities embraces the community's culture, wisdom, languages, spiritualities, religions, ancestors, and ways of being, seeing, and acting in the world. And self-love includes a love of nature, animals, birds, plants, fish, air, water, earth, and the minerals of the earth.

Jesse Battle and Archbishop Emeritus Desmond Tutu, *Reconciliation: The Ubuntu Theology of Desmond Tutu* (Cleveland, OH: Pilgrim Press, 1997). Also examine Frederick L. Hord, ed., *I Am Because We Are: Readings in Black Philosophy* (Amherst: University of Massachusetts Press, 1995); Betty Press, *I Am Because We Are: African Women in Image and Proverb* (Jackson: University Press of Mississippi, 2011); Bogobe B. Ramose, "The Philosophy of *Ubuntu* and *Ubuntu* as a Philosophy," in *The African Philosophy Reader,* ed. P. H. Coetzee and A. P. J. Roux, 2nd ed. (New York: Routledge, 2003), 230–38; and Nkonko M. Kamwangamalu, "Ubuntu in South Africa: A Sociolinguistic Perspective to a Pan-African Concept," in *The Global Intercultural Communication Reader,* ed. Molefi Kete Asante, Yoshitaka Miike, and Jing Yin, 2nd ed. (New York: Routledge, 2014), 226–36.

[17] For various perspectives on human dignity, see Gilbert Meilaender, *Neither Beast Nor God: The Dignity of the Human Person* (New York: Encounter Books, 2009); George Kateb, *Human Dignity* (Cambridge, MA: Belknap Press of Harvard University Press, 2011); and Michael Rosen, *Dignity and Meaning* (Cambridge, MA: Harvard University Press, 2012).

[18] This section on human dignity comes from a statement I proposed to (and that was adopted by) the International Association of Black Religions and Spiritualities after having traveled widely and listened to people from a wide range of educational and social backgrounds. I initiated and managed the association, consisting of thirteen countries: Fiji, Japan, Australia, India, England, South Africa, Zimbabwe, Botswana, Ghana, Cuba, Jamaica, Brazil, and the United States, including Hawaii.

Next is *self-esteem*. Self-esteem happens when a people who love themselves put value on themselves. There is worth to their very being. They hold themselves in high regard. When a community loves itself, it values its history, ancestry, land, language, and traditions, its unborn, very existence, right to live on earth, and connections to the sacred, all of nature, and the cosmos.

When an individual and a community love themselves and hold themselves in high esteem, they then become more *self-confident* to change the world. Two sayings from oral traditions of African American folk wisdom are relevant here. One states that "God will make a way out of no way."[19] The second is a complement to the first and asserts that "God helps those who help themselves."[20] It is important to stress that, in African American religious beliefs and practices, both thoughts go together. Taken in tandem, they lift up both God's presence and God's call on us to use our created gifts to glorify God by working to help the poor. God will do; and God calls on humans to do, too. With certain divine accompaniment, we boldly move forward to change the world.

Self-confidence helps us to act out our love and esteem of self in the world around us, especially as a people's movement to change the world for justice and harmony. With confidence we protect our individual healthy self and our collective healthy communities. We move in the world to challenge those obstacles that prevent the health of human beings, nature, and the cosmos. We have strong confidence in the future and the future of our unborn. We struggle for justice now. And we have a deep hope in a better society and better relations between humans and all of the nonhuman realities. We have hope that healthy societies will one day appear on earth. Self-confidence encourages a people to define its own self and the space around it in such a way that we are in harmony and balance with our selves, families, neighbors, ancestors, nature, the cosmos, and the sacred—all that there is.

In a related fashion, the Second Vatican Council document *Gaudium et Spes* ("Joy and Hope," December 7, 1965) touches directly on the question of human dignity. For me, it complements a similar notion from a black liberation theology perspective. The document states:

> At the same time, however, there is a growing awareness of the exalted dignity proper to the human person, since he stands above all things, and his rights and duties are universal and inviolable. Therefore, there must be

---

[19] For a womanist perspective, see Monica A. Coleman, *Make a Way Out of No Way: A Womanist Theology* (Minneapolis: Fortress Press, 2008). For slavery's contextual origin of this phrase, see Dianne Swann-Wright, *A Way Out of No Way: Claiming Family and Freedom in the New South* (Charlottesville: University of Virginia Press, 2002), and Hopkins, *Down, Up & Over*.

[20] For example, former black American slave James L. Bradley proclaimed, "God will help those who take part with the oppressed." See John W. Blassingame, ed., *Slave Testimony: Two Centuries of Letters, Speeches, Interviews, and Autobiographies* (Baton Rouge: Louisiana State University Press, 1977), 690.

made available to all people everything necessary for leading a life truly human, such as food, clothing, and shelter; the right to choose a state of life freely and to found a family, the right to education, to employment, to a good reputation, to respect, to appropriate information, to activity in accord with the upright norm of one's own conscience, to protection of privacy and rightful freedom even in matters religious.[21]

Like black liberation theology, *Gaudium et Spes* links human dignity to the material well-being of human communities. Thus it opens a dialogue about the concrete material life of the poor in the United States and throughout the world. Relying on sound biblical interpretation, the document draws us to the story of Lazarus in Luke 16:19–31, where a rich man refused the material needs of a poor man, Lazarus. Consequently, God gives justice to Lazarus by bringing him into glory upon his death. But the rich man suffers a horrible death because he refused to recognize the human dignity of Lazarus beneath his external poverty. As *Gaudium et Spes* notes:

> Coming down to practical and particularly urgent consequences, this council lays stress on reverence for man [*sic*]; everyone must consider his every neighbor without exception as another self, taking into account first of all His life and the means necessary to living it with dignity, so as not to imitate the rich man who had no concern for the poor man Lazarus.[22]

With these three dimensions of human dignity (self-love, self-esteem, and self-confidence), another world is possible, based on social justice. And coupled with *Gaudium et Spes*, *Nostra Aetate*, like black liberation theology, points us in that ultimate direction of a potential (but realizable) healthy community with healthy individuals.

Indeed, *Nostra Aetate* and black liberation theology suggest similar concerns about antidiscrimination and human dignity. Restated, the social justice of *Nostra Aetate* and black liberation theology requires a theological imagination about the revelation of antidiscrimination and human dignity on earth. Thus far in our comparative analysis, however, we lack a vision of the practice of healthy communities embracing healthy individuals. To this end, black liberation theology draws on the Bible's witness, one of its foundational sources for constructing a forward-looking theology.

---

[21] *Pastoral Constitution on the Church in the Modern World—Gaudium et Spes*, promulgated by Pope Paul VI (Vatican City, 1965), sec. 26, http://www.vatican.va/archive/hist_councils/ii_vatican_council/documents/vat-ii_cons_19651207_gaudium-et-spes_en.html.

[22] Ibid., sec. 27.

Living Out the Preaching and Practice of Jesus

Reading the sacred text from a perspective of black liberation theology, we find that three major stories emerge.[23] First, when we step back and frame the story line of the entire Old Testament, we can make a good case that the theological glue in those books is that Yahweh God liberated enslaved workers from material poverty and slavery. We see this narrative play out in Exodus 3:7–8:[24]

> The Lord said, "I have indeed seen the misery of my people in Egypt. I have heard them crying out because of their slave drivers, and I am concerned about their suffering. So I have come down to deliver them from the hand of the Egyptians and to bring them up out of that land into a good and spacious land, a land flowing with milk and honey."

Consequently in Exodus 6, Yahweh created a covenant with these enslaved workers.[25] Yahweh said that he would deliver them from earthly poverty and provide them with concrete material resources. The freed slaves, in the covenant, would own and control their own material resources. Exodus talks about the God–slave workers covenant. The Book of Numbers tells the story about scouts going into Canaan land and bringing back food, and it gives us an eyewitness account of the fertility and abundance of the earth. In other words, the content of the Yahweh–slave workers covenant is for workers and the oppressed to own their own land and resources for their families and their future offspring. That way, the lamb and lion can be together. That way, every family and community can live under their own vine and fig tree. The Old Testament witnesses to the primordial interactions and duties between Yahweh and humanity.[26]

The New Testament picks up on this Old Testament covenant theme and further clarifies the content of black liberation theology.[27] For example, the first public speech of Jesus had a specific and unique agenda: declare to the human community the sole purpose why the Spirit had anointed him to be incarnated on earth. This first public address is eschatologically significant, for it teaches Jesus'

---

[23] The elaboration of these three biblical threads can be found in Cone, *Black Theology and Black Power*, Cone, *Black Theology of Liberation*, and Roberts, *Liberation and Reconciliation*.

[24] This and subsequent quotations come from the New International Version unless otherwise noted.

[25] Michael Joseph Brown, *Blackening of the Bible: The Aims of African American Biblical Scholarship* (Harrisburg, PA: Trinity Press International, 2004), and Cain Hope Felder, ed., *Stony the Road We Trod: African American Biblical Interpretation* (Minneapolis, MN: Fortress Press, 1991).

[26] See Itumeleng J. Mosala, *Biblical Hermeneutics and Black Theology in South Africa* (Grand Rapids, MI: William B. Eerdmans, 1989).

[27] See Brian K. Blount, *Then the Whisper Put on Flesh: New Testament Ethics in an African American Context* (Nashville, TN: Abingdon Press, 2001).

ultimate goal. When God through Jesus explicitly tells us why God decided to reveal Godself decisively in the Incarnation, such a public declaration is like a presidential State of the Union address. What is the sole reason why God incarnated Godself in Jesus? We find the answer in Luke 4:16–20, the second passage on how to follow Jesus:

> He went to Nazareth, where he had been brought up, and on the Sabbath day he went into the synagogue, as was his custom. He stood up to read, and the scroll of the prophet Isaiah was handed to him. Unrolling it, he found the place where it is written: "The Spirit of the Lord is on me, because he has anointed me to proclaim good news to the poor. He has sent me to proclaim freedom for the prisoners and recovery of sight for the blind, to set the oppressed free, to proclaim the year of the Lord's favor." Then he rolled up the scroll, gave it back to the attendant and sat down. The eyes of everyone in the synagogue were fastened on him.

Now this is how the savior and liberator describes the criteria of his mission on earth.

Martin Luther King Jr. (a source of black liberation theology's intellectual and faith claims) stood in this spiritual tradition when he paraphrases Luke 4:18 and proclaims: "Jesus said the spirit of the Lord is upon me, because he's anointed me to heal the broken hearted, to preach the gospel to the poor, to bring deliverance to those who are in captivity and to proclaim the acceptable year of the Lord. And I must confess that the spirit of the Lord is upon me."[28]

Not only does Jesus unambiguously elaborate his criteria for healthy communities and individuals in the community, he also enunciates plainly the requirements for human flourishing. For black liberation theology, to be a Christian is to want to go to heaven ultimately. Whether one believes that heaven exists after death, where we will eventually be rejoined with our father, grandfather, mother, and grandmother, or whether heaven means a better life on earth, the primary reward of being a Christian is to get to heaven to meet Jesus. Whatever it looks like, heaven is a new life with Jesus. In Luke Jesus has already revealed his sole purpose and where we can find him—that is to say, with the poor, the prisoners, the blind, and the oppressed. It is no accident that these are the same criteria for Christians to achieve ultimate new life. To my knowledge, there is only one place in the sixty-six books of the Protestant Bible where Jesus explicitly gives the criteria for Christians to enter heaven. They are found in Matthew 25:31–40, the third biblical story on how to follow Jesus:

> When the Son of Man comes in his glory, and all the angels with him, he will sit on his glorious throne. All the nations will be gathered before him, and he will separate the people one from another as a shepherd separates

---

[28] Martin Luther King Jr., *The Trumpet of Conscience* (New York: Harper & Row, 1967), 4.

138   DWIGHT N. HOPKINS

the sheep from the goats. He will put the sheep on his right and the goats on his left. Then the King will say to those on his right, "Come, you who are blessed by my Father; take your inheritance, the kingdom prepared for you since the creation of the world. For I was hungry and you gave me something to eat, I was thirsty and you gave me something to drink, I was a stranger and you invited me in, I needed clothes and you clothed me, I was sick and you looked after me, I was in prison and you came to visit me."

The disciples of Jesus remain confused with this direct instruction. Their befuddlement originates from their initially equating the achievement of potential new life based on their self-centered practices. As a result, Jesus has to make it plain. All human beings will reach their new existence in glory only when earthly living flows from service to and liberation of the least in society. Jesus then resumes his narrative form of a salvific decree.

Then the righteous will answer him, "Lord, when did we see you hungry and feed you, or thirsty and give you something to drink? When did we see you a stranger and invite you in, or needing clothes and clothe you? When did we see you sick or in prison and go to visit you?" The King will reply, "Truly I tell you, whatever you did for one of the least of these brothers and sisters of mine, you did for me."

This prophetic passage, somewhat partial to the poor, was a favorite for Martin Luther King Jr.'s ministry that influenced black liberation theology. Toward the end of his life, King summed up all that he had done and asked that his eulogy convey the following message: "I don't want a long funeral. . . . But I hope I can live so well that the preacher can get up and say he was faithful. . . . That's the sermon I'd like to hear." Defining the nature of Christian faith by servanthood, he finishes his statement with these words:

"Well done thy good and faithful servant. You've been faithful; you've been concerned about others." That's where I want to go from this point on, the rest of my days. "He who is greatest among you shall be your servant." I want to be a servant. I want to be a witness for my Lord, do something for others.[29]

In the list of his own earthly achievements, King does not detail his Nobel Peace Prize, his many speaking and preaching engagements, his prestigious educational degrees, or his books and articles. In contrast, he hopes the living will remember him for his lifelong service to the physical poor and society's powerless

---

[29] Quoted in Garrow, *Bearing the Cross*, 555. Also see Martin Luther King Jr., "The Drum Major Instinct," in *A Testament of Hope: The Essential Writings of Martin Luther King, Jr.*, ed. James M. Washington (San Francisco: Harper & Row, 1986), 266–67.

victims. King based the servant trait of the Christian faith on his interpretation of the Bible. Specifically, he refers to Matthew 25:31–40. Here Jesus uses
the parable about the ultimate judgment day, when exact criteria deny or permit
passage into heaven.

Unpacking Jesus' words in Matthew 25 (and its application by King), I suggest
that they imply various levels of theological leadership needed today to attend to
workers and the wounded. For instance, black liberation theologians are called by
their spiritual vocation to be practical, priestly, and prophetic leaders. The practical
vocation calls us to accumulate as many material resources and wealth as necessary
to build a material reality so that the poor, the workers, and the oppressed can live
life abundantly. The Old Testament describes how God provided material resources
for the Hebrew ex-slaves in the land of Canaan. In Luke, Jesus said that he is the
fulfillment of the liberation year of Jubilee, when the oppressed become materially
free on earth. And Jesus' criteria for entering heaven explicitly demand giving water,
food, clothing, health, shelter, and sympathy to the poor, the workers, and the
oppressed in every nation throughout the land.[30] The priestly vocation commands
us to bind up the injuries of the physically broken and the emotionally wounded.
And the prophetic vocation commands to speak truth to power. The Old Testament Yahweh called Moses to go tell Pharaoh to let his people go. Similarly, Luke 4
and Matthew 25 relay stories about fighting structures that keep workers, the poor,
and the oppressed in chains. In a word, we construct practical ways to help our
people. We heal the emotional bruises of our people. And we speak on behalf of
their obtaining social justice.

Indeed, the Spirit of liberation brings good news to all who are forced to the
margins of the nation's vision. In the Book of Acts, we see what the new human
community can become: "All the believers were together and had everything in
common. They sold property and possessions to give to anyone who had need"
(2:44–45). This new common wealth, on the economic level, will have all of society
sharing the wealth among its citizens. God gave creation for all of humanity. But a
few individuals and a very small group of families have monopolized the inheritance
and distribution of these resources. Here wealth is very different from income. Even
when working people earn an income, they still are subject to the profit decisions
of the people for whom they work because the employers privately own wealth.
Wealth determines income.[31]

Martin Luther King Jr. differentiated the two concepts toward the end of
his life. More and more King began to deepen his analysis of class relations in the
United States when he underscored the distinction between those who own wealth
and those who are poor. Earlier in his public career, he had tried to aid "the discouraged

---

[30] Obery Hendricks, *The Politics of Jesus: Rediscovering the True Revolutionary Nature
of Jesus' Teaching and How They Have Been Corrupted* (New York: Three Leaves Press, 2006).

[31] See Kim Yong-Bock, "Covenant with the Poor: Toward a New Concept of
Economic Justice," in *Healing for God's World: Remedies from Three Continents*, eds. Kofi Asare
Opoku, Kim Yong-Bock, and Antoinette Clark Wire (New York: Friendship, 1991), 80.

beggars in life's market place." But a year before his death, he saw the need to not only help the beggar, but also reconstruct the causes forcing people to beg:

> We are called upon to help the discouraged beggars in life's market place. But one day we must come to see that an edifice which produces beggars needs restructuring. . . . When you deal with this, you begin to ask the question, "Who owns the oil?" . . . "Who owns the iron ore?" . . . "Why is it that people have to pay water bills in a world that is two-thirds water?"[32]

Here King makes a clear contrast between income and wealth. Income is money someone pays you for working for them. But wealth raises questions such as who owns the shopping malls, who owns the land in the city, who owns airline, television, radio, and information technology industries, and where is the concentration of wealth in the United States?

Therefore, poverty for all of humanity will disappear when the poor are no longer people whose only option is to work for others and are forced to receive an income.[33] Poverty will disappear when the poor share in the abundance of wealth and break the current global monopolization of the earth's resources, thereby bringing about a democracy in economics. Again, the Book of Acts helps us understand this difference between income and wealth:

> Now the whole group of those who believed were of one heart and soul, and no one claimed private ownership of any possessions, but everything they owned was held in common. . . . There was not a needy person among them, for as many as owned lands or houses sold them and brought the proceeds of what was sold. They laid it at the apostles' feet, and it was distributed to each as any had need. (4:32, 34–35, NRSV)

The key to a society that allows everyone access to wealth is to foster a shared will, faith, and vision among the poor. To achieve this degree of clarity and resolve, the bottom sectors of society will have to develop a lifestyle in line with the purpose of the Spirit of liberation. This Spirit calls for the majority of the world and, through them, the entire global community to act as stewards and to accept natural resources, human potentialities, and technological knowledge as divine gifts. By achieving the ultimate goal of this Spirit of liberation, the poor will be able eventually to realize new social relationships on earth in which everyone is on an equal level in their access to wealth.

This essay has drawn out the implications of *Nostra Aetate*'s final section by explicating them from the perspective of black liberation theology. Such a reading concludes that social justice is the foundation for any theory or practice to enhance

---

[32] King, Jr., "President's Address," 162.

[33] See Manning Marable, *From the Grassroots: Social and Political Essays Towards Afro-American Liberation* (Boston: South End Press, 1980).

antidiscrimination, human dignity, and living out the preaching and practice of
Jesus. Black liberation theology concurs that what is congruent with the mind of
Christ is that affirmation of and solidarity with all men and women regardless of
race and color. Intentionally crafting healthy communities with healthy individuals
in communities moves us toward social justice that eagerly accepts the varieties of
who we are as diverse religious citizens on earth.

In this religious way, a theology of social justice is intertwined with interreligious dialogue. Indeed, various aspects of black liberation theology offer one
model for such a dialogue. For instance, representatives from multiple local and
national religious denominations created black liberation theology in the late
1960s. They came together around the need for a multipronged response to the
religious, cultural, social, and political crises in 1960s America. In addition to its
origin in uniting various religious strands, black liberation theology continues to
bring variegated religious meanings to the discussions of pastors and academics.
The diversified *theological content* shared in such venues includes literal readings
of the Bible all the way to liberal readings by God-believers who are humanists.
These deliberations have occurred in various multireligious *institutional* locations,
encouraging black liberation theology to expand the range of its conversational
partners. Specifically, the 1975 Black Theology Project was part of the larger (multiracial, multireligious) Theology in the Americas organization, an umbrella network
consisting of Third World, or non-European, religious thought leaders. And based
on providing evidence for claims and presenting logical reasoning, the 1989 Black
Theology program unit of the American Academy of Religion placed black liberation theology into discussions with all the world's religions.

The *method* of black liberation theology likewise can engender interreligious
dialogue. Black theology does liberation theology by working with and speaking
about vulnerable communities among us. All religions are eagerly encouraged to
participate in this "doing," because collaboration hinges on practical projects. Here,
the first commitment is solidarity with our oppressed citizens. Similarly, black liberation theology's *reading* of the Bible interprets this sacred text as a living document
guiding the daily lives of all people and religions. This interpretation follows from
the *norm* of black liberation theology that affirms Jesus' mission as an offer of new
life to any group of people, of any belief or lifestyle, which has compassion for the
poor. And the basic *worldview* of black liberation theology is that two truths can
coexist in families, communities, and among nations. In a word, Jesus is decisive for
the faithful while maintaining interreligious dialogue with the truths of other world
religions. What holds the two (or more) truths together is that they both sustain a
commitment to working for justice for all people, especially for the oppressed and
marginalized.

Human activities of social justice and numerous religious conversations exem-
plify a hope that another world is possible if we hold tight to the sacredness of all
creation. Indeed, the *imago dei* (image of God) obligates us to celebrate and rejoice
in our racial, color, and gender complementarities. We are all equal children of

God, since we all reflect the divine image equally. Consequently, how best to implement social justice (i.e., ending all categories of discrimination, conferring human dignity on everyone, and following Jesus' path) remains an unfolding interreligious dialogue. And a comparison between *Nostra Aetate* and black liberation theology is one important strand in that ongoing process of forging healthy communities and healthy individuals in community.

8

Nostra Aetate: Views from a Sibling on Inclusivism and Pluralism

Peter C. Bouteneff

The request for an Orthodox Christian response to *Nostra Aetate*[1] presents several options. One might be an Orthodox critique of Roman Catholic ecclesiology, but *Nostra Aetate* is not primarily about the church's doctrine or papal structure. Another might be a rigorous Orthodox theological exploration of interreligious questions, but this would present the danger either of losing sight of *Nostra Aetate* entirely or of effectively repeating what it says, since Orthodox and Roman Catholic theological approaches to other faiths are essentially aligned. Given the text under review, and the theological proximity of our churches on relevant questions, the Orthodox confessional identity of this response will serve mostly to affirm the text, both in its theological underpinnings and especially its inclusive orientation.

An Orthodox vantage on *Nostra Aetate* may be of interest in that it emanates from a church that is both theologically close to Roman Catholicism and yet still outside it. Our theological proximity and ecclesiastical distance permit some observations about this text that focus on its apparent starting point and goals, with particular attention to how it might—and might not—have gone further in its inclusive stance toward other faiths. Exploring this inclusive stance will be an opportunity to discuss the spectrum of inclusive and pluralistic approaches to interreligious relationships.

Despite some strictly isolated theological disputes (e.g., the *filioque* clause added to the Nicene-Constantinopolitan Creed),[2] disagreements over the nature of primacy,

I am grateful to all the participants in the colloquium from which this book is drawn, especially the late Rita Gross, for their thoughtful and candid engagement during its proceedings. They have helped shape this chapter in its current form.

[1] *Declaration on the Relation of the Church to Non-Christian Religions—Nostra Aetate*, proclaimed by Pope Paul VI (Vatican City, 1965).

[2] Considerable progress has been made in the bilateral discussions of this issue. See the 2003 agreed-upon statement of the North American Orthodox-Catholic Consultation, at http://www.usccb.org/beliefs-and-teachings/ecumenical-and-interreligious/ecumenical/orthodox/filioque-church-dividing-issue-english.cfm.

with special reference to the papacy,[3] and ecclesiastical tensions limited to certain times in specific localities (notably disputes over "canonical territory" in Eastern Europe),[4] the Orthodox Church generally views the Roman Catholic Church as a close relative, a sibling.[5] Our respective ecclesiologies present some divergences from each other.[6] But they are united in the essential question of what the church is: the Body of Christ. Jesus Christ is himself the head; the church is his body. Roman Catholics and Orthodox also have similar theological approaches to both the integrity and the fragmentation of the Christian world. There is one Body, and the divided Christianity that we see today reflects historic divisions *from* that Body. The Orthodox identify the One Church with the Orthodox Church, from which others have, over time and to different extents, separated. And the Roman Catholic Church would make something like that same statement about itself. Each of these two churches, then, self-identifies with the church, and although it sounds like this dual claim would drive a powerful wedge between us, it ironically unites us. We are united in that we do not see the Christian church as one great tree with different branches, each representing the countless denominations, together constituting the One Church. Our position means that we see some Christian divisions as representing genuine separations, and not merely surface symptoms, or occasions of healthy diversity.

This common understanding of the church's coherence and identity leads each church, Orthodox and Roman Catholic, to the challenge of reckoning how those *outside* our respective bodies are understood vis-à-vis the Body of Christ. The Orthodox Church has reflected in a limited way on this issue, and tends toward the stance that the Body of Christ does not end at the canonical borders of the Orthodox Church.[7] Roman Catholics have expressed their version of such a view in

---

[3] The nature of primacy has in recent years been the reigning theme of the Joint International Commission for the Theological Dialogue between the Roman Catholic Church and the Orthodox Church. See the so-called Ravenna Statement, *Ecclesiological and Canonical Consequences of the Sacramental Nature of the Church—Ecclesial Communion, Conciliarity and Authority* (Vatican City, 2007), http://www.vatican.va/roman_curia/pontifical_councils/chrstuni/ch_orthodox_docs/rc_pc_chrstuni_doc_20071013_documento-ravenna_en.html.

[4] Among the relevant ecumenical texts is a report of the Joint Working Group between the Roman Catholic Church and the World Council of Churches, which discusses issues of canonical territory and the challenge of proselytism. See "Seventh Report of the Joint Working Group" (December 1, 1998), https://www.oikoumene.org/en/resources/documents/commissions/jwg-rcc-wcc/seventh-report-of-the-joint-working-group.

[5] The term "sister churches" has frequently been deployed by both sides, though not without controversy. See Will Cohen, "The Concept of 'Sister Churches' in the Orthodox-Catholic Relations in the 12th and 21st Centuries," *St. Vladimir's Theological Quarterly* 53 (2009): 375–406.

[6] The most commonly cited divergences concern the nature of the papacy; these are both jurisdictional—what is the nature and scope of papal authority?—and theological—what is the relationship between the universal church and local churches?

[7] The leading essay on this score remains Father Georges Florovsky, "The Limits of the

more formalized texts, most notably *Lumen Gentium*, *Unitatis Redintegratio*, and more recently, *Dominus Iesus*.

This essentially common ecclesiological stance vis-à-vis other Christian churches is based on a shared reverence for the experience and authority of the great Christian writers and ecumenical councils of the first millennium. Might it logically translate into a similarly unified approach toward non-Christian religions? In the ensuing pages I argue that, within the range of exclusive, inclusive, and pluralistic approaches to religious diversity—however flawed that taxonomy may be—Roman Catholics and Orthodox tend to experience a gravitational pull toward the inclusive. Beginning with a brief examination of the function and theology of *Nostra Aetate* as I perceive it, I go on to discuss the subsequent calls to push the text further in the direction of religious pluralism. I do so from the perspective of Orthodox theology, or more precisely, from the vantage of the shared Orthodox and Catholic recourse to early patristic and conciliar theology.

Nostra Aetate and Conceptions of the Non-Christian Sphere

Most modern Catholic and Orthodox thinking on other faiths has been founded not on ecclesiology, but on basic convictions about the human person and about Jesus Christ. This observation applies to *Nostra Aetate*, and the observations I offer about that document apply equally to convictions expressed within the Orthodox Church.

The Human Person and Truth

The main theological presupposition underlying the anthropology of *Nostra Aetate* is that human beings find their final goal in God. This speaks to the conviction that, whether or not a person believes in God, God (a) exists, (b) is universal, and therefore (c) is the source and goal of *everything*—and in a special way every*one*—that exists.

Paragraph 2 of the text recalls Saint Paul's preaching at the Areopagus, as recounted in Acts 17:19–34. *Nostra Aetate* suggests a near-universal perception of a "hidden hovering power"—what the Greek pagans of Acts 17 may have called "the unknown god . . . in whom we live, and move, and have our being" (Acts 17:23, 28).

Apart from this faith conviction, *Nostra Aetate* founds itself on the observation that human hearts are "restless" for God—and furthermore, that human beings of all faith convictions and of no particular faith position ask similar questions about life's origins and its aim, especially (and this is one place that *Nostra Aetate* can sound rather imperialist) where they are part of "an advanced culture."

Church," *Church Quarterly Review* 117 (October 1933): 117–31, which (rather unusually for an Orthodox theologian) draws on Augustine as its primary criterion.

Nostra Aetate points finally to the fundamental dynamic of love as the motivator for listening genuinely to others and treating their positions with genuine respect. The Catholic Christian is urged to engage with people of other faiths, not only because they "reflect a ray of that [Christ-] Truth which enlightens all men [*sic*],"[8] but because it is the decent and loving thing to do. For all are made in God's image.[9]

Jesus Christ and Truth

Nostra Aetate includes as one of its central features the conviction that, effectively, truth is truth, wherever it is found. Furthermore, it does so on the basis that Jesus Christ is, in his own person, the Truth, specifically "the way, the truth, and the life" (Jn 14:6, cited in *Nostra Aetate* sec. 2). In so doing, the document stands in direct continuity with the theology commonly attributed to the second-century apologist Justin Martyr, who wrote about the "seeds of the Word" that are sown among all people. Justin's inclusivist teaching, to which I shall return further on, is in turn grounded in the New Testament. Saint Paul, in his preaching to the Gentile converts, and in his message to the Jews to *justify* his approach to the Gentiles, is of the conviction that the truth and the way of God is written on human hearts, whether or not people know it or have come upon it through scriptures.[10]

Paul's understanding finds further expression elsewhere in the New Testament, in the conviction that a right morality transcends Jewish or Gentile identity: "You may be sure that everyone who does right is born of Him" (1 Jn 2:29). Right action and awe before God—above and beyond national identity—have clear implications even for salvation: "Truly I perceive that God shows no partiality, but in every nation any one who fears him and does what is right is acceptable to him" (Acts 10:34–35).

Returning to Justin Martyr, another of his celebrated sayings carries the understanding that not only is truth something universal, but since Christ *is* "the Truth," it means that all truth is Christ-truth. In his words, "Whatever things were rightly said among all people are the property of us Christians."[11] *Nostra Aetate* section 2 is reminiscent of this spirit, where it says,

---

[8] *Nostra Aetate*, sec. 2.

[9] This imperative of love and the conviction of human dignity in God's image run throughout the text. In its concluding (fifth) paragraph, *Nostra Aetate* states, "We cannot truly call on God, the Father of all, if we refuse to treat in a brotherly way any man, created as he is in the image of God."

[10] This theme, which underlies the Epistle to the Romans, is found explicitly in Romans 1:19–20, 2:14–15, 5:5.

[11] *Apol.* 2.13. See *I, II Apologiae,* ed. A. Wartelle (Paris: Études Augustiniennes, 1987). As it happens, L. W. Barnard finds a nearly identical phraseology in Seneca, who claimed anything that is said well or true as "his own." See Leslie William Barnard, *St. Justin Martyr: The First and Second Apologies*, Ancient Christian Writers 56 (New York: Paulist, 1997), 200, at n. 73.

[The Catholic Church] regards with sincere reverence those ways of conduct and of life, those precepts and teachings which, though differing in many aspects from the ones she holds and sets forth, nonetheless often reflect a ray of that Truth which enlightens all men. Indeed, she proclaims, and ever must proclaim Christ "the way, the truth, and the life" (John 14:6), in whom men [sic] may find the fullness of religious life, in whom God has reconciled all things to Himself.

Much of *Nostra Aetate* implicitly evokes the concept of what Karl Rahner has called "anonymous Christianity."[12] This idea suggests that when people believe things that are true and live in God's grace through their manner of living—even if they employ names and terminology that are not explicitly Christian—they draw nearer to Christ and are enlightened by Christ, who is "the true light who enlightens every human being" (Jn 1:9). "Anonymous Christianity" does not mean that everybody is a Christian whether they know it or not. It means that truth, as such, is impartial. And that the Christian, who believes that Truth is identified with the person of Christ, may thus appropriately affirm truth wherever it is found. This idea in turn carries the conviction that, when people are doing or believing the truth, whatever their religious "location," they are drawing closer to Christ.[13]

As discussed above, in its basic approach to the human person and to Christ-as-truth, *Nostra Aetate* locates itself decisively with what would come to be identified as an inclusive approach to other faiths. This text, thoroughly grounded in the doctrine of the *Imago Dei,* assumes that every human person is going to seek—and potentially find—the God in whose image he or she was created. The text likewise sides with Christian writings from the earliest centuries (Pauline and Johannine writings, Justin Martyr's *Apology*, et al.),[14] which have demonstrated and articulated how truth and righteousness are not relativized categories, but are identifiable with the person of Christ, regardless of their geographic or religious location.

---

[12] Rahner promulgated this idea in his essay, originally published just prior to Vatican II, "Christianity and the Non-Christian Religions," in *Theological Investigations* (London: Darton, Longman and Todd, 1966), 5:115–34.

[13] Other faiths have availed themselves of similar expressions, such as where Christians can be considered anonymous Muslims. See Seyyed Hossein Nasr, "The Islamic View of Christianity," in *Christianity among World Religions,* ed. H. Küng, J. Moltmann, M. Lefebure, Concilium vol. 183 (Edinburgh: T. & T. Clark, 1986), 3–12. Paul Knitter has informed me that the Zen Master Nishitani once identified Karl Rahner as an "anonymous Zen Buddhist." See J. Kellenberger, *God-Relationships with and without God* (New York: Palgrave Macmillan, 1989), 103.

[14] Numerous other arguments for inclusivism can be made from the gospels, such as Christ's finding equal if not greater faith and righteousness among the non-Israelites than among the Jews (e.g., Luke 7:9) together with all the passages that praise the (foreign) Samaritans, Luke 17:11–19, 10:30–37.

What is *Nostra Aetate* up against, in its inclusivism? A strict, theologically articulated interreligious *exclusivism* is usually associated with Protestant theologians, most notably Karl Barth and Hendrik Kraemer.[15] Yet the architects of *Nostra Aetate* evidently saw fit to deliver a sharp rebuke to exclusivist theologies and missionary practices. And this is what *Nostra Aetate* ultimately represents, as it promulgates inclusivism: a clear censure—really a rebuke—of exclusivism. It will no longer do to say that "the non-Christian religions seem like stammering words from some half-forgotten saying."[16] Or that salvation can be accessed only within the visible, canonical church. Salvation, says *Nostra Aetate*, is in the name of Jesus Christ alone, but there is truth—and all truth is Christ-truth—outside the visible Christian church. It would be difficult to overstate the significance of *Nostra Aetate* in enshrining inclusivism within the Second Vatican Council, and therefore within the life and thought of the Roman Catholic Church.

Exclusivism, Inclusivism, Pluralism: Assessing the Taxonomy

My observations about *Nostra Aetate* identify it with an inclusive approach to other faiths. Before I ask the question, "Should it have gone further, or in any case, should *we* go further?" it would be useful to examine further the existing range of orientations toward other faiths and how people have made sense of that range. *Nostra Aetate* does not speak explicitly of "inclusivism," since it had not yet become common to identify exclusivism, inclusivism, and pluralism as three models of interreligious relationship. That taxonomy[17] has become widespread, though increasingly imperfect, as the landscape of approaches becomes more complex. As typically presented, exclusivism is the understanding that there is effectively no saving truth in any religion other than one's own. Inclusivism perceives truth outside one's own faith, interpreting that truth in terms of one's own faith teachings—as seen where ancient and modern Christian theologians have identified all truth with the person of Jesus Christ. Pluralism sees all the great religious traditions as having equal access to the truth—ultimately an unknowable entity—such that it is impossible or at least unreasonable to identify the teachings or deities of any one tradition as absolute.

All such categorizations are flawed, and others have been proposed. Especially helpful in this regard is Paul Knitter's four-point schema[18] that effectively adds nuance

---

[15] Others, from a wider swath of the Protestant spectrum include Lesslie Newbigin, Hendrik Kraemer, D. A. Carson, and William Lane Craig.

[16] Emil Brunner, *Revelation and Reason,* trans. Olive Wyon (London: SCM, 1947), 270.

[17] These categories, as applied to the interreligious landscape, are commonly attributed to Alan Race, in his *Christians and Religious Pluralism: Patterns in the Christian Theology of Religions* (Maryknoll, NY: Orbis Books, 1982).

[18] See Paul Knitter, *Introducing Theologies of Religions* (Maryknoll, NY: Orbis Books, 2002).

to "inclusivism." It does so by identifying a "fulfillment model," wherein one's own faith is seen as the full realization of others' (which nonetheless contain truths), and a "mutuality model" which maintains something of the unique location of truth within one's own faith, but posits that not only are there truths in other religions, but that people must learn from other faiths in order to arrive at comprehensive truth.

Knitter's analysis is especially useful in pointing out that there are different forms of inclusivism, some of which are closed and some of which are open, and different ways to arrive at them; he likewise identifies a range of exclusivist positions. But might it be possible to identify a whole spectrum of positions from the strictest exclusivism to fully fledged relativism, and then to point to certain markers that would help indicate where someone stands along that spectrum? It might indeed. Yet I propose rather to identify one spectrum along the exclusive-inclusive span, and a different spectrum within pluralism. One's location within each of these ranges would depend on answers to the following kinds of questions:

Exclusive-Inclusive

- Is there holiness, as manifest in human beings, outside the Christian church?
- Can there be true statements about God in non-Christian faiths?
- Is there something to be profitably learned, in doctrine, philosophy, or way of life, by a Christian from non-Christian faith traditions?
- Is salvation, now and in the age to come, possible outside the visible Christian church?

Even as the diverse answers to these questions testify to a range of positions, I would point out that the exclusivist-inclusivist Christian spectrum is based on common beliefs that (a) there is an absolute truth, (b) it can be known, even if not comprehensively, and (c) this truth is identified with the person of Jesus Christ, in a way that it is not identified with any other person or concept. If I am correct in identifying these beliefs with the exclusivist-inclusivist spectrum, we might pose a quite different set of questions that may help define a perhaps more subtle range of positions within pluralist positions.

Pluralist

- Is there such a thing as absolute truth?
- If there is, can that truth be known?
- Is it philosophically possible to identify one's own faith position with the absolute (which is not necessarily to say *exclusive*) truth?

A fully fledged relativist position would answer the first of these questions in the negative. The second question, if answered in the negative, would identify someone who does not rule out absolute truth but is led to the conviction that it cannot be decisively located in any single faith tradition—and who would therefore answer "no" to the third question as well.

With the above, I am suggesting a sharper dividing line between pluralism and inclusivism than is properly drawn between exclusivism and inclusivism. The latter two both presume the existence and identifiability of absolute truth, and (in the Christian case) associate it with Jesus Christ. The move toward pluralism is radical, both epistemologically (positing that absolute truth, if it exists at all, cannot be known or identified) and doctrinally (Jesus Christ cannot properly be identified as the Truth, nor as the sole savior or unique name by which we are saved). Indeed, the advent of an articulated pluralism was heralded with the kind of metaphors that would emphasize its far-reaching, even revolutionary character. John Hick likened it to the Copernican Revolution, which required a complete reconception of one's place in the physical, or, in this case, religious universe.[19] Several authors have spoken of pluralism as the crossing of the theological Rubicon.[20] No one would posit a Rubicon or other revolution in the subtler movement between exclusivism and inclusivism, both of which are predicated (in the case of Christianity) upon the faith in Jesus Christ as the unique Son of God the Father and unique savior of the world.

Why do I emphasize the above? Because if pluralism does represent a more radical ideological, philosophical, and theological move than that between exclusivism and inclusivism, this consideration would be significant when evaluating *Nostra Aetate*. It should not undermine the document's importance in opening the door of truth to other faiths, but it may well inform a response to the question of whether *Nostra Aetate* should have, or ought to be, pushed beyond its inclusivist position into a pluralist one. I will argue, by way of a reflection on issues in pluralism, that the movement from *Nostra Aetate*'s inclusivism into interreligious pluralism would constitute not only a philosophical and theological revolution but also an ecclesiastical one, in that it would distance the text from conciliar Roman Catholicism.[21]

Philosophical Issues in Pluralism

The diverse iterations of pluralism and inclusivism, and their defenses and critiques (complete with mutual charges of arrogance) have been the subject of a body of literature that found an early apex in the late 1980s with John Hick and Paul Knitter's edited volume *The Myth of Christian Uniqueness: Toward a Pluralistic Theology*

---

[19] John Hick, *God and the Universe of Faiths*, rev. ed. (1973; London: Oneworld, 1993), chap. 9, "The Copernican Revolution in Theology."

[20] In John Hick and Paul F. Knitter, eds., *The Myth of Christian Uniqueness: Toward a Pluralistic Theology of Religions* (Maryknoll, NY: Orbis Books, 1987), 16, 22, 90, and passim.

[21] By "conciliar" I mean Catholicism faithful to the ancient Ecumenical Councils as well as to Vatican II.

of Religions and the response volume edited by Gavin D'Costa, *Christian Unique-ness Reconsidered: The Myth of a Pluralistic Theology of Religions*.[22] But these rich exchanges have to be relived and re-received by subsequent generations. Among the points I would like to see rescued from that earlier dialogue is the identification of pluralism as a bona fide philosophical/religious and epistemological worldview, with profound implications for each of the world's main religious faiths. This fact needs to be re-emphasized because pluralism, to many pluralists, is not actually a "position" at all. It is the uber-position, a para-worldview. It is enlightenment; it is evident reality. Again, the Copernican metaphor is indicative: Pluralism, like the Copernican Revolution, is presented as a matter of crossing into what was at first strenuously, hopelessly, even foolishly resisted, but now universally accepted as *objective reality*. But pluralism, like any view, is a philosophical stance with its own trajectory in the history of ideas,[23] its own ontological presuppositions[24] that may be defended or challenged, and its own potential for humility, integrity, and wisdom, as well as for absolutism, superiority, and imperialism.

Theological Issues in Pluralism

More relevant to *Nostra Aetate*, and to religious faiths generally speaking, the adop-tion of a rigorous and self-consistent pluralism requires substantial realignments within virtually every religious tradition, sometimes to the sacrifice of its fundamental principles.[25] In the case of Christianity, the assertions (pervasive in the New Testa-ment) of Jesus Christ's unique identity as the Son of the Living God, the one in whom all things have their origin and coherence (Col 1:17), the only name by which people are saved (Acts 4:12, Eph 1:21, Phil 2:9–11), the sole "door" or point of access to the One God (Jn 10:7–9), must inevitably be done away with. This reality is openly acknowledged by some of the founders of pluralism: "Jesus was not . . . the second

---

[22] Hick and Knitter, eds., *Myth of Christian Uniqueness*; Gavin D'Costa, ed., *Christian Uniqueness Reconsidered: The Myth of a Pluralistic Theology of Religions* (Maryknoll, NY: Orbis Books, 1990). Most if not all of the issues I raise in the coming pages were signaled already within these and subsequent volumes; my hope will be to bring a few fresh insights into each, within the specific context of evaluating *Nostra Aetate*.

[23] See Kenneth Surin, "A 'Politics of Speech': Religious Pluralism in the Age of the McDonald's Hamburger," in *Christian Uniqueness Reconsidered*, ed. D'Costa, 192–212.

[24] Some forms of pluralism may be associated with essentialism. Just as Roman Cath-olics are periodically accused of a view of a church-essence that subsists in the different churches, some pluralists seem to suggest a truth or reality-essence (a *noumenon*) that subsists in the different religions. This observation was made by John Cobb in "Beyond 'Pluralism,'" in *Christian Uniqueness Reconsidered*, ed. D'Costa, 81–95.

[25] In one among many iterations of this problem, Gavin D'Costa argues that John Hick replaces "one form of 'arrogance' with another," in that "all religious claims are deemed myth-ological, whether or not adherents recognize this." See his "The New Missionary: John Hick and Religious Pluralism," *International Bulletin of Missionary Research* 15 (April 1991): 69.

person of a divine Trinity living a human life and having both a divine and human nature, but was a man responding totally to divine grace and doing the will of God."[26] John Hick is editor and co-editor, respectively, of *The Myth of God Incarnate* and *The Myth of Christian Uniqueness*. The interdependence of the demythologization of the Incarnation and of Christ's uniqueness is further underscored by the title (and naturally the content) of Hick's later book, *The Metaphor of God Incarnate: Christology in a Pluralistic Age*.[27] Even as the views within these volumes are diverse, and Hick's pluralism can be complex and brilliantly nuanced, the fact remains that pluralism and the de-literalization of the Incarnation are mutually dependent logical/theological positions. As Hick puts it, "A non-traditional Christianity based upon this [metaphorical] understanding of Jesus can see itself as one among a number of different human responses to the ultimate transcendent Reality that we call God."[28]

Hick's Jesus is a man, one who is extraordinarily attuned to the divine. He is no more attuned, necessarily, than Muhammad, or Gautama Buddha. He is extraordinary, but he is, ontologically speaking, nothing more or less than a human being; only in this way can he coexist on a par with the prophets and deities particular to other faiths. The incongruity of Jesus' status as mere man with the New Testament has been alluded to above. I will argue further that the doctrine articulated during the first Christian millennium, notably in the Ecumenical Councils to which the Roman Catholic and Orthodox churches accord clear authority, is incompatible with identifying Jesus as one-among-other possible saviors, or with seeing him as consubstantial with human beings but not with God.

The New Testament presents a certain diversity of Christologies, but such diversity was soon narrowed within the church community that Roman Catholics and Orthodox consider their ecclesiological root. Some pluralists have argued that the clear teachings about Jesus' incarnation and unique character were not codified until the fifth century,[29] but this statement is inaccurate. As an early example, "Psilanthropism"—the teaching associated with several figures, such as the third-century Paul of Samosata and Artemon, that Christ was "merely human" (*psilos anthropos*) and not divine—was condemned decisively before the early fourth century. The tendency toward adoptionism was also consistently rejected.[30] The Councils of Nicaea (325 CE) and Constantinople (381 CE) had as their *raison d'être* the defeat of Arianism, which had taught that Jesus Christ was, in his essence

---

[26] John Hick, *The Metaphor of God Incarnate: Christology in a Pluralistic Age* (London: SCM, 1993), 108.

[27] Hick and Paul Knitter, eds., *Myth of Christian Uniqueness*; John Hick, ed., *The Myth of God Incarnate* (London: SCM, 1977); Hick, *Metaphor of God Incarnate*.

[28] Hick, *Metaphor of God Incarnate*, ix.

[29] See Wesley J. Wildman, *Fidelity with Plausibility: Modest Christologies in the Twentieth Century* (Albany: State University of New York Press, 1998), 267, 153–54, cited in Knitter, *Introducing Theologies of Religion*, 170.

[30] On psilanthropism and adoptionism, see, e.g., John Behr, *The Way to Nicaea* (Crestwood, NY: SVS Press, 2001), 207–35.

or being, less than divine. Christ's consubstantiality (*homoousion*) with God the Father has been an explicit mainstay of the conciliar (i.e., authoritative) theology of the church at least since that time. In an attempt to soften that consensus and make way for his own psilanthropist Christology, Hick has insisted that traditional language about the Incarnation and about Christian uniqueness is not meant to be scientific.[31] This is true and potentially helpful, but cannot operate as a general principle that softens early Christology. Identifying the language of the patristic and conciliar teachings about the Incarnation as poetic or metaphorical ignores, for example, the Christian heresies that this language was invoked specifically, urgently, and with philosophical-ontological precision, to reject.

Anyone is free to disagree with the idea that Christ was not ontologically of the same essence/nature/character as God. One may dispute that teaching with the best intentions, and with no lack of intelligence or rigor. But, for what it is worth, the teaching that Christ is consubstantial with God constitutes an expressed fundamental tenet of Orthodox and Roman Catholic theology—not merely a hard-line or "traditionalist" tenet, but one that lies at the very doctrinal and conciliar roots of the church.

Which brings us back to the point that pluralism necessitates a sometimes elemental realignment of the faiths that it purports to respect. Thus altered (Muhammad is not "the seal of the prophets," Jesus is not the unique Son of God in any literal sense, the unity of the Hindu pantheon is identical to that of the Trinity),[32] these faiths are rendered all but unrecognizable to their main adherents, through whatever theological work or demythologizing needs to be done in order to denude them of their universal claims. Such distortions could not withstand Catholic Christianity, which is why *Nostra Aetate*, as a Roman Catholic conciliar text, takes an inclusivist and not a pluralist position.

Moral Issues in Pluralism

One compelling argument for pluralism has been that, by according potentially equal place to all faiths and privileging none, it promotes a deep tolerance that is so evidently needed. The premise is that holding any one faith exclusively and absolutely is—or leads to—fundamentalism and violence.

Intolerance and violence carry a special relevance to relationships with Judaism, which has been historically persecuted in the name of both Christianity and Islam. Indeed, given the very real specter of antisemitism in history, notably in its horrific twentieth-century apex, it is within Christian-Jewish relationships that one must be especially mindful and prayerful, and especially humble in one's portrayals of the interreligious landscape, wherever one is on the exclusive, inclusive, and even pluralist spectrum. We would take note, then, that when *Nostra Aetate* appropriately devotes special attention to relationships with Judaism and

---

[31] See Hick, *Metaphor of God Incarnate,* esp. 99–111.
[32] Hick, *God and the Universe of Faiths,* 140.

Jews, it does not yield Jesus' unique divine identity, but acknowledges the Jewish roots of Christianity and condemns the scourge of antisemitism, singling out the perversity of justifying it through the New Testament. *Nostra Aetate* attempts to tread the path of a humbly expressed form of inclusivism akin to what Knitter calls the "fulfillment model," manifesting strengths and weaknesses typical of a 1960s European context.[33]

The question then becomes, can someone be convicted in their faith without being unhealthily attached to it? Without, effectively, being a tyrant? In the case of Christian-Jewish relations, can someone believe that Jesus in fact is the promised Messiah—in disagreement with the Jewish belief that he is not—without being antisemitic, or intolerant?

Issues in Inclusivism

This type of question lies at the heart of inclusivism: Is it possible to see Jesus Christ as the unique Son of the Living God, to identify Jesus' name as the one by which all are saved, and remain genuinely open to truth and wisdom everywhere, and to do so without being patronizing, hateful, or violent, and without minimizing the full impact of that truth? Of course it is. The world has seen its share of condescending and intolerant expressions of inclusivism. It has also seen stunningly arrogant pluralism.[34] But let us remind each other of what inclusivism, in its various expressions, actually stands for. Like pluralism, and exclusivism, inclusivism too is a stance, a worldview, with its own logic that can be defended or argued against. It evidently bears the potential both for arrogance and humility, closed-mindedness and openness. It encompasses a range of positions, some more and some less willing to embrace and learn from truths outside its faith teachings. In identifying Christ with The Truth, Christian inclusivist principles of themselves dictate neither a genuine inquisitive openness to wisdom outside Christianity nor a paternalistic condescension to non-Christian faiths. In other words, inclusivism, in and of itself, is not about "exclusive ownership" of truth; it is merely the logical extension of belief in Christ as savior and Son of God.

As shown above, inclusivism has been theologically defended with reference to the New Testament and the early Apologists, Justin Martyr chief among them. Contemporary Orthodox missiologists continue to rely (perhaps even too consistently) on these same seminal texts for their own inclusivist positions.[35] But

---

[33] I spoke earlier of the latent imperialist character in parts of *Nostra Aetate*. Its language is also non-gender-inclusive and can frequently sound terribly sexist to our ears today.

[34] Pluralism has been subject to charges of arrogance, primarily through its alleged claims to have attained a vantage superior to that of any religion's actual adherents. See, for example, Lesslie Newbigin, *The Gospel in a Pluralist Society* (Grand Rapids, MI: William B. Eerdmans, 1989), 9–10.

[35] See, e.g., Archbishop Anastasios (Yannoulatos), "Sharing the Good News in a Multi-Religious Country: Theological Reflections on Other Religions," delivered at Fordham

Orthodox and other inclusivists are left with options as to how to orient themselves. For some, the truths in other traditions can be seen as "rays of light" that happen periodically to fall on them, much as the sun shines indiscriminately on both the good and the bad. For others, there are elements of other faith traditions whose truth does not directly reflect recognizable elements of one's own tradition, and yet those elements genuinely enrich one's own tradition. The Indian Orthodox theologian Paulos Mar Gregorios, together with many Roman Catholics, speaks in this way of Hinduism.[36] There are countless examples of inclusivist Christians who see their faith as enriched through their experience of other traditions.

It would therefore be all too simple to equate anything short of religious pluralism with elitism, imperialism, exclusivism, tyranny, and the ignorance of the evident wisdom of other faiths. It would likewise be tempting to equate, for example, Pope Francis's openness, embrace, and even his expressed conviction that non-Christians can be saved, with pluralism, and therefore as a retreat from traditional Catholic teaching. These are two sides of the same coin: they both assume the identity between pluralism and open-mindedness, the identity of exclusivism and fundamentalism, and the identity of inclusivism and imperialism.

In this essay, as an Orthodox Christian and a citizen of the twenty-first-century West, I argued two points.

My first is that, rather than posit a taxonomy of exclusivist, inclusivist, and pluralist approaches that a Christian may adopt vis-à-vis other faiths, where exclusivism is all closed, pluralism is all open, and inclusivism is somewhere in between, it may be more helpful to identify two basic orientations:

a. One locates truth and salvation uniquely with Jesus Christ. We have in mind here the whole spectrum of exclusivist and inclusivist positions. Salvation, within this range, is or is not possible outside the church, but, in either case, it is Christ who saves. There is more or less interest in other faiths, more or less openness to their genuine truths and their holiness. But Jesus is Lord.

b. Within the other orientation, it is unwise, uncharitable, and logically or epistemologically inadmissible to locate truth and salvation uniquely with Christ or any other figure or deity.

These two orientations are indeed separated by a Rubicon.

My second point—to which I arrived through an Orthodox/Catholic critique of pluralism—is that *Nostra Aetate* represents a hugely important movement within

---

University, January 28, 2014, http://www.fordham.edu/downloads/file/2070/anastasios_lecture. See also George C. Papademetriou, "An Orthodox Christian View of Non-Christian Religions," http://www.goarch.org/ourfaith/ourfaith8089.

[36] See "The Challenge of Hinduism: What Can Christians Learn from It?" in *Christianity among World Religions*, ed. Küng et al., 38–45.

the exclusivist-inclusivist spectrum, but that a move into pluralism would have transformed *Nostra Aetate* into something foreign to the fundamental expressed teachings of the Roman Catholic Church. Its status as a text of the Second Vatican Council gives *Nostra Aetate* significant weight. But it also indicates the text's location within the heart of Roman Catholic teaching. Vatican II's role, like that of any great churchwide council, was to revitalize the church's teaching and life, embodying the principle that the church must be always renewing itself (*Ecclesia semper reformanda*). But that renewal is in the service of fidelity to the church's foundations, which would be incommensurate with the relativizing of Christ's identity.

Part IV

Jewish Perspectives

9

"Who Do You Say That I Am?"

Jewish Responses to Nostra Aetate *and Post-Holocaust Christianity*

Rabbi David Fox Sandmel

Though *Nostra Aetate* is but one of scores of Christian statements about Jews and Judaism that have been issued since the end of the Second World War,[1] for both Jews and Christians it has become emblematic of all post-Holocaust Christian reconsideration of Christianity's relationship to Jews and Judaism. *Nostra Aetate's* prominence is the result of several factors, among them the size of the Catholic Church, its antiquity, and the attention generally given to popes and Vatican documents. The Jewish community, in contrast, has produced only a few statements on its relationship to Christianity or other religious traditions. This lack does not mean that Jews have been silent about Christianity—indeed, Jews have had a lot to say about both it and Jesus[2]—but, for reasons that I will consider below, they have

---

In this chapter I focus on "Dabru Emet: A Jewish Statement on Christians and Christianity." I played a role in the production of that statement. When I joined the staff of the Institute for Christians & Jewish Studies (now the Institute for Islamic, Christian & Jewish Studies) as Jewish Scholar in 1998, managing the Jewish Scholar's Project was one of my responsibilities. I participated in the final editing sessions for "Dabru Emet," and came up with the title of the statement. I also look at a document written by Samuel Sandmel, my father. Although I have attempted to maintain scholarly distance and objectivity, I believe the reader should be aware of these connections.

[1] Many of these can be found on the Dialogika section of the website of the Council of Centers of Jewish-Christian Relations, http://www.ccjr.us/dialogika-resources. See also Franklin Sherman, *Bridges: Documents of the Christian-Jewish Dialogue* (New York: Paulist Press, 2011).

[2] Much of this scholarship has focused on Jesus or Paul. See, for example, Samuel Sandmel, *We Jews and Jesus* (New York: Oxford University Press, 1965); Matthew Hoffman, *From Rebel to Rabbi: Reclaiming Jesus and the Making of Modern Jewish Culture* (Palo Alto, CA: Stanford University Press, 2007); Daniel R. Langton, *The Apostle Paul in the Jewish Imagination: A Study of Modern Jewish-Christian Relations* (Cambridge: Cambridge University Press, 2007).

159

generally expressed themselves in scholarship and theology rather than in public pronouncements.

The web resource "Dialogika," a project of the Council of Centers for Christian-Jewish Relations, lists twenty-one items under the rubric "Jewish Documents and Statements."[3] Seven fit the definition of an individual Jew or group of Jews issuing a proclamation on the relationship between Judaism and Christianity. One of these, Jules Isaac's "The Rectification Necessary in Christian Teaching: Eighteen Points" (1947),[4] predates *Nostra Aetate*. It calls on Christians to reject what Isaac famously referred to as "the Teaching of Contempt." Refuting such long-standing attitudes is precisely what *Nostra Aetate* and other such documents did. All six Jewish statements written after it challenge Jews to reconsider Christianity in light of the changes it represents. None of the statements limits its response to the Roman Catholic Church; rather, they address Christians of any denominational identification wherever they have embraced a new attitude toward Jews and Judaism.

The best known of the six statements is "Dabru Emet: A Jewish Statement on Christians and Christianity," published in 2000.[5] When it was published, "Dabru Emet" caused a sensation, and it has since taken its place as a major "event" in the world of interfaith relations. The controversies and critiques it produced provide a window into the debate among Jews about Christianity. The other Jewish statements include:

- a proposed "declaration" from Samuel Sandmel's 1967 book, *We Jews and You Christians*;
- a document from the French rabbinate written in 1973 but published only in 2001;
- a 2011 statement from the Center for Jewish-Christian Understanding & Cooperation;
- a 2015 statement from representatives of the French Jewish community;
- a 2015 statement from a group of Orthodox rabbis.

That the last two appeared the same year as the *Nostra Aetate* jubilee is no coincidence.

None of these latter statements have had the impact or generated the kind reaction of "Dabru Emet," but, taken together, they can provide insight into how post-Holocaust Christian theology about Jews and Judaism has affected Jewish attitudes toward Christians and Christianity.

---

[3] See http://www.ccjr.us/dialogika-resources/documents-and-statements/jewish.

[4] See http://www.ccjr.us/dialogika-resources/documents-and-statements/jewish/1257-isaac1947.

[5] http://www.ccjr.us/dialogika-resources/documents-and-statements/jewish/319-dabru-emet. "Dabru Emet" means "speak truth" and comes from Zec 8:14.

Samuel Sandmel's "Proposed Declaration:
The Synagogue and the Christian People" (1967)

My father, Samuel Sandmel, was a scholar of Tanach/Old Testament and New Testament, as well as a pioneer in post-Holocaust Jewish-Christian relations.[6] He was a Reform rabbi and, for most of his career, professor of Bible and Hellenistic Literature at the Hebrew Union College-Jewish Institute of Religion in Cincinnati, Ohio. In 1956, he published *A Jewish Understanding of the New Testament* (1956), followed in 1965 with *We Jews and Jesus*. In 1967, after the promulgation of *Nostra Aetate*, *We Jews and You Christians: An Inquiry into Attitudes* appeared. The final chapter of this book is "A Proposed Declaration: The Synagogue and the Christian People." This was the first such Jewish effort to respond to *Nostra Aetate* of which I am aware.

Sandmel, speaking in the voice of the "The Synagogue," proposed that it "views the Christians as its offspring," who "spread the message of the Synagogue" to the world. It "laments" past hostility and welcomes Christian statements that repudiate "irreligious hatred."[7] Today's Christians are not responsible for the persecutions of the past. The synagogue anticipates a time of global spiritual unity, while it is also committed to its own self-perpetuation. It understands God's election of Israel in terms of obligation, not preference. The synagogue welcomes proselytes, and hopes that the church will "attain and maintain the spiritual heights [it has] often nobly expressed."[8] Many of the points Sandmel made appear in some or all of the subsequent statements to be examined. He recognized a relationship or kinship between Judaism and Christianity, acknowledged Christian efforts at reconciliation with the Jews, valued Christianity's role in disseminating Judaism's message, and awaited a shared messianic future.

There are also ideas not found in the other statements. My father felt very strongly that acknowledging and repudiating Jewish prejudices against Christians and Christianity was as incumbent upon Jews as the opposite was among Christians. This sentiment might strike some as odd, since the past persecution of Jews by Christians is a significant focus of much Jewish-Christian dialogue. However, referencing past Jewish hostility to Christianity suggests that he considered repudiation of past wrongs a sine qua non for authentic Jewish-Christian relations and dialogue. Although not willing to abandon the concept of election, he nonetheless wanted to assure Christians that Judaism rejects elitist interpretations of "chosenness." Elsewhere, he had written, "I do not regard Judaism as objectively superior to Christianity nor Christianity to Judaism. Rather Judaism is mine and I consider it good and I am at home in it and love it. That is how I want Christians to feel about their Christianity."[9]

---

[6] Samuel Sandmel, *A Jewish Understanding of the New Testament* (Cincinnati, OH: Hebrew Union College Press, 1956); idem, *We Jews and Jesus* (New York: Oxford University Press, 1965); idem, *We Jews and You Christians* (Philadelphia: J. B. Lippincott, 1967).

[7] Sandmel, *We Jews and You Christians*, 144–45.

[8] Ibid., 146.

[9] Sandmel, *We Jews and Jesus*, 151.

Missing from Sandmel's "Proposed Declaration" is any mention of Jesus or discussion of Christian faith. Indeed, other than acknowledging Christian efforts at reconciliation with the Jewish community, Sandmel's declaration says much more *to* "Christian people" than it says *about* them or their beliefs. *We Jews and You Christians* explores Jewish attitudes toward Christianity, and, while Sandmel attempts to explain differences between Judaism and Christianity in the body of the book, it may be that, in his declaration, he did not consider it proper to offer a Jewish evaluation of Christian beliefs. Second, Sandmel was keenly aware of the diversity within both Judaism and Christianity; perhaps he felt that this diversity could not be adequately represented in a brief statement. The very fact that this document is a "proposed declaration" suggests a hesitancy to speak on behalf of the "Synagogue"; perhaps the "proposal" should be understood as being offered for discussion.

Sandmel's statement is not well known, even among those active in Jewish-Christian dialogue; none of the authors of "Dabru Emet" was aware of its existence until that document was nearly finished, and the editor of *Dialogika* learned about it only from an earlier draft of this essay. Nonetheless, it is the first of such efforts, and it shares important similarities to subsequent statements.

A Committee of the Chief Rabbinate of France: "Christianity in Jewish Theology" (1973)

The second "statement" was completed in 1973 but not published until 2001. In 1968, the Catholic bishops of France asked the (Orthodox) Chief Rabbi of France for a description of Jewish views on Christianity. "Christianity in Jewish Theology" was then written on behalf of the French rabbinate by a committee composed of the noted philosopher Emmanuel Levinas (1906–1995), Georges Vajda (1908–1981), a well-respected Hebraist, Arabist, and scholar of Islam and Jewish thought, and Charles Touati (1925–2003), a scholar of rabbinic literature and head of the French rabbinate's doctrinal commission. The original intention was that the committee's work would become an official statement of the rabbinate. The committee proposed six points, each supported by citations from recognized and authoritative Jewish sources. One unique aspect of this document is that it speaks to both Islam and Christianity, and in its three final paragraphs addresses them together. The other documents under consideration address only Christianity.

The committee finished its work in 1973, but the rabbinate did not discuss the statement until 1978. The rabbis were unable to reach consensus, and the Chief Rabbi withdrew it from consideration. Since it was never officially approved, the statement must be regarded as a work in progress, rather than a finished piece. Indeed, compared to the others, in its current form it is terse and void of context. After "Dabru Emet" appeared in 2000, Touati, the only surviving member of the committee, recommended that the document be released; it appeared in the *Revue des Etudes Juives*, a French scholarly journal, in 2001. Two representatives of the French rabbinate, former Chief Rabbi Rene-Samuel Sirat and Chief Rabbi of Paris

David Messas, expressed their hesitations about the statement in a February 12, 2001, article in *Le Monde*. Messas emphasized that the document did not reflect the official views of the rabbinate. Sirat also intimated that, if the rabbis again addressed the issue, there would be new ideas.[10]

The main points of the statement are:

• The separation from Christianity could have been avoided.
• Christians are not idolaters; they adore the God who created the world, and they have a certain number of beliefs in common with the Jews.
• Christians can achieve eternal life.
• The people, Israel, should be inspired by Christians and Muslims.
• Christianity and Islam contributed to the improvement of humanity.
• Christianity and Islam clear the way for the Messiah.

"Christianity in Jewish Theology" includes two Talmudic texts describing an encounter between Joshua ben Perahya and his student, Jesus, that support the first point.[11] In these passages ben Perahya rejects Jesus and refuses to be reconciled. It seems unlikely, given their academic credentials, that the authors limited their interpretation of this text to the specific incident described. More likely, they are making the historical point that, had ben Perahya and, by extension, the Jews in general, behaved differently, Christianity either might not have emerged or might somehow have stayed within Judaism. The statement does mention Jesus, but it does so only in the context of these Talmudic passages. It neither analyzes who Jesus was nor assesses Christian claims about him. The major point, however, is that the French rabbis were promoting a more open and respectful approach to Christianity (and Islam) rather than absolute and uncompromising rejection.

Turning the above positive statements into negatives reveals the image that the committee was trying to counter: Christians are idolaters; they are beyond redemption; by definition they can be neither wise nor righteous; they bring only evil into the world; and they prevent the coming of the Messiah. This Jewish construction of Christians and Christianity, while extreme, can just as easily be supported with citations from rabbinic writings and still finds expression in some segments of the Jewish community.[12] The authors of this statement, however, want to affirm the spiritual and ethical value of Christianity and Islam and to acknowledge their role in the ultimate redemption of the world.

This statement makes no reference to *Nostra Aetate* or other Christian pronouncements, but, since the original impetus for its composition came from

---

[10] http://www.ccjr.us/dialogika-resources/documents-and-statements/jewish/765-fr-jewish-comm1973.

[11] Babylonian Talmud, *Sanhedrin* 107b and *Sota* 47a.

[12] See, for example, "Head of Extremist Jewish Group calls Christians 'Blood-sucking Vampires,'" *Times of Israel*, December 22, 2015, http://www.timesofisrael.com/head-of-extremist-jewish-group-calls-christians-blood-sucking-vampires.

the French bishops just three years after *Nostra Aetate*, the monumental shift in Christian thinking that the proclamation represents must have had an influence on the authors. Nevertheless, like Sandmel's statement, it has garnered little attention beyond a small circle of scholars and interfaith activists. We do not know what issues prevented the French rabbinate from approving the document; writing twenty-five years after the fact, Touati tersely described its discussion in 1978 as "very rough," leading to the document's being "withdrawn" and remaining "private."[13] Whatever may have underwritten their rationale, the rabbis' hesitation to proceed highlights the controversy that can be engendered in the Jewish community when speaking about Christianity.

The Jewish Scholars' Project, "Dabru Emet: A Jewish Statement on Christians and Christianity" (September 10, 2000)

Background

On September 10, 2000, "Dabru Emet: A Jewish Statement on Christians and Christianity," appeared as a full-page ad in the *New York Times* and the *Baltimore Sun*.[14] It was released with great fanfare and became an international media event, generating a significant amount of both popular and scholarly interest. It remains an important milestone in the development of contemporary Jewish-Christian relations and a unique document in Jewish literature.

"Dabru Emet" was written by four Jewish scholars working at North American universities—Tikva Frymer-Kensky, David Novak, Peter Ochs, and Michael Signer—and endorsed by over two hundred rabbis and Jewish scholars. It did not come from any organization within the Jewish community, neither the denominational movements nor communal organizations such as the Anti-Defamation League or the American Jewish Committee. The authors all worked in university settings where they regularly interacted with Christian colleagues, rather than in synagogal or communal settings. They were not constrained by institutional policy or communal politics. When they presented the statement for endorsement, they did so as individuals.[15] The statement sparked a flurry of debate in the American

---

[13] Charles Touati, "Le Christianisme dans la Théologie Juive (1968–1973)," in Jean Dujardin, *L'Église catholique et le peuple juif: Un autre regard* (Paris: Calmann-Lévy, 2003), Annexe XVII, 462 ("le débat fut très houleux et il fut décidé de retirer le dossier . . . [il] resta donc un document privé").

[14] The *New York Times* was chosen because of its prominence and reach, the *Baltimore Sun* because Baltimore is the location of what was then the Institute for Christian & Jewish Studies (ICJS), whose work generated "Dabru Emet." It is now the Institute for Christian, Islamic & Jewish Studies.

[15] At the same time that we were finalizing the statement, the four authors and I edited a collection of scholarly essays; see Tikva Frymer-Kensky, David Novak, Peter Ochs, Michael Signer, and David Fox Sandmel, eds., *Christianity in Jewish Terms* (Boulder, CO: Westview

Jewish community. It has been translated into French, German, Hebrew, Spanish, Italian, Polish, Russian, Portuguese, and Dutch. Symposia and conferences on it were held in Germany, the Netherlands, Poland, and Israel, some of which have produced volumes of essays. It continues to be referenced in theological writing today.[16]

"Dabru Emet" begins with a two-paragraph preamble. It acknowledges the changes in Christian theology since the Shoah as seen in *Nostra Aetate* and various official Protestant statements,[17] as well as in the work of individual theologians (such as Paul van Buren, Alice and Roy Eckhardt, Father John Pawlikowski, and Sister Mary Boys) whose writings "put them at odds with many of their colleagues and with the consensus of many people who were within their Church."[18] "Dabru Emet" proposes that, in light of these changes, Jews might begin to reassess their relationship to a Christianity that is no longer hostile. It then makes eight points, each of which is followed by a brief but essential explanatory paragraph:

- Jews and Christians worship the same God.
- Jews and Christians seek authority from the same book—the Bible (what Jews call "Tanakh" and Christians call the "Old Testament").
- Christians can respect the claim of the Jewish people upon the land of Israel.
- Jews and Christians accept the moral principles of Torah.
- Nazism was not a Christian phenomenon.
- The humanly irreconcilable difference between Jews and Christians will not be settled until God redeems the entire world as promised in scripture.
- A new relationship between Jews and Christians will not weaken Jewish practice.
- Jews and Christians must work together for justice and peace.[19]

Press, 2000). In addition, my colleagues at the ICJS and I edited a volume for congregational study groups, ideally including both Jews and Christians: David F. Sandmel, Rosann M. Catalano, and Christopher M. Leighton, eds., *Irreconcilable Differences? A Learning Resource for Jews and Christians* (Boulder, CO: Westview Press, 2001). The ICJS had hoped that it would be able to initiate dialogue groups around the country using the statement and the two books, but most of those plans were not realized. This was a disappointment for me and for the ICJS.

[16] Rabbi Abraham Skorka dedicated a significant part of his paper and the opening session of the recent meeting of the International Conference of Christian and Jews to "Dabru Emet."

[17] For example, the Episcopal Church (USA)'s "A Resolution of the 1964 General Convention: 'Deicide and the Jews,'" http://www.ccjr.us/dialogika-resources/documents-and-statements/protestant-churches/na/episcopalian/685-ecusa64oct, and the United Methodist Church's "Bridge in Hope: Jewish-Christian Dialogue" (1972), http://www.ccjr.us/dialogika-resources/documents-and-statements/protestant-churches/na/methodist/690-umc72apr.

[18] Michael A. Signer, "Some Reflections on Dabru Emet," http://www.jcrelations.net/Some+Reflections+on+Dabru+Emet.2222.0.html?L=3.

[19] One of the most helpful ways to read "Dabru Emet" comes from Michael Signer. Keeping in mind that the document was not intended to be definitive but rather to promote

As the authors had hoped, "Dabru Emet" provoked discussion among both Jews and Christians and between them.[20]

Origins: Scholars Groups and Statements

In 1995, the Institute for Christian & Jewish Studies in Baltimore announced the formation of the Jewish Scholars Group on Christianity, a body analogous to the Christian Scholars Group on Jews and Judaism, which had, in 1973, issued a statement called "A Statement to Our Fellow Christians."[21] Subsequently, about twenty-five Jewish scholars from various academic disciplines and locations within the Jewish community met several times a year to discuss the relationship between Judaism and Christianity and how, as Jewish scholars, they should relate to Christianity.

There were two broad perspectives within the group of scholars. One held that Christianity was important only as an object of research. *Nostra Aetate* and similar statements were positive developments, these individuals maintained, but they affected only a select group within a few specific churches. The vast majority of churches continued to be hostile to Jews and Judaism, or actively sought to convert Jews. Michael Signer described the second group, to which he himself belonged, as committed Jews no longer threatened by a hostile Christianity, who were able to see Christianity not only "as a series of texts" but also "as a coherent body of practices and doctrines that transformed the lives of its believers into human beings who shared a vision of the future of humankind with us as Jews."[22] Those who shared Signer's perspective sensed that some in the Christian world were beginning to wonder when—or whether—a Jewish response to Christian initiatives like *Nostra Aetate* would be forthcoming. At the group's first meeting, philosopher and theologian Michael Wyschogrod recommended precisely that kind of theological reevaluation of Christianity. This endeavor soon became the group's focus; those who were not committed to it dropped out. Wyschogrod himself later withdrew in "principled disagreement" with the statement's final content.

---

discussion and dialogue, he suggested that each of the bolded statements that make it up be read as questions. So, where "Dabru Emet" says that Jews and Christians worship the same God, one should ask: Do Jews and Christians worship the same God, or what does it mean to say that Jews and Christians worship the same God? What does it mean to say that Jews and Christians seek authority from the same book? Is it really the same book, especially if both traditions interpret it so differently? Reading the statement this way is an invitation to dig deeper in order to learn both what Judaism and Christianity hold in common and what are the irreconcilable differences that define the uniqueness of each tradition.

[20] Some compared "Dabru Emet" to *Nostra Aetate*. See note 35. The latter, however, is an authoritative document of the Roman Catholic Church, whereas "Dabru Emet" has no institutional authority; it speaks only for its authors and those who signed it.

[21] Full text is available at http://www.ccjr.us/dialogika-resources/documents-and-statements/ecumenical-christian/947-csg1973.

[22] Signer, "Some Reflections on Dabru Emet."

"Dabru Emet" was published initially over the names of about 170 rabbis and Jewish academics, mostly American. In the weeks after its appearance, a number of additional names were added. Among the signers were leaders of the Reform, Conservative, and Reconstructionist movements, as well as a smaller number of Orthodox rabbis and scholars. At that time, the Orthodox community had not embraced Jewish-Christian relations to the same extent as the other, more liberal movements.[23] As we will see below, that situation is changing.

Response to "Dabru Emet"

The release of "Dabru Emet" generated a brief frenzy of media attention. The initial reports in newspapers and other media sources were overwhelmingly positive, and major church bodies welcomed the statement.[24] The general positive reception of "Dabru Emet" contrasted sharply with the reaction to *Dominus Iesus*, released the same week by the Vatican's Congregation for the Doctrine of the Faith (then under the leadership of Cardinal Joseph Ratzinger, later Pope Benedict XVI).[25] *Dominus Iesus* addresses the church's relation to other religious communities, Christian and non-Christian. The description of non-Catholic Christianity and other religions as "gravely deficient" regarding their access to the full "means of salvation,"[26] among

---

[23] This attitude can, in part, be traced to the thinking of Rabbi Joseph Soloveitchik, who cautioned about engagement in theological dialogue with Christians; see his essay "Confrontation," *Tradition: A Journal of Orthodox Thought* 6, no. 2 (1964): 5–29. See also a reconsideration of his views: Soloveitchik's "Confrontation"—Forty Years Later, a symposium held at Boston College, November 23, 2003, https://www.bc.edu/content/dam/files/ research_sites/cjl/texts/center/conferences/soloveitchik/index.html.

[24] This welcome can be seen from a selection of headlines, such as Laurie Goodstein, "Leading Jewish Scholars Extend a Hand to Christians," *New York Times*, September 8, 2000, A14. The same article appeared in the *Cleveland Plain Dealer,* September 8, 2000, A1, as "Jews Urge Détente with Christianity," and the *International Herald Tribune* as "Jewish Group Urges a Nod toward Christianity." See also Religion News Service (September 8, 2000), http://religionnews.com/2000/09/08/news-story-jewish-leaders-affirm-common-roots-with-christians-in-historic-s/, "Jewish Leaders Affirm Common Roots with Christians in Historic Statement." Others spoke about a "gesture of good will" (*Portland Oregonian,* September 16, 2000, B08) or a "rare praise of Christianity" (*Fort Lauderdale Sun-Sentinel,* September 9, 2000, 1A).

[25] *U.S. News and World Report* 129, no. 11 (September 18, 2000), 74, wrote, "Pull back or reach out: interfaith statements seem to differ markedly." Caryle Murphy wrote in the *Washington Post* (September 9, 2000), B09: "Interfaith dialogue encountered a chilly wind and an earnest caress this week with the release of two strikingly different documents on the delicate matter of how believers in one religion should regard those of other faiths."

[26] Congregation for the Doctrine of the Faith, *Declaration—Dominus Iesus: On the Unicity and Salvific Universality of Jesus Christ and the Church* (Vatican City, 2000), sec. 22, http://www.vatican.va/roman_curia/congregations/cfaith/documents/rc_con_cfaith_doc_20000806_dominus-iesus_en.html.

other aspects of *Dominus Iesus*, elicited extensive criticism, especially from non-Catholic Christians.[27] This controversy drew added media attention to "Dabru Emet."

Several official Christian bodies responded to "Dabru Emet." The National Conference of Catholic Bishops[28] issued a statement of appreciation, as did the Committee on Christian Unity of the American Baptist Churches,[29] the Interfaith Relations Commission of the National Council of Churches in Christ in the USA,[30] the European Lutheran Commission on the Church and the Jewish People,[31] and the Consultative Panel on Lutheran Jewish Relations of the Evangelical Lutheran Church of America.[32] Cardinal Walter Kasper, then President of the Pontifical Commission for Religious Relations with the Jews, praised it in his keynote address to the 2001 International Conference of Christians and Jews.[33]

Many in the Jewish community welcomed "Dabru Emet." Edward Kessler, a leading British proponent of interreligious relations, compared its impact to that of *Nostra Aetate*.[34] Stanislaw Krajewski, a Polish Jewish leader, immediately translated it into Polish and had it published because he was "delighted" and "thrilled" that "Dabru Emet" expressed his own approach to Jewish-Christian relations.[35] There was also criticism, some of it quite sharp. Some who applauded the intention of "Dabru Emet" nonetheless took issue with one point or another.[36] Rabbi David

---

[27] See, for example, Edmund Doogue and Stephen Brown, "Dominus Iesus a 'Public Relations Disaster' for Ecumenism Say Critics," *Christianity Today*, September 1, 2000, http://www.christianitytoday.com/ct/2000/septemberweb-only/34.0a.html.

[28] "Catholic Leaders Express Appreciation for '*Dabru Emet*,' a Jewish Statement on Christians and Christianity," http://www.jcrelations.net/The_Power_of_Words__A_Catholic_Response_to__Dabru_Emet.2401.0.html?id=720&L=0&searchText=dabru+emet&searchFilter=%2A.

[29] "An American Baptist Response to 'Dabru Emet,'" http://www.ccjr.us/dialogika-resources/documents-and-statements/protestant-churches/na/baptist/712-abc2002june.

[30] "An Ecumenical Response to 'Dabru Emet,'" http://www.ccjr.us/dialogika-resources/documents-and-statements/ecumenical-christian/716-nccc01feb24?highlight=WyJkYWJydSIsImVtZXQiLCJkYWJydSBlbWV0Il0=.

[31] "A Response to Dabru Emet," http://www.ccjr.us/dialogika-resources/documents-and-statements/protestant-churches/eur/711-lekkj03may12?highlight=WyJkYWJydSIsImVtZXQiLCJkYWJydSBlbWV0Il0=.

[32] "Lutheran-Jewish Panel Welcomes 'Dabru Emet,'" http://archive.wfn.org/2000/11/msg00147.html.

[33] "Spiritual and Ethical Commitment in Jewish-Christian Dialogue," http://www.jcrelations.net/Spiritual_and_Ethical_Commitment_in_Jewish-Christian_Dialogue.2333.0.html?id=720&L=0&searchText=dabru+emet&searchFilter=%2A&page=2.

[34] Edward Kessler, "Understanding Christianity Today—Jewish Perspectives: *Dabru Emet: A Jewish Statement on Christianity*," *Reviews in Religion & Theology* 9, no. 5 (November 2002): 479–87.

[35] Stanislaw Krajewski, "*Dabru Emet* in Poland: A Personal Account" (January 6, 2003), http://www.jcrelations.net/i_Dabru_Emet__i__in_Poland_____A_Personal_Account.2743.0.html?searchText=Israel&L=&page=7.

[36] See, for instance, David Rosen, "*Dabru Emet*: Its Significance for Jewish-Christian

Berger, a scholar of Jewish-Christian relations, was asked by the Rabbinical Council of America (a major Orthodox institution) to evaluate the document. He wrote a brief response that became that organization's official policy. Berger praised the document's "exquisitely skillful formulation," including the paragraph on Nazism, but was concerned about the "theological reciprocity" implicit in the desire to respond to Christian "reassessments of Judaism." He also thought that "Dabru Emet" needed a stronger, explicit rejection of the worship of Jesus by Jews as *avodah zarah* (foreign worship).[37] Finally, he cautioned against the relativism implied in the statement that neither community should insist "that it has interpreted Scripture more accurately than the other."[38]

Berger touched on some of the primary points of contention in "Dabru Emet." The first is the statement that Nazism was not a Christian phenomenon, a claim with which he agreed. Many others did not. The Holocaust was and remains a very sensitive subject in the Jewish community, and this statement outraged some. Rabbi A. James Rudin, for many years the National Director of Interreligious Affairs for the American Jewish Committee, refused to sign because of the "inadequate and surprisingly diffident description" of Christianity's role in the "rise of genocidal Nazism."[39] Equally controversial was the statement that "Jews and Christians worship the same God." While agreeing with that basic premise, Berger was troubled that "Dabru Emet" did not explicitly reject the association of Jesus with

---

Dialogue," Address delivered at the twentieth anniversary celebration of the Dutch Council of Christians and Jews (OJEC) at Tilburg, the Netherlands, November 6, 2001, https://www.bc.edu/content/dam/files/research_sites/cjl/texts/cjrelations/resources/articles/rosen.htm.

[37] In the Talmud, Gentile worship is classed either as *avodah zarah,* literally "foreign worship," whose object, ultimately, is God or as a*vodat elilim,* "idolatry," whose object is something other than God. Medieval Jewish authorities differed over Christian worship, a question that had practical as well as theological ramifications, since Jewish law prohibits certain kinds of interactions with idolaters. The doctrine of the Trinity, which many Jewish authorities considered polytheism, and the prevalence of images and icons in Christian architecture and worship, influenced Jewish opinion. Other authorities, such as Menachem ha-Meiri (1249–c.1310), ruled that Christian worship was *avodah zarah.* In the eyes of these rabbis, both Christians and Muslims accept the seven Noahide Laws, including the prohibition of idolatry. Nonetheless, while they may be monotheists, their worship, which for Christians includes the invocation of Jesus, is forbidden to Jews. See David Novak, *Jewish-Christian Dialogue: A Jewish Justification* (New York: Oxford University Press, 1989), 53–56. Berger agrees with the designation of *avodah zarah,* but thinks that "Dabru Emet" does not clearly state that Judaism cannot affirm the religious validity of Christian beliefs about Jesus.

[38] "Statement by Dr. David Berger regarding the *New York Times* ad by Dabru Emet," September 14, 2000, http://advocacy.ou.org/2000/statement_by_dr_david_berger_regarding_the_new_york_times_ad_by_dabru_emet/.

[39] A. James Rudin, "'Dabru Emet': A Jewish Dissent," http://www.jcrelations.net/Dabru_Emet_A_Jewish_Dissent.2349.0.html?L=5.

God, a position that, he points out, violates the rabbinic prohibition of *shituf,* the association of anything other than God with God. Berger was also concerned with relativism, a point he made twice. Though recognizing that the comment about neither community insisting that it possesses a more accurate interpretation of scripture was intended to ward off proselytizing, he was concerned that it would be taken as an affirmation that both Jewish and Christian interpretations are "valid." In this case, Berger's criticism was not with the overall substance of the "Dabru Emet," but with deficiencies in its "exquisitely skillful formulation."

Other Jewish scholars raised additional difficulties. Amy-Jill Levine, a leading Jewish scholar of the New Testament, found the suggestion that "Jews and Christians seek authority from the same book" problematic. The Christian Bible, she countered, contains the New as well as the Old Testament, the former of which is not scriptural for Jews. She also questioned whether the Old Testament and the Tanach are really the same book.[40]

Jon Levenson, a well-known biblical scholar at Harvard Divinity School, leveled the harshest critique. Levenson was originally part of the Jewish Scholars Group, but he declined to sign "Dabru Emet." After analyzing it statement by statement, he found it lacking on every count. The central flaw, he claimed, was that "Dabru Emet suffers from one of the great pitfalls of interfaith dialogue": it "avoid[s] any candid discussion of fundamental beliefs" and "adopt[s] instead the model of conflict resolution or diplomatic negotiation. . . . Commonalities are stressed, and differences . . . denied altogether," while "critical judgments" that define each tradition are subsumed in order to reach "agreement." Levenson pointed to the rising rate of interfaith marriage and its "striking acceptance . . . on the part of many Jewish organizations." Given the commonalities articulated in "Dabru Emet," he asks, why should Jews resist either intermarriage or conversion to Christianity? He concludes:

> None of this need deter anyone from "speaking the truth" about the relationship of Jews and Christians as he sees it. But for the authors and signatories of *Dabru Emet* to assert that their version of this truth poses no hazards to Jewish practice and identity is not just wishful thinking; it is whistling in the dark.[41]

---

[40] "A Slight Judeo-Christian Warming Trend," *New York Times,* October 1, 2000, http://www.nytimes.com/2000/10/01/weekinreview/01GOOD.html. Note here the language of "Dabru Emet": "Jews and Christians seek authority from the same book." This is one of the areas where the religious difference between the authors surfaces. Given the spectrum of Jewish belief that they represented, finding a way of expressing the relationship between Jews and their scripture on which all four could agree was challenging and provoked lengthy discussion and debate. The phrase "seek authority" skirts the questions of divine authorship, inerrancy, and the like.

[41] Jon D. Levenson, "How Not to Conduct Jewish-Christian Dialogue," *Commentary* 112, no. 5 (December 1, 2001): 33, 37, available at http://www.commentarymagazine.com/article/how-not-to-conduct-jewish-christian-dialogue/.

Levenson's article stimulated vigorous debate in the pages of *Commentary* magazine.[42] Michael Wyschogrod agreed with him that "Dabru Emet" does not address crucial theological differences—most intractably, the divinity of Jesus and Christianity's abrogation of Mosaic Law. "Its authors would argue," Wyschogrod supposed, "that they wished to focus on what unites us rather than on what divides us. But if the document's aim is to show how Jews evaluate Christianity, omission of the difficulties Mr. Levenson enumerates is fatal."[43] The authors responded that Levenson had fundamentally misunderstood the statement's nature. "Dabru Emet," they explained, is not a scholarly or theological document but "a political statement, offered to arouse attention and to provide the minimal common ground needed for any serious discussion." They found it "bizarre" that a "serious scholar" would "base his criticisms on such a statement alone," while totally ignoring *Christianity in Jewish Terms*, since that book answers most of Levenson's specific criticisms directly.[44]

Evaluation

Although "Dabru Emet" raises substantial theological questions, I think that some of the negative reaction to it turns on this question of trust.[45] Are the changes in the Christian world upon which the statement is premised sufficient, and, perhaps more importantly, has the face of Christianity changed to an extent that warrants what the document proposes? In historical terms, the new era of Jewish-Christian relations is in its infancy. Furthermore, even those most enthusiastic about it would admit that official pronouncements do not immediately lead to the complete elimination of anti-Jewish thinking or attitudes; celebrating this new era might be premature. Since no one can claim to speak for the Jewish community, making pronouncements that are perceived as "letting down" the community's guard against what has been a perennial threat understandably provokes strong reaction

---

[42] "Jewish-Christian Dialogue: An Exchange between Jon D. Levenson and Critics on His December 2001 Piece, 'How Not to Conduct Jewish-Christian Dialogue,'" *Commentary* 113, no. 4 (April 1, 2002): 8–21, available at http://www.commentarymagazine.com/article/jewish-christian-dialogue/.

[43] Ibid., 16.

[44] Ibid., 8.

[45] In this vein, Hanspeter Heinz, a German Catholic theologian, has written about the novelty of "Dabru Emet," which he considers a "courageous" document. After a brief survey of the ups and downs of institutional relations between the Catholic Church and the Jewish community, he states: "The irritation, which often goes deep, even to the point of breaking off the conversation, is an indication of how unstable the relationship of trust towards the churches still is. In current crises, the question of trust is often expressed: Has the Church really done an about-face since the Shoah, or isn't the truth that everything is still as it always was?" Hanspeter Heinz, "*Dabru Emet*: A German Perspective: Results of a Research Period in the USA," http://www.jcrelations.net/Dabru_Emet__A_German_Perspective__Results_of_a_Research_Period_in_the_USA.2720.0.html?L=2.

from other Jews who are yet to be convinced that the changes in Christianity are permanent or sincere.

For Peter Ochs trust and confidence are central. He sees "Dabru Emet" as the expression of "a renewed Judaism that is recovering its confidence and sense of purpose after the devastations of the Holocaust." Jews must respond to Christianity as it is today, and therefore need to understand, not avoid, it: "We have learned from the horrors of the past century that secular humanism is an insufficient bulwark against Western tendencies toward nihilism and totalitarianism. . . . We need to locate friends within the Christian world who will help us protect the next generations from such influences. 'Dabru Emet' is an invitation to these Christians to join us."[46]

Underlying "Dabru Emet," then, is the belief that it is no longer Christianity that threatens the existence of the Jewish people. The differences between Christians and Jews, treated respectfully, need not be a source of enmity or conflict. And what Jews and Christians share—scripture, moral values, a vision of the future—make it possible for Jews and Christian to work together against common challenges and for common goals. In this regard, if *Nostra Aetate* represents an invitation from the Christian world to a new relationship with the Jewish people, "Dabru Emet" accepts that invitation and challenges the rest of the Jewish community to do so as well.

Center for Jewish-Christian Understanding and Cooperation: "A Jewish Understanding of Christians and Christianity" (2011)

In 2008, Rabbi Shlomo Riskin, an American-born Israeli rabbi, founded the Center for Jewish-Christian Understanding and Cooperation, located in Efrat, south of Jerusalem.[47] It has described itself as "the first Orthodox Jewish entity to engage in dialogue with the Christian world."[48] The center runs programs for tour groups and conducts seminars through its Institute for Theological Inquiry. CJCUC has strong ties with conservative Catholics and the Evangelical community, including Christian Zionists. In 2011, the center published "A Jewish Understanding of Christians and Christianity," written by Riskin, Rabbi Eugene Korn, the center's academic director, and David Nekrutman, its executive director. In an introduction, Riskin writes,

> This statement only represents the view of our center but should also be used as a catalyst for other orthodox Jews and Jewry worldwide to consider fostering relationships with Christian communities. Leaders within the

---

[46] "Jewish-Christian Dialogue: An Exchange," 8.

[47] See http://cjcuc.com/site/.

[48] http://www.ccjr.us/dialogika-resources/documents-and-statements/jewish/950-cjcuc2011may24.

Catholic and mainline Protestant churches as well as the non-denominational movements of Evangelical Christianity have become sincere friends of the Jewish people and the State of Israel. It is vital that we strengthen our relationship with them. We are certain that through these relational dialogues we will find far more which unites us than divides us.[49]

The document makes the following points:

- Christians have repudiated replacement theology and affirm the Jews' ongoing role in God's plan.
- Christians see themselves as grafted into the Abrahamic covenant and as spiritual partners with the Jewish covenant, while recognizing the Jews' "unique covenantal relationship."
- In light of these changes, Jews need not fear "a sympathetic understanding of Christianity" and should "work together" with Christians for "universal morality, peace and redemption under God."
- Christianity, by spreading monotheism, is helping fulfill "the main vocation of Abraham."
- Jews and Christians must respect "each other's theological beliefs and eschatological convictions."
- "Christians respect the right of all Jewish peoples to exist as Jews with complete self-determination—free from any attempts of conversion to Christianity."
- "Judaism must respect Christian faithfulness to their revelation, value their role in divine history, and acknowledge that Christians have entered a relationship with the God of Israel."
- A partnership between Jews and Christians after 2,000 years of enmity would be a powerful witness to God's presence in human history.

Many of these points can be found in previous documents, and some of the same classical rabbinic sources cited by the French rabbis appear here as well.[50] What stands out is the call for Jews to recognize that Christians are in "relationship" with God, and that they have a "system of commandments," a "revelation," and a "role in divine history." Although affirming that Christians are in covenant with God, the document does not mention Jesus, though the reference to "revelation" is tantalizing.

Two other phrases bear closer examination. The term "grafted in," while not exclusive to Evangelical discourse, is more prevalent there than in other segments

---

[49] "CJCUC's Statement on a Jewish Understanding of Christians and Christianity," http://cjcuc.com/site/2011/05/24/cjcuc-statement-on-a-jewish-understanding-of-christians-and-christianity/.

[50] Despite the similarity between the two Orthodox statements, Rabbi Korn informed me in an email that, at the time of the writing of the CJCUC statement, he was unaware of the effort of the French rabbinate.

of the Christian community. Additionally, though neither the state nor the land of Israel is mentioned, it is difficult to imagine "self-determination" in anything but political terms. Given the profile of the center, neither of these emphases is surprising. The statement has not generated discussion or response in either interfaith circles or among the broader public.

"Declaration for the Upcoming Jubilee of Brotherhood: A New Jewish View of Jewish-Christian Relations"

On November 23, 2015, at a festive public event at the Collège des Bernardins in Paris, the Chief Rabbi of France, Haim Korsia, presented a "Declaration for the Upcoming Jubilee of Brotherhood: A New Jewish View of Jewish-Christian Relations"[51] to Cardinal André Vingt-Trois, the Archbishop of Paris, and Pastor François Clavairoly, President of the Fédération Protestante de France. The statement was written by Jean-François Bensahel, Rabbi Philippe Haddad, Rabbi Rivon Krygier, Raphy Marciano, and Franklin Rausky, each of whom is a respected leader in the French Jewish community, and was endorsed by forty additional leaders, representing both Orthodox and liberal sectors of the community. The declaration begins by noting that *Nostra Aetate* opened an era of Jewish-Christian reconciliation. This fiftieth anniversary should be seen "as a sacred calling, as a pivotal moment, as a challenge and a commitment." The authors then ask, "*What have we Jews learned from you Christians during these last 50 years?*"[52] They answer that the church has undergone a massive, positive transformation in its attitudes toward Jews. It has rediscovered the Jewishness of Jesus and his earliest followers, and rejected the charge of deicide. It considers anti-Judaism a sin and has recognized the State of Israel. This change is "a reversal . . . of exemplary character for all religions and spiritual beliefs on the planet."[53]

They then ask: "*What can we, the Jews, hope to build with you Christians in the next 50 years?*" Once again, the answer affirms a trust in Jewish-Christian relations. "Jews should welcome Christianity as the religion of our brothers and sisters in synergy with Judaism." Both should recognize the common goal of "the universal brotherhood of humanity gathered around the One and Only God." Although each tradition is unique, "many Christian teachings are in perfect agreement with those of rabbinic tradition."[54] This statement is cautious, as can be seen in the choice of the word "synergy," a thoroughly modern term with no obvious theological implica-

---

[51] The French original can be found at http://www.ajcf.fr/Le-23-novembre-2015-au-College-des.html. An English translation can be found at http://www.ccjr.us/dialogika-resources/documents-and-statements/jewish/1356-declaration-for-the-upcoming-jubilee-of-brotherhood.

[52] Emphasis in the original.

[53] "Declaration for the Upcoming Jubilee of Brotherhood."

[54] Ibid., emphasis in the original.

tions. It celebrates the changes in the Christian world and focuses on commonalities, including the obligation to work together for the good of humanity, but says nothing about what Christians believe or what Christianity might mean for Jews.

"To Do the Will of Our Father in Heaven: Toward a Partnership between Jews and Christians"

Ten days after the Paris event, an international group of twenty-five Orthodox rabbis published "To Do the Will of Our Father in Heaven: Toward a Partnership between Jews and Christians."[55] Since then, another thirty rabbis have signed on. The statement is posted on the website of the Center for Christian Jewish Understanding and Cooperation. Though Rabbi Shlomo Riskin signed the statement, and Rabbi Eugene Korn is its primary author, the statement is not an official document of the center.[56]

The document's premise is that, after 2,000 years, Christianity has changed, and, as a result, Jews should "accept the hand offered to us by our Christian brothers and sisters."

It supports this contention with seven points:

- The Shoah was the result of the failure to overcome "mutual contempt and engage in constructive dialogue."
- Noting *Nostra Aetate*, the document acknowledges "the Church's affirmation of Israel's unique place in sacred history" and affirms that Jews have experienced "sincere love and respect from many Christians," especially in dialogue settings.
- "Christianity is neither an accident nor an error, but the willed divine outcome and gift to the nations," a statement that invokes rabbinic sources, both medieval and modern, notably Maimonides and Yehudah ha-Levi. Jews "can acknowledge the ongoing constructive validity of Christianity as our partner in world redemption, without any fear that this will be exploited for missionary purposes."
- Jews and Christians share a common covenantal mission to perfect the world, but first Jews and Christians must overcome their fears and establish trust.
- Jews and Christians have more in common than what divides them.
- Despite the difference, "We believe that G-d employs many messengers to reveal His truth."
- Jews and Christians will remain dedicated to the Covenant by playing an active role together in redeeming the world.

---

[55] "Orthodox Rabbinic Statement on Christianity," http://cjcuc.com/site/2015/12/03/orthodox-rabbinic-statement-on-christianity/. French and Korean versions are also available on the site.

[56] Dr. Korn confirmed this identification in an email.

Though the statement was prepared by Orthodox rabbis, it is important to note that most, if not all, of the fifty or so rabbis who have endorsed the document are identified with the progressive or liberal segment of the modern Orthodox world; in other words, the authors represent a subset of a subset of the diverse world of Orthodox Judaism. This statement makes bold assertions, including that Christianity is the "willed divine outcome" that shares "a covenantal mission" with Judaism. The implication of "many messengers" remained unexplored: Is this a reference to Jesus or Christians in general? I think it is fair to say that many Orthodox scholars and authorities, and perhaps other non-Orthodox Jews as well, will reject these claims as unsupportable by the tradition and, more specifically, as well the interpretation of Maimonides and ha-Levi that the authors cite.[57]

Conclusions:
What Do These Statements Tell Us and
Why Are There So Few of Them?

All six of the statements examined above are predicated on the belief that Christian teachings about Jews and Judaism have changed for the better, as represented primarily by *Nostra Aetate*, but also by efforts within some Protestant churches.[58] Though the French rabbis' document made no reference to any contemporary events, it was formulated after *Nostra Aetate* and at the request of the French bishops. Furthermore, all of them contend that, in light of these changes, Jews can and should approach Christians and Christianity without the trepidation of the past. All either explicitly or implicitly draw on rabbinic tradition going back to the

---

[57] See David Berger, "Vatican II at 50: Assessing the Impact of '*Nostra Aetate*' on Jewish Christian Relations," http://www.tabletmag.com/jewish-life-and-religion/195761/vatican-ii-at-50. A number of significant Orthodox institutions released a joint statement that became available only in February 2017, too late to be considered in this essay. This new document, according to one of its authors, was written both to present an Orthodox appreciation of *Nostra Aetate* and the changes it represents, and to provide a statement that avoids the aforementioned problematic assertions. It can be found at: http://www.ccjr.us/dialogika-resources/documents-and-statements/jewish/1421-cer-rca-2016.

[58] The Orthodox Christian community has not engaged in Jewish-Christian dialogue to the same extent as either the Catholics or the Protestants, though there have been periods of "academic consultations" since the 1970s, the most recent one in Thessaloniki, Greece, in 2013. Ecumenical Patriarch Bartholomew has addressed the Jewish community on several occasions. For example, in 2009, he addressed a group of Jewish leaders at the Park East Synagogue in New York, highlighting the shared scriptural heritage and common challenges of the environment and rising fundamentalism, but avoiding theological issues. Also of interest is "The final declaration by the Christian Roundtable of Eastern Orthodox priests and cultural representatives from Greece, Georgia, Italy, Russia, and Ukraine visiting Jerusalem, April 20–24, 2007." See http://www.ccjr.us/dialogika-resources/documents-and-statements/e-orthodox.

Middle Ages that assigns Christianity (and, for the French rabbis, Islam) a role in the ultimate redemption of the world. Three of the six statements recognize that Christians are not idolaters and that they worship the same God as the Jews (even if their form of worship is inappropriate for Jews).

The common denominators in these statements are the recognition of changes in Catholic and other Christian theologies, as well as their repudiating the enmity and violence of the past, including the Shoah, and their affirming Judaism as a vital religion. Jews, according to this consensus, should approach Christianity similarly. Finally, Christians and Jews share certain texts, beliefs, and moral values, though there are what "Dabru Emet" calls "irreconcilable differences" that define each community's uniqueness. The CJCUC statement and the Orthodox rabbis' statement both make bold assertions about the theological significance of Christianity.

Barely present in any of the statements is Jesus. Neither Sandmel nor the CJCUC refer to him at all. The other four statements contain his name, but none attempts to engage from a Jewish perspective what Christians hold most sacred. While Jews, it seems, can acknowledge that Christians are monotheists and value the Tanach/Old Testament, they deny (or are agnostic about) what Christians hold most sacred. In the kind of statements under consideration here, it would be difficult for Jews to evaluate Christian claims about Jesus that did not, by necessity, involve a critique or rejection of what lies at the core of Christian faith: Jesus, the son of God, is the risen Christ foretold by the prophets of Israel. This would be self-defeating in a statement intended to move beyond a contentious past and promote better relationships.

This observation leads to some reflection on the very nature of statements, which are, by definition, brief.[59] None of those under consideration here exceeds 1,200 words. This brevity precludes depth and nuance, and therefore also makes it difficult to discuss complex or potentially divisive issues adequately, though, as we have seen with "Dabru Emet," divisiveness seems hard to avoid. In this regard, it is worth remembering that Sandmel's statement is the final chapter of a much larger book, or, more accurately, a trilogy. Similarly, the authors of "Dabru Emet" insisted that their statement also be accompanied by books.

A second problem with Jewish "statements" is the matter of authority. For whom do these documents speak? Sandmel's "declaration" is "proposed," while "Dabru Emet" and the CJCUC speak "only" for themselves. The sole document that might have been issued with some institutional authority is the French statement—but the members of that very institution rejected it. Although the Catholic Church and some Protestant denominations have issued authoritative documents, Jews, by and large have not. Jews have produced an extensive literature on Christians and Christianity, but they have done so as individuals. This phenomenon may be frustrating for Christians looking for parallels to their own statements, and may

---

[59] See also Danny Burkeman, "Why Are There So Few Jewish Statements on Christianity or Jewish-Christian Relations?" *European Judaism: A Journal for the New Europe* 37, no. 1 (Spring 2004): 111–23.

explain why "Dabru Emet," despite its own modesty about whom it represents, achieved prominence and has had more authority ascribed to it than it claims for itself. The Jewish statements propose the broad parameters for the contemporary Jewish consideration of Christianity; those who want more will find much to contemplate in the works of individual scholars but must remember that nobody speaks for "the Jews."

In the final analysis, these statements demonstrate that a broad spectrum of Jewish communal leaders and scholars has paid attention to *Nostra Aetate* and similar Christian efforts. This segment—if not all Jews everywhere—is confident that those changes are both real and permanent. Jews who have assumed this perspective can now approach those Christians who speak in that manner as partners rather than adversaries. *Nostra Aetate* has been described as "sea change" in Christian relations to Jews and Judaism; these Jewish statements represent the resulting "sea change" among Jews.

10

LOT'S WIFE

On The Dangers of Looking Back

Rabbi Shira L. Lander

On October 28, 1965, the United States was at war in Vietnam. That week's cover of *Time* magazine pictured American helicopters dropping off US Marines during action in the Pacific arena.[1] The front page of the *New York Times* featured gun-wielding troops abroad and protesting students stateside.[2] Across the Atlantic, in the bustling, ancient city of Rome, a church council had been meeting at the Vatican since 1962. In four sessions originally convened by Pope John XXIII and presided over by Pope Paul VI after his election in June 1963, over two thousand bishops and thousands of observers, members of religious orders, scholars, laymen, and laywomen met to craft Catholic responses to a rapidly changing world. Sixty-three official non-Catholic observers, and numerous unofficial members of religious orders, scholars, laymen, and laywomen served as consultants.[3] The council introduced vast reforms within the Catholic Church: prayer in the vernacular, priests facing the congregation, women taking on new public roles, and the embrace of modern methods of biblical interpretation.

Of greatest interest to Jews is the document known by the opening words of its Latin text, *Nostra Aetate* ("In Our Time"), which reconsiders the relation of

---

A portion of this essay appeared in Shira L. Lander, "Jewish Identity," in *Toward the Future: Essays on Catholic-Jewish Relations in Memory of Rabbi León Klenicki*, ed. Celia Deutsch, Eugene J. Fisher, and James Rudin (Mahwah, NJ: Paulist Press, 2013), 55–68.

[1] *Time* 8, no. 17 (October 22, 1965), cover drawing by Henry Koerner, http://content. time.com/time/covers/0,16641,19651022,00.html.

[2] See the photograph accompanying Charles Mohr, "Siege at Pleime: Americans Marvel at Tough Foe," *New York Times*, October 28, 1965, 1, Associated Press Radtopphoto, and Will Lissner, "Students Clash on Saigon Policy after Manhattan College Rally," ibid., http://proxy.libraries.smu.edu/login?url=http://search.proquest.com.proxy.libraries.smu. edu/docview/117015348?accountid=6667.

[3] "Vatican II: 50 Years Ago Today," https://vaticaniiat50.wordpress.com/2013/09/ 27/63-non-catholic-observers-attending-second-session; Colleen McDannell, *The Spirit of Vatican II: A History of Catholic Reform in America* (New York: Basic Books, 2011), 116.

Catholics to non-Christians.[4] The council advocated "mutual understanding and respect."[5] The fourth section, which focuses on Catholic-Jewish relations, acknowledges the Jewish origins of Christianity.[6] More important, it asserts the irrevocability of God's gifts and covenant with the Jewish people.[7] Most notably, it affirms the view that the suffering and death of Jesus "cannot be charged against all the Jews, without distinction, then alive, nor against the Jews of today."[8] Although the church had promulgated this position in earlier centuries, it was not always heeded.[9] *Nostra Aetate* goes on to condemn using the Bible to promote anti-Judaism: "Jews should not be presented as rejected or accursed by God, as if this followed from the Holy Scriptures," and declares that the church "decries hatred, persecutions, displays of anti-Semitism, directed against Jews at any time and by anyone."[10]

The church's repudiation of anti-Judaism and the deicide charge was heralded as a watershed breakthrough by American Jewish leaders such as Rabbi Ben Zion Bokser.[11] Jewish organizations lauded and eagerly welcomed the church's declaration. Morris B. Abram, president of the American Jewish Committee (AJC), issued a press release that characterized the pronouncement as "a turning point in 1,900 years of Jewish-Christian history" and "the climax to an unprecedented effort to bring about a new era in relations between Catholics and Jews."[12] Remarking that the rejection of the charge of Jewish collective guilt for the crucifixion and the repudiation of anti-Semitism are "significant clarifications of Church teachings," Abram

---

[4] *Declaration on the Relation of the Church to Non-Christian Religions—Nostra Aetate*, proclaimed by Pope Paul VI (Vatican City, 1965), sec. 1, http://www.vatican.va/archive/hist_councils/ii_vatican_council/documents/vat-ii_decl_19651028_nostra-aetate_en.html.

[5] Ibid., sec. 4.

[6] Ibid.: "The beginnings of her [the Church's] faith and her election are found already among the Patriarchs, Moses and the prophets. . . . She also recalls that the Apostles, the Church's main-stay and pillars, as well as most of the early disciples who proclaimed Christ's Gospel to the world, sprang from the Jewish people."

[7] Ibid.: "He does not repent of the gifts He makes or of the calls He issues—such is the witness of the Apostle."

[8] Ibid.

[9] "This guilt seems more enormous in us than in the Jews" ("Reasons Why Christ Suffered," in *Roman Catechism* 1.4.11, trans. Robert I. Bradley, SJ, and Eugene Kevane (Boston: St. Paul Editions, 1985). The document is also known as the "Catechism of Trent," since it was produced in the aftermath of the church's Council of Trent (1545–63). Historically speaking, the confessional creeds of the early church ascribe responsibility for Jesus' death solely to Pontius Pilate.

[10] *Nostra Aetate*, sec. 4.

[11] Ben Zion Bokser, "Vatican II and the Jews," *Jewish Quarterly Review* 59, no. 2 (October 1968): 136–51.

[12] Press Release of the American Jewish Committee, New York, October 28, 1965, http://ajcarchives.org/ajcarchive/DigitalArchive.aspx?panes=2.

hoped that they would "help purify the climate of relations between Christians and Jews throughout the world."[13]

To a great extent, Abram's hopes have been realized. Jews and Catholics have, in the half-century since *Nostra Aetate*, achieved a degree of mutual understanding and affirmation. This is a remarkable achievement given the nearly two millennia of distrust and hostility that defined Jewish-Catholic relations. *Nostra Aetate* notwithstanding, the Jewish-Catholic dialogue has not always acknowledged the complexity and dynamism of Jewish identification, on the one hand, or the variety of Catholic faith and practice, on the other. This failure to understand the fullness of the other is evidenced on the Catholic side by attempts to detach theological issues from political concerns, and on the Jewish side by recurrent suspicion of Catholic ambiguity on the theological validity of the Judaic covenant.[14] This essay addresses lingering Jewish reservations about Catholic-Jewish relations.

Jewish qualms about *Nostra Aetate* began to emerge even before the publication of the final pronouncement. The American Jewish Committee's public statement of October 15, 1965, stated, "We regret keenly some of the assertions in the Declaration, especially those that might give rise to misunderstandings."[15] In an op-ed piece published by the *New York Herald Tribune* on October 17, 1965, Rabbi Marc Tanenbaum, director of interreligious affairs of the American Jewish Committee, explained these concerns: "The document appears not to have resolved conclusively the ancient ambivalence of love and contempt for Jews and Judaism which has dominated Church literature and practice for almost two millennia," a failure that might allow "bigots and anti-Semites" to "exploit negative teachings about Jews."[16] In particular, Tanenbaum expressed disappointment that the council had retreated from its November 1964 version of the declaration, which directed the clergy in their catechetical work and preaching not to "teach anything that could give rise to

---

[13] Press Release of the American Jewish Committee, October 28, 1965.

[14] As Judith Hershcopf Banki has stated, "A mistrust of the Church's motives [was undergirded by] a suspicion that theological dialogue was a honeyed approach to conversion." See "The Interfaith Story behind *Nostra Aetate*," a roundtable discussion held at the United States Holocaust Memorial Museum on December 7, 2005, https://www.ushmm.org/research/the-center-for-advanced-holocaust-studies/programs-ethics-religion-the-holocaust/programs/the-interfaith-story-behind-nostra-aetate/the-interfaith-story-behind-nostra-aetate.

[15] "Statement by the American Jewish Committee on the Adoption of the Vatican Council's Declaration (October 15, 1965)," in American Jewish Committee, "The Second Vatican Council's Declaration on the Jews: A Background Report," private communication (New York: n.d.), 3, http://www.ajcarchives.org/AJC_DATA/Files/6A5.PDF.

[16] Rabbi Marc H. Tanenbaum, "Future Test," *American Jewish Archives* MS-603: Rabbi Marc H. Tanenbaum Collection, 1945–92. Series A: Writings and Addresses. 1947–91 Box 1, Folder 36, "The Catholics and the Jews: Two Views," October 17, 1965, reprinted from the *New York Herald Tribune*, October 17, 1965, http://collections.americanjewisharchives.org/ms/ms0603/ms0603.001.036.pdf.

hatred or contempt of the Jews in the hearts of Christians [and] . . . never present the Jewish people as one rejected, cursed, or guilty of deicide. All that happened to Christ in His Passion cannot be attributed to the whole people then alive, much less to those of today."[17] Tanenbaum further cited the appearance in *Nostra Aetate* of two additional paragraphs reaffirming Jewish opposition to the gospel and reattributing a measure of culpability for "the death of Christ" to "the Jewish authorities and those who followed their lead."[18] He attributed these changes to "the demand of conservative theologians who insisted that a proper New Testament portrait of the Jews required 'severe' judgements [*sic*] against them."[19]

Beyond initial reactions to *Nostra Aetate*, Jews as a community have been slow to respond to Catholic gestures of reconciliation. The reasons for this hesitance are vast and complicated. Some involve internal dissension about the propriety of theological dialogue and political differences over who constitutes the best representatives of the Jewish people, but I propose to discuss two other reasons for Jewish reticence:

1. Attachments to a particular kind of memory of and relationship with the collective past; and
2. The structural asymmetry between Jewish and Catholic communities.

As will become apparent, the two causes are intertwined; the first operates on an ideological as well as a theological level, while the second works in the social and political realms.

Although Catholics and Jews continue to learn from each other and work together on shared social agendas, memories of their collective pasts can sometimes interfere with the ability of each community to effectively manage the present. Jewish imagination remains deeply linked to a perception of the Jewish people as unjustly victimized and constantly endangered by the threat of disappearance.[20] In order to overcome this corporate sense of marginalization and insecurity, Jews have often tried to position themselves as "indispensable" contributors to the project of Western culture.[21] This tendency is especially evident in Jewish-Catholic relations, where Catholics often cite the Old Testament (and, to a lesser extent, the historical Jesus) as their "patrimony" inherited from, and shared with the Jewish people.[22]

---

[17] Tanenbaum, "Future Test."

[18] Ibid., quoting from *Nostra Aetate*, sec. 4.

[19] Ibid.

[20] Moshe Rosman, *How Jewish Is Jewish History?* (Oxford: Littman Library of Jewish Civilization, 2007), 111–30. Rosman points out that such fears are often harbored by minorities whose position among majority cultures is unstable and unpredictable. This view was first noted by Salo Baron in his famous article, "Ghetto and Emancipation: Shall We Revise the Traditional View?" *Menorah Journal* 15, no. 6 (June 1928): 515–26.

[21] Rosman, *How Jewish Is Jewish History?* 116.

[22] See, for example, *Nostra Aetate*, sec. 4.

The Jewish expectation of exceptionalism has sometimes produced disappointment for Jewish participants in interreligious dialogue. As Judith Hershcopf Banki, one of the few Jewish women who attended the council, noted:

> The fact that it [*Nostra Aetate*] had been compromised at all, and that the pure and spontaneous spirit which had prompted the late Pope John XXIII to initiate such a statement had given way to the demands of caution and expediency, created dissatisfaction among many Jews.[23]

Negative responses to *Nostra Aetate* resulted in part from unrealistic expectations, as Rabbi Noam Marans has pointed out in his reflections on the document half a century later.[24] Expectations that the church would, with a single declaration, overturn two millennia of what the French Jewish historian Jules Isaac termed the Christian "teaching of contempt [l'enseignement du mépris]" were misplaced.[25] For the AJC, these expectations were likely also rooted in the perception of its own role as Jewish representatives to the Catholic Church. From its inception, the AJC expressed its mission as "to aid in securing the civil and religious rights of the Jews in all countries where these are denied or endangered."[26] Since the Alliance Israélite Universelle was founded in 1860, modern Jewish organizations have pursued a strategy of pleading their case to advance Jewish rights rather than simply explicating Jewish religious thought and practices for Christian audiences.[27] By following the well-established path of advocacy "since nearly its founding in 1906," the AJC was somewhat less successful in the religious realm than anticipated.[28] This advocacy approach, still employed by Jews in interreligious dialogue, has a well-established history in Jewish-Catholic relations.

Although by 1965 the circumstances of Jews had dramatically changed with the establishment of a Jewish state and the political inroads they had made in the context of Western democratic countries, Jews were in some ways still following patterns of intergroup relations held over from a not-so-venerable past, inscribed in their collective memories through historical narratives, liturgical litanies, and

---

[23] Judith Hershcopf (Banki), "The Church and the Jews: The Struggle at Vatican Council II," *American Jewish Yearbook* 67 (1966): 46.

[24] Noam Marans, "Celebrating 50 Years of the Catholic Church's Dialogue with Jews," address at Catholic University of America, Washington, DC, May 20, 2015, http://www.ajc.org/site/apps/nlnet/content3.aspx?c=7oJILSPwFfJSG&b=9291855&ct=14736165&notoc=1.

[25] Isaac, *L'Enseignement du mépris: Vérité historique et mythes théologiques* (Paris: Fasquelle, 1962).

[26] AJC Minutes, Preliminary Conferences, February 3–4, 1906, [13], http://ajcarchives.org/ajcarchive/DigitalArchive.aspx?panes=2.

[27] *L'Alliance israélite universelle: Publié à l'occasion du vingt-cinquième anniversaire de sa fondation célébré le 1er mars 1885* (Paris: Siège de l'Alliance israélite universelle), 3.

[28] Marans, "Celebrating 50 Years."

ritual practices.[29] Jews retell the Exodus story on Passover with the added refrain, "In every generation an enemy has arisen to destroy us";[30] they also make noise to drown out the name of the villain from the biblical book of Esther as it is read aloud on the festival of Purim.[31] Because of the historically unstable position of Jews in Western civilization, reinscribed by the experience of the Shoah, Jews continued to deploy the premodern role of self-advocacy in interreligious relations. Undoubtedly the shock of the Shoah set Jewish communities back, retreating from the optimism with which they had previously welcomed citizenship and inclusion in America and Europe. Yet decades after the Shoah, Jews still retreated to the familiar dynamic of political advocacy in their approach to the Second Vatican Council.

Jewish groups submitted well-researched reports on Catholic teachings about Jews and Catholic liturgy, and lobbied Catholic clergy, from the local bishop of San Antonio on up to the pope. Representatives from the AJC, the Anti-Defamation League of B'nai B'rith, the World Jewish Congress, l'Amitié Judéo-Chrétienne de France, and the World Conference of Jewish Organizations (with its president, Nahum Goldmann, dubbed by the Jesuits the "Jewish Pope")[32] were explicitly invited by the pope as observers and consulted. Some met with Vatican representatives in secret, while the pope held private audiences with individual emissaries such as Rabbi Abraham Heschel, Jules Isaac, and UN Ambassador and US Supreme Court Justice Arthur J. Goldberg.[33] Catholic opinions were divided on whether such advocacy had deleterious or beneficial effects on the document's rapprochement toward Jews.[34] The proclamation's near derailment by Arab interests, who saw

---

[29]   Viz., *Eleh Ezkerah* of the Yom Kippur liturgy and the Passover Seder.

[30]   Moshe ben Maimon [Moses Maimonides], *Mishneh torah le-ha-Rambam*, ed. Shabse Frankel, vol. 2 (Jerusalem: Hotzaat Shabse Frankel, 2000), Book of Seasons: Laws of Leavened and Unleavened Bread, 9:13.

[31]   In ancient times they burned Haman in effigy. See the fourth-century incident at Callinicium recorded by the church historian Socrates Scholasticus, *Historia Ecclesiastica* 7.16 (viz. edition by Günther Christian Hansen and Manja Širinjan, *Die Griechischen Christlichen Schriftsteller* NS 1 [Berlin: Akademie Verlag, 1995]), which may have prompted the imperial ban on such Purim rites (Theodosian Code 16.8.18).

[32]   Thomas Stransky, "The Genesis of *Nostra Aetate*, An Insider's Story," in *Nostra Aetate: Origins, Promulgation, Impact on Jewish-Catholic Relations.* Proceedings of the International Conference, Jerusalem, October 30–November 1, 2005, ed. Uri Bialer, Neville Lamdan, and Alberto Melloni (Berlin: LIT Verlag, 2007), 37.

[33]   Joseph Roddy, "How the Jews Changed Catholic Thinking," *Look* 30, no. 2 (January 25, 1966): 18–23. Humanities scholar Edward K. Kaplan condemns this article as containing "numerous errors of fact and egregious distortions," labeling it "dangerously misleading" because it "gave credence to the claim that without pressure from the Jews, the declaration would not have been accepted"; see *Spiritual Radical: Abraham Joshua Heschel in America, 1940–1972* (New Haven, CT: Yale University Press, 2007), 276.

[34]   For the former, see Thomas F. Stransky, "The Catholic-Jewish Dialogue: Twenty Years after 'Nostra Aetate'" *America*, February 8, 1986, 92–93; for the latter, see Monsignor George Higgins of the National Catholic Welfare Conference in Washington, DC,

Jewish involvement as politically motivated by a Zionist agenda, supported the view of naysayers.[35] Jews, too, disagreed over the success of their involvement; as Banki has observed, the Jewish community "ended up turning on some of its own leadership and people who had led the struggle at the Vatican Council had a very difficult time of it. They were sometimes accused of selling out Jewish interest and Jewish self-respect."[36]

Such internal Jewish divisions continue to complicate Jewish-Catholic relations, despite the fact that both Jews and Catholics have developed more nuanced understandings of each other's internal dynamics.

Thus far my examination of the historical context of the promulgation of *Nostra Aetate* in 1965 reveals that Jewish reactions were divided, for deeply embedded cultural and historical reasons. One of the reasons for this division relates to the structural asymmetry of the Jewish and Catholic communities mentioned earlier. Many Jews assume that, because the Catholic Church is headed by a pope and operates with a well-defined hierarchy, it is monolithic. They contrast this arrangement with the decentralized structure of organized Jewish religious life, which not only lacks a hierarchy, but is divided along denominational lines.[37] Other Jews do recognize that the church is not a monolith. Nevertheless, many of the historically and culturally conditioned patterns evident in 1965 persist into the present, as the incidents discussed subsequently demonstrate.

Jews who have been consistently involved in the dialogue over the decades since *Nostra Aetate*, like myself, understand the diversity and conflicts within the church, rather than taking the appearance of monolithic authority of the Catholic hierarchy at face value. Catholics, too, have a deeper grasp of intra-Jewish tensions, as reflected by the bilateral consultations conducted with two different Jewish

---

private correspondence to Marc Tanenbaum, December 14, 1965 (Monsignor George Higgins papers, courtesy of the American Catholic History Research Center and University Archives), reproduced at https://jnjrelations.files.wordpress.com/2014/10/higgins_correspondence.pdf.

[35] Hershcopf (Banki), "Church and the Jews," 110–16. The distinction between political and religious motivations was necessary for the document's success; yet that distinction would hinder Jewish-Catholic understanding for decades to come. According to Hershcopf (Banki), this dichotomy was explicitly expressed by "Cardinal Bea, in a statement published in *Osservatore Romano* on November 30: . . . 'This is a religious question in which the Council aims at nothing else but the promotion of peace everywhere; it hopes that a religious matter will not be misused in order to justify political discrimination and prejudices'" ("Church and the Jews," 136).

[36] Banki, "Interfaith Story." See also Hershcopf (Banki), "Church and the Jews," 127–35.

[37] David Rosen, Unpublished papers of the symposium on the Future of Jewish-Catholic Relations in the World and in Israel/The Holy Land (February 10–11, 1997), in the Van Leer Institute, Jerusalem, quoted in Edward Cardinal Cassidy, "Catholic–Jewish Relations: A New Agenda," in *A Legacy of Catholic-Jewish Dialogue: The Joseph Cardinal Bernardin Jerusalem Lectures*, ed. Thomas A. Baima (Chicago: Liturgy Training Publications, 2012), 49.

organizations since 1987 by the US Conference of Catholic Bishops (USCCB) through the Bishops Committee on Ecumenical and Interreligious Affairs (BCEIA). Recognizing Orthodox Jews' self-imposed limitations on theological conversation, the USCCB meets with their rabbinic and congregational organizations (Orthodox Union and Rabbinical Council of America), as well as with the National Council of Synagogues (representing the Central Conference of American Rabbis, the Rabbinical Assembly of Conservative Judaism, the Union of Reform Judaism, and the United Synagogue of Conservative Judaism; hereafter NCS) to which I have been a Reform representative and consultant since 1998.

Jews and Catholics have long memories. In the US context, this trait makes both groups countercultural. Yet Jewish attachment to the past sometimes clouds emotions in the present, producing unfortunate outcomes. Three such examples arose in this century: responses to Mel Gibson's 2004 film, *The Passion of the Christ*; Pope Benedict's 2007 permission to celebrate the Tridentine Mass as an extraordinary form of the Roman rite; and the 2009 controversy over the document *Reflections on Covenant and Mission* that had been issued jointly in 2002 by the Consultation of the NCS and delegates of the Bishops Committee for Ecumenical and Interreligious Affairs.

Audiences of Jews and Catholics who had been engaged in productive dialogue for decades chose to watch the Gibson film together. I was part of one such group in Baltimore, which included Cardinal William Keeler and Rabbi Joel Zaiman. At the time, the two men co-chaired the Consultation of the BCEIA and the NCS. Deeply disturbed by what he saw in the film, Rabbi Zaiman sought to obtain a public denunciation of its negative portrayal of Jews from the Consultation. What resulted was a joint declaration from the NCS and the USCCB (May 19, 2004), which declared that:

> While for many Christians, the movie represents a work of artistic beauty that can provide the opportunity for faith values to be expressed on the screen in a way that has broad appeal, for other Christians and most Jews it recalls the Passion Plays of the past. Those dramatizations of Jesus' death in medieval and indeed modern European history often precipitated violence against Jews by triggering the insidious notion that "the Jews" were and are collectively guilty of the death of Jesus.[38]

For the Jewish members of the Consultation, and what the document calls "most Jews," the movie evoked the ancient specter of deicide charges and mob attacks on Jews incited by Passion Plays during Easter Holy Week, while "many Christians" found the film spiritually moving, a vivid and soul-searching reenact-

---

[38] "National Catholic-Jewish Dialogue Warns against Antisemitic Uses of Gibson's *Passion*," Communiqué of the Catholic-Jewish Consultation Committee, May 19, 2004, https://www.bc.edu/content/dam/files/research_sites/cjl/texts/cjrelations/news/News_May2004.htm.

ment akin to the stations of the cross found in Catholic churches around the world. The divide portrayed in the opening words of this document revealed a deep, long-standing wound, one that the film had ripped open once again.

These disparate reactions to the movie revealed that Jews and Christians cherish different, and sometimes conflicting, collective memories of their past. Despite their apparent success, Jews in the United States retain a collective consciousness of themselves as a vilified and persecuted people, a national self-image forged largely through the "lachrymose conception," in the words of Columbia University historian Salo Baron, of remembering Jewish history as a vale of tears.[39] Jewish history was traditionally learned through ritual and recitation as a litany of tragic historical events that illustrated Jews' ostracism by every people among whom they had settled, from the Babylonian exile and the Greco-Roman destruction of the Jewish polity in the first century through the Crusades and other massacres of Jews in the wake of the Black Death, or the forced expulsion across Europe, from thirteenth-century England to fifteenth-century Spain, not to mention periodic blood libels and synagogue appropriation and destruction. Jews' identification as a scorned people—punished for its own sins—perpetuated a particular kind of collective memory that inculcated self-criticism, distrust of outsiders (often characterized as "tribal"),[40] and a quickness to see anti-Semitism as motivating all kinds of problematic behavior.

The series of events surrounding the Gibson film led to unfortunate consequences. Unrealistic expectations that Catholic members of the Consultation would unequivocally condemn the movie's depiction of Jews as anti-Semitic and caution Catholic viewers against interpreting the film as a faithful rendering of the gospel led to Jewish disappointment. Rabbi Zaiman stepped down as co-chair of the Consultation and eventually resigned his membership. Perhaps even more tragically, the long-standing friendship between the cardinal and the rabbi was destroyed.

A second episode illustrates how Jewish vision was clouded by hindsight. In 2007, Pope Benedict XVI issued the *Motu Proprio* (apostolic letter) "Summorum Pontificum," "which expanded and simplified the permissions to celebrate the whole liturgy according to the norms of 1962."[41] The Catholic motivation was clearly expressed: "Not a few of the faithful continued to be attached with such love and affection to the earlier liturgical forms which had deeply shaped their culture and spirit."[42] Jewish concerns immediately erupted over the renewed permission to

---

[39]   Baron, "Ghetto and Emancipation," 515–26.

[40]   See Ze'ev Chafets, *Members of the Tribe: On the Road in Jewish America* (New York: Bantam Books, 1988).

[41]   United States Conference of Catholic Bishops, "Extraordinary Form of the Mass," http://www.usccb.org/prayer-and-worship/the-mass/extraordinary-form.

[42]   Pope Benedict XVI, "*Apostolic Letter Given Motu Proprio—Summorum Pontificum: On the Roman Liturgy Prior to the Reform of 1970*," July 7, 2007, http://w2.vatican.va/content/benedict-xvi/en/motu_proprio/documents/hf_ben-xvi_motu-proprio_20070707_summorum-pontificum.html.

use a liturgy that contained a Good Friday prayer for the Jews, which they considered to be offensive because of its request that God not "exclude from your mercy even Jews," whose "blindness" keeps them from "acknowledging the light of your truth, which is Christ."[43]

Abraham H. Foxman, national director of the Anti-Defamation League, in addition to voicing his concerns privately to Vatican officials in Rome, issued a statement on July 6 in which he lamented that the Vatican would now permit Catholics to utter such hurtful and insulting words by praying for Jews to be converted. "This is a theological setback in the religious life of Catholics and a body blow to Catholic-Jewish relations."[44] Later that week, Foxman published his view in the *Jewish Telegraphic Agency*, in which he charged that "such a conversion call and condescending references conjure up the great suffering and pain imposed on the Jews by the church through the centuries . . . [and it] threatens to undermine the conceptual underpinnings of so much that has happened over 40 years."[45] Foxman's invocation of "great suffering and pain" illustrates the Jewish attachment to lachrymose history.

For many of us who had been working so hard to build relationships of trust and mutual understanding, Foxman's use of public media to conduct dialogue generated dismay and discomfort, even if we also shared his views of "Summorum Pontificum." The ambiguity of the papal letter on whether the Good Friday prayer was in or out called for elucidation, not recriminations. The International Jewish Committee for Interreligious Consultations, the American Jewish Committee, and the International Council of Christians and Jews requested clarification.[46] Rev. Dr. Norbert Hofmann, secretary to the Pontifical Commission for Religious Relations with the Jews, responded on July 21, suggesting that here was an opportunity to study the prayer for possible revision.[47] Just prior to Lent, on February 4, 2008, the Vatican issued a revised version of the prayer:

> Let us pray for the Jews. May the Lord Our God enlighten their hearts so that they may acknowledge Jesus Christ, the savior of all men [*sic*]. Almighty and everlasting God, you who want all men to be saved and to

---

[43] Sandro Magister, "A Bishop and a Rabbi Defend the Prayer for the Salvation of the Jews," http://chiesa.espresso.repubblica.it/articolo/193041?eng=y&refresh_ce.

[44] "ADL Calls Vatican Prayer for Conversion of Jews 'A Theological Setback' and 'A Body Blow to Catholic-Jewish Relations,'" http://archive.adl.org/presrele/vatican-jewish_96/5093_96.html?_ga=1.70274576.1049517890.1459353552#.Vv1nLFK-Xco.

[45] Abraham Foxman, "Latin Mass Cause for Concern," *Jewish Telegraphic Agency*, July 11, 2007, reprinted at http://www.adl.org/press-center/c/latin-mass-cause-for-concern.html#.Vv1oRFK-Xco.

[46] Philip A. Cunningham, "The 1962 Roman Missal and Catholic-Jewish Relations," http://www.jcrelations.net/The+1962+Roman+Missal+and+Catholic-Jewish+Relations+-+Updated+August+8,+2007.3168.0.html?L=3.

[47] See the section "Further Modifications," in Cunningham, "1962 Roman Missal."

reach the awareness of the truth, graciously grant that, with the fullness of peoples entering into your church, all Israel may be saved.[48]

Although the prayer no longer referred to the "blindness" of Jews, some Jewish leaders objected to what they perceived as its proselytizing implications.

The March 14 issue of *Commonweal* published a series of Catholic and Jewish reflections on the controversy. Banki wrote that, due to the recognition that this was an "internal debate involving the church's theological self-understanding . . . the response by Jews has been muted."[49] Nevertheless, she cautioned,

> Those who have insisted that Jews stay out of internal Catholic theolog-
> ical debate should remind themselves that the practical consequences of
> Christian "theology" have led to persecution and pogroms in the past, and
> that concern about what Christians learn, teach, preach, and pray about
> Jews is motivated more by self-protection than by intrusiveness.[50]

Banki, like Foxman, rang the note of the persecuted Jewish past. Her critique of the prayer's revised wording rehearsed a litany of historical calamities: "For many Jews the very word 'conversion' will recall campaigns, not prayerful hopes: the Crusades, the forced disputations and sermons, the expulsions, the Inquisition, the ghettos."[51] Notwithstanding her sympathy for "many Jews," Banki concluded that "to allow only these bitter memories to determine our response to the pope's prayer would be a big mistake. . . . To recognize this history without being mired in it is a task incumbent on both Catholics and Jews."[52] Like Banki, I felt my relationships with Catholics were unaffected by this series of events. Some of my colleagues, however, felt differently. The Rabbinical Assembly issued a statement charging that the prayer would "cast a harsh shadow over the spirit of mutual respect and collaboration that has marked these past four decades, making it more difficult for Jews to engage constructively in dialogue with Catholics."[53] This sentiment was affirmed by thousands of other rabbis worldwide.[54]

---

[48] John Thavis, "Pope Reformulates Good Friday Prayer for Conversion of Jews, Removes Offensive Language," *American Catholic*, February 5, 2008, www.americancatholic.org/News/Lent2008/goodfridayprayer.asp.

[49] Judith Banki, "Praying for the Jews," *Commonweal* 135, no. 5 (March 14, 2008): 12.

[50] Ibid.

[51] Ibid.

[52] Ibid.

[53] Neela Banerjee, "Conservative Rabbis to Vote on Resolution Criticizing Pope's Revision of Prayer," *New York Times*, February 9, 2008, A9, http://www.nytimes.com/2008/02/09/us/09prayer.html?_r=0.

[54] "'Insulting to Jews': Leading German Rabbi Condemns Pope's Good Friday Prayer," *Spiegel Online International*, March 21, 2008, http://www.spiegel.de/international/world/insulting-to-jews-leading-german-rabbi-condemns-pope-s-good-friday-prayer-a-542872-2.html.

The last episode to be discussed is the confrontation that arose over the document *Reflections on Covenant and Mission* (hereafter RCM).[55] This series of events illustrates how the structural asymmetry of the two communities and the way in which mutual misperception of those structures can sometimes produce unfortunate results and create unproductive tension. On August 12, 2002, the Consultation of the NCS and the Bishop's Committee for Ecumenical and Interreligious Affairs, the same group that responded to the Gibson film, published RCM, the results of its March 13, 2002, meeting, with the intent that it "be read and discussed as part of an ongoing process of increasing mutual understanding."[56] The document spoke with two voices, one Catholic, the other Jewish. The Catholic contribution to RCM addressed the validity of the Mosaic covenant, quoting John Paul II, who "has explicitly taught that Jews are 'the people of God of the Old Covenant, never revoked by God,'[57] 'the present-day people of the covenant concluded with Moses,'[58] and 'partners in a covenant of eternal love which was never revoked.'"[59] It noted that "the post-*Nostra Aetate* Catholic recognition of the permanence of the Jewish people's covenant relationship to God has led to a new positive regard for the post-biblical or rabbinic Jewish tradition that is unprecedented in Christian history."[60] This recognition of the ongoing validity of the Jewish Mosaic covenant garnered praise from those Jewish delegates present at the meeting as well as others in the Jewish and interreligious dialogue communities.[61]

A second passage in RCM offered a nuanced definition of evangelization within the context of Catholic-Jewish dialogue as "the Church's activities of presence and witness; commitment to social development and human liberation; Christian worship, prayer, and contemplation; interreligious dialogue; and proclamation and catechesis."[62] It further explained "proclamation and catechesis [as] the

---

[55] Consultation of the National Council of Synagogues and delegates of the Bishops Committee for Ecumenical and Interreligious Affairs, "Reflections on Covenant and Mission" (hereafter RCM), August 12, 2002, http://www.usccb.org/beliefs-and-teachings/ecumenical-and-interreligious/jewish/upload/Reflections-on-Covenant-and-Mission.pdf.

[56] RCM, [2].

[57] RCM, reference to John Paul II, "Address to the Jewish Community in Mainz, West Germany," November 17, 1980 [footnote 2 in original].

[58] RCM, reference to John Paul II, "Address to the Jewish Community in Mainz" [footnote 3 in original].

[59] RCM, reference to John Paul II, "Address to Jewish Leaders in Miami," September 11, 1987 [footnote 4 in original].

[60] RCM, 3.

[61] Michael Kogan called the document "a revolutionary Catholic pluralism" ("Into Another Intensity: Christian-Jewish Dialogue Moves Forward," *Journal of Ecumenical Studies* 41 (Winter 2004): 14.

[62] RCM, reference to Pontifical Council for Interreligious Dialogue and the Congregation for the Evangelization of Peoples, *Dialogue and Proclamation* (Vatican City, 1991), sec. 2 [footnote 15 in original]. Note Pope John Paul II's similar comments in *Encyclical of Pope John Paul II—Redemptoris Missio: On the Permanent Validity of the Church's Missionary*

'invitation to a commitment of faith in Jesus Christ and to entry through baptism into the community of believers which is the church'"[63] and distinguished these activities from evangelization. The section concluded that, for Catholics, interreligious dialogue entailed "mutually enriching sharing of gifts devoid of any intention whatsoever to invite the dialogue partner to baptism."[64] This type of evangelization was a "way of engaging in the Church's mission" that included "witnessing to their own faith in the kingdom of God embodied in Christ."[65] The document thereby identifies dialogue as a form of evangelization. The description of dialogue as "mutually enriching" and nonconversionary presumably reflected the writers' own experiences and theological perspectives, and was intended as a contribution to, not a definition of, the meaning of evangelization and dialogue for Catholics.

Both RCM's approach to the Mosaic covenant and its understanding of nonconversionary evangelism in the context of Catholic-Jewish dialogue elicited critique from some bishops who did not participate in the consultation. Over the subsequent six years, dissent roiled. In an attempt to consider these opposing views along with the perspective of RCM, the Committee on Doctrine and the BCEIA issued a document on June 18, 2009, titled "A Note on Ambiguities Contained in Covenant and Mission" (henceforth "Note"). "Note" sought to address concerns that "some theologians, including Catholics, have treated the document as authoritative."[66]

After clarifying the document's unofficial status within the church, "Note" discusses RCM's portrayal of the Sinaitic covenant as continuous with Jewish faithfulness to Torah and its understanding of "evangelization" in the particular

---

Mandate (Vatican City, 1990), sec. 41, http://w2.vatican.va/content/john-paul-ii/en/encyclicals/documents/hf_jp-ii_enc_07121990_redemptoris-missio.html: "Mission is a single but complex reality, and it develops in a variety of ways. Among these ways, some have particular importance in the present situation of the Church and the world." The pope went on to cite these various ways: "Witness" (secs. 42–43), "Proclamation" (secs. 44–47), "Forming local churches" (secs. 48–49), "Ecumenical activity" (sec. 50), "Inculturation" (secs. 52–54), "Interreligious Dialogue" (secs. 55–57), and "Promoting Development and Liberation from Oppression" (secs. 58–59).

[63] RCM, reference to Pontifical Council, *Dialogue and Proclamation*, sec. 10 [footnote 16 in original].

[64] RCM, 4–5.

[65] Ibid.

[66] As noted below, the USCCB issued a revised version of "Note," dated October 13, 2009, which removed some (but not all) of the language to which Jews had objected, and placed this version on its website at http://www.usccb.org/about/doctrine/publications/upload/note-on-ambiguities-contained-in-reflections-on-covenant-and-mission.pdf. This action deleted the unrevised version—which, however, can be found on the website of the International Council of Christians and Jews. Unless noted, all quotations come from the unrevised version. See Committee on Doctrine and Ecumenical and Interreligious Affairs, United States Conference of Catholic Bishops, "A Note on Ambiguities Contained in *Reflections on Covenant and Mission*" (hereafter "Note on Ambiguities"), June 18, 2009, para. 2, http://www.iccj.org/redaktion/upload_pdf/201011271849120.covenant09e.pdf.

context of Catholic-Jewish dialogue. "Note" finds certain phrases in RCM worthy of disambiguation, three of which I will discuss. Item 5 of "Note" corrects RCM's impression of "the enduring quality of the [i.e., Israel's] covenant" by asserting: "The long story of God's intervention in the history of Israel comes to its unsurpassable culmination in Jesus Christ, who is God become man."[67] This point of view may be aptly characterized as supersessionist, since, by stating that Jesus Christ is the end of the Israelite narrative, it claims that the "history of Israel" has no other trajectories except the church. According to this ecclesiology, "the Synagogue"—the complement of the medieval typology of "the Church"—is not a legitimate heir to "God's promises to Israel," which, "Note" asserts, "is found only in Jesus Christ."[68] This position may be what Catholics affirm, but both Jews and Catholics need to openly acknowledge that such a view negates a central Jewish claim. Can Jews and Catholics form a meaningful relationship if each thinks the other's claim to Israelite patrimony is unwarranted and illegitimate? This issue constitutes an impasse to future Catholic-Jewish dialogue; much more work needs to be done within the two respective communities before dialogue will be able to move forward.[69]

On the topic of evangelism, paragraph 7 of "Note" quotes RCM's description of interreligious dialogue as "devoid of any intention whatsoever to invite the dialogue partner to baptism."[70] "Note" then explains that "though Christian participation in interreligious dialogue would not normally include an explicit invitation to baptism and entrance into the Church, the Christian dialogue partner is always giving witness to the following of Christ, to which all are implicitly invited."[71]

The word "implicitly" begs elaboration—who is being invited, and to what? The original version of "Note" invokes Romans 11:25–26, "all Israel will be saved" by a deliverer out of Zion, to account for the Catholic expectation that conversion, in relation to the Jews, is communal rather than individual. I hesitate to introduce my own biblical reading into Catholic theological debates, but the way this passage is used poses problems for a Jewish reader. In my reading, Paul believed that Jews who did not have faith in Jesus would not be saved, a view rooted in his eschatology, which presumed Christ's imminent return, that is, before all living Jews would likely affirm Jesus as messiah by baptism and faith. Yet the unrevised version of "Note" uses these verses to claim that "Paul's complete teaching about the inclusion of the Jews in Christ's salvation" leads us to "look forward to the

---

67 "Note on Ambiguities," unrevised version, para. 5.

68 Ibid., para. 10.

69 Recent work such as that in this volume's essays, by Catholic theologians like Philip Cunningham, John Pawlikowski, and Mary Boys, and by Jewish theologians like Leon Klenicki, Michael S. Kogan, and Eugene Korn need to be discussed more broadly within each community. See Philip A. Cunningham, Mary C. Boys et al., eds., *Christ Jesus and the Jewish People Today* (Grand Rapids, MI: Eerdmanns, 2011).

70 "Note on Ambiguities," unrevised version, para. 7. The revised version omits this sentence.

71 Ibid.

inclusion of the whole people of Israel."[72] Whatever Paul himself may have meant, this claim is problematic. The "whole people" in the church's (or, at least, the document authors') eyes cannot include nonbaptized Jews, as paragraph 9—which warns against "mistakenly" thinking that Christians have no obligation to baptize Jews—makes clear. "Note" may be inviting all Israel to salvation, but the cost of the R.S.V.P. is clear: baptism. In cautioning that RCM "could lead some to conclude mistakenly that Jews have an obligation *not* to become Christian and that the Church has a corresponding obligation *not* to baptize Jews," the "Note's" invitation ignores the vast differences between Jewish and Catholic soteriology, most importantly the Jewish emphasis on ethical behavior as the barometer of eligibility.[73] To leave any portion of Jews outside salvation based on their rejection of Christ transgresses Jewish understandings of the covenant, of course, not to mention Catholic pronouncements that the covenant with Israel abides even after the Resurrection (see my discussion below). Soteriology, thus construed, presents an impasse for the dialogue, if Catholics believe—as "Note" suggests they should—that Jews must be baptized to be saved, and Jews disagree, what fruit can a dialogue that fundamentally negates Jewish existence bear?

Jewish reactions to the RCM controversy were exacerbated by a vote taken at the June 2008 meeting of the USCCB, later recognized by the Vatican as in keeping with Catholic teaching. The decision was to replace the sentence in the American adult catechism—"Thus the covenant that God made with the Jewish people through Moses remains eternally valid for them"—with:

> To the Jewish people, whom God first chose to hear his word, "belong the sonship, the glory, the covenants, the giving of the law, the worship and the promises; to them belong the patriarchs, and of their race, according to the flesh, is the Christ." (Rom 9:4–5; cf. CCC, no. 839)[74]

The replacement of an unequivocal statement about the Mosaic covenant that recognizes its validity among current Jews with an enigmatic Pauline passage about the ancient heritage of biblical Jews struck many in the Jewish community as a retreat from the church's original affirmation.

On August 18, 2009, a coalition of American Jewish groups responded to the "Note," expressing concern that "the document's assertion that the remark in the earlier RCM that interreligious dialogue is 'devoid of any intention whatso-

---

[72] Ibid., para. 8.

[73] Ibid., para. 9. For two classic formulations of Jewish salvation, see "all Israel merits a place in the world to come" (m. *Sanh.* 10:1) and "the righteous among the nations merit a place in the world to come" (t. *Sanh.* 13:2).

[74] USCCB, "Backgrounder for Recognition of Change in Adult Catechism," August 27, 2009, which cites the revision to the 2006 *Catechism* on pages 130–31, http://www.ccjr.us/dialogika-resources/documents-and-statements/roman-catholic/us-conference-of-catholic-bishops/577-usccb09aug27. In the original, this quotation is boldfaced.

ever to invite the dialogue partner to baptism' needs to be qualified."[75] The writers concluded that, unlike the original RCM, the "Note"

> informs us that Catholics engaging in dialogue with Jews must have the intention of extending an implicit invitation to embrace Christianity and that one can even imagine a situation in such a dialogue where this invitation would be made explicit. . . . Section 10 . . . appears to posit that the Mosaic covenant is obsolete and Judaism no longer has a reason to exist.[76]

In response to these concerns, the USCCB issued a revised version of its "Note" on October 13, 2009. The passage from the original paragraph 7 regarding dialogue as a form of evangelization and implicit invitation to baptism was deleted.[77] The document left intact, however, the claim that it is mistaken for Catholics to believe that "the Church has a corresponding obligation not to baptize Jews."[78] Concerns about the validity of the Jewish Mosaic covenant were left unaddressed.

Such statements by church leaders understandably arouse Jewish concerns, exacerbated by centuries of Christian triumphalism. Nevertheless, despite such fractures and tensions as I have explored in this essay,[79] as the second half of this

---

[75] "Letter to U.S. Conference of Catholic Bishops: Jewish Organizations Express Concern about Future of Interfaith Dialogue," August 18, 2009, http://www.adl.org/Interfaith/usccb_letter.asp, accessed September 10, 2015. Representatives of the (Orthodox) Rabbinical Council of America and Union of Orthodox Jewish Congregations of America expressed similar concerns over "Note" in a meeting with representatives of the US Bishops on June 25 in New York.

[76] "Letter to U.S. Conference of Catholic Bishops: Jewish Organizations Express Concern about Future of Interfaith Dialogue," August 18, 2009, http://www.adl.org/Interfaith/usccb_letter.asp. Representatives of the (Orthodox) Rabbinical Council of America and Union of Orthodox Jewish Congregations of America expressed similar concerns over "Note" in a meeting with representatives of the US Bishops on June 25 in New York.

[77] The unrevised "Note on Ambiguities" read: "For example, *Reflections on Covenant and Mission* proposes interreligious dialogue as a form of evangelization that is 'a mutually enriching sharing of gifts devoid of any intention whatsoever to invite the dialogue partner to baptism.' Though Christian participation in interreligious dialogue would not normally include an explicit invitation to baptism and entrance into the Church, the Christian dialogue partner is always giving witness to the following of Christ, to which all are implicitly invited," para. 7.

[78] "Note on Ambiguities," para. 9.

[79] Other moments of tension emerged in reaction to *Dialogue and Proclamation* (see note 62 above), which, although invoking *Nostra Aetate* (secs. 1, 16), made no attempt to make an exceptional case for Jews in evangelism, and to the *Declaration—Dominus Iesus: On the Unicity and Salvific Universality of Jesus Christ and the Church* (Vatican City, 2000), issued by the Congregation for the Doctrine of the Faith, http://www.vatican.va/roman_curia/congregations/cfaith/documents/rc_con_cfaith_doc_20000806_dominus-iesus_en.html, which asserted that "It was . . . through Jesus Christ in the Spirit (cf. *Eph* 1:3–14), that the first Christians encountered the Jewish people, showing them the fulfilment of salvation that went beyond the Law" (sec. 13).

century of Jewish-Catholic relations dawns, we need to bear in mind the historical novum that this dialogue represents. The first flowers of *Nostra Aetate* have already blossomed in subsequent documents from multiple Catholic offices. Taken as a whole, these statements have clarified just how fundamentally the church has reconsidered its relationship to the Jewish people. Over several decades, the Pontifical Commission for Religious Relations with the Jews, established by Pope Paul VI in 1970 for "promoting and fostering relations of a religious nature between Jews and Catholics,"[80] issued three sets of guidelines for implementing a revised evaluation of Jews and Judaism: "Guidelines and Suggestions for Implementing the Conciliar Declaration, Nostra Aetate No. 4" (1974), which advocated dialogue to improve mutual understanding, closer attention to how homilies treat Jews, teaching the basic principles of *Nostra Aetate*, section 4, and joint social action; "Notes on the Correct Way to Present Jews and Judaism in Preaching and Teaching in the Roman Catholic Church" (1985), which recognized Israel (i.e., the Jewish people) as "a historic fact and a sign to be interpreted within God's design";[81] and "We Remember: A Reflection on the Shoah" (1998), which recognized how "the fact that the Shoah took place in Europe, that is, in countries of long-standing Christian civilization, raises the question of the relation between the Nazi persecution and the attitudes down the centuries of Christians towards Jews," and called the church's repentance for its complicity in the sins of the Shoah "*teshuva.*"[82] The document's use of the Hebrew term for atonement, so deeply rooted in Jewish liturgy and theology, demonstrated an unprecedented degree of appreciation and respect for Jewish self-understanding.

Most recently, in December 2015, the commission issued the monumental document, *The Gifts and Calling of God Are Irrevocable: A Reflection on Theological Questions Pertaining to Catholic-Jewish Relations on the Occasion of the 50th Anniversary of Nostra Aetate (No. 4)*. The reflection expresses "gratitude" for "all that has been achieved over the last decades in the Jewish-Catholic relationship" and recognizes the "unique status of this relationship within the wider ambit of interreligious dialogue."[83] The reflection also describes the structural asymmetry discussed

---

[80] *Commission for Religious Relations with the Jews* (Vatican City, n.d.), http://www.vatican.va/roman_curia/pontifical_councils/chrstuni/relations-jews-docs/rc_pc_chrstuni_doc_19740101_commission-jews_en.html.

[81] Commission for Religious Relations with the Jews, *Notes on the Correct Way to Present Jews and Judaism in Preaching and Teaching in the Roman Catholic Church* [June 24, 1985] (Vatican City, 1985), sec. 6, para. 1, http://www.vatican.va/roman_curia/pontifical_councils/chrstuni/relations-jews-docs/rc_pc_chrstuni_doc_19820306_jews-judaism_en.html.

[82] Commission for Religious Relations with the Jews, *We Remember: A Reflection on the Shoah* (Vatican City, 1998), sec. 5, http://www.vatican.va/roman_curia/pontifical_councils/chrstuni/documents/rc_pc_chrstuni_doc_16031998_shoah_en.html.

[83] Commission for Religious Relations with the Jews, *The Gifts and Calling of God Are Irrevocable: A Reflection on Theological Questions Pertaining to Catholic-Jewish Relations on the Occasion of the 50th Anniversary of Nostra Aetate (No. 4)* (Vatican City, 2015), "Preface," http://www.vatican.va/roman_curia/pontifical_councils/chrstuni/relations-jews-docs/rc_pc_chrstuni_doc_20151210_ebraismo-nostra-aetate_en.html.

earlier in this essay.[84] The document's history of the strides made over the past half-century mentions how "communities that once faced one another with skepticism" have become "reliable partners and even good friends, capable of weathering crises together and negotiating conflicts positively."[85] These lessons learned from dialogue are expressed in the assertion that "texts and documents, as important as they are, cannot replace personal encounters and face-to-face dialogues."[86] These relationships, as noted in this Vatican reflection and throughout this essay, have deepened and strengthened over the years. The reflection devotes substantial space to rehearsing these achievements, highlighting "successful cooperation," "positive conflict management," and "resilient and fruitful mutuality," and noting that "the bonds of friendship . . . have proved to be stable, so that it has become possible to address even controversial subjects together without the danger of permanent damage being done to the dialogue."[87]

Quite remarkably, the reflection describes Jews as inherently related to the church on a theological level: "From a theological perspective it also makes good sense to link this commission with the Council for Promoting Christian Unity, since the separation between Synagogue and Church may be viewed as the first and most far-reaching breach among the chosen people."[88] This theological interpretation is explicated later in the document:

> Christians and Jews are irrevocably inter-dependent, and . . . the dialogue between the two is not a matter of choice but of duty as far as theology is concerned. . . . Without her Jewish roots the Church would be in danger of losing its soteriological anchoring in salvation history and would slide into an ultimately unhistorical Gnosis.[89]

This theology occasions the rejection of supersessionism and an emphasis on historical continuity: "In spite of the historical breach and the painful conflicts arising from it, the Church remains conscious of its enduring continuity with Israel. Judaism is not to be considered simply as another religion; the Jews are instead our 'elder brothers' (Saint Pope John Paul II), our 'fathers in faith' (Benedict XVI)."[90] This continuity is challenged most prominently by the meaning and significance of Jesus; how his figure is to be evaluated represents the "fundamental difference between Judaism and Christianity."[91] Regarding salvation, the reflection asserts a dialectic whose tension must remain until the End of Time, or in Catholic

---

[84] Commission for Religious Relations with the Jews, *Gifts and Calling of God*, 1.9.

[85] Ibid., 1.2.

[86] Ibid., 1.8.

[87] Ibid., 1.10.

[88] Ibid., 1.3.

[89] Ibid., 1.13.

[90] Ibid., 2.14.

[91] Ibid.

terms, a "mystery." Although "the Church and Judaism cannot be represented as 'two parallel ways to salvation,'" and "the Church must 'witness to Christ as the Redeemer for all' (No. I, 7)," it nevertheless "does not in any way follow that the Jews are excluded from God's salvation because they do not believe in Jesus Christ as the Messiah of Israel and the Son of God." The Jews are "participants in God's salvation," but "how that can be possible without confessing Christ explicitly, is and remains an unfathomable divine mystery."[92] Regarding evangelization, the document explicitly affirms that "the Catholic Church neither conducts nor supports any specific institutional mission work directed towards Jews [and asserts a] principled rejection of an institutional Jewish mission."[93] The repudiation of a particular mission to convert Jews breaks new and fertile ground.

The Pontifical Justice and Peace Commission, established by Pope Paul VI in 1967 to apply the church's social teachings to promoting global human rights, justice, and peace, issued "The Church and Racism" (1988), which both decried the horrors of anti-Semitism that culminated in the Holocaust—which, it lamented, have "unfortunately not yet entirely disappeared"[94]—and, for the first time, asserted the church's stance that Anti-Zionism "serves at times as a screen for anti-Semitism."[95] Five years later, after much negotiation, the Vatican Secretariat of State attained a "Fundamental Agreement between the Holy See and the State of Israel" (1993) that acknowledged the "unique nature of the relationship between the Catholic Church and the Jewish people" and "the historic process of reconciliation and growth in mutual understanding and friendship between Catholics and Jews."[96] It also laid out expectations for how the State of Israel would treat Catholics and Catholic property, "respect[ing] the 'Status quo' in the Christian Holy Places."[97]

The International Theological Commission, established by Pope Paul VI in 1969 to examine major doctrinal issues, published "Memory and Reconciliation: The Church and the Faults of the Past" (1999), which invited all Catholics to engage in a process of *teshuva*, "to keep [in mind] a 'moral and religious memory' of the injury inflicted on the Jews."[98] The century-old Pontifical Biblical Commis-

---

[92] Ibid., 5.35–36.

[93] Ibid., 6.40. Note that the goal of conversion is noticeably absent in section 7, "The goals of dialogue with Judaism."

[94] Pontifical Commission Justice and Peace, "The Church and Racism: Toward a More Fraternal Society," 2.15, https://www.ewtn.com/library/curia/pcjpraci.htm.

[95] Pontifical Commission, "Church and Racism," 2.15.

[96] *Conventio Inter Apostolicam Sedem Atque Israelis Statum—Fundamental Agreement between the Holy See and the State of Israel*, "Preamble," http://www.vatican.va/roman_curia/secretariat_state/archivio/documents/rc_seg-st_19931230_santa-sede-israelc_en.html.

[97] *Fundamental Agreement*, art. 4, sec. 1.

[98] International Theological Commission, *Memory and Reconciliation: The Church and the Faults of the Past* (Vatican City, 1999), 5.4, http://www.vatican.va/roman_curia/congregations/cfaith/cti_documents/rc_con_cfaith_doc_20000307_memory-reconc-itc_en.html5.

sion, restructured in 1971 as an advisory body of biblical scholars and re-tasked with investigating theological issues in biblical context, issued three important statements. "Scripture and Christology" (1984) affirmed the Jewishness of Jesus and Paul, and recognized the importance of studying first-century Judaism, including works authored by Jewish scholars, "so that the personality of Jesus may be understood."[99] "The Interpretation of the Bible in the Church" (1993) noted the usefulness of noncanonical "ancient Jewish traditions" like the Targums and the Midrashic literature as well as the work of "Jewish commentators, grammarians and lexicographers" and biblical scholars from "antiquity down to the present day."[100] It also reiterated the caution of *Nostra Aetate*:

> to avoid absolutely any actualization of certain texts of the New Testament which could provoke or reinforce unfavorable attitudes to the Jewish people [and] . . . to keep unceasingly in mind that, according to the New Testament, the Jews remain "beloved" of God, "since the gifts and calling of God are irrevocable" (Rom 11:28–29).[101]

Finally, "The Jewish People and Their Sacred Scriptures in the Christian Bible" (2001) rejected supersessionism when it wrote that "the Christian Church has no wish to suggest that the Jewish Scriptures are outdated or surpassed."[102] The document also contextualized those New Testament passages that have been used to promote anti-Judaism,[103] promoted a dual covenant theory—the Old and New Testaments—while preserving continuity between the two,[104] and affirmed that "the Jewish reading of the Bible is a possible one, in continuity with the Jewish Sacred Scriptures from the Second Temple period."[105]

The USCCB and its committees have also issued many relevant documents, including "Guidelines for Catholic-Jewish Relations" (1967, 1985); "Criteria for

---

[99] Pontifical Biblical Commission, "Instruction on Scripture and Christology" (n.p.: 1984), trans. Joseph A. Fitzmyer, SJ, https://www.bc.edu/content/dam/files/research_sites/cjl/texts/cjrelations/resources/documents/catholic/pbc_christology.htm, 1.1.5.1.

[100] Pontifical Biblical Commission, "The Interpretation of the Bible in the Church," Presented on March 18, 1994 [first presented September 21, 1993], 1.C.2, https://www.ewtn.com/library/CURIA/PBCINTER.HTM5.

[101] Ibid., 4.A.3.

[102] Pontifical Biblical Commission, *The Jewish People and Their Sacred Scriptures in the Christian Bible* (Vatican City, 2002 [Eng. ed.; orig. 2001]), 2.A.1[.19], http://www.vatican.va/roman_curia/congregations/cfaith/pcb_documents/rc_con_cfaith_doc_20020212_popolo-ebraico_en.html.

[103] Pontifical Biblical Commission, *Jewish People and Their Sacred Scriptures*, 3.B.1–5.70–78, C.1–3.79–83, analyzing multiple citations in the gospels, Acts, the Pauline and other epistles, and Revelation.

[104] Ibid., 2.B.5.37–42.

[105] Ibid., preface, 2.A.7, para. 22.

the Evaluation of Dramatizations of the Passion" (1988); "God's Mercy Endures Forever: Guidelines on the Presentation of Jews and Judaism in Catholic Preaching" (1988); and "Catholic Teaching on the Shoah: Implementing the Holy See's We Remember" (2001). All of these expand the understanding of the Jewish-Catholic relationship and ideas about Jews first expressed in *Nostra Aetate,* while demonstrating their application to and implementation within Catholic religious life.

John Borelli, with whom I had the pleasure of working when he served as associate director of the Secretariat for Ecumenical and Interreligious Affairs of the USCCB, astutely observed about the RCM affair: "Exchanging public statements is a poor way to conduct dialogue."[106] Offering a critique of the process, both from the perspective of trusting one's dialogue partners and episcopal protocol, Borelli has advocated further dialogical study instead of "more unilateral actions that ignore the fruits of the Catholic-Jewish dialogue of the past 45 years." Joint study can certainly help further understanding about deeply complex and controversial issues, but will it repair the breach of trust that has occurred in the relationships between the Catholic and Jewish participants in this dialogue?

In addition to exploring shared social and theological concerns, Jewish-Catholic dialogues could benefit from exploring the types of structural issues exposed by the missteps I have analyzed in this chapter. Why does the Jewish-Catholic relationship suffer when Catholics have internal theological conflicts? Why are the two religious communities so intimately connected, to the extent that one cannot be discussed without implicating the other? How have the ways that Jews (and Catholics) have constructed their religious identities, tracing their very survival to the ability to withstand influence from the other, at odds with this historical symbiosis of the Jewish-Catholic relationship?[107] These foundational questions might go a long way to understanding the fragility of Jewish-Catholic relations, and help chart a way forward that is built on mutual understanding and respect.

Understanding the *roles* that collective memories of the past play in current dialogue may help Jews move beyond the attachment to a lachrymose recitation of history. Although it is deceptive and disloyal to forget the past, understanding how the past shapes Jewish behavior in the context of current Jewish-Catholic dialogue can begin opening the door to a radically different future. No one who enters into dialogue with a truly open heart should be able to imagine that future, but hoping that it be different than the past is an honest place to start.

---

[106] John Borelli, "Troubled Waters," *America,* February 22, 2010, 20.

[107] For Catholics, the resistance to Jewish influence can be found in the myriad canonical laws against Judaizing, or observing Jewish practices, like eating unleavened bread of the Jews (Syn. Trull, dated 692, ap. Gratian, *Caus.* 28, Qu. 1, c. 13).

Part V

Islamic Perspectives

11

Beyond the Rays of Truth?

Nostra Aetate, *Islam, and the Value of Difference*

Jerusha Tanner Lamptey

The formal decrees of the Second Vatican Council are remarkable in their nature and scope. The topics broached, the tensions engaged, and the strategic silences invoked are ripe for ongoing analysis and theological reflection. One striking characteristic of these decrees is the manner in which they negotiate religious sameness and religious difference. The decrees move beyond earlier trends of absolute rejection of all manifestations of religious difference to a more nuanced discussion. This trend is evident not only in the council's brief but explicit discussion of Islam in *Nostra Aetate*—the topic of this essay—but also in its engagement with Judaism, with the Orthodox Church, and the "separated Protestant brethren" in the Decree on Ecumenism (*Unitatis Redintegratio*),[1] and with secularism in the Pastoral Constitution on the Church in the Modern World (*Gaudium et Spes*).[2] The nuanced approach is also present in the emphasis placed on dialogue—a form of interaction that transcends mere rejection and mere acceptance—found throughout the final decrees of the council. The council decrees begin to articulate parameters for such interaction with diverse communities.

Although *Nostra Aetate* exemplifies the more nuanced approach, in this essay, I argue that it does nevertheless prioritize religious commonality and sameness as the basis of dialogue and positive interactions among Catholics and Muslims. This position results in a lack of engagement with religious difference and a form of inclusive domestication of the Muslim religious other. In order to illustrate this claim, I begin by critically exploring the content of *Nostra Aetate* that addresses the Islamic tradition, Muslim practice, and Muslim persons. I place this content in the broader context of *Nostra Aetate* and in juxtaposition to the decree's discussion of

---

[1] *Decree on Ecumenism—Unitatis Redintegratio*, promulgated by Pope Paul VI (Vatican City, 1964), http://www.vatican.va/archive/hist_councils/ii_vatican_council/documents/vat-ii_decree_19641121_unitatis-redintegratio_en.html.

[2] *Pastoral Constitution on the Church in the Modern World—Gaudium et Spes*, promulgated by Pope Paul VI (Vatican City, 1965), http://www.vatican.va/archive/hist_councils/ii_vatican_council/documents/vat-ii_cons_19651207_gaudium-et-spes_en.html.

Judaism, Jewish tradition, and Jewish persons. I then examine the manner in which subsequent elaborations of *Nostra Aetate* by Pope John Paul II and recent statements by Pope Francis reveal more intricate engagement with and re-envisioning of religious difference. I conclude by arguing that Pope Francis's affirmation of religious difference offers a marked departure from the inclusivism of *Nostra Aetate* and thereby redefines dialogue as an engagement that necessitates deep knowledge of and appreciation of the particularities of both religious self and other.

Nostra Aetate, Muslims, and Religious Difference

The content of *Nostra Aetate* that specifically addresses Islam, Muslim practice, and Muslim persons is found in section 3. However, that content is best illuminated in reference to the larger context of *Nostra Aetate*, and with particular reference to its discussion of Judaism.

Nostra Aetate commences by invoking three central concepts. The first two are those of "relationship" and "fellowship." These concepts echo the council's overriding emphasis on appropriate interaction and especially dialogue; *Nostra Aetate*, like many other decrees, is not premised on the notion of an isolated or withdrawing church. The church is very much in the world, and the world is a world of diversity.

The third concept *Nostra Aetate* introduces is that of unity. The decree speaks of "promoting unity" (*Nostra Aetate*, sec. 1) and of the unity of people in "origin" and "final goal."[3] Unity is also evident in the litany of "unsolved riddles of the human condition" (*Nostra Aetate*, sec. 1) and the "perception of that hidden power" (*Nostra Aetate*, sec. 2) found in many religious traditions. Notably, this unity arises from and is facilitated by "what men [*sic*] have in common" (*Nostra Aetate*, sec. 1). *Nostra Aetate* thus prioritizes an emphasis on unity, commonalities, and sameness. Unity is the goal of interaction and dialogue, and unity arises from commonality in experience, origin, destination, and human nature.

Unity, though, is not all that exists. In section 2, the decree states that in response to riddles, perceptions, and human restlessness, "religions found everywhere"—with explicit mention of Buddhism and Hinduism—propose "'ways,' comprising teachings, rules of life, and sacred rites" (*Nostra Aetate*, sec. 2). The decree here acknowledges diversity and religious difference, stating that every religion makes such proposals "in its own manner" (*Nostra Aetate*, sec. 2). It then pointedly and astonishingly states that the church "rejects nothing that is true and holy in these religions" (*Nostra Aetate*, sec. 2). There are aspects—and they are aspects, not entireties—of other traditions that are to be regarded with "sincere

---

[3] *Declaration on the Relation of the Church to Non-Christian Religions—Nostra Aetate*, promulgated by Pope Paul VI (Vatican City, 1965), sec. 1, http://www.vatican.va/archive/hist_councils/ii_vatican_council/documents/vat-ii_decl_19651028_nostra-aetate_en.html.

reverence" because they often reflect a "ray" of the Truth, the Truth of Christ, and the Truth found fully in Catholic religious life (*Nostra Aetate*, sec. 2). Dialogue and collaboration are then invoked as the forms of interaction equipped to promote these "rays" or "good things" found among other "men" (*Nostra Aetate*, sec. 2).

But what aspects are these? Are they the unique features of each tradition? Are they the theological particularities or practices of other religions? While acknowledging the existence of religious diversity, *Nostra Aetate* does not claim that religious difference is an asset in positive interaction or in unified work for the good of all humankind. Thus, in response to the question of which aspects are positively evaluated—which are the "rays of Truth"—the decree values those areas of practice, thought, and moral action that have significant overlap with the already outlined and affirmed practices, thought, and moral action of the church.

This perspective becomes clearer in section 3, with the discussion of Islam, Muslims, and Muslim practice. The section begins by expressing "esteem" for Muslims. This esteem is connected to their adoration of God as Creator and Revealer; to their desire to "submit wholeheartedly" to God's decrees; to their reverence of Jesus and Mary; to their belief in the Day of Judgment and Resurrection; and to their valuing of "moral life and worship" (*Nostra Aetate*, sec. 3). Section 3 concludes with an explicit, albeit general, recognition of "quarrels and hostilities" among Christians and Muslims, and a call to "forget the past" and work for "mutual understanding" and the benefit of all humankind (*Nostra Aetate*, sec. 3).

When Muslim people—conspicuously not the Islamic tradition—are esteemed in the decree, they are esteemed for beliefs and practices (such as those related to God, God's decrees, Jesus and Mary, the Day of Judgment and Resurrection, and moral life and worship) that are familiar to the church. Similar praise of Muslims grounded in the recognition of commonalities and sameness is also found in *Lumen Gentium*[4] and in the papal encyclical of Pope Paul VI *Ecclesiam Suam*.[5] The esteemed beliefs and practices—with the potential exception of "revering" Jesus—are not Islamic particularities. They are very important aspects of the Islamic tradition, but they are not features that distinguish Islamic thought and practice from other (especially Catholic) forms of thought and practice. They are not

---

[4] *Dogmatic Constitution on the Church—Lumen Gentium*, promulgated by Pope Paul VI (Vatican City, 1964), http://www.vatican.va/archive/hist_councils/ii_vatican_council/documents/vat-ii_const_19641121_lumen-gentium_en.html: "But the plan of salvation also includes those who acknowledge the Creator. In the first place amongst these there are the Muslims, who, professing to hold the faith of Abraham, along with us adore the one and merciful God, who on the last day will judge mankind" (sec. 16).

[5] *Pastoral Constitution on the Church in the Modern World—Ecclesiam Suam,* promulgated by Pope Paul VI (Vatican City, 1964), http://w2.vatican.va/content/paul-vi/en/encyclicals/documents/hf_p-vi_enc_06081964_ecclesiam.html: "Then we have those worshipers who adhere to other monotheistic systems of religion, especially the Moslem religion. We do well to admire these people for all that is good and true in their worship of God" (sec. 107).

aspects that require great "exegetical effort"[6] on behalf of the church or Catholics; they do not require extensive explanation nor do they provoke theological dialogue or self-reflection.

Nostra Aetate thus is novel in its inclusive statement that value can be found outside of the church and among some Muslims in some beliefs and practices. This statement, though, is not the same as valuing other traditions holistically or valuing the distinctive features of other traditions. Nor is it the same as entertaining the possibility that other traditions may have something unfamiliar yet valuable to offer the church and Catholics. In *Nostra Aetate*, the "rays" found outside of the church must always emanate from and reflect the familiar contours of the "sun" that is Christ.

Section 4, which discusses the relationship of the church with Jewish people and tradition, offers an illuminating juxtaposition to the approach to sameness and difference adopted in relation to Islam and Muslims. To begin, the content of this section is much longer than others and references historical, scriptural, and theological claims in a manner absent in the rest of the decree. Section 3, for example, glosses only Christian and Islamic theological differences over Jesus. This superficial treatment is striking in light of a vast and fiery history of theological and rhetorical debate on the subject, and in light of the centrality of claims about Jesus in both traditions.

Section 4 also introduces the relational concepts of "bonds of spirituality" and "spiritual patrimony" between Christians and Jews. This particular form of relationship arises in part from the fact that "the Apostles, the Church's main-stay and pillars, as well as most of the early disciples who proclaimed Christ's Gospel to the world, sprang from the Jewish people" (*Nostra Aetate*, sec. 4). In taking this stance, the decree distinguishes the relationship between Christianity and Judaism from relationships with other religious traditions. Relational proximity between Christianity and Judaism is not asserted solely on the basis of commonality or familiarity, as with other traditions, including Islam, but rather on the basis of spiritual, textual, and theological genealogy.

Section 4 then echoes earlier calls for interaction based on "mutual understanding and respect," but adds that, in the case of Christianity and Judaism, understanding and respect would arise from "biblical and theological studies" as well as from "fraternal dialogues" (*Nostra Aetate*, sec. 4). This statement is significant for two reasons. First, it broaches the topic of scriptural and theological discussions. And second, such recommendations are not explicitly made in reference to other traditions. In other words, the decree is silent, perhaps intentionally so, on the process whereby mutual understanding and respect would be generated with Islam, Hinduism, and Buddhism. The concern for greater specificity in regard to Judaism is also evinced by the 1974 issuance of the *Guidelines and Suggestions for Implementing the Conciliar Declaration* Nostra Aetate *(n. 4)*.[7] These *Guidelines*

---

[6] Jonathan Z. Smith, *Relating Religion: Essays in the Study of Religion* (Chicago: University of Chicago Press, 2004), 269. Smith uses this phrase to describe the conceptual and interpretative grappling demanded by the encounter with various "others."

[7] Commission for Religious Relations with the Jews, *Guidelines and Suggestions for*

reinforce the shared patrimony of Judaism and Catholicism, stress the importance of dialogue, and offer concrete and pragmatic suggestions in terms of liturgy, education, and joint social action. It is worth noting that similar, more complex negotiations of religious sameness and difference, and practical suggestions for interaction, are found in relation to Orthodox and Protestant churches (the "separated brethren") in *Unitatis Redintegratio*, the Decree on Ecumenism.[8]

What the juxtaposition of *Nostra Aetate*'s approaches to Islam and to Judaism illustrates is that religious particularities—or those aspects of traditions that are not shared in common—are engaged in different ways and to different degrees dependent on both the tradition engaged and Catholic self-understanding. To borrow the rubric of Jonathan Z. Smith, as I have done elsewhere in analyzing the Second Vatican Council's treatment of Orthodox and Protestant churches, some religious others are treated by *Nostra Aetate* as "proximate others" and some are treated as "distant others."[9] Distant others are recognized as being different, but their difference is envisioned as being far removed and unrelated to the religious self. As such, they do not demand or require deep theological engagement because they present no real challenge to religious self-understanding. In contrast, proximate others claim to be "us" (e.g., Protestant churches) or are claimed by "us" as part of our own self-understanding and religious identity (e.g., Judaism and Orthodox churches). They, therefore, demand self-reflection and theological contemplation. As Smith contends, "The 'other' emerges only as a theoretical issue when it is perceived as challenging a complex and intact worldview."[10] The distant other does not do this; they are simply other. The proximate other, however, is problematic and provocative, and thus of "supreme interest."[11]

Nostra Aetate appears to treat Islam as a distant other distinctive from the proximate other of Judaism. Shared history, genealogical and theological connections, and the necessity of study or mutual investigation are not mentioned in reference to Islam and Muslims. Moreover, no "Guidelines and Suggestions for Implementation" were ever drafted in reference to *Nostra Aetate* section 3, or, for that matter, section 2. This disparity underscores the reality that the general approach of *Nostra Aetate* to Islam and Muslims is premised on affirming and domesticating the familiar while avoiding the complexities, challenges, and potential resources of religious difference found in that religious other.

Implementing the Conciliar Declaration Nostra Aetate *(n. 4)* (Vatican City, 1974), http://www.vatican.va/roman_curia/pontifical_councils/chrstuni/relations-jews-docs/rc_pc_chrstuni_doc_19741201_nostra-aetate_en.html.

   [8] I have written about this subject elsewhere. See Jerusha T. Lamptey, "'Mapping' the Religious Other: The Second Vatican Council's Approach to Protestantism," *Journal of Ecumenical Studies* 45, no. 4 (Fall 2010): 604–16.

   [9] Smith, *Relating Religion*, 245.

   [10] Ibid., 269.

   [11] Ibid., 253.

Nostra Aetate and Beyond:
Elaborations by Pope John Paul II

Throughout the duration of his almost twenty-seven-year papacy, Pope John Paul II frequently invoked the teachings of *Nostra Aetate* on Islam and Muslims. This interest is manifest in numerous papal addresses and documents[12] in which the bulk of his discourse is made up of direct quotations from the decree. However, to understand Pope John Paul II's approach solely as repetition would overlook the unique intricacy and scope of his engagement with Islam and Muslims. Pope John Paul II did echo the Second Vatican Council, but he also expanded on and strove to explicate its basic assertions. He also, in a move from *Nostra Aetate*, struggled explicitly to reconcile affirmations of Islam and Muslims with clear areas of difference and contention between the two religious traditions. As such, Pope John Paul II continues the prioritization of religious commonality evident in the Second Vatican Council and *Nostra Aetate*, but he also grapples with theological and practical complexities related to religious difference.

Pope John Paul II draws on *Nostra Aetate* in verbalizing a "high regard" for Muslims, but his esteem is more specifically and explicitly directed toward the religiosity, or the religious practices, of Muslims. He highlights the praiseworthiness of practices such as prayer, almsgiving, and fasting. Prayer, though, clearly garners the most attention. For Pope John Paul II, the Muslim commitment to habitual performance of prayer, even in minority settings, is commendable and worthy of emulation. In *Crossing the Threshold of Hope*, he writes,

> The religiosity of Muslims deserves respect. It is impossible not to admire, for example, their fidelity to prayer. The image of believers in Allah who, without caring about time or place, fall to their knees and immerse themselves in prayer remains a model for all those who invoke the true God, in particular for those Christians who, having deserted their magnificent cathedrals, pray only a little or not at all.[13]

He assumes this stance for two particular reasons. First, he is concerned with the encroachment of secularism and atheism.[14] Prayer, especially in societies that

---

[12] The impressive scope of his engagement is evinced in over sixty-four written documents at various levels of authority, ranging from short public speeches to apostolic letters to papal encyclicals to his more personal theological reflections in Pope John Paul II, *Crossing the Threshold of Hope*, ed. Vittorio Messori and trans. Jenny McPhee and Martha McPhee (New York: Knopf, 1994).

[13] Ibid., 93.

[14] See Pope John Paul II, [*Address*]—*General Audience, Wednesday 5 May 1999* (Vatican City, 1999), https://w2.vatican.va/content/john-paul-ii/en/audiences/1999/documents/hf_jp-ii_aud_05051999.html. Here, he references the "world where God is

may be heavily influenced by such worldviews, serves as an observable and public contestation. It is a public witness to belief in God, a witness that he urges Catholics and other Christians to adopt more widely.

Second, he depicts prayer as a shared necessity for all humanity. Describing people as spiritual beings, he argues that all humans need to engage in prayer in order to live successfully and to thrive. This is apparent in his description of the human heart as "withered" when deprived of prayer.[15] Although Pope John Paul II's esteem for Muslim religiosity is clear, it should not be misconstrued as a blanket expression of respect or acceptance. It is a specific and limited expression. By praising Muslim religiosity, he does not aim to praise or elicit respect for all aspects of Muslim practice, nor all aspects of Islamic belief. In line with *Nostra Aetate*, Pope John Paul II focuses on specific aspects—or rays—of truth and goodness present in Islam and Muslim practice.

The focus on rays of truth and goodness is clear in Pope John Paul II's discussion of commonalities between Islam and Catholicism. Religiosity is one significant area of overlap between the two traditions, but he does not confine his discussion of commonalities to practice alone. Like *Nostra Aetate*, he also delves into common religious beliefs and views of God and humanity. In particular, he unequivocally asserts that Muslims and Catholics believe in the same God, and emphasizes that Muslims view God as one, just, merciful, and almighty.[16] Like Catholics, Muslims

---

tragically forgotten" (sec. 4). Also see Pope John Paul II, *Homily of the Holy Father—"Day of Pardon," Sunday, 12 March 2000* (Vatican City, 2000), https://w2.vatican.va/content/john-paul-ii/en/homilies/2000/documents/hf_jp-ii_hom_20000312_pardon.pdf, sec. 4: "Let us confess, even more, our responsibilities as Christians for the evils of today. We must ask ourselves what our responsibilities are regarding atheism, religious indifference, secularism, ethical relativism, the violations of the right to life, disregard for the poor in many countries."

[15] Pope John Paul II, *Address of the Holy Father—Meeting with the Muslim Leaders, Omayyad Great Mosque, Damascus, Sunday, 6 May 2001* (Vatican City, 2001), https://w2.vatican.va/content/john-paul-ii/en/speeches/2001/may/documents/hf_jp-ii_spe_20010506_omayyadi.html: "The fact that we are meeting in this renowned place of prayer reminds us that man is a spiritual being, called to acknowledge and respect the absolute priority of God in all things. Christians and Muslims agree that the encounter with God in prayer is the necessary nourishment of our souls, without which our hearts wither and our will no longer strives for good but succumbs to evil" (sec. 2),

[16] For example, see Pope John Paul II, *Address of His Holiness John Paul II to Young Muslims, Morocco, Monday, 19 August 1985* (Vatican City, 1985), https://w2.vatican.va/content/john-paul-ii/en/speeches/1985/august/documents/hf_jp-ii_spe_19850819_giovani-stadio-casablanca.html, accessed February 25, 2016; and Pope John Paul II, *Address of John Paul II to the Muslim Religious Leaders, Kaduna (Nigeria), Sunday, 14 February 1982* (Vatican City, 1982), https://w2.vatican.va/content/john-paul-ii/en/speeches/1982/february/documents/hf_jp-ii_spe_19820214_musulmani-nigeria.html: "All of us, Christians and Muslims, live under the sun of the one merciful God. We both believe in one God who is the Creator of Man. We acclaim God's sovereignty and we defend man's dignity as

view God as the creator, the ultimate judge, and the grantor of mercy. In line with this, Pope John Paul II highlights a shared universal humanity; all humans are created by God, serve God, repent to God, will be judged by God, and will undergo resurrection.[17] Other areas of commonality invoked include a desire to emulate Abraham's model of submission and a great respect for Jesus.[18]

Up to this juncture, Pope John Paul II's discussion of commonalities aligns closely with *Nostra Aetate* and *Lumen Gentium*. His elaboration becomes evident in his use of these commonalities as the basis of envisioning a new community, the "one community of believers." This community is woven together with the various strands of commonality. But this community is not homogeneous. In order to capture this, he invokes the analogy of a family; each member has particularities, but the family group is also profoundly unified.[19] Expanding further, he indicates that families have not only particularities but significant conflicts as well. He argues, though, that what ties the family—the community of believers—together is stronger than that which divides it. Although this contention is certainly debatable, it does indicate that Pope John Paul II is aware of significant differences between the religious traditions and that he is involved in a tensive struggle to simultaneously account for commonalities and differences.

Further indications of this struggle are found in Pope John Paul II's attempt to balance *Nostra Aetate*'s affirmation of rays of truth and goodness with his unequivocal assertion that perfect and complete truth is found only in Christ. Although he states that Muslims respect Jesus[20] and share a common belief in the same God, he delves further into the nature of these beliefs to reveal pointed distinctions. In *Crossing the Threshold of Hope*, for example, he outlines his understanding of the

God's servant. We adore God and profess total submission to him. Thus, in a true sense, we can call one another brothers and sisters in faith in the one God. And we are grateful for this faith, since without God the life of man would be like the heavens without the sun" (sec. 2).

[17] For example, see Pope John Paul II, *Address of His Holiness John Paul II to the Representatives of the European Islamic Community, Sacred Convent of Saint Francis—Assisi (Perugia) Sunday, 10 January 1993* (Vatican City, 1993), sec. 2, https://w2.vatican.va/content/john-paul-ii/en/speeches/1993/january/documents/hf_jp-ii_spe_19930110_islam-assisi.html; and Pope John Paul II, *Discorso del Santo Padre Giovanni Paolo II ai Rappresantanti della Comunità Musulmana, Aeroporto di Davao, 20 febbraio 1981* (Vatican City, 1981), https://w2.vatican.va/content/john-paul-ii/it/speeches/1981/february/documents/hf_jp-ii_spe_19810220_davao-comunita-musulmana.html.

[18] Pope John Paul II, *Discorso di Giovanni Paolo II alla Comunità Armeno-Cattolica di Istanbul, Istanbul, 20 novembre 1979* (Vatican City, 1979), https://w2.vatican.va/content/john-paul-ii/fr/speeches/1979/november/documents/hf_jp-ii_spe_19791129_istanbul-turchia.html.

[19] Pope John Paul II, *Meeting with the Muslim Leaders, Omayyad Great Mosque*; Pope John Paul II, *Address to the Representatives of Muslims of the Philippines*.

[20] Pope John Paul II, *Meeting of John Paul II with the Muslim Leaders, Nairobi (Kenya), Wednesday, 7 May 1980*, https://w2.vatican.va/content/john-paul-ii/en/speeches/1980/may/documents/hf_jp-ii_spe_19800507_musulmani-kenya.html.

implications of the Islamic view of God. He contends that, since Muslims deny incarnation, they do not view God as redemptive. Describing the Muslim denial of incarnation as a "reduction" of divine revelation, he states that it results in a God that is outside of or uninvolved with the world.[21] He then astutely notes that this significant theological divergence results in equally significant divergences in respect to anthropology.[22] In other words, the view of God and God's action is directly correlated to the view of humanity and human action. The way in which one envisions God does indeed affect how one envisions the needs, capabilities, and goals of humanity. As a result, Pope John Paul II seems to be arguing that the two traditions have significant differences in both realms. The tension that exists between this assertion and his (and *Nostra Aetate*'s) assertion of a shared universal humanity and unity in origin and ends is clear.

It would be tempting to explain this and other tensions by arguing that Pope John Paul II proffered a message of commonality to Muslim audiences and discussed differences only with fellow Catholics. This differentiation of audiences, though, does not appear to have been the case. What does appear to be true is that Pope John Paul II's direct addresses to Muslim audiences tended to focus on issues of religiosity and social action, and not on issues of theology. This distinction is noteworthy because the main divergences that he identifies are largely theological in nature, and the central commonalities tend to be largely practical in nature. He does state that theological dialogue between scholars should occur,[23] but this dialogue is not manifest in his written documents.

One final area of *Nostra Aetate* that Pope John Paul II elaborates upon is that of relations between Muslims and Catholics, particularly the topics of reconciliation, dialogue, and mission. Explicitly acknowledging a somewhat troubled history, he states that there is a need to move beyond this history and toward a new relationship.[24] Such "moving beyond," however, is not, for Pope John Paul II, simply a matter of forgetting the past; rather, there are certain requirements for reconciliation. Two requirements that are discussed frequently are freedom of religion (especially for Christian minorities in Muslim majority countries) and protection of human rights.[25] Another crucial component of reconciliation is forgiveness.

---

[21] Pope John Paul II, *Crossing the Threshold of Hope*, 92–93.

[22] Ibid., 93.

[23] For example, Pope John Paul II, *Meeting with the Muslim Leaders, Omayyad Great Mosque*.

[24] Ibid.

[25] Ibid.; see also Pope John Paul II, *Crossing the Threshold of Hope*, 94; Pope John Paul II, *Post-Synodal Apostolic Exhortation—Ecclesia in Africa* (Vatican City, 2000), secs. 44, 66, 112, http://w2.vatican.va/content/john-paul-ii/en/apost_exhortations/documents/hf_jp-ii_exh_14091995_ecclesia-in-africa.html; Pope John Paul II, *Speech of the Holy Father John Paul II at the Welcome Ceremony in Jordan, International Airport "Queen Alia" in Amman, March 20, 2000* (Vatican City, 2000), sec. 2, https://w2.vatican.va/content/john-paul-ii/en/speeches/2000/jan-mar/documents/hf_jp-ii_spe_20000320_jordan-arrival.html; and Pope John Paul II, *Post Synodal Apostolic Exhortation—Pastores Gregis* (Vatican

He argues that the ultimate goal of peace will never be achieved without justice, but justice will never be achieved without forgiveness.[26] Moreover, he describes forgiveness as the "assiduous practice of human brotherhood," in which individuals recognize and prioritize commonalities, especially a common anthropology.[27]

Closely connected to reconciliation is the process of dialogue. While dialogue between religious traditions can assume many forms, Pope John Paul II is categorical in his vision of its conditions, types, and goals. The primary conditions are a genuine desire to know the other and a firm rooting in one's own religious tradition.[28] The first expresses his view that dialogue is willed by God; God desires for us to know our differences. The second is his refutation of secularism, indifferentism, and irenicism; religious dialogue is motivated by particular religious commitment, rather than a lack of religious commitment or a syncretic religious commitment.[29] He also endorses different types of dialogue, including the practical dialogue that occurs in the daily lives of people living in multireligious settings—the "dialogue of life"[30]—and the philosophical or theological dialogue of scholars.[31] He is adamant that no other types of dialogue are possible without the foundation of practical, daily dialogue. Heaping extensive praise on such encounters, he depicts them as an organic and stable foundation for achieving the goals of dialogue.[32]

City, 2003), secs. 67, 68, http://w2.vatican.va/content/john-paul-ii/en/apost_exhortations/documents/hf_jp-ii_exh_20031016_pastores-gregis.html.

[26] Pope John Paul II, *Message of His Holiness Pope John Paul II for the Celebration of the World Day of Peace* (Vatican City, 2002), http://w2.vatican.va/content/john-paul-ii/en/messages/peace/documents/hf_jp-ii_mes_20011211_xxxv-worldday-for-peace.html.

[27] Pope John Paul II, *Exhortation Apostolique Post-Synodale—Une Esp*érance Nouvelle pour Le Liban (Vatican City, 1997), sec. 97 ["la pratique assidue de la fraternité humaine"], https://w2.vatican.va/content/john-paul-ii/fr/apost_exhortations/documents/hf_jp-ii_exh_19970510_lebanon.html.

[28] For example, Pope John Paul II, *Discorso di Giovanni Paolo II ai Vescovi Nordafricani in Visita "Ad Limina Apostolorum," 23 novembre 1981* (Vatican City, 1981), https://w2.vatican.va/content/john-paul-ii/fr/speeches/1981/november/documents/hf_jp-ii_spe_19811123_vescovi-nordafrica.html.

[29] For example, *Encyclical of Pope John Paul II—Redemptoris Missio: On the Permanent Validity of the Church's Missionary Mandate* (Vatican City, 1990)," secs. 55–57, http://w2.vatican.va/content/john-paul-ii/en/encyclicals/documents/hf_jp-ii_enc_07121990_redemptoris-missio.html; and Pope John Paul II, *Post-Synodal Apostolic Exhortation—Ecclesia in Asia* (Vatican City, 1999), sec. 31, http://w2.vatican.va/content/john-paul-ii/en/apost_exhortations/documents/hf_jp-ii_exh_06111999_ecclesia-in-asia.html.

[30] Pope John Paul II, *Redemptoris Missio*, secs. 55–57; and Pope John Paul II, *Discorso di Giovanni Paolo II ai Capi Religiosi Musulmani, Camera di Comercio di Dakar (Senegal)—Sabato, 22 febbraio 1992* (Vatican City, 1992), sec. 3 ("dialogo di vita"), https://w2.vatican.va/content/john-paul-ii/fr/speeches/1992/february/documents/hf_jp-ii_spe_19920222_musulmani-dakar.html.

[31] Pope John Paul II, *A New Hope for Lebanon*; and Pope John Paul II, *Address to the Muslim Religious Leaders*.

[32] Pope John Paul II, *Meeting with the Muslim Leaders, Omayyad Great Mosque*, sec. 4:

One initial goal of dialogue is gaining knowledge about each other, which in turn fosters respect, reduces conflict, creates freedom, and allows people to progress spiritually.[33] It also serves as the basis of cooperation in the service of humanity, which he describes as the most important objective. However, in addition to this central goal, he indicates that dialogue, arising from both genuine openness and particular religious commitment, has another objective: cultivation of greater self-awareness and moral development.[34] By "gazing" on the other, one learns more about the self.[35] It is necessary to reiterate that his stated goal of dialogue is never reconciliation of religious differences or consensus. This does, of course, land Pope John Paul II in another tensive discussion about the relationship of dialogue and mission, that is, the relationship of cooperative action and deep learning to the effective communication of the one Truth across religious boundaries. He tackles this head-on, asserting that there is no conflict between mission and dialogue because dialogue is an expression of mission; it is a facet or part of mission.[36] This statement could be construed as indicating that dialogue is simply a ruse for conversion, but it appears that he is again seeking to navigate the inherent tensions that arise from engaging both commonalities and differences across traditions.

In sum, although Pope John Paul II does echo *Nostra Aetate* in great measure, his elaborations begin to reveal new trajectories in Catholic engagements with Islam, Muslim practice, and Muslim persons. Specifically, he invokes the familiar and common (e.g., prayer) as an exhortation to Catholics. This is a novel usage of the familiar that assigns more agency to the religious other. Also, he is much more explicit and detailed about religious differences, especially theological differences, and about the fact that theological differences have implications that are not easily overlooked. He does nevertheless strive to maintain references to commonalities and unity, but must do so through more complex analogies, such as that of the one community of believers and the family of believers. And finally, he extends the value and goal of dialogue beyond collective moral action. Although he does prioritize such action, he also states that dialogue requires a genuine desire to know the religious other and that it can potentially lead to spiritual progression and better understanding of the religious self.

"Interreligious dialogue is most effective when it springs from the experience of 'living with each other' from day to day within the same community and culture."

[33] For example, Pope John Paul II, *Apostolic Letter—Novo Millennio Ineunte* (Vatican City, 2001), sec. 55, https://w2.vatican.va/content/john-paul-ii/en/apost_letters/2001/documents/hf_jp-ii_apl_20010106_novo-millennio-ineunte.html; and Pope John Paul II, *Meeting with the Muslim Leaders, Omayyad Great Mosque.*

[34] For example, Pope John Paul II, *Ecclesia in Asia*, sec. 31.

[35] Pope John Paul II, *Discorso di Giovanni Paolo II—Incontro con i Rappresentanti Mondo Politico, Culturale e Religiosio* [Carthage, Tunisia, April 14, 1996] (Vatican City, 1996), http://w2.vatican.va/content/john-paul-ii/en/speeches/1996/april/documents/hf_jp-ii_spe_19960414_world-culture.html.

[36] Pope John Paul II, *Redemptoris Missio*, secs. 4, 55–57; and Pope John Paul II, *Pastores Gregis*, sec. 68.

"Richness and Fruitfulness":
Pope Francis and the Reassessment of Difference

Pope Francis has a much smaller corpus of written statements related to Islam, Muslim practice, and Muslim persons. However, his statements are notable for the manner in which they build on some of the new trajectories evident in the statements and writings of Pope John Paul II, and thus present a new vision of religious difference. In this final section of the essay, I focus on two particular features of the statements of Pope Francis: his depiction of the process of dialogue and his reassessment of the value of religious difference.

In November 2013, Pope Francis issued the apostolic exhortation *Evangelii Gaudium*, in which he devoted two paragraphs to the discussion of dialogue with Muslims.[37] Paragraph 252 largely repeats sentiments from *Lumen Gentium* and *Nostra Aetate*, stressing Abrahamic connections, veneration of Jesus and Mary, religiosity as manifest in prayer, devotion to God, and ethical commitment. Two aspects of this paragraph begin to hint at a new layer of complexity in the engagement with religious difference. The first is the opening sentence, which stresses the "great importance" that relations with Muslims have now assumed because of the presence of many Muslims in Christian contexts. The second is the statement that "the sacred writings of Islam have retained some Christian teachings" (*Evangelii Gaudium*, sec. 252). Both of these begin to problematize and complicate the depiction of Islam and Muslims as being the distant other. Islam and Muslims in these descriptions are becoming spatially and scripturally proximate.

The second paragraph of *Evangelii Gaudium* devoted to Islam and Muslims explicitly discusses dialogue. Dialogue itself, of course, is not a new theme; it colors the vast majority of the decrees of the Second Vatican Council and the writings of Pope John Paul II. What is new in this apostolic exhortation is the emphasis placed on "suitable training . . . for all involved" (*Evangelii Gaudium*, sec. 253) in dialogue. According to Pope Francis, this training is required to ground people in their own tradition, but also to enable them to "acknowledge the values of others, appreciate the concerns underlying their demands and shed light on shared beliefs" (*Evangelii Gaudium*, sec. 253). Dialogue may entail some component of affirming commonalities, but this is not all it entails. The call here is to learn about one's religious self-identity and to then develop the capacity to see and hear the religious other in all of their particularity and familiarity. Acknowledgment and appreciation of differences and particularities are thus elevated in this exhortation, rather than glossed over or minimized as in *Nostra Aetate*. Moreover, according to Pope Francis, true dialogue and peaceful interaction are not possible without this form of training and knowledge.

---

[37] Pope Francis, *Apostolic Exhortation—Evangelii Gaudium* (Vatican City, 2013), secs. 252–53, https://w2.vatican.va/content/francesco/en/apost_exhortations/documents/papa-francesco_esortazione-ap_20131124_evangelii-gaudium.html.

A similar emphasis on education about religious difference is found in Pope Francis's 2013 *Message to Muslims at the End of Ramadan*, which he himself signed in divergence from earlier and subsequent custom. The stated theme of this message is "Promoting Mutual Respect through Education," and in it he calls on all people to respect the integrity of each individual life and to "think, speak and write respectfully of the other." He states that "families, schools, religious teaching and all forms of media" have a large role to play in promoting respect. Although he does not outline specific educational steps, respect of this type—respect that does not defame or attack the religion, teachings, symbols, values, religious leaders, and places of worship of the other—requires knowledge of the particularities of other traditions, knowledge of the ways in which other traditions are and are not familiar. Respect of this kind may even, and more provocatively, require appreciation, that is, positive valuation of religious differences.[38]

Hints of this possibility—of a reassessment of religious difference which significantly diverges from *Nostra Aetate*'s prioritization of sameness—are clear in the last statement of Pope Francis's that I will discuss, an address given to participants at the Pontifical Institute for Arabic and Islamic Studies' (PISAI) 50th Anniversary Conference in January 2015. Pope Francis begins this address by acknowledging misunderstandings and highlighting the centrality of "Listening" as a "necessary condition in a process of mutual comprehension and peaceful coexistence" and as a "pedagogical duty" aimed at facilitating the acknowledgment and appreciation mentioned in *Evangelii Gaudium*, sec. 253. He then cautions against the "snare of a facile syncretism" and an "accommodating approach" that affirms all things in interreligious engagement.[39]

What then is the proper approach to dialogue across traditions according to Pope Francis? He states that the first step is encounter and that, out of encounter, knowledge is born. Remarkably, he acknowledges that this encounter and resultant knowledge will "ask us and lead us to question our own spirituality." If the encounter is only an encounter of commonalities or a domestication of commonalities, then there would be nothing that would provoke such questions. Pope Francis is here speaking of deep encounters with real differences. While he maintains the groundwork of a shared human nature, he states that this foundation enables us to then truly engage differences and particularities; it allows us to "go beyond prejudices and fallacies and begin to understand the other according to a new perspective."

---

[38] Pope Francis, *Message to Muslims throughout the World for the End of Ramadan ('Id al-Fitr)* (Vatican City, 2013), https://w2.vatican.va/content/francesco/en/messages/pont-messages/2013/documents/papa-francesco_20130710_musulmani-ramadan.html.

[39] Pope Francis, *Address of His Holiness Pope Francis to Participants in the Meeting Sponsored by the Pontifical Institute for Arabic and Islamic Studies on the 50th Anniversary of Its Establishment in Rome* (Vatican City, 2015), https://w2.vatican.va/content/francesco/en/speeches/2015/january/documents/papa-francesco_20150124_pisai.html6. Quotations in the next three paragraphs come from this document.

Turning to discuss the efforts and history of the Pontifical Institute for Arabic and Islamic Studies, Pope Francis underscores the imperative and value of scholarly (rather than just practical) engagement across traditions. This form of study investigates sources, involves languages, and proposes "hermeneutics of dialogue." Two additional phrases invoked in this context are of particular import. First, he describes scholarly contributions in interreligious engagement and dialogue as "inspired by astonishment and wonder." Astonishment and wonder certainly transcend affirmation of the familiar. They are expressions of awe, insight, and positive questioning. Second, he states that in this form of dialogue "one tip-toes toward the other without stirring up the dust that clouds one's vision." One approaches the other with humility and esteem, and one endeavors to see the other as they see themselves, rather than as they are seen through the lens of religious self-identity. This address concludes with Pope Francis discussing dialogue in relation to violence. He contends that the best antidote to such violence is re-envisioning and teaching people to re-envision "the discovery and acceptance of difference as richness and fruitfulness."

In this brief survey, Pope Francis's approach to Islam, Muslim practice, and Muslim people appears to grow out of and grow beyond that of *Nostra Aetate* and Pope John Paul II. Pope Francis is concerned not only—or primarily—with religious commonalities. He does not depict dialogue as a practical encounter alone, nor as an encounter that achieves respect and cooperation based on avoidance of tensive theological questions. He outlines specific requirements for dialogue, many of which circle around the cultivation of knowledge of religious self-identity, along with accurate and nuanced knowledge of the identity of the religious other. Finally, he extends Pope John Paul II's discussion of the value of gazing on the other and presents difference as an asset, as "richness and fruitfulness." Difference is not just acknowledged and then avoided. Difference can, should, and must be engaged to foster true knowledge and appreciation of both the religious self and religious other. Thus, the unfamiliar—not just the familiar—becomes invaluable in the process of dialogue

In this essay, I explored the manner in which *Nostra Aetate* addresses Islam, Muslim practice, and Muslim persons, and argued that the decree prioritizes religious commonalities and sameness while neglecting religious differences. I then compared this approach to that of *Nostra Aetate*'s treatment of Judaism, to elaborations of *Nostra Aetate* by Pope John Paul II, and to recent statements by Pope Francis. Throughout these juxtapositions, I have highlighted the emergence of new trajectories in the approach to and evaluation of religious difference, and ultimately argued that Pope Francis's affirmation of religious difference offers a marked departure from the inclusivism of *Nostra Aetate*.

In conclusion, while Pope Francis's approach to religious difference and dialogue does diverge from that of *Nostra Aetate*, I would contend that *Nostra Aetate* set this trajectory in motion. The adoption of an inclusive stance to the religious other in the decree permitted the possibility of value outside of the church, even if only as a reflection of the Truth found within. It has been argued that inclusivism as a theological stance in response to religious diversity is a somewhat tensive and perhaps unstable position. I would refine this assessment slightly and state that inclusivism raises many questions that are easily silenced in more exclusive and more pluralist theologies. Inclusivism raises a host of questions about the degree of truth, the location of truth, the manifestations of truth, the vehicles of truth, and the reason for the existence of religious diversity. Inclusivism tends to step headlong into the divine mystery at its finest, and once these questions are asked—as is evident in Pope John Paul II's tensive elaborations of *Nostra Aetate*—we start looking for information and answers. We begin to have encounters and gain knowledge that transcends the somewhat superficial or one-dimensional depictions of religious others that are easily amenable to standard formulations of inclusivism. Encounters with real religious others tend not to fit the mold of the imagined and domesticated religious other.

In my estimation, such encounters with real religious others give rise to deep and provocative questions about the purpose and value of religious difference and diversity. Is there a value to religious difference in and of itself? If so, what is it? What is the purpose of religious difference? Pope John Paul II begins to reflect on these questions in his discussion of gazing and spiritual progression, but he ultimately prioritizes unified moral action. Pope Francis similarly extols moral action, but he appears to have adopted an alternative stance on the value and purpose of religious difference and interreligious dialogue. Dialogue cannot take place without deep knowledge of, appreciation of, and "unclouded" engagement with religious differences. These are prerequisites for Pope Francis. As such, dialogue remains concerned with moral action, while being transformed into a unique opportunity to foster awareness of both the religious self and religious other in all of their particularities and commonalities.

12

A Muslim Woman's Perspective
on Interreligious Dialogue
in the Light of *Nostra Aetate*

Riffat Hassan

"The Declaration on the Relation of the Church with Non-Christian Religions," commonly referred to as *Nostra Aetate*, passed by the Second Vatican Council and proclaimed by His Holiness Pope Paul VI on October 28, 1965, is certainly a document of profound historic significance not only for Roman Catholics but also for non-Christians, especially those who are specifically mentioned in it. It set the church on a new course vis-à-vis Muslims—a course which has been profoundly influential for me both personally and professionally.

Nostra Aetate, Section 3:
Affirmation of Commonalities between Christianity and Islam

Nostra Aetate begins by affirming the unity of the origin of all people and the fact that they will all return to God. Continuing in this spirit, it states in section 3, which pertains to Muslims, that the church holds Muslims in "high regard," since they worship the One God, endeavor to submit themselves to God as did "Abraham," revere Jesus "as a prophet," honor "Mary, His virgin Mother," await the "day of judgment," and "value the moral life."[1] I consider it highly significant that, among the reasons cited in the above passage for the church's "esteem" for Muslims, reference is made, first and foremost, to *Tawhid*—belief in God who is one, unique, and self-subsistent—which Muslims regard as the cardinal principle of Islam and the foundation of world unity. Among the three prophetic figures highly revered by Muslims who are mentioned in *Nostra Aetate*, section 3—Abraham, Jesus, and Mary—the first-named is especially important in the context of *Tawhid*. The special eminence accorded by the Islamic tradition to Abraham is due primarily to his identification as the first true monotheist, who "turned to his Sustainer with a heart free

---

[1] *Declaration on the Relation of the Church to Non-Christian Religions—Nostra Aetate*, proclaimed by Pope Paul VI (Vatican City, 1965), sec. 3, http://www.vatican.va/archive/hist_councils/ii_vatican_council/documents/vat-ii_decl_19651028_nostra-aetate_en.html.

of evil" (Surah 37: *As-Saaffat*: 84).[2] The Qur'an portrays Abraham's passionate quest for God.[3] It repeatedly describes him as *hanif*, one true in faith; as a verse highly meaningful for Muslims puts it, "Abraham was neither a 'Jew' nor a 'Christian' but was one who turned away from all that is false, having surrendered himself to God; and he was not of those who ascribe divinity to aught beside Him."[4] It is customary now to refer to Judaism, Christianity, and Islam as "Abrahamic" faiths, but Christians and Jews do not always fully grasp the centrality of Abraham in the Islamic tradition. I am, therefore, deeply touched that *Nostra Aetate*, section 3, likens the submission and self-surrender of Muslims to God's will to that of Abraham, with whom Muslims "take pleasure in linking [themselves]."[5] Although there are significant differences in the way in which Jews, Christians, and Muslims see Abraham, particularly with regard to his family life and descendants, their "common recognition of Abraham as a model of faith and submission"[6] forms a critical link among them. A powerful testament to this shared perspective is provided by the emergence of the concept of the "Abrahamic faiths" as perhaps the most important rubric within which the discipline of interreligious dialogue has developed since the 1970s.

Nostra Aetate, section 3, identifies another commonality between Christians and Muslims in their high estimate of Jesus and Mary, pointing out that Muslims venerate Jesus as a prophet even though they do not acknowledge him as the Son of God. While the fact that Muslims do not acknowledge the divinity of Jesus is regarded as the greatest theological obstacle to Christians and Muslims coming together, many Christians are unaware of the exceptional dignity that the Qur'an accords "'Isa ibn Maryam" (Jesus, son of Mary). It affirms that he was born of a virgin mother and declares that he shall be "of great honor in this world and in the life to come."[7] Muslims love Jesus deeply, not only on account of his miraculous birth and his miracles, but also, according to Fathi Osman, an eminent Muslim scholar and pioneer of Muslim-Christian dialogue, because of his message and how he presented it: Jesus "was taught by God not merely the 'letter' of the Book, but the 'essence' and the 'deep of wisdom' of God's revelations that is beyond the letter, and thus he could complement the Torah, with its strictness and legality, with the Gospel in its impressiveness and spirituality."[8]

---

[2] Muhammad Asad, *The Message of the Qur'an: The Full Account of the Revealed Arabic Text Accompanied by Parallel Transliteration* (Bristol, UK: Book Foundation, 2003), 774. All English translations come from this text.

[3] To cite just two: Surah 6: *Al-'An'am*: 74–81, and Surah 37: *As-Saaffat*: 88–89.

[4] Surah 3: Al-'Imran: 67. See Asad, *Message of the Qur'an*, 91.

[5] *Nostra Aetate*, sec. 3.

[6] Archbishop Michael L. Fitzgerald, MAfr, "From Heresy to Religion: Vatican II and Islam," in *Christian-Muslim Relations—A Road to Understanding*, Hospitallers Newsletter, Circular Paper # 3, 7, https://orderofmaltaamerican.org/files/pages/0047-newsletter_hospitallers_20_islam.pdf.

[7] Surah 3: *Al-'Imran*: 45, in Asad, *Message of the Qur'an*, 87.

[8] Fathi Osman, *Concepts of the Quran: A Topical Reading*, 2nd ed. (Los Angeles: MVI Publications, 1999), 480.

Nostra Aetate, section 3, further mentions that Muslims "honor, and at times devoutly invoke" Mary. I would amplify this statement by noting that the Qur'an names an entire chapter, Surah 19, for her. Though Muslims generally believe that all prophets were men, in my view there is strong evidence for regarding Mary as a prophet who received direct revelations from God. The place that she occupies in the hearts of Muslim women is unique. Surah *Maryam* is one of the most often recited chapters of the Qur'an, and its earlier part—which narrates the story of how she received the divine revelation announcing the birth of her gracious son, the travails she endures during childbirth, and the difficulties she faces when she returns to her people with her infant child—is recited by many Muslim women, especially during pregnancy and childbirth. A large number of Muslim girls are named after her. The portrayal of Jesus and Mary in the Qur'an is different, in a number of ways, from their portrayal in the Christian tradition, but it has a beauty and profundity of its own. It is my deep-felt desire that the opening of the closed spaces of the heart and mind that *Nostra Aetate* made possible will lead, one day, to an appreciation of the love and reverence for Jesus and Mary that is contained in the Qur'an and in the hearts of Muslims.

After identifying prophetic figures important to both Christians and Muslims, section 3 of *Nostra Aetate* takes up a belief that is central to each tradition. Both Christians and Muslims believe that human beings are accountable for their actions, and that, on the Day of Judgment, when the dead are resurrected, they will be rewarded or punished for their deeds during their lifetime. This belief provides the framework of the ethics that guides the daily life of both Christians and Muslims who seek to live in accordance with the will and pleasure of God. According to Qur'anic teaching, believers in God are required to honor both *Haquq Allah* (Rights of God) and *Haquq al-'ibad* (Rights of creatures). For Muslims the essence of "an upright life" is the fulfillment of one's duties to God and humankind, which constitutes righteousness. The religious practices common to Christians and Muslims that *Nostra Aetate*, section 3, highlights are "prayer, alms-deeds and fasting." Muslims refer to these practices as *salat, zakat,* and *siyam,* respectively, and include them in the "Pillars" of their faith, which connect them both to God and to other human beings. I have no doubt that Christians in general would endorse the spirit of piety underlying these practices as described in Surah 2: *Al-Baqarah*: 177, which teaches that true piety consists not in ritual observance, but in believing "in God, and the Last Day," spreading one's "substance" among family, orphans, and the needy, freeing "human beings from bondage," devoting oneself to prayer, and keeping one's promises.[9]

By stressing that Christians and Muslims follow common religious practices, *Nostra Aetate*, section 3, charts a realistic course for interreligious cooperation. As Anthony Cirelli, associate director of the Secretariat of Ecumenical and Inter-religious Affairs of the US Conference of Catholic Bishops, has noted, "The first thing to acknowledge when speaking of the Church's relationship with Muslims is

---

[9] Asad, *Message of the Qur'an*, 46.

not our differences, however real and theologically significant these might be, but rather those aspects or practices of our faith traditions that we share in common," such as prayer, fasting, and charitable acts. Emerging "plainly" from "the sacred texts of both Christianity and Islam," these practices are—far from being "insignificant virtues"—in fact "the keys to living in harmony and relative peace." I much appreciate his conclusion: "To the extent, therefore, that we Catholics, with the cooperation of our Muslims brothers and sisters, endeavor to highlight these foundational commonalities between our traditions, as well as point out together where such are lacking, we will, in fact, make an enormous contribution to the overall well-being of the world."[10]

Developments in Christian-Muslim Relations in the Catholic Church since *Nostra Aetate*

Having first offered compelling reasons why Christians should show "high regard" for Muslims, section 3 of *Nostra Aetate* recognizes the "many quarrels and hostilities" that have roiled Christians and Muslims over the centuries but pleads with them "to forget the past," urging that they sincerely work together to achieve "mutual understanding" and promote "social justice and moral welfare, as well as peace and freedom" for all humankind.[11] I regard this statement as a masterpiece— both for what it states and what it does not. It acknowledges the long and troubled history of the conflict between Christians and Muslims without specifying the multifarious areas of confrontation, including theological, political, and cultural. This "silence" is understandable in view of the plea the Second Vatican Council made to both Christians and Muslims "to forget the past" and engage in a sincere, collaborative effort to "preserve and promote peace, liberty, and social justice and moral values." I appreciate the Council's wisdom in not opening Pandora's box, for there is no easy way to resolve the multifaceted, multidimensional issues that have divided Christians and Muslims since the advent of the new faith.[12]

Although I admire the sagacity and skill of the authors of section 3 of *Nostra Aetate*, who covered so much ground in so few words, I am nevertheless intrigued by the exhortation "to forget the past." George Santayana, literary philosopher, has stated insightfully that "those who cannot remember the past are condemned to repeat it."[13] I am sure the learned authors knew that those who do "forget" their history can only replicate it, and I am inclined to think that what they were advocating was not "forgetting" the past

---

[10] Anthony Cirelli, "The Church in Relationship with Muslims" (September 15, 2012), http://www.usccb.org/beliefs-and-teachings/how-we-teach/catechesis/catecheticalsunday/human-dignity/nostra-aetate-cirelli.cfm.

[11] *Nostra Aetate*, sec. 3.

[12] In that spirit, I want to acknowledge those individuals who assisted in writing the passage relating to Muslims: Georges Anawati, OP, Robert Caspar, MAfr, Joseph Cuoq, MAfr, Father Jean Corbon, and John Long, SJ. See John Borelli, "Fifty Years Ago at Vatican II: The Critical Year for Interreligious Dialogue," *Origins* 44, no. 3 (May 22, 2014): 45.

[13] George Santayana, *Life of Reason* (New York: Charles Scribner's Sons, 1905), 1:284.

but "letting go" the rancor and bitterness that has been a legacy of the past especially for Muslims. Catholics and Muslims are the two largest religious blocs in the world, together constituting more than 55 percent of the human race. Underlying the poignant plea for advancing "mutual understanding" between Christians and Muslims in *Nostra Aetate*, section 3, I believe, was the recognition that the goals of global peace, liberty, and social justice could not be actualized without it. In this context, it is important to note how much of a practical nature has been accomplished,[14] including a number of concrete advances made in Christian-Muslim relations.[15]

Regarding theological matters beyond shared practices, the picture is mixed. Here it is useful to keep in mind Archbishop Michael Fitzgerald's distinction between the official teachings of the church regarding Islam and Muslims, and the statements of individual popes. "On the reflective level," he states, "there has been very little change in the position of the Church with regards to Islam," as witnessed by *Catechism of the Catholic Church* promulgated by Pope John Paul in 1992, which refers to *Nostra Aetate*, section 3, only in a note.[16] Rhetorically, however, much has changed. Subsequent to the promulgation of *Nostra Aetate*, every pope has underscored the need for dialogue with Muslims. Fitzgerald cites significant papal statements by Pope Paul VI and Pope John Paul II that "strike a slightly different tone" with reference to common bonds and brotherhood.[17]

Pope John Paul II appealed to the Catholic community in Ankara (1979) "to recognize and develop the spiritual bonds that unite us" (i.e., Christians and Muslims) and declared to the young Muslims in Casablanca (1985) that "the Catholic Church regards with respect and recognizes the quality of your religious progress, the richness of your spiritual traditions. I believe that we, Christians and

---

[14] Popes have felicitated Muslims on the occasion of *'Eid al-Fitr* since 1974. Further, the Vatican formed the Commission for Religious Relations with Muslims (CRRM) (1974), co-organized the Christian-Islam Congress in Tripoli with the World Islamic Call Society (WICS) (1976), established the *Nostra Aetate* Foundation (1990), sponsored a conference co-led by the Pontifical Council for Interreligious Dialogue (PCID) and the Muslim World League, the Organisation of the Islamic Conference, and the Muslim Congress in Cairo (1994), set up the Muslim-Christian Liaison Committee with four international Muslim organizations (1995), and established the Permanent Committee for Dialogue as a joint committee with Al-Azhar University's Monotheist Religions Committee (1998). See Salih Yusel, "Muslim-Christian Dialogue: Nostra Aetate and Fethullah Gulen's Philosophy of Dialogue," *Australian eJournal of Theology* 20, no. 3 (December 2013), 197–206. https://www.academia.edu/6274681/Muslim-Christian_Dialogue_Nostra_Aetate-and-Fethullah_Gulens-Philosophy_of_Dialogue.

[15] Including, for instance, the expansion of diplomatic ties between the Holy See and Muslim countries, academic agreements between Catholic and Islamic universities, many publications on Christian-Muslim relations by Catholic Churches, and positive papal actions. Pope John Paul II made a point of meeting Muslims on many of his journeys and included Muslims in all his invitations to pray together for peace. See Fitzgerald, "From Heresy to Religion," passim.

[16] Ibid., 9.

[17] Ibid.

Muslims, must recognize with joy the religious values which we have in common, and give thanks to God for them."[18] With reference to brotherhood, Pope Paul VI emphasized to the Islamic communities in Uganda (1969) "that what we hold in common may serve to unite Christians and Muslims ever more closely in true brotherhood." Pope John Paul II addressed Muslims in Paris (1980) as "our brothers in faith in one God," and affirmed to Muslims in the Philippines (1981) that "I deliberately *address you as brothers*: that is certainly what we are, because we are members of the same human family . . . but we are especially brothers in God, who created us and whom we are trying to reach, in our own ways, through faith, prayer and worship, through the keeping of his law and through submission to his designs."[19] I agree with Fitzgerald that the reference to brotherhood has special significance, since the term "brother" was traditionally reserved for fellow Christians. By calling Muslims "brothers" (rather than "neighbors of other faiths," as was generally done by the World Council of Churches in its documents), the popes were demonstrating "openness and friendship."[20]

Subsequent to the promulgation of *Nostra Aetate*, every pope has underscored the need for dialogue with Muslims.[21] The degree to which this perspective has become normative for the church can be gauged by remarks Pope Benedict XVI made to the Muslim community in Cologne, Germany, in 2005. Referencing the concluding words of section 3 or *Nostra Aetate*, the pope stated: "For us, these words of the Second Vatican Council remain the *magna carta* of the dialogue with you, dear Muslim friends, and I am glad that you have spoken to us in the same spirit and have confirmed these intentions."[22]

"A Common Word between Us and You": An Islamic Theological Response to Pope Benedict XVI's Remarks Subsequent to *Nostra Aetate*

Only a year after these remarks, ironically, Pope Benedict XVI threw Catholic-Muslim relations into turmoil. Lecturing an audience at the University of Regensburg, the pope examined the historical and philosophical differences

---

[18] Ibid.

[19] Ibid.

[20] Ibid.

[21] Barely a week into his papacy, Pope Francis declared that "it is important to intensify dialogue among the various religions, and I am thinking particularly of dialogue with Islam." *Address of Pope Francis—Audience with the Diplomatic Corps Accredited to the Holy See, Friday*, 22 March 2013 (Vatican City, 2013), http://w2.vatican.va/content/Francesco/en/speeches/2013/march/documenta/papa-frncesca_20130322_corpo-diplomatico.html).

[22] John Borelli, "Interreligious Dialogue as a Spiritual Practice," in *Islam in the Age of Global Challenges: Alternative Perspectives of the Gulen Movement Conference*, University International Conference Proceedings (Washington, DC: Georgetown University, 2008), 146, http://en.fgulen.com/conference-papers/gulen-conference-in-washington-dc/3100-Interreligious-dialogue-as-a-spiritual-practice.

between Christianity and Islam, and the relationship between violence and faith. He quoted the fifteenth-century Byzantine Emperor Manuel II Palaeologos, who had said, "'Show me just what Muhammad brought that was new, and there you will find things only evil and inhuman, such as his command to spread by the sword the faith he preached."[23] This quotation was widely denounced by Muslim religious leaders as well as governments of Islamic countries, and it led to public protests, including some violent ones in the West Bank. The pope was forced to issue an apology, stating that the offending quotation had a "startling brusqueness, a brusqueness which leaves us astounded," that it did not "express my personal thought," and that "the true meaning of my address . . . was and is an invitation to frank and sincere dialogue, with mutual respect."[24]

As a Muslim who has been engaged in Muslim-Christian dialogue for almost four decades, I am all too familiar with the way in which Islam has been maligned, sometimes to the point of demonization, since it first appeared in the world of Christendom. Given this history, it should not be difficult to understand why Muslims react so strongly to what they perceive as an erroneous and misleading presentation of Islam, often in slanderous terms meant to evoke hatred, ridicule, and contempt. But while the public outrage against Pope Benedict's lecture was not surprising, "An Open Letter to His Holiness," written by thirty-eight Muslim intellectuals a month later, was an unexpected—and salutary—response. It was intended to be "a very gentle and polite way of pointing out some factual mistakes" in Pope Benedict XVI's "controversial and potentially incendiary Regensburg lecture."[25] No "satisfactory answer from the Vatican" was received, and, exactly a year later, an expanded version of the letter, now titled "A Common Word between Us and You," written by Prince Ghazi bin Muhammad bin Talal of Jordan, was issued.[26] Signed by 138 prominent Muslims from several countries, including religious scholars, academics, writers, politicians, and the Grand Muftis of Egypt, Syria, Jordan, Oman, Bosnia, Russia, and Istanbul, this letter was addressed to the leaders of all Christian churches and denominations.[27]

"A Common Word" begins by clarifying what makes this initiative "so necessary at this time in history"—the current state of tension between Christian and Muslim communities, which could lead to "a growing popular consensus (on both

---

[23] Pope Benedict XVI, *Lecture of the Holy Father—Faith, Reason and the University: Memories and Reflections,* Aula Magna of the University of Regensburg, Tuesday, September 12, 2006, http://w2.vatican.va/content/benedict-xvi/en/speeches/2006/september/documents/hf_ben-xvi_spe_20060912_university-regensburg.html.

[24] "Pope Benedict VI in His Own Words," http://www.bbc.com/news/world-europe-21417767.

[25] H. R. H. Prince Ghazi bin Muhammad of Jordan, "On 'A Common Word between Us and You,'" in *A Common Word: Muslims and Christians on Loving God and Neighbor,* ed. Miroslav Volf, Ghazi bin Muhammad, and Melissa Yarrington (Grand Rapids, MI: William B. Eerdmans, 2010), 8.

[26] Ibid., 8–9.

[27] Ibid., 3.

sides) for worldwide (and thus cataclysmic and perhaps apocalyptic) Muslim/ Christian *jihad*/crusade."[28] The document categorically asserts that its goal is "to try to spread peace and harmony between Christians and Muslims all over the world, not through governments and treaties but on the all-important popular and mass level, through precisely the world's most influential popular leaders—that is to say, through the leaders of the two religions."[29] While recognizing that religious leaders are not makers of public policy, "A Common Word" firmly believes that "their opinions matter," not only because they have large public followings, but also because they are "the ultimate touchstones for morality and thus the final safety net for public opinion and non-governmental actors."[30]

Underscoring the fact that knowledge is a precondition for peace, "A Common Word" aimed to disseminate "proper basic knowledge" of Islam "in order to correct and abate the constant and unjust vilification of Islam, in the West especially."[31] The essence of this knowledge, stated in the opening paragraph of "A Common Word," consists of "*the twin 'golden' commandments*" shared by Islam and Christianity, namely, "*the paramount importance of loving God and loving one's neighbor.*"[32] Regarding these two commandments as the "*joint common ground*" between Muslims and Christians, "A Common Word," like *Nostra Aetate*, section 3, calls "*for peace and harmony between Christians and Muslims worldwide.*"[33] The very title of "A Common Word" comes from the Qur'an:

> Say: O People of the Scripture! Come to a common word between us and you: that we shall worship none but God, and that we shall ascribe no partner unto Him, and that none of us shall take others for lords beside God. (Surah 3: *Al-'Imran: 64*)[34]

The reference to the "People of the Scripture" (*Ahl al-Kitab*) in the above verse includes the adherents of the three Abrahamic faiths, namely, Jews, Christians, and Muslims, for all of whom loving God with total devotion is the greatest commandment, as is reiterated categorically in the Qur'an, the Torah, and the New Testament.[35] The emphasis in "A Common Word" on loving others as oneself came from its effort

---

28 Ibid., 4–9.

29 Ibid., 9.

30 Ibid., 12.

31 Ibid., 9.

32 Ibid., 3.

33 Ibid.

34 "The ACW Letter: A Common Word between Us and You," The 5-Year Anniversary Book, http://www.acommonword.com/the-acw-document.

35 Compare, for instance, the *hadith* recording the Prophet Muhammad's statements that faith encompasses love for one's brother as for oneself (*Sahih Al-Bukhari, Kitab al-Iman, Hadith* no. 13, and *Sahih Muslim, Kitab al-Iman, 67-1, Hadith* no.45), Jesus' articulation of the "Golden Rule" (Mt 22:38–40), and the Levitical injunction to "love your neighbor as yourself" (Lv 19:17–18). *A Common Word* cites all of these texts.

to find a theologically correct, preexisting *essential* common ground (albeit interpreted perhaps differently between Islam and Christianity), rooted in our sacred texts and in their common Abrahamic origin, in order to stop our deep-rooted religiously mutual suspicions from being an impediment to behaving properly toward each other. It was, and is, an effort to ensure that religions behave as part of the solution and are not misused to become part of the problem.[36]

The launching of both *Nostra Aetate* and "A Common Word" have been watershed events in the history of Christian-Muslim relations even though Islam has no centralized ecclesiological structure similar to that of the Catholic Church. "A Common Word" has received "unprecedented global acceptance" as the world's leading Muslim-Christian interfaith initiative, to which a large number of Christian religious leaders, including Pope Benedict XVI, Orthodox Patriarch Alexi II of Russia, Archbishop of Canterbury Rowan Williams, and the Presiding Bishop of the Lutheran World Federation, Bishop Mark Hanson, have responded.[37] In November 2007, more than three hundred leading Protestant leaders and academics (including evangelicals) responded to it in an open letter in the *New York Times*, while Muslim signatories, including individuals and Islamic organizations and associations, have continued to grow significantly in number.[38]

In the first year (2008) of the launching of "A Common Word," its impact became visible in many countries in diverse responses ranging from grassroots, community-based initiatives to academic dialogues, research, and publication to international conferences at important forums.[39] "A Common Word" has also had political influence[40] and was cited[41] during the Post-Inauguration Service for President Obama (January 21, 2009). In subsequent years, "A Common Word," like the Charter for Compassion launched by Karen Armstrong (2009), has continued to have worldwide impact.[42]

Nostra Aetate and "A Common Word": Commonalities versus Interreligious Dialogue

I have been extensively and intensively engaged in interreligious dialogue since 1979 and am one of the pioneers of Jewish-Christian-Muslim dialogue (often referred to as "trialogue") in the United States. My experiences in this arena, multifaceted

---

[36] Muhammad, "On 'A Common Word,'" 10.

[37] Ibid., 13.

[38] Ibid.

[39] For examples, see ibid.,14.

[40] For instance, it was the inspiration for the successful Wamp-Ellison Resolution (2008), which explicitly supported *A Common Word*'s initiative for interfaith dialogue, in the US House of Representatives, Muhammad, "On 'A Common Word,'" 14.

[41] By Reverend Sharon E. Watkins, General Minister and President of the Disciples of Christ Church in the United States and Canada, Muhammad, "On 'A Common Word,'" 14.

[42] Muhammad, "On 'A Common Word,'" 14.

and multilayered, have been life-transforming. Before I relate that experience to the ongoing debates about Muslim-Christian relations, I would like to make a point that seems to me fundamental: the basic purpose of neither *Nostra Aetate* nor "A Common Word between Us and You" was to promote the academic discipline or exercise commonly known as "interreligious dialogue." Indeed, I would assert that they tacitly recognize the limits of "interreligious dialogue" for effectively reconciling Christians and Muslims.

The complete title of *Nostra Aetate* is "Declaration on the Relation of the Church with Non-Christian Religions." The central concern of both it and "A Common Word" is to enable Christians and Muslims to have a *relationship* with each other based on what their respective authors perceived to be *essential moral and devotional commonalities between Christianity and Islam.* These authors were well aware of the theological differences between the two religious traditions as well as the long history of conflict and confrontation between their adherents, and chose not to delve into them. I believe that underlying this choice were two realizations: (1) that exploring the theological and historical dissensions between Christians and Muslims would not be conducive to building a positive relationship between them, and (2) that it is possible to develop a mutually respectful and beneficial relationship between Christians and Muslims on the basis of the common ground that the two ground-breaking documents have identified. In my judgment, the authors' choice was wise given their goal to move their respective communities from an attitude of mutual belligerency, suspicion, and exclusivism to one of cooperation and goodwill that would lead to global peace and well-being.

I came to the United States in 1972, a thirty-six-year-old Muslim woman of Pakistani origin who wanted to teach at the university level. Most Americans at that time had little knowledge of or regard for either Islam or Muslims. These attitudes were not surprising, since negative stereotyping of Muslims began in the seventh century, when the new faith started to move into territories largely occupied by Christians, who came to see Muslims not only as "'the Other" but also as "the Adversary." The grievous "sin" for which Dante Alighieri, the celebrated poet of medieval Christianity, placed the Prophet of Islam into all but the lowest levels of hell was that he "divided" the world of Christendom. Since Dante's description of the sinners matched their sins, he portrayed Prophet Muhammad as similarly cleaved, a "bloody" figure having a "mangled and split body" with his guts hanging out.[43] This gruesome portrait has left an unforgettable mark on the Muslim psyche. Edward Said has very ably documented how unfavorably Islam, Muslims, and Arabs have been misrepresented by "Orientalist" writers, who have played a major part in shaping Western perceptions of all three. One major result of his landmark work was that non-Muslims who have written about Islam subsequently no longer call themselves "Orientalists," a term now discredited.[44] However, the mind-set exhibited by so-called scholarly experts on Islam from Bernard Lewis (writing about "the

---

[43] Dante Alighieri, *The Inferno*, trans. John Ciardi (New York: Mentor, 1954), 236.
[44] Edward W. Said, *Orientalism* (New York: Pantheon Books, 1978).

Rage of Muslims") to Samuel Huntington (writing about "the Clash of Civilizations") as well as by numerous Western media experts, and now also by the US
president, is very similar to that of the non-Muslim detractors of Islam of earlier
times.[45]

By the late 1970s, interest in Islam had exploded in the West, fueled notably
by the Islamic Revolution in Iran, which overthrew Shah Reza Pahlavi, a staunch
ally of the United States, and brought to power Ayatollah Ruhollah Khomeini,
who identified the United States as "the great Satan." The long-drawn-out crisis
surrounding Americans held hostage by the Revolutionary Guard exacerbated the
tension many Americans felt at what was miscalled "the return of Islam."[46] Suddenly
there seemed to be an overwhelming interest in understanding Muslims/Arabs/
Iranians who had become a visible threat to "the American way of life." Since I was
a Muslim teaching about Islam, I was called upon with increasing frequency to talk
about Islam and Muslims in the context of contemporary issues. In March 1979, Dr.
Leonard Swidler, professor of religion at Temple University, invited me to take part
in a Jewish-Christian-Muslim "trialogue" of scholars, which included two Muslims
and two women. Sponsored by R. Sargent Shriver, head of the Kennedy Institute
of Ethics in Washington, DC, the trialogue attempted to enlarge Christian-Jewish
dialogue to include Muslims, since Islam was one of the three Abrahamic religions
and had begun to play a role in current affairs that was seen increasingly as both
prominent and problematic.

From 1979 to 1982, that trialogue became an open and direct conversation
among Jewish, Christian, and Muslim scholars motivated, for the most part, by
an earnest desire to listen to, and learn from, one another. We talked about many
subjects—including difficult ones such as conflicting biblical and Qur'anic texts—
without eroding the mutual trust and respect that had developed over time among
most of the group members. Although being in the trialogue was a great learning
and growing experience, two issues continued to trouble me. The first was that,
while the Jewish and Christian scholars in the group regarded it as self-evident that
acquiring knowledge of one another's religious tradition required a long period of
serious study, some of them tended to assume that Islam was a religion that one
could understand by reading a brochure over the weekend. It was very disappointing
to find out, for instance, that, although well-intentioned, a number of them knew
very little about Islam, and they tended, therefore, to think of it in simplistic or
reductionist terms. "A Common Word" has stated that knowledge is a precondition
for peace; I would add that it is also necessary for authentic dialogue. I made this
point frequently and was somewhat gratified to see that some non-Muslim partners
began to consider undertaking a systematic study of Islam.

---

[45] Bernard Lewis, "The Roots of Muslim Rage," *Atlantic Monthly* 266, no. 3 (September
1990): 47–60; Samuel P. Huntington, *The Clash of Civilizations and the Remaking of World
Order* (New York: Simon and Schuster, 1996).

[46] See Bernard Lewis, "The Return of Islam," *Commentary* 61, no. 1 (January 1, 1976),
39–49.

The other issue that troubled me was the lack of women in the group, as well as the lack of interest in investigating women's marginalization in both the world's major religious traditions as well as ecumenical dialogue in general. It took me a significant amount of time and effort to persuade my very liberal and liberated dialogue partners in the trialogue to devote a part of our meetings to issues regarding women in the three Abrahamic traditions. It continues to amaze me how even groups of men who regard themselves as staunch proponents of equal human rights for all people do not see the near-invisibility of women (especially those who have a strong voice) in their dialogues. It is unfortunate that women's presence is also not seen or felt in any significant way in *Nostra Aetate* or "A Common Word."

Despite these shortcomings, the original trialogue retained its visionary character as long as Sargent Shriver supported it. Once that backing ended, the group, which came to be known as the "International Scholars' Abrahamic Trialogue" (ISAT), became, in my opinion, a different entity, more bureaucratized and less intimate. The personal relationships that had sustained its spirit of cordiality and mutuality gave way to hard-line groupings of competing interests whose dynamics reminded me of Arnold Toynbee's profound observation that the three religions which sprang from a common historical root—Judaism, Christianity, and Islam—all have a tendency not only toward exclusivism and intolerance, but also to ascribe to themselves an ultimate validity against each other.[47]

The world has changed much between 1979 and 2016, but I do not see substantive changes in underlying Western ideas and attitudes toward Muslims. With Islamic Studies as an academic discipline now being taught at many more colleges and universities than was the case four decades ago, the ever-increasing volume of literature on Islam and Muslims by post-Orientalist writers, and the internet revolution, there appears to be little excuse for Westerners to remain ignorant about the subject. But looking at the Islamophobia pervasive in the United States today in every possible medium, I am reminded of T. S. Eliot's immortal lines:

Where is the wisdom we have lost in knowledge?
Where is the knowledge we have lost in information?
The cycles of Heaven in twenty centuries
Bring us farther from GOD and nearer to the Dust.[48]

The escalation in terrorism associated primarily with individuals and organizations self-identifying with militant Islam is regarded by many as the main reason for Islamophobia, and there is no doubt that the horrendous brutalities perpetrated by Al-Qaeda, Islamic State, and other participants in the global terror network upon both Muslims and non-Muslims have done irreparable damage to the image of Islam as a religion of peace and mercy. However, it remains pertinent to ask why, with so much interreligious dialogue going on in the Western world and other regions, atti-

---

[47] Arnold Toynbee, *An Historian's Approach to Religion* (Oxford: Oxford University Press, 1956).

[48] T. S. Eliot, *The Rock* (New York: Harcourt, Brace, 1934), 7.

tudes toward Muslims appear to have become much more negative than they were when we began this enterprise. There is no simple answer to this complex question. I have examined these issues more extensively elsewhere,[49] but here I would like to draw attention to one relatively unnoticed factor.

Until recently, virtually all interreligious dialogues in the West were sponsored by Christian and/or Jewish organizations. What this meant in practical terms was that these dialogues were dominated largely by Christian concepts, categories, and terminology, since Christians held center stage organizationally and structured the proceedings. It was not uncommon for the partners on either side—Jews and Muslims—to be expected to dialogue in terms that were not only alien to their particular religious ethos but sometimes even hostile to it. The fact that Muslims—including myself—had become culturally colonized due to our historical (and educational) experience made us collaborate, consciously or otherwise, in this unequal and unfair conversation. It took me more than a decade to realize that I could not give authentic answers to inauthentic questions, after which I refused to use terms that did not represent what I held to be the truth of my religious faith or perspective.

One major reason why Muslim participants in interreligious dialogue with their Abrahamic cousins felt like poor relations was that these meetings—held mostly in the United States or Europe—were almost always funded by Christians and/or Jews. The landscape has now changed significantly with the establishment of three interfaith organizations by Muslims from ruling families: the Royal Institute for Interfaith Studies by Prince Hassan bin Talal in Jordan (1994); the Doha International Center for Interfaith Dialogue by Sheikh Hamad bin Khalifa Al-Thani, Emir of Qatar (2007); and the King Abdullah bin Abdulaziz International Centre for Interreligious and Intercultural Dialogue (KAICIID) by King Abdullah of Saudi Arabia (2011). Although a new era seems to have dawned in the world of interreligious dialogue—at least in terms of political appearances, and especially with the huge influx of Saudi money—I have serious concerns about the integrity of any interreligious dialogue in which the process is controlled by imperial donors who desire to change their image abroad while the injustices in their societies remain unchallenged, and have the means to utilize the services of "experts" (some of whom may be well-intentioned) who can use politically correct rhetoric to create an aura of authenticity.

---

[49]   See, for instance, "The Burgeoning of Islamic Fundamentalism: Towards an Understanding of the Phenomenon," in *The Fundamentalist Phenomenon: A View from Within; A Response from Without*, ed. Norman J. Cohen (Grand Rapids, MI: William B. Eerdmans, 1990), 151–71; "A Muslim's 'Dialogue' with Abraham Heschel," in *No Religion Is an Island: Abraham Joshua Heschel and Inter-religious Dialogue*, ed. Harold Kasimow and Byron L. Sherwin (Maryknoll, NY: Orbis Books, 1991), 151–62; "Trialogue among the Abrahamic Faiths," *Global Dialogue: The New Universe of Faiths* 2, no. 1 (Winter 2000): 43–52; and "Engaging in Interreligious Dialogue: Recollections and Reflections of a Muslim Woman," *Journal of Ecumenical Studies*, Special Issue on Celebrating Fifty Years of Ecumenism and Interreligious Dialogue, 49, no. 1 (Winter 2014): 134–39.

Experience has made me increasingly skeptical about the ability of interreligious dialogue to bring people together. What started as a conversation among scholars and practitioners of two or more religions now also refers to conversations among representatives of diverse religious institutions, or even different religious cultures or civilizations. Furthermore, it has evolved into an academic discipline which is being taught in more and more educational academies in several countries, particularly in the West. Given the wide variety of persons who are today engaged in it, there is bound to be a multiplicity of differing or overlapping motivations underlying such engagement. To be sure, a number of scholars, students, and religious practitioners regard interreligious dialogue as a necessary pedagogical tool for dealing with the challenges of peaceful coexistence in a world with ever-increasing plurality as well as polarity. They often cite Hans Küng's famous words: "No peace among the nations without peace among the religions. No peace among the religions without dialogue between the religions. No dialogue between the religions without investigation of the foundations of the religions."[50]

Although the first of Küng's statements would have been endorsed by the authors of *Nostra Aetate* and "A Common Word" (as well as Sargent Shriver, who would probably have affirmed the second statement too), fostering a "dialogue between the religions" was not—as I have stated earlier—their primary purpose. Both documents identify what they regard as core commonalities between Christianity and Islam and urge their respective communities to accept them as a sufficient basis for global peace, but neither of them pay serious heed to an "investigation of the foundations of the religions." A major reason for this approach, in my judgment, is that such an investigation is bound to lead to what I call "nonnegotiable theological propositions," which have historically played a pivotal role in bringing the interreligious dialogue to a bitter impasse.

In my experience of Muslim-Christian dialogue, I have seen that the issue of Christology, which for the vast majority of Christians is "a nonnegotiable proposition," has been the rock upon which this dialogue has floundered because of the inability of Muslims to accept the divinity of Jesus. Dr. Fathi Osman has trenchantly observed that "the person of Jesus has probably raised some of the most heated disputes in the history of God's messages, and these disputes arise not only between those who follow him and those who do not, but even among his very followers."[51] For Muslims the nonnegotiable proposition is the belief that the Qur'an is the literal Word of God transmitted by the Archangel Gabriel to Prophet Muhammad, who transmitted it without change or error to his followers. My experience has taught me that if one wants interreligious dialogue to lead to open and positive understandings and appreciations of each other's traditions, it is almost mandatory to steer clear of "nonnegotiable" theological propositions.

By grounding the possibility of, and the necessity for, peace between the two largest religious communities in the world on core commonalities between Christianity and Islam, *Nostra Aetate* and "A Common Word" offer signs of hope in a

---

[50] Hans Küng, *Islam: Past, Present and Future* (Oxford: Oneworld, 2007), xxiii.

[51] Osman, *Concepts of the Quran*, 478.

sorely divided world. The successful public outcomes of these two documents testify to their ability to secure agreements between governments, international organizations, and a host of institutional or professional groupings. Still, one may fairly ask if this consensus will be able to set aside or transcend the attachment that the vast majority of devout Christians and Muslims have for the nonnegotiable theological beliefs that they regard as the bedrock of their religions? Should one not expect extreme difficulties, including strong negative reactions, when desire for peace on earth comes into conflict with deeply held religious beliefs?

Concluding Personal Reflections

I search for answers by looking at my own past life—not in further academic or intellectual exploration, but in the realm of the spirit. Muslims—like Christians and Jews—believe that God's Spirit has been breathed into them, which makes them the recipients of special capabilities as well as responsibilities. Muslims have been told by the Qur'an that human beings have been appointed *khala'if al-'ard* (God's vicegerents on earth), who must take care of the earth that sustains us. They are also commanded to strive to develop their potentialities to the fullest, having been created by God "in the finest configuration" (Surah 95: *At-Tin*: 4).[52] This imperative has been embodied in the beloved Islamic tradition: "Create in yourselves the attributes of God."

Islamic mystics often talk about God's ninety-nine Names, each of which has a particular signification. The two most essential names are *Rahman* and *Rahim*, terms which signify the highest degree of mercy, compassion, and grace. The invocation with which Muslims start not only their five daily prayers but also every other important activity in their everyday lives is *Bismil-laah ir Rahman ir Rahim* ("In the Name of God, the Most Merciful and Gracious, the Most Compassionate and the Dispenser of Grace"). Two Qur'anic verses in Surah 6: *Al-An'am*, deserve particular attention for what they reveal about God's mercy. The first (verse 12) reads: "Say: 'Unto whom belongs all that is in the heavens and on earth?' Say: 'Unto God, who has willed upon Himself the law of grace and mercy.'"[53] The second (verse 54) reads: "And when those who believe in Our messages come unto thee, say: 'Peace be upon you. Your Sustainer has willed upon Himself the law of grace and mercy.'"[54] Explicating these two verses, Muhammad Asad[55] points out that:

the expression "God has willed upon Himself as a law" [*kataba 'ala nafsihi*] occurs in the Qur'an only twice—and in both none of the other divine attributes has been similarly described. This exceptional quality of God's grace and mercy is further stressed in Surah 7: *Al-'A'raf*: 156: "My grace

---

[52] Asad, *Message of the Qur'an*, 1097.

[53] Ibid.,199.

[54] Ibid., 206.

[55] Muhammad Asad's *Message of the Qur'an* is regarded by most modern Muslim Qur'anic scholars to be the best translation and explanation of the Qur'an in English.

overspreads everything"—and finds an echo in the authentic Tradition in which according to the Prophet (Muhammad), God says of Himself, "Verily, My grace and mercy outstrips My wrath" (Bukhari and Muslim).[56]

The strong emphasis on God's mercy and compassion present in the Qur'an makes it self-evident that all human beings irrespective of religious identity are recipients of God's unbounded grace. Muslims and other believers in God must recognize what this means in terms of how they relate to their brothers and sisters who profess a different faith. As a Muslim woman who has fought countless battles to secure justice for my sisters in Islam—perhaps the most disadvantaged group in the world—my effort today is focused on rebuilding so much that is broken in our world by meditating on, and internalizing, the essence of God as *Rahman* and *Rahim*. The statements by Popes John Paul II and Pope Paul VI cited earlier, in which they refer to the fundamental importance of recognizing, honoring, and developing the spiritual kinship and brotherhood (and sisterhood, even though it remains unmentioned) that exists between Christians and Muslims, strikes a deeper chord in my heart than any intellectual argumentation or academic theorizing that I have come across during my lengthy sojourn in the wonderland/wasteland of interreligious dialogue.

I would like to end by remembering two mystics—one Catholic, the other Muslim—who were able to realize the essential unity of human beings despite everything that separated them. In 2015 the people of Kentucky—the state in which I live—celebrated the hundredth anniversary of the birth of Thomas Merton, whom Pope Francis in his recent address to Congress named as one of four great Americans to whom he wanted to draw attention. In 1957, as Merton stood at the corner of Fourth and Walnut (now Muhammad Ali Boulevard) in Louisville, he had an epiphany as he saw people walking by. "I was suddenly overwhelmed with the realization," he recounted, "that I loved all those people, that they were mine and I was theirs, that we could not be alien to one another even though we were total strangers."[57]

And finally, I want to place in the sacred silence of my spirit's sanctum the immortal words of Jalal ad-Din Rumi, who invites us all to a higher place beyond the reach of common humanity:

Out beyond ideas of wrongdoing and rightdoing,
there is a field. I'll meet you there.

When the soul lies down in that grass,
the world is too full to talk about.
Ideas, language, even the phrase *each other*
doesn't make any sense.[58]

---

[56] Ibid., 199n10.

[57] Gregory Hillis, "Kentucky's Own Merton Embodies the Pope's Call for Cialogue," *Louisville Courier-Journal* (October 5, 2015), 12A.

[58] *The Essential Rumi*, trans. Coleman Barks, new exp. ed. (New York: HarperCollins, 2004), 36.

Part VI

Buddhist and Hindu Perspectives

13

A BUDDHIST RESPONSE TO *NOSTRA AETATE*

Rita M. Gross

I am grateful for this opportunity to offer a Buddhist response to *Nostra Aetate*, the classic Roman Catholic statement on religious diversity, due to my lifelong involvement in issues of religious diversity and my profound dislike of any claims to exclusive truth claims on the part of any religion. In my book *Religious Diversity—What's the Problem? Buddhist Advice for Flourishing with Religious Diversity*,[1] I wrote extensively about several things essential to Buddhist sensibilities that I think could improve interreligious interchange and theology of religions. I briefly discuss some of them in this essay.

The Main Matter:
Attitudes toward Religious Diversity

Regarding theology of religions and issues of religious diversity, I have long contended that the main task facing every religion is to acknowledge that religious diversity is normal and inevitable, not a religious or theological mistake, and presents no ultimate theological problem for any religion. This is my position as a Buddhist constructive thinker who is deeply influenced by the modern academic study of religions. I cannot claim that this is the Buddhist position historically, only that it is completely compatible with major Buddhist claims, but I also want to offer the claim that, given contemporary conditions, every other religion needs to incorporate this reality into its theology of religions.

Therefore, some issues that have been much debated in theology of religions seem beside the point to me because they do not concede the inevitability of religious diversity. If religious diversity is inevitable and not a deep theological problem, the question for theologians of religions becomes, "Why do we dislike religious diversity so much and have such a preference for religious uniformity?" not the question currently uppermost in the work of many theologians of religions: "Are the other religions enough like ours to be worthy of our respect?" All of the major options in theology of religions, even the pluralist option, circle primarily

---

[1] Rita M. Gross, *Religious Diversity—What's the Problem? Buddhist Advice for Flourishing with Religious Diversity* (Eugene, OR: Cascade Books, 2014).

around that question, and it seems to me that that is the question behind *Nostra Aetate*. That document asks the question: Do non-Catholics really have anything worthy of respect and reverence? Listen carefully to the wording:

> The Catholic Church rejects nothing that is true and holy in these religions. She regards with sincere reverence those ways of conduct and of life, those precepts and teachings which, though differing in many aspects from the ones she holds and sets forth, nonetheless often reflect a ray of that Truth which enlightens all men [*sic*! Note the androcentrism].[2]

But who asks and answers the question? Although one can applaud the concessions in this document and its realization that non-Christian religions include many worthy teachings and practices, it still presumes that one religion alone (Catholicism in this case) contains The Truth and is qualified to judge the truth of other religions.

In other publications I have argued that it simply is not religiously cogent to imagine that any one of the world's current religions could or should become the sole surviving religion on the planet or could meet the spiritual and religious needs of everyone on the planet, any more than everyone would or should adopt the same language, the same culture, or the same diet. I do not want to repeat those arguments here.[3] If we don't concede that religious diversity is inevitable and not theologically problematic, we wind up with the same kinds of hierarchical dualisms that result in racism, sexism, nationalism, and the suffering that results when one group of people claims superiority over those who are different. It is hard to understand the urge to rank alternatives hierarchically into true/false, better/worse dichotomies whenever differences are perceived. But given that oppositional dualism seems to be a default mode for human consciousness, such alleged dichotomies are common. It is very sad that such thinking has been so pervasive regarding religious diversity.

Therefore, I claim that, for theology of religion, the paramount task is finding the right questions, and that those questions have largely been unasked in the exclusivism, inclusivism, pluralism discussions. The question is not "Are other religions enough like ours to be acceptable?" It is not even, "Are the various religions essentially the same or congruent at some deep level?" The relevant questions are, "Why does religious diversity seem to be a problem to us?" and "How do we flourish with religious diversity, given that it is inevitable?" These are the questions theologians of religions should be asking of their religions. They also need to be asking what resources their traditions have for flourishing with inevitable religious diversity.

---

[2] *Declaration on the Relation of the Church to Non-Christian Religions—Nostra Aetate*, proclaimed by Pope Paul VI (Vatican City, 1965), sec. 2.

[3] Rita M. Gross, "Excuse Me but What's the Question? Isn't Religious Diversity Normal?" in *The Myth of Religious Superiority: A Multifaith Exploration*, ed. John Hick and Paul F. Knitter (Maryknoll, NY: Orbis Books, 2005), 75–87, and Gross, *Religious Diversity*, chap. 5, 118–35.

The much loved question—whether the various religions all teach essentially the same thing, the "the Fatherhood of God and the brotherhood of man," as it is often put (note the triple androcentrism)—needs to be dispensed with succinctly. As a lifelong student of comparative studies in religion, I am very suspicious of claims that religions teach essentially the same thing, though claims that they are structurally similar or have similar ethical ideals are cogent. Many commentators seem to prefer unity and universalism over nonduality and diversity, a topic that I addressed in an entire chapter of my book on religious diversity.[4] Nonduality, the deeply internalized recognition that subject and object do not exist independently of each other and cannot be isolated from one another, is a deep-seated Buddhist sensibility. Buddhists claim that nonduality, rather than the duality of their independent, separate existence, or their unity and uniformity, more accurately represents "things as they are." I contend that nonduality needs to be much more deeply explored by theologians of religions and others who deal with issues of religious diversity. It has much to offer such discussions. One should not assume that "unity" is obviously more worthy than diversity and uniqueness, as so many do. In nature, diversity, not sameness and unity, is the norm, and it also seems to be the norm among human beings. The question is why human diversity is so troubling to so many, given how much human suffering is caused by rejection of that diversity.

Among the many other Buddhist sensibilities that I claim could greatly benefit discussions of religious diversity, in this short chapter, I can present only one, and I have chosen to highlight Buddhism's suspicion that verbal and conceptual propositions cannot be trusted to be reliable absolute truths, or to be "most certainly true," as I was taught to regard them as a child. There are many examples of how Buddhists have fallen short of taking these sensibilities seriously, including a disappointing history of intra-Buddhist sectarianism. Nevertheless, these Buddhist teachings are both central to *Buddhist* sensibilities and could be extremely helpful in a religiously diverse world if they were deeply internalized by religious leaders and practitioners. Consistently, this has been one of the most basic points of my writing and teaching on flourishing with religious diversity, being the subject of a whole chapter of *Religious Diversity*.[5]

Problems that occur with undue or inappropriate reliance on words and concepts are consistent in Buddhist commentaries on the four main attachments to which people are easily subject. To understand why attachment to words and concepts is so dangerous, clear understanding of the way that Buddhists understand the role of attachment or grasping (*trsna*) in causing human suffering is required. These teachings are at the heart of Buddhism. As is well known, the first truth of the Noble Ones is that suffering is inevitable in conventional ways of living, and the second truth of the Noble Ones is that suffering is caused by attachment, which is desperately wanting what we cannot have or wanting things to be different than they are. In turn, when explaining the Second Truth, teachings on *pratityasumut-*

---

[4] See Gross, *Religious Diversity,* chap. 8, 135–50.

[5] See ibid., chap. 6, 101–17.

pada, conditioned genesis, the twelve *nidanas*, or teachings on interdependence, develop these teachings further. These twelve trace out the conditioning links that connect all phenomena, which means that all phenomena are interdependent, and none of them is independent. In a single word, they are "empty" of inherent or independent existence.

Important texts represent the Buddha as teaching: "Bhikkhus, there are these four kinds of clinging. What four? Clinging to sensual pleasures, clinging to views, clinging to rules and observances, and clinging to a doctrine of self."[6] Thus, clinging to views, including religious views, is one of the four major things to which we habitually cling. Thus, rather than being a virtue, holding religious views strongly, which could be defined as being too convinced of one's own religious views, is an impediment, a problem. The link between suffering and clinging to religious views is important to explore. Most, if not all, wars and persecutions stem from too much conviction in the rightness and correctness of one's own views, as well as self-centeredness. Few people reflect seriously on the aggression inherent in ideology, aka holding views strongly. Holding one's own views strongly often results in aggression and disrespect toward those with whom one disagrees. One also experiences the suffering of one's own anger, one of the most painful of all emotions. Religions often encourage their followers to adhere to the religion's doctrines with unquestioning, unreflective allegiance. The more fiercely people adhere to the religious doctrines of their sect, the more they are praised for "having true faith."

In politics, anyone who thinks through a situation or an issue and changes his or her mind is derogatively called a "flip-flopper." Just reflect on how much more pleasant life could be if people's beliefs about many things, including religion and politics, were held less dogmatically, with less attachment. Think how much personal and family discord is caused when close friends and family members, who do not know how to flourish with diversity and discord in their midst, argue with their relatives and friends about religion or politics, even "unfriending" them when people refuse to change their views until they accord with those of the one with strong views.

No wonder so many spiritual teachers regard opinionatedness or rigid conviction of the correctness of one's own views, religious and otherwise, as one of the greatest obstacles on the spiritual path. Religions often decry self-centeredness and attachment to sensual pleasure as great obstacles for realizing deep spirituality, but few realize that attachment to one's own version of religious truth is just as big an obstacle to spiritual attainment. It completely destroys the equanimity and evenness of mind so prized by Buddhists, which bring so much peace and which make religious diversity and religious coexistence unproblematic. It is very interesting and insightful to realize that attachment to views could be as unhelpful as attachment to sensual pleasures or self-centeredness. I would argue that this is one of the most important contributions Buddhists could make to discussions of religious diversity and coexistence.

---

[6] Bhikkhu Nanamoli and Bhikkhu Bodhi, *The Middle Length Discourses of the Buddha: A Translation of the Majjhima Nikaya* (Boston: Wisdom Books, 1995), 161.

People who are very attached to their own opinions are often under the illusion that the world would be a better place and everyone would be happier if only everyone else would adopt their opinions, not realizing that such a vision is no more realistic than the dream of a universally comprehensible language, which is a much more practical and desirable outcome than universally accepted religion or political/social systems. One of the most insightful comments about the aggression inherent in such conviction and opinionatedness is by Chögyam Trungpa:

> While everyone has a responsibility to help the world, we can create additional chaos if we try to impose our ideas or our help upon others. Many people have theories about what the world needs. Some people think that the world needs communism; some people think that the world needs democracy; some people think that technology will save the world; some people think that technology will destroy the world. The Shambhala teachings [or any nonoppressive vision] is not based on converting the world to another theory.[7]

The operative word here is "theory," as in "converting the world to another theory." *The problem is never with one's views, but with the desire to universalize or absolutize them,* to think they could or should be relevant for everyone. As I stated over and over throughout my book, the problem with universalized religious truth claims, such as that Jesus is the "only universal savior of the world" is not the belief itself but how it is held—with attachment and dogmatically. Those to whom such a belief is dear would not be harmed in any way if they changed the way those beliefs were held. A belief that is not universalized or absolutized is not less meaningful if it is held in a more flexible and relaxed manner. It is the same with most of the "hot button" social issues. Those who advocate for marriage equality never claim that everyone should enter same-sex unions, whereas those who oppose marriage equality often claim that only the form of marriage they prefer, heterosexual unions, should be allowed.

Why the arrogance and aggression of thinking everyone else should adopt one's views and preferences, for Jesus, for Christianity, or for Buddhism, or for heterosexuality? Given that, regarding religion, I prefer diversity and coexistence to intolerance and universal truth claims, I am sometimes asked if such preferences are not "intolerant" of those who prefer universalism to valuing diversity, intolerant of those who advocate stridently for their own religion out of intense conviction that it is the only worthwhile religion on the planet? I answer "No," because a situation in which many religious views flourish does not diminish any specific view unless it claims that it is worthy of being absolutized and universalized, and I would claim that no view rises to that standard.

---

[7] Chögyam Trungpa, *Shambhala: The Sacred Path of the Warrior* (Boston: Shambhala Publications, 1998), 29.

There are many Buddhist images for the inadvisability of clinging to religious views, even the Buddhist teachings themselves. Two of the most relevant similes compare "truth" or dharma held with grasping and fixation to a snake grabbed by the wrong end and to a raft that has already served its purpose of getting one across a body of water but which one still wants to carry around. The snake simile is better known for its later use by Nagarjuna in explaining how teachings on emptiness are totally misunderstood and become damaging if they are taken literally or nihilistically, but it is also used in Pali texts. The statement attributed to the Buddha states:

> Suppose a man needing a snake, seeking a snake, wandering in search of a snake, saw a large snake and grasped its coils or its tail. It would turn back on him and bite his hand or his arm or one of his limbs and because of that he would come to death or deadly suffering.[8]

In the much-quoted raft parable, found in the same collection of sutras, the Buddha talks of a man who, on a dangerous shore of a body of water, sees the peaceful and pleasant other shore and decides to build a raft out of grass and branches and paddles himself to the other shore using his hands and his feet. He then thinks that because the raft was so useful, he should continue to carry it around on dry land. The Buddha says of that plan:

> Bhikkhus, when you know the Dhamma to be similar to a raft, you should abandon even the teachings, how much more so things contrary to the teachings.[9]

This principle is stated even more forcefully by the contemporary Tibetan teacher Dzongsar Khyentse, Rinpoche, who says,

> At the point of total realization, you must abandon Buddhism. The path is a temporary solution, a placebo to be used until you understand emptiness.[10]

Later in the same book, he writes, "If you still define yourself as a Buddhist, you are not a Buddha yet."[11]

These two similes, especially the raft parable, present an insight about what religion can and should do in our lives that is often missed by those commenting on religious diversity or those who think that diversity is a mistake or a problem. It is often thought that religion is about certainty or absolute truth, that it should provide us with answers to questions about which there can be no certainty, but

---

[8] Nanamoli and Bodhi, *Middle Length Discourses*, 227.

[9] Ibid., 229.

[10] Dzongsar Jamyang Khyentse, *What Makes You Not a Buddhist?* (Boston: Shambhala Publications, 2007), 77–78.

[11] Ibid., 106.

only speculation and culturally transmitted beliefs, which hopefully are also credible hypotheses. *Religions are not about "truth." But they should work. They should do something. What? They cannot provide certain answers to questions about which only speculation is possible. But they should "get us to the other shore," to use the raft analogy. In other words, their job or function is to be a skillful means for transformation, to transform those who follow them from self-centeredness toward greater kindness and flexibility.*

There is no reason to suppose that there is only one tool or skillful means for meaningful transformation, which nicely answers the question about how to think about the multiplicity of religions. The question we need to ask of other religions is not, "Are they true or 'more true' (whatever that might mean)?" but "Do they work?" Are their believers kind to women, animals, the unfortunate, and nature? Are they kinder and more flexible, less rigid and dogmatic than they were formerly? I would contend that this question about the practicality of religion, about how effective they are as skillful means for relevant ethical transformation, is the question about religious diversity that should be uppermost but is most often unasked and overlooked because so many commentators are far too concerned with questions of truth in religion.

But in my work, I have consistently claimed that the effectiveness of religious teachings and practices in promoting meaningful transformation is much more relevant than questions of the "truth" of religious claims, something that is impossible to determine. That effectiveness is what Buddhists sometimes call "skillful means," the ability of religious practices and teachings to promote meaningful and auspicious transformation. Flourishing with religious diversity is much more likely to occur if people are more concerned with the utility and effectiveness of religions, that is to say their track record as skillful means, than with their truth. Concern with religious teachings and practices as skillful means rather than as truth claims opens up many possibilities for flourishing with religious diversity.[12]

My suggestions for evaluating the diverse religious teachings and practices as skillful means, methods for spiritual transformation, is Buddhist-inspired rather than purely Buddhist. The concept of skillful means is authentically Buddhist and is part of a complex of teachings involved in the common pairing of wisdom (*prajna*), gendered feminine, on the one hand, and skillful means (*upaya*), gendered masculine, on the other, especially as is common in Vajrayana Buddhism. They are paired because the one without the other is relatively useless. In other words, having answers or "truth" without knowing how to work with the situation at hand is useless, even ineffective. One also has to have enough skill to put knowledge or information into effect, to get practical results. Knowledge is meaningful only when paired with appropriate skills. Contemplating that pairing led me to conclude that teachings or ideas are, in fact, more in the realm of *upaya*, not the realm of *prajna*, which initially strikes even many Western Buddhists as counterintuitive. I would

---

[12] For my full discussion of this point, see Gross, *Religious Diversity*, chap. 5.

argue that this insight accords with the Buddhist emphasis on not speculating on metaphysical questions or theoretical knowledge, as in the famous "arrow parable," in which the Buddha likens the futility of pursuing philosophical speculations to the behavior of a man shot with a poisoned arrow who refuses help until someone answers every query he can pose about the circumstances of the attack. His questions prevent his healing.

This discussion of religious teachings as skillful means rather than truth claims is part of my presentation of the Buddhist emphasis that I think could offer the most to discussions of religious diversity and interreligious exchange. Buddhism's suspicion is that verbal or conceptual propositions cannot be trusted to be totally reliable absolute truths, or to be "most certainly true," as I was taught to regard them as a child. Though this suspicion is expressed in the point that attachment to views is actually spiritually problematic, it is also often expressed in the much later analogy, extremely common in Zen Buddhism, of the moon and a finger pointing to the moon. This analogy asks us to consider someone who sees someone else pointing a finger at the moon and focuses on the tip of the finger while ignoring the moon to which the person is pointing. The point of his analogy is to emphasize the difference between theoretical teachings and insight into the (nonconceptual) meaning of teachings, in keeping with frequent Buddhist advice regarding how to take teachings—rely on the meaning, not the words. The point is not that there is nothing to "know," but that that knowledge cannot be captured in words and concepts, much as Western apophatic theology points out—God is always beyond our theologies. Instead, we must pursue the disciplines, the skillful means of teachings and practices that put us in touch with the "god beyond god," to quote Paul Tillich. This relationship between words or concepts and deep understanding is pointed out in the words of a great twentieth-century meditation master Thrangu Rinpoche:

> When you rest in this experience of the mind, which is beyond extremes or elaborations, what is the experience of that like? It is characterized by a profound state of ease, which means an absence of agitation or discomfort. Therefore, the experience is comfortable and pleasant. The term comfortable does not indicate pleasure in the sense of something you're attached to, or the pleasure of acting out an attachment or passion. It's simply the absence of any kind of discomfort or imperfection in the nature of the mind itself. Therefore, the experience of that nature is characterized by comfy blissfulness. This is as close as we can come in words to what you experience when you look at your mind. You couldn't actually communicate what you experience. It's beyond expression . . . [it] is inexpressible, indescribable and even inconceivable.[13]

---

[13] Khenchen Thrangu Rinpoche, *Pointing Out the Dharmakaya: Teaching on the Ninth Karmapa's Text* (Ithaca, NY: Snow Lion Publications), 71.

Conceding what words and concepts can do, as well as acknowledging their limits, would really go far to promote the flourishing of religious diversity. Doing so would significantly limit the tendency toward "competitive theology," which is often expressed, as in *Nostra Aetate*, in looking for an underlying similarity between "their" religion and "ours," a method of dealing with religious diversity that does not really concede that religions are diverse and that difference is not necessarily a problem and need not promote negative comparison, as it so often does. Conceding that all theologies or conceptual systems encounter the same limits regarding their verbal formulations puts them on a level playing field, which fosters flourishing with religious diversity.

One of the problems, in my view, is that many theologians and religious thinkers seem confused about the inevitable nature of religious language. They tend to talk as if the language of their own religious tradition is unmediated, directly from a nonhuman and nonnatural source, as if the deity speaks only Hebrew or Arabic, or whichever language they prefer. But if one understands interdependence and emptiness, one would not suppose that one's own language is unmediated (though some Tibetans seem to think that of Tibetan!). Both Buddhism and the modern comparative study of religion would agree that, because phenomena are conditioned, unconditioned religious language is impossible. I would not claim that in general Buddhists recognize this fact more readily than adherents of other religions.

Religious and theological language, if one is honest about it, is speculative, metaphysical, and/or mythological. I am not one who thinks this is a problem unless one insists that religious claims are of some other order, are not speculative, metaphysical, mythological, therefore, metaphorical in the long run. Such language is conditioned by its cultural matrix, a fact recognized more thoroughly by comparative studies in religion than by most Buddhists or by most theologians of other traditions. Nevertheless, it is because of the limits and nature of speculative, metaphysical, or mythological language, that it is so important not to become attached to views, concepts, and teachings, and to make a sharp distinction between words and meaning when deciphering religious texts and teachings. The major problem here is a post-Enlightenment tendency to mistake the nature of religious language and religious claims, to take them as facts rather than as symbols, analogies, or metaphors. This is a very serious problem, both in popular religion and in formal theology these days.

Another Problem

However, *Nostra Aetate* has another serious failing, which many might not notice, but which I should point out. The generic masculine language and consistent androcentrism of this document is deeply troubling. The early date of its proclamation (1965) may help explain this unfortunate language. At that time, I still wrote in the generic masculine myself, but, very soon thereafter, I completely remedied my writing style. Should one expect less of a religious institution that expects the whole world to take seriously what it has to say about itself and its view of its relationship with the rest of the world? Language that so disregards my own humanity but collapses me into a generic "mankind" from an institution that has never taken women's lives and subjectivities seriously makes it difficult for me to take this document seriously. I expect at least some note of editorial correction or acknowledgment of the problem. Women do not assume that they can or should enter a room labeled "Men," nor are we intended to enter that room, so why should we assume that we are actually included in "mankind"? The arrogance of assuming that men represent the norm and ideal of humanity, which such language implies, is so alienating for the rest of us. Such language reflects the Christian/Catholic view, drawn from the Hebrew Bible, that women are derived from a prior creature that most people assume to have been a male, though the language of the Hebrew does not actually imply such. If women are indeed derived, secondary creations, generic masculine language might be accurate. Those who insist on continuing to use such language need to be aware of and acknowledge that implication.

Though Buddhist institutions do not reflect fundamental Buddhist insights about female/male relationships, Buddhist literature does contain what seems to me to be a much more insightful account of the essentials of male/female relationships. As is well known, there is no creation story, per se, in Buddhism, no story of a time before there was something and how the world then came out of nothing. There is, however, a story of how humans came to be as they currently are from an earlier condition in which there were no gender signs and "people" were able to subsist on spontaneously appearing food that required no work. However, people gradually began to develop greed and clinging (*tanha*) regarding this spontaneously appearing food and began to hoard and store it. Their bodies changed, becoming "coarser," and they begin to differentiate between those who are more attractive and less attractive. This kind of cycle went through many permutations until finally, as bodies became coarser and coarser, "the females developed female sex-organs, and the males developed male organs. And the women became excessively preoccupied with men, and the men with women. Owing to this excessive preoccupation with each other, passion was aroused, and their bodies burned with lust."[14]

In the main Western narrative, as usually interpreted, first a male creature is made. Then from him, a female is drawn out. In the Western story, the male is primary and the female is a secondary creature who was made to serve his needs. Freud's view of women as incomplete and inadequate, castrated human beings is a direct descendant of this biblical story. To make things even worse, the female is routinely blamed for the "fall." That Eve misled Adam into eating the "apple" has been used for centuries to justify not letting women speak in public or religious gatherings. Because a woman taught once and got it all wrong, better never

---

[14] Maurice C. O'Walshe, *The Long Discourses of the Buddha: A Translation of the Digha Nikaya* (Boston: Wisdom Publications, 1995), 411.

to let women have any teaching role in the future! Included in the modern fallout of this story is the deep androcentrism of Western culture with its view that men represent the normal and ideal human, while women are an exception to the norm and are not able to meet it. This position lies behind a common Western view that women "think with their glands," which makes their thinking untrustworthy. Men's thinking, by contrast, results in a correct view of the world because men's bodies are regarded as providing a normal, direct connection with the world around them, conveniently ignoring the extent to which men's bodies are also governed by hormones.[15] If hormones are so determinative, one would think that a hormone which promotes aggression, testosterone, would be a supreme disqualifier for worthiness. Nevertheless, even in the contemporary political scene, we still find claims that women have the "wrong" hormones, which disqualifies them for political leadership.

Nostra Aetate, now fifty years old, was a breath of fresh air when first articulated and very refreshing in the context of what I had been taught as a child about Christian exclusive truth claims, dogmatism, and ridicule of other religions. I taught this statement to my undergraduate students many times in an attempt to shift their own attitudes about religious diversity, trying to show them that there is Christian warrant for being more positively disposed toward other religions, and good Christian theological grounds for doing so.

Yet today, after many years of reflecting on what a Buddhist theology of religions could be, using all the resources and sensibilities of Buddhism, even those that many Buddhists may ignore to some extent, and also years of studying religion using the methods of the contemporary academic study of religion, I find the statement inadequate. Fundamentally, I would fault *Nostra Aetate* for not recognizing the inevitability and normalness of religious diversity, and for still regarding religious diversity as an issue or a problem. This tendency is, in my view, the great fault of contemporary, mainly Christian theologies of religion, with their exclusivist, inclusivist, and pluralist typologies, all of which focus on religious teachings as truth claims rather than as skillful means for relevant transformation.

There are many reasons why it is important to regard religious diversity as a fact, not a problem, not the least of which is that *it is a fact* that is not likely to change anytime soon. In my view, until religious leaders concede that religious diversity is not a problem and that it is possible for every religion to flourish in situations of religious diversity, not much progress in theology of religions or interreligious relations can be made. *Nostra Aetate*, it seems to me, is far from conceding that teachings that may be unknown to or quite different from Catholic

---

[15] Simone de Beauvoir first articulated this point in the early feminist classic *The Second Sex* (1949), written well before modern gender studies, which severely undercut these stereotypical assumptions. Such thinking nevertheless remains strong in many segments of folk and popular culture.

or Christian teachings might be workable and worthwhile, not just those that are similar to what the church already proclaims. It also seems to me that *Nostra Aetate* is quite far from recognizing that unanimity may not be desirable or necessary for us all to flourish with religious diversity.

14

THE ETERNAL VEDA AND THE
"TRUTH WHICH ENLIGHTENS ALL"

Correspondences and Disjunctures
between Nostra Aetate and
Swami Vivekananda's Vedantic Inclusivism

Jeffery D. Long

In this essay, I present a Hindu response to *Nostra Aetate*, the declaration of the Catholic Church on its relationship to non-Christian religions. I must first point out that there can be no generic Hindu response to *Nostra Aetate*—or to anything— any more than there can be a generic Buddhist response, Islamic response, or Jewish response, for there are many Hindu traditions and many Hindu perspectives on the topic of relations to the religious other (a topic on which I have written elsewhere).[1] My response reflects my adherence to the tradition of Vedanta established by Sri Ramakrishna Paramahansa and popularized in the Western world by Swami Vivekananda and subsequent teachers of the Ramakrishna Order and Ramakrishna Mission. I shall, however, also point out the ways in which this response reflects the sensibility of the broader Hindu community; for this response, while it is distinctive to the Ramakrishna tradition, is not therefore idiosyncratic within the larger realm of Hindu thought.

My response takes the shape of a comparative analysis of the understanding of the relationship between the church and the world's religions expressed in *Nostra Aetate* and that between the Vedic tradition and the world's religions found in the teachings of Swami Vivekananda, specifically in an essay titled "Hinduism and Shri Ramakrishna," in which Swamiji presents his perspective on this relationship.[2] Interestingly,

---

[1] Jeffery D. Long, "Hindu Relations with the Religious Other," in *Understanding Interreligious Relations*, ed. David Cheetham and Douglas Pratt (New York: Oxford University Press, 2014), 37–63.

[2] Swami Vivekananda, "Hinduism and Shri Ramakrishna," in *The Complete Works of Swami Vivekananda* (Calcutta, India: Advaita Ashrama, Mayavati Memorial Edition, 1973–79), 6:181–86.

a structural similarity can quickly be discerned between the approach of Swami Vivekananda and the approach of the Second Vatican Council in how each conceptualizes the relationship of its own tradition to the other world religions.

What is this structural similarity? Both of these approaches are examples of what theologians and philosophers of religion call *inclusivism*. This is the view that one's own religion possesses a final, definitive truth available only imperfectly in other traditions, and that it provides the standard in terms of which the truth of a religion is to be measured. This approach is sometimes seen as a middle path between exclusivism, which holds that one's own tradition alone possesses salvifically relevant truth, with other traditions being false or delusory, and pluralism, which sees the world's religions as more or less equal in terms of their ability to express and embody truth and salvation. An inclusivist approach to religion has the advantage of avoiding the condemnation of most human beings to eternal damnation that one finds in exclusivism. It instead affirms the compassionate and hopeful side of religion—but, at the same time, by holding up a specific vision of truth to be normative for all traditions, it avoids the trap of relativism to which a pluralistic view can lend itself. The common charge of relativism against pluralistic approaches is itself sometimes apt and sometimes not (for there are many models of religious pluralism). It can be said, though, that all pluralistic models need to contend with this issue, with some doing so more successfully than others.

Religious pluralists such as John Hick have criticized inclusivism as retaining the paternalism of exclusivism, pointing out that the choice of which tradition is to serve as normative for evaluating the rest is as arbitrary as exclusivist claims that only those who adhere to a particular tradition are eligible to receive salvation. Instead of saying that all religions find their fulfillment in Christ, or in Brahman, or in Allah, or in the realization of one's Buddha Nature, pluralists commend the "Copernican Revolution" of perceiving the world's religions as leading their adherents toward a shared transcendent reality that is not identifiable exclusively or definitively with any particular religious conception of it.

Although the vision of religious diversity expressed by the Second Vatican Council and by Swami Vivekananda share the same inclusivist structure, there are also important differences between these two visions. The most obvious difference is, of course, the identity of the tradition each identifies as best conveying ultimate truth. For the Second Vatican Council, this truth is found preeminently in the Roman Catholic Church. For Swami Vivekananda, it is to be found in the *Vedas*.

Another important way in which these two visions differ, though, is in the manner in which Swami Vivekananda conceives of the *Vedas*—not as simply identical to the collection of Hindu texts that go by this name, but as the sum total of what he calls "supersensuous truths."[3] Although he sees the text of the

---

[3] Ibid., 181. One may note both structural and substantive similarities between Swami Vivekananda's conception of "supersensuous truths" and pluralistic thinker John Hick's concept of "the Real." This correspondence is likely not coincidental, given the influence of Vedantic thought, largely via Sri Aurobindo and Sarvepalli Radhakrishnan, on Hick's thought.

Vedas as the preeminent embodiment of these truths among the world's religions, he does not see these texts as exhaustive of truth, or as the only place where truth may be found; nor does he preclude the possibility that truth not expressed in the written *Vedas* might be found elsewhere, including both non-Hindu religions and modern science.

The question I would like to raise is whether resources might exist in the Catholic tradition to similarly conceive of the ultimate locus of truth as nonidentical with the visible church. One such resource might be the mystical Body of Christ as preeminently manifested in, but not exclusively identified with, the church. I am raising this question because Swami Vivekananda's emphasis on the nonidentity of the written *Veda* and the eternal *Veda* opens his inclusivist theology of religions in a pluralistic direction, on the boundary between inclusivism and pluralism; it allows the possibility that adherents of other traditions might conceptualize the same eternal *Veda*, the same supersensuous truth, but under many names, similarly nonexhaustive of the totality of ultimate truth. Adherents of other traditions thus become fellow travelers on the way to the goal of the highest realization, with their own perfectly valid ways of conceptualizing that goal and the path or paths appropriate to it.

Is a similarly pluralistic move available to the Roman Catholic Church, under the terms defined by *Nostra Aetate*? Concepts, such as the aforementioned mystical Body of Christ, clearly do exist within the rich theological conversation that is the heritage of this great tradition for seeing the adherents of other religions as fellow travelers on the way to truth, rather than—not in addition to, but *rather than*—as potential converts to Christianity, and for reconceiving ideas such as evangelization and mission in ways that reflect this.

I shall seek here to bring *Nostra Aetate* and Swami Vivekananda into dialogue with one another, in the hope that this dialogue will be both mutually illuminating and conducive to better relations between the Catholic Church and the Hindu community all over the world. Such a dialogue is essential; for I can say, not only as an adherent of the path of Sri Ramakrishna, but as a member of the global Hindu family, that the greatest single obstacle to positive Hindu-Christian relations, at least from a Hindu perspective, is the insistence of Christians on pursuing an evangelical mission that aims at conversion of Hindus from Hindu Dharma to Christianity. Such a mission is seen by Hindus, in the words of the recently departed Swami Dayananda Saraswati, as a form of violence.[4]

I would also like to note that an inclusivist approach to religious diversity of the kind that I outline here is not the only, nor even necessarily the most popular, one for an adherent of the Vedanta tradition of Sri Ramakrishna to take. Far too much, in my judgment, has been made by some authors of differences in the teaching of Ramakrishna and his most prominent disciple, Swami Vivekananda, with some even implying (or flat-out stating) that Vivekananda deliberately

---

4   Swami Dayananda Saraswati, *Conversion Is Violence* (Chennai, India: Arsha Vidya Research and Publication Trust, 2009).

misrepresented the teaching of his master to promote his own agenda and vision of Vedanta.[5] My view is closer to that of interpreters within the Ramakrishna Order, who see a deep harmony between the teachings of these two foundational figures. It is true, though, that, particularly in regard to the question of religious diversity, one can note distinctions in their approaches. Sri Ramakrishna was a deep mystic, who eagerly embraced all spiritual paths as ways to God-realization. His is a thoroughgoing pluralism. Vivekananda, however, while affirming the teaching of Sri Ramakrishna in this regard, was keenly aware, especially through his travels in the West, of the many ways in which Hinduism existed under the yoke of European imperialism and was being denigrated by missionary interests.

Swami Vivekananda's need to affirm the distinctive greatness of Hinduism was, therefore, one could argue, more of a factor in his thought than in that of Ramakrishna, particularly in the wider context of Vivekananda's efforts to awaken the people of India and to arouse a sense of pride and dignity within them—a sense that would do much to fuel the Indian movement for independence from the British Empire. In our time of global conflict, many of us are now rightly suspicious of religious nationalisms of all kinds. It is important, though, to recall that nationalism can also play a positive role during a particular phase of a people's liberation struggle. Thus even such a well-known and thoroughgoing religious pluralist as Mohandas K. Gandhi—who arguably gave his life for his commitment to pluralism—once made a highly inclusivist statement: "What of substance is contained in any other religion is always to be found in Hinduism. And what is not contained in it is insubstantial or unnecessary."[6]

I feel that a comparison of Swami Vivekananda's inclusivism with that of *Nostra Aetate* shows Hindu and Catholic thought to be closer than they might otherwise appear if the point of comparison were to be the radical pluralism of Sri Ramakrishna (a pluralism to which Vivekananda's position points and to which it invites its adherents to approach). One generally compares things that are like one another in some significant way. This is why I have taken the approach that I have in this essay.

The Inclusivism of *Nostra Aetate*

With *Nostra Aetate*, its 1965 "Declaration on the Relationship of the Church to the Non-Christian Religions," the Second Vatican Council, as it had done in so many other areas of church life, clarified that Catholic teaching regarding religions other than Christianity could be far more open-minded and open-hearted than had all

---

[5] The work of Narasingha Sil comes to mind as an example of this interpretation of these two teachers. See Narasingha Sil, *Swami Vivekananda: A Reassessment* (Selinsgrove, PA: Susquehanna University Press, 1997).

[6] Mohandas K. Gandhi, "All Religions Are True," in *Collected Works* (New Delhi, India: Publications Division, Ministry of Information and Broadcasting, Government of India, 1958–99), 28:194.

too often been the case in the past. Rather than *extra ecclesiam nulla salus*, "outside the church there is no salvation," the council proclaimed a doctrine of inclusivism.

Speaking of the non-Christian religions, the council declared, "The Catholic Church rejects nothing of what is true and holy in these religions. She regards with sincere reverence those ways of conduct and life, those precepts and teachings which, though differing on many points from the ones she herself holds and sets forth, nonetheless often reflect a ray of the Truth which enlightens all men [*sic*]."[7] If one reads these words through the lens of the tradition of Sri Ramakrishna and Swami Vivekananda, one becomes elated. A devout Hindu could say exactly these same words about non-Hindu traditions.

At the same time, these words allow for a considerable scope of interpretation. It may be that what one finds to be true and holy in other religions may not be very much at all, or it may be quite peripheral to the self-understanding of the communities that adhere to them. And it may be that what one regards as false and pernicious nevertheless forms a considerable part of a community's life and practice. But the idea of rays of truth that enlighten all is very much in keeping with a Vedantic Hindu understanding that the light of Brahman, the inherent divinity within all beings, does indeed make its presence felt in all our lives, for the veil of ignorance that separates us from the highest realization is not opaque. It is, in fact, translucent, and manifests in many ways in the lives of all beings.

Nostra Aetate, however, does not end here. It continues by saying that, although the church respects the truths of the other religions, "She proclaims, and must ever proclaim Christ 'the way, the truth, and the life' (John 14:6), in whom men [*sic*] find the fullness of religious life, and in whom God has reconciled all things to Himself."[8] This statement, of course, is essential to the church's Christian vision and to its identity as Christian. It is the church founded by Christ precisely to proclaim his truth to the world.

The question from a Hindu perspective is, of course, how this truth is conceived. Is Christ simply identical to the figure of Jesus Christ? Or, as Raimon Panikkar suggests, might the reality called Christ be known by other names in the other religions of the world, names that capture other dimensions of this infinite being?[9]

So what are the pragmatic implications—the "cash value," to use William James's famous phrase—of the council's declaration? To cite *Nostra Aetate*, "The Church, therefore, exhorts her sons [*sic*], that through dialogue and collaboration with the followers of other religions, carried out with prudence and love and in witness to the Christian faith and life, they recognize, preserve, and promote the

---

[7] *Declaration on the Relation of the Church to Non-Christian Religions—Nostra Aetate*, proclaimed by Pope Paul VI (Vatican City, 1965), sec. 2, http://www.vatican.va/archive/hist_councils/ii_vatican_council/documents/vat-ii_decl_19651028_nostra-aetate_en.html.

[8] Ibid.

[9] Raimon Panikkar, *The Unknown Christ of Hinduism* (Maryknoll, NY: Orbis Books, 1981), 14, 27.

good things, spiritual and moral, as well as the socio-cultural values found among these men [*sic*]."[10]

The balancing act entailed by religious inclusivism—the need to affirm openness and love toward the religious other while simultaneously maintaining fidelity to the truth of one's own tradition—can be discerned in this exhortation. One is to engage in loving dialogue and collaboration with the followers of other religions, but also "prudently," and "in witness to the Christian faith and life." One is not only to acknowledge, but even to help preserve and promote the spiritual and moral goods and the sociocultural values other traditions affirm while maintaining one's own stance as a Christian, as a disciple of Jesus Christ.

The Inclusivism of Swami Vivekananda

The Vedanta tradition with which Swami Vivekananda is affiliated as a disciple of Sri Ramakrishna is well known for its pluralistic stance toward the world's religions, seeing them as many paths to the same ultimate goal, or different experiences of varied aspects of the same infinite, ultimate Reality. The work of Sri Aurobindo and of Sarvepalli Radhakrishnan, both of whom were profoundly influenced by this tradition, in turn exerted profound influence on pluralistic thinkers in the West, such as John Hick.[11]

In his essay "Hinduism and Shri Ramakrishna," Swami Vivekananda articulates an interpretation of the *Veda* that places his thought in more of an inclusivist mold, akin to what would be expressed more than sixty years later in *Nostra Aetate*. He declares, in quite unequivocal terms, the supremacy of the *Veda* as one's guide to the spiritual life. "In matters of religious duty the *Vedas* are the only capable authority."[12] He also affirms that "the authority of the *Vedas* extends to all ages, climes and persons; that is to say, their application is not confined to any particular place, time, [or] persons," and that, "The *Vedas* are the only exponent of the universal religion."[13]

To what, though, is Swamiji referring when he speaks of the *Vedas*? "Truth," he says, "is of two kinds: (1) that which is cognizable by the five ordinary senses of man, and by reasonings based thereon; [and] (2) that which is cognizable by the subtle, supersensuous power of Yoga. Knowledge acquired by the first means is called science; and knowledge acquired by the second is called the *Vedas*."[14] The *Vedas*, in other words, refer preeminently not to a collection of texts, which can be located in time and space. "The whole body of supersensuous truths, having no beginning or end, and called by the name of the *Vedas*, is ever-existent. The

---

[10] *Nostra Aetate*, sec. 2.

[11] Sharada Sugirtharajah, scholar and former student of John Hick, personal communication.

[12] Vivekananda, "Hinduism and Shri Ramakrishna," 181.

[13] Ibid.

[14] Ibid.

Creator Himself is creating, preserving, and destroying the universe with the help of these truths."[15]

Swami Vivekananda is here affirming an ancient Hindu teaching: that the *Vedas* are *apauruṣeya*—that is, "non-man-made"—and eternal, existing outside of time and space, and providing the foundation—the support, or *dharma*—upon which the cosmos depends, and through which Īśvara, the Lord, engages in the actions of creation, preservation, and destruction that define the life cycle of the universe. One is tempted to say that the *Vedas* are the Word "that was with God in the beginning, through which all things were made, and without which nothing was made that has been made" (Jn 1:2–3).

As he elaborates further elsewhere,

> But by the *Vedas* no books are meant. They mean the accumulated treasury of spiritual laws discovered by different persons in different times. Just as the law of gravitation existed before its discovery, and would exist if all humanity forgot it, so is it with the laws that govern the spiritual world. The moral, ethical, and spiritual relations between soul and soul and between individual spirits and the Father of all spirits, were there before their discovery, and would remain even if we forgot them.[16]

What, then, is the relationship between the eternal *Vedas* and the collected texts of the Hindu tradition, which the Hindu tradition regards as *Śruti*, or "heard," by the *ṛṣis* or sages of the distant past in the depths of their meditation? Swami Vivekananda proclaims that the eternal truth is present in many texts, not only of the Hindu tradition, but of other world religions as well. His vision, however, is inclusivist inasmuch as he sees the texts called the *Vedas* as the standard by which the truth of other texts and other traditions is to be measured. He writes,

> Although the supersensuous vision of truths is to be met with in some measure in our *Purāṇas* and *Itihāsas* [ancient lore and history which form part of the *Smṛti* or "remembered" portion of Hindu scripture] and in the religious scriptures of other races, still the fourfold scripture known . . . as the *Vedas* being the first, the most complete, and the most undistorted collection of spiritual truths, deserve to occupy the highest place among all scriptures, command the respect of all nations of the earth, and furnish the rationale of all their respective scriptures.[17]

Vivekananda does not see the *Vedas* as the only true scripture. In an essay titled "The Hindu Religion," he says of them: "These are a series of books which, to our

---

[15] Ibid.

[16] Vivekananda, "Paper on Hinduism Read at the Parliament on 19th September, 1893," in *Complete Works*, 1:7–8.

[17] Vivekananda, "Hinduism and Shri Ramakrishna," 182.

minds, contain the essence of all religion; but we do not think they alone contain the truths."[18] The *Vedas* are the scripture providing the *fullest* vision of truth in textual form.

This inclusivist move is important to the integrity of Vivekananda's thought, for he is also, in keeping with the teaching and lived example of his master, Ramakrishna, deeply committed to religious pluralism. He says of the Hindu community, in his famous first address to the Parliament of the World's Religions, which he delivered on September 11, 1893, "We believe not only in universal toleration, but we accept all religions as true."[19]

In this same address, Vivekananda cites two Hindu scriptural sources—the *Śiva Mahimna Stotra* and the *Bhagavad Gītā*—in support of Hindu religious pluralism. "As the different streams having their sources in different places all mingle their water in the sea, so, O Lord, the different paths which men[20] take through different tendencies, various though they appear, crooked or straight, all lead to Thee." And, "Whosoever comes to Me, through whatsoever form, I reach him; all men are struggling through paths which in the end lead to me."[21]

The assertion that Swami Vivekananda is both an inclusivist and a pluralist may appear to be confusing, as these two views have, along with exclusivism, generally been seen as opposing options in the academic discourse of the last few decades on truth and religious diversity. As mentioned earlier, one could see Swami Vivekananda's views on this topic as occupying a position on the boundary between inclusivism and pluralism. It is the case that he affirms, in numerous places throughout his *Complete Works*, the ability of all religions to serve as efficacious means toward the attainment of God-realization. It is also the case, though, that he is a Vedic inclusivist, and that it is this fact that prevents his pluralism from sliding into the kind of "debilitating relativism" to which Alan Race refers in his landmark work, *Christians and Religious Pluralism*.[22] The *Vedas* provide a logical standard in terms of which the truth of other texts may be measured.

At the same time, Swami Vivekananda's distinction between the eternal *Vedas*—the sum total of supersensuous truths available, in principle, to all human beings, with the traces of these truths discernible in the scriptures of many religions—and the texts known by this name decenters the Vedic text in his model, opening a space for the pluralism that is a centerpiece of his master's teaching: *yato mat, tato path*.

---

[18] Vivekananda, "The Hindu Religion," in *Complete Works*, 1:329.

[19] Vivekananda, "Response to Welcome at the World's Parliament of Religions, Chicago, September 11, 1893," in *Complete Works,* 1:3.

[20] Though Swami Vivekananda, a product of his times, did not use gender-inclusive language, he certainly intends to refer to all people—all of humanity—here. The original Sanskrit term being translated here, *manushya*, refers to human beings, and need not be read as referring exclusively to the male gender.

[21] Vivekananda, "Response to Welcome at the World's Parliament of Religions," 4.

[22] Alan Race, *Christians and Religious Pluralism: Patterns in the Christian Theology of Religions* (Maryknoll, NY: Orbis Books, 1982), 90.

Yato mat, tato path means that every religion is a genuine path to God-realization. When coupled, however, with Swami Vivekananda's affirmations about the *Veda*, this statement comes to mean not necessarily that truth and salvific efficacy are *equally* distributed among the world's religions, as many religious pluralists would affirm. And this position is not relativism, because there does exist a standard by which truth claims can be measured. But truth and salvific efficacy are, in fact, abundantly available to all sincere seekers. It is up to the spiritual aspirant to pursue the path that is made available in his or her tradition to its final conclusion. And there is no fear that anyone is left out in any final way from the ultimate aim of salvation, for the teaching of reincarnation, or rebirth, that is central to a Hindu understanding of existence allows for infinite second chances for those who do not choose to avail themselves in a given lifetime of the spiritual wisdom that can be found in many traditions.

Nostra Aetate and Swami Vivekananda in Conversation with Each Other

The structural similarity of the approach to religious diversity outlined in *Nostra Aetate* and to that in the teachings of Swami Vivekananda should be fairly clear. To again quote from *Nostra Aetate*, "The Catholic Church rejects nothing of what is true and holy in these religions. She regards with sincere reverence those ways of conduct and life, those precepts and teachings which, though differing on many points from the ones she herself holds and sets forth, nonetheless often reflect a ray of the Truth which enlightens all men." The Hindu tradition as characterized by Vivekananda, in a similar vein, though somewhat more radically, "believes not only in universal toleration, but accepts all religions as true."

But the Catholic Church, "proclaims, and must ever proclaim Christ 'the way, the truth, and the life' (John 14:6), in whom men [*sic*] find the fullness of religious life, and in whom God has reconciled all things to Himself." And the Hindu tradition affirms, "The authority of the *Vedas* extends to all ages, climes and persons." And "The *Vedas* are the only exponent of the universal religion." Each tradition sees truth as abundantly available, but differs on the precise locus of the fullest expression of truth in the world's religions.

If one is attentive to Vivekananda's identification of the *Vedas*—the eternal *Vedas*—with the universal law, or *Sanātana Dharma*, by which "The Creator Himself is creating, preserving, and destroying the universe," and to the Gospel of John's understanding of Jesus as the incarnation of the eternal Word that was "With God in the beginning," through whom "all things were made," then it is very tempting to affirm, as many Hindus do (though not all, to be sure), that the similarity here is more than merely structural: that the Christ who is proclaimed by the Catholic Church is the very eternal truth proclaimed by the *Vedas*.

This, at least, is a Hindu understanding, informed by the impulse toward pluralism that can be discerned not only in the teaching of Swami Vivekananda and in the teaching and lived example of Sri Ramakrishna, but also in Hindu texts harking back to the *Ṛg Veda*, with its proclamation, "*Ekaṃ sat bahudha viprā vadanti:*" "Truth is one, though the wise speak of it in many ways" (*Ṛg Veda* 1.164:46c). To be sure, there are also many Hindus who are deeply uncomfortable with—or who would even angrily reject—an identification of Christ—the cosmic Christ, the divine Word—with the eternal Word of the *Vedas*. This rejection is based not on Vedic scriptural study or theological or philosophical reflection, but on the historical realities that make a conversation between *Nostra Aetate* and the thought of Swami Vivekananda so urgent in the twenty-first century. Even as many Christians, in the open-minded, open-hearted spirit of *Nostra Aetate*, pursue respectful dialogue with the Hindu community and its texts and traditions, many more continue to pursue an evangelical mission conceived not in terms of mutual respect or deep learning across religious borders or an ethic of global responsibility, but in the old colonial terms of conversion, and the demonization of Hindu deities, teachings, and practices.

Rather than seeing Christianity as a tradition that converges in many important respects on the same profound truths as are revealed in the *Vedas*, many Hindus—for good reason—see Christianity as a tradition fueled by a predatory desire to win adherents at the expense of other religions.

I alluded earlier to the wide latitude of interpretation to which *Nostra Aetate* lends itself—from what one could call a maximalist reading, in which the emphasis is on the truths that the Catholic Church shares with the other religions, to a minimalist reading, in which a few glimmers of truth are available in other religions that are, fundamentally, to be seen as standing in need of fulfillment in Christ (meaning adherence to faith in Jesus Christ in an explicit mainstream Christian sense, and conversion to Christianity). This width of interpretation unfortunately enables the church to send a decidedly mixed signal to the Hindu community. Are we fellow travelers on the path of truth, standing to benefit from a mutually respectful and mutually enriching dialogue, in which we speak honestly about and learn from our differences, as well as acknowledging those places in which we seem to be arriving at a common insight, or even talking about the same divine realities? Or are we objects of potential conversion? My own sense is that Christians more broadly, and Roman Catholics in particular, are divided on this topic: divided both among themselves, but also at times inwardly conflicted, finding themselves to be torn between the conflicting impulses that their tradition commends, toward respectful and compassionate engagement pursued in a sincere desire for the truth, and toward bringing about that day when "every knee shall bend and every tongue confess that Jesus Christ is Lord" (Phil 2:10–11). To a Hindu sensibility, these words from Paul's letter to the Philippians sound like a call to global domination.

Certainly, the resources do exist in Christian tradition for reading *Nostra Aetate* in a way that will render it the clarion call for global interreligious harmony which it has the potential to be—the mystical Body of Christ, the cosmic Christ, the eternal Word—or more modestly, the simple affirmation of shared values and the need for all communities to set aside differences as a source of conflict and work toward the betterment of life on earth for all. And again, many Christian thinkers, including many involved in this conference, have dedicated their careers to developing precisely these resources, and to cultivating shared insight across religious boundaries.

All too often, however, the understanding generated by these excellent thinkers does not find its way easily into the wider church. And this is not simply an elitist claim that more rank-and-file Christians should read the works of people like Paul F. Knitter, Francis X. Clooney, and John Thatamanil—though that would certainly be a good thing. The hierarchy of the church itself tends to send mixed signals in this regard. In 2004, at the Parliament of the World's Religions in Barcelona, I lamented the tone and content of a document issued in 2000 by the Congregation for the Doctrine of the Faith, *Dominus Iesus*, with its assertion that interreligious dialogue is "part of the Church's evangelizing mission," and its caution *against* seeing other world religions as equal dialogue partners.[23]

I should note that the issue here is *not* with the church's claim to being the locus, among the world's religions, of the fullness of truth revealed in Christ. Each religion will naturally see itself as being in possession of unique access to truth. My tradition is not an exception to this. Again, Swami Vivekananda sees the *Vedas*—the written *Vedas*—as "the first, the most complete, and the most undistorted collection of spiritual truths," and he further asserts that these texts "deserve to occupy the highest place among all scriptures, command the respect of all nations of the earth, and furnish the rationale of all their respective scriptures."[24] Unlike most religious pluralists, I do not see the claim of some Christian religious inclusivists (such as Karl Rahner) that sincere adherents of the non-Christian religions are "anonymous Christians" to be especially problematic, so long as those making this claim accept that I may just as well see them as "anonymous Hindus," while others may see them as "anonymous Muslims," and still others as "anonymous Buddhists." One scholar, Matt Lopresti, calls my stance a "Hindu Pan-Inclusivism."[25] The important exception must of course be noted that the use of power to *enforce* such a view of the other is absolutely unacceptable. People have a right to define themselves.

It seems simply to be an epistemic fact, though, that we will all begin our inquiry into the nature of reality from the perspective of some tradition, some received discourse. If one did not believe that one's tradition had something that others did not, it would not make sense to continue adhering to it. There is

---

[23] Congregation for the Doctrine of the Faith, *Declaration—Dominus Iesus: On the Unicity and Salvific Universality of Jesus Christ and the Church* (Vatican City, 2000), secs. 2, 22. http://www.vatican.va/roman_curia/congregations/cfaith/documents/rc_con_cfaith_doc_20000806_dominus-iesus_en.html.

[24] Vivekananda, "Hinduism and Shri Ramakrishna," 181.

[25] Matt Lopresti, "*Sanātana Dharma* as a Whiteheadian Religious Pluralism?" *Journal of Process Studies* 36, no. 1 (Spring–Summer 2007): 108–20.

a minimal sense, I maintain, in which we are all inclusivists—including religious pluralists, who see pluralism as a fuller truth than nonpluralism.

The issue is the relationship between our attitudes about where truth is to be found and the ways in which we treat actual human beings. The church's absolutely integral need to "proclaim Christ, 'the way, the truth, and the life' (John 14:6), in whom men [sic] find the fullness of religious life, and in whom God has reconciled all things to Himself" has, for most of the history of this tradition, been taken to imply a mission to convert adherents of other traditions to Christianity. This implication, however, does not follow necessarily from one's duty to proclaim the truth as one sees it. The Buddhist tradition possesses a similar imperative to spread the Buddha's *dharma* to all, but, in Buddhist history, this dictum has not led to the eradication of the traditions which Buddhist monks have encountered and with which they have engaged. Rather, to the extent that other traditions do not conflict radically with Buddhist practice, their adherents have continued to follow them even while embracing Buddhism. In China and Japan, therefore, it has not been uncommon at all for Buddhists to simultaneously be adherents of Confucianism and Daoism (in the case of China) or adherents of Shinto (in the case of Japan). In Tibet and Southeast Asia, the indigenous shamanisms have not been uprooted, but continue to be practiced by the side of, and in some cases as part of, Buddhism. The situation would be analogous to an alternative history in which Europeans embraced Christianity while continuing to revere the old deities of their various pantheons. (And, of course, shadows of the pre-Christian religions of Europe persist even in Christian practices associated with Christmas, Easter, the feasts of various saints, and so on.)

Hinduism, however, certainly as conceived in the contemporary period, is generally a nonproselytizing tradition.[26] Swami Vivekananda and subsequent gurus of various Hindu traditions have proclaimed their teachings and practices far and wide in the modern era, but they have typically not seen themselves as promulgating Hinduism. Indeed, Swamiji affirms not that adherents of other traditions should convert to Hinduism. "God forbid!" he says, quite firmly. "But each must assimilate the spirit of the others and yet preserve his individuality and grow according to his own law of growth."[27]

It is possible to proclaim a religious truth, and even to receive new adherents into one's community, without insisting that others abandon their own paths, particularly if one is able to see these paths as filling an important role in a larger economy of salvation, in which even those paths with which one does not fully agree can be seen as cultivating some important salvific value and contributing positively toward the eventual attainment by their adherents of the highest aim of human existence.

---

[26] Although D. N. Jha notes significant premodern exceptions to this pattern in his *Rethinking Hindu Identity* (London: Equinox, 2009).

[27] Swami Vivekananda, "Address at the Final Session, September 27, 1893," in *Complete Works*, 1:24.

Such breadth of vision is possible, and even commended, from a Vedantic point of view, without giving up the core commitment to a Vedic vision of reality, in which the divine Reality is present in all beings, in which we are all pursuing, through many lives and in myriad forms and myriad ways, the manifestation of this potential divinity in our own being and in the being of all. It may be that the Hindu teaching of reincarnation is able to facilitate such a view in a way not available to religions that deny this view of the afterlife. But the possibility of a posthumous encounter with Christ has been affirmed by a number of Christian theologians—a possibility which, like the Hindu doctrine of rebirth, can have the effect of mitigating a felt need to convert others to one's own path, since all souls will one day encounter the ultimate truth.

If *Nostra Aetate* can be read in a way that similarly commends and positively values the paths of others, enabling those paths to be appreciated and their practitioners seen not as potential converts, but as adding to the richness of the wisdom available to all, while frankly affirming one's own sense of where the fullest expression of truth is to be found, then the potential of this document to transform interreligious relations—to lead to a world of less conversion and more conversation—can be fully realized.

Part VII

Moving with and beyond *Nostra Aetate*

15

IN OUR TIME

Coformation as a Modality for
Interreligious Teaching and Learning

Jennifer Howe Peace

The beauty of the literal translation of *Nostra Aetate*—"In Our Time"—is that we are invited to constantly update this document, to translate and explore its relevance for us, *now*. I appreciate the invitation to ponder its impact from my perch on a hilltop in Newton, Massachusetts, in my position as associate professor of Interfaith Studies and co-director of the Center for Interreligious and Communal Leadership Education (or CIRCLE) at Andover Newton Theological School (ANTS). My observations are filtered through the lens of my work as an interfaith organizer and educator for the past twenty years. Extending my reading of *Nostra Aetate* to its relevance for today, I explore some of the promising ways in which interfaith work is evolving, as well as some of the limits of existing models.

In Our Time

In our time, when day by day [humankind] is being drawn closer together and the ties between different peoples are becoming stronger, the Church examines more closely her relationship to non-Christian religions.[1]

Three points strike me when I read this opening line. The last phrase in the sentence gives us the orienting frame of this declaration: the church is examining its "relationship" to non-Christian religions. Beyond the theological and ethical arguments, the appreciative characterizations of various faiths, and the assertions of our common human concerns that follow, the declaration is first and foremost about *relationships*. This stance resonates with the work I do now.

---

[1] *Declaration on the Relation of the Church to Non-Christian Religions—Nostra Aetate*, proclaimed by Pope Paul VI (Vatican City, 1965), sec. 1, http://www.vatican.va/archive/hist_councils/ii_vatican_council/documents/vat-ii_decl_19651028_nostra-aetate_en.html.

Second, the trend toward greater proximity and stronger ties noted fifty years ago is even more significant today. With all the avenues for communication and access to social media, we are more connected than ever. Religious diversity is on the rise. We are in a period of dramatic population shifts, which are contributing to demographic changes. The UN refugee agency estimates there are currently more than 6 million people displaced because of conflicts globally. With ongoing refugee resettlement in the United States, many of our smaller cities and towns will be reshaped in profound ways. Promoting constructive models for how we engage this increasing diversity is something those of us committed to interreligious education should be actively concerned about and working on.

Finally, the phrase "the Church examines" was striking to my Protestant (United Church of Christ) ears; in my religious community, we are, given our polity, more likely to talk about the actions or attitudes of a single congregation than about the Church with a capital "C." This realization led me to read *Nostra Aetate* with an eye for what else the church as an institution is *doing* in this text.

When I went through the text noting the verbs attributed to the church, this is what I found: The church examines, considers, and rejects nothing that is true and holy in these religions. It regards, proclaims, exhorts, searches, acknowledges, professes, awaits, and decries hatred. In the final paragraph it reproves as foreign to the mind of Christ any discrimination against people or harassment of them because of their race, color, condition of life, or religion.

It is the verb tucked into the second paragraph of the declaration—arguably the strongest action verb and the only one that invites a response from the reader—on which I want to focus. The church "exhorts" its sons and daughters "through dialogue and collaboration with the followers of other religions . . . to promote the good things, spiritual and moral, as well as the socio-cultural values found among these men" and women. The church *exhorts* its followers to engage with people across religious lines. This is, for me, the most impactful and relevant point in the document as I consider the future of interfaith work.

I am certainly not the first to highlight the significance of this passage. As Paul Knitter writes: "What was the most surprising statement of 'Nostra Aetate'—and what turned out to be, as I look back, its most transformative announcement—was the new 'obligation,' or challenge, that the bishops were laying before all Christians: they were 'exhorting' the people of God prudently and lovingly to dialogue and collaborate with followers of other religions." This invitation to dialogue was now, as Knitter describes it, part of the "job description of a follower of Christ."[2]

The ripple effects of this obligation are hard to overstate. A recent collection edited by James Fredericks and Tracy Tiemeier, *Interreligious Friendship after Nostra Aetate*, is one long testimony to the power and impact of interreligious friendships for the Catholic scholars and religious professionals who

---

[2] Paul Knitter, "Theological Goosebumps: A Turning Point in My Interfaith Journey," in *My Neighbor's Faith: Stories of Interreligious Encounter, Growth, and Transformation*, ed. Jennifer Howe Peace, Or N. Rose, Gregory Mobley (Maryknoll, NY: Orbis, 2012), 123.

contributed to the volume.[3] Beyond the pews and the halls of academia, in the soccer fields and grocery stores, this impact, though perhaps less documented, is no less significant. In the next section of this chapter, I explore some of the implications of this exhortation to dialogue and collaboration for models of interfaith work today.

Coformation as a Modality for Interreligious Teaching and Learning

If we are to extend the promise of *Nostra Aetate* to our times, we need to think carefully about how to create the conditions for dialogue and collaboration. Although casual encounters in the public square are increasingly common, the tools and opportunities to unpack, process, and reflect critically on these encounters are not necessarily keeping pace. Although perhaps some of the required skill-building and religious literacy belong under the purview of civic education, my primary interest is in thinking about the ways a reimagined model of seminary education might better prepare our future religious leaders for the multireligious world they will be serving. Although a depth of understanding of one's own faith tradition remains central to seminary formation, in isolation, I argue, it is insufficient for our times.

My experiences at Andover Newton have convinced me that not only do we have an obligation to train students with the skills, knowledge, and resources for dialogue and collaboration across religious lines but also that doing so produces more mature, inspired, and effective clergy. This insight is something we hear again and again reflected in the reports of our CIRCLE fellows. As one 2011 CIRCLE fellow wrote:

> As I reflect on my seminary experience, I feel that my involvement with CIRCLE's Prison Justice Ministry has been one of the most valuable things I've done. Sharing in this experience with Hebrew College students has been an important aspect of the ministry. I have seen how both of our faith traditions have something to offer to the task at hand whether it is a pearl of ancient wisdom, a song, or a prayer. Because this interfaith experience has been so rich and rewarding, I am very motivated to become the kind of pastor who reaches out and connects with clergy from other traditions and forms connections with other houses of worship. I will be a better pastor because of the time I've spent with this group![4]

---

[3] James Fredericks and Tracy Tiemeier, *Interreligious Friendship after Nostra Aetate* (New York: Palgrave Macmillan, 2015).

[4] From an unpublished CIRCLE fellowship report by an Andover Newton student submitted to the author, May 2011.

Creatively reimagining the model for seminary formation requires resources. Sometimes providence provides the pivotal resources, such as when, in 2002, Hebrew College relocated from Brookline, Massachusetts, to the hilltop adjacent to Andover Newton. Sometimes the resources come from the hard work of individuals, such as when dedicated students, staff, and faculty members at ANTS and HC began to build bridges across our two campuses. Sometimes the resources come from outside supporters, such as when, in 2008, Andover Newton and Hebrew College jointly applied for and received a significant grant from the Henry Luce Foundation. The Luce Foundation has a long history of supporting seminaries and recognizing the need for a wider interreligious frame for seminary education. Their ongoing support since 2008 has allowed us to move from ad hoc interfaith programming to a dynamic set of curricular and extracurricular offerings, faculty professional development, a jointly appointed Islamic scholar, and most recently, a pioneering new MA program in global interreligious leadership.

The broadest mandate of our shared work is to create an ethos of interreligious understanding on each campus. We realized early in the process that building such a perspective would require attention to the full range of institutional stakeholders and involve working with students, staff, faculty, administration, board members, and alums. As we began to articulate the foundational approach that weaves through our work with all of these stakeholders, the phrase "interreligious learning through relationship-building" emerged as an important frame of reference. It continues to serve as a core value embodied through co-taught classes, the CIRCLE fellowship program, and the extracurricular activities sponsored by the center.

Another way to describe the paradigm of interreligious learning through relationship-building is to say that our work privileges the importance of learning *with* the religious other as opposed to learning *about* the religious other. As a seminary professor concerned with the formation of my Christian and Unitarian Universalist (UU) students, I think a lot about the impact of designing an environment where Christian and UU students study alongside Jewish and now increasingly Muslim students. As one CIRCLE fellow reflected in his year-end report, there is a prevalent idea among UU's that they are "doing interfaith" each Sunday because of the wide range of references and sources from various religions that are included in many services. After his fellowship year, this routine no longer meets his definition. He commented that readings and references may open the door or lay the groundwork for interfaith understanding, but that his new definition is predicated on engagement with people of strong conviction from faiths other than his own.

When students do this work together, side-by-side, year after year, something new happens that I call "coformation." As I described this concept in an essay published in the journal of the Association of Theological Schools, *Colloquy*:

> To add the prefix "co" to "formation" and apply it to seminary education
> is to assert that students are not formed in isolation but in connection
> to a dynamic web of relationships. Making formation an intentionally

interfaith process reflects the reality that our particular beliefs exist in a larger and complex multireligious (and nonreligious) human community, a community we want to prepare our students to both encounter and engage on multiple levels—theological, ethical, and pastoral—as community organizers, educators, preachers, and citizens.[5]

Creating spaces where these coformation processes can unfold, I am convinced, is one of the best ways to nurture a culture of interfaith understanding. This practice is at the heart of CIRCLE's work inside and outside the classroom. As I think about the future of interfaith work, I draw from the data embedded in the insights and questions that have emerged in the context of this work over the past eight years. The transformative power of the relationships and experiences that are possible when we learn together is something I see in my work every day.

Creating New Spaces for
Coformation Experiences

In January 2015 I taught a course with my CIRCLE co-directors, Rabbi Or Rose and Celene Ibrahim. Or Rose is a founding director of CIRCLE, and Celene Ibrahim joined us in 2014 as the third co-director after being appointed jointly by Hebrew College and Andover Newton in a historic move to add an Islamic scholar to our faculties. The course was a weeklong intensive colloquy called "Religious Leadership in a Multireligious Society: Jewish, Christian, and Muslim Perspectives." We focused on the rich and diverse religious landscape in the Boston area and designed the course to include multiple field trips. We capped the class at thirty and found ourselves with a lively group of Jewish, Christian, Muslim, and UU students learning alongside their multireligious trio of instructors. Beyond the religious diversity in the group, we discovered the importance and impact of other intersecting identities, including culture, race, gender, class, sexual orientation, and a surprisingly diverse spectrum of theological positions and political opinions. The class was a learning experience in many ways, but what has lingered with me in its wake was a comment by one of the quietest students.

Basma sat near the back of the room each day. She had come to the United States from Egypt with her husband, who was enrolled in a PhD program at a nearby university. While taking care of two young children, Basma was also continuing her own work as a PhD student at Al-Azhar University in Cairo, where she was focusing on perceptions of Arab and Muslim women in a particular body of Hebrew literature. Fluent in Arabic, Hebrew, and English, Basma was also leading a CIRCLE peer group with a Christian student from Andover Newton exploring attitudes toward the religious "other" in Jewish, Christian, and Muslim texts.

---

[5] Jennifer Peace, "Coformation through Interreligious Learning," *Colloquy* 20, no. 10 (Fall 2011): 24.

Basma was auditing the class and tended to listen more than speak. But there was one comment that she made twice, and, like the exhortation to "dialogue and collaboration" in *Nostra Aetate*, it was a simple statement with significant implications. She described how limited her encounters with people beyond the Muslim tradition were before she came to America and how varied and rich her experiences had been since arriving here. Then she commented: "Our experiences change who we are." The next day in class discussions she said it again, and this time I heard it more clearly, "Our experiences change who we are."

This point is so obvious that it is easy to overlook, but it encapsulates the hope and promise of the interfaith work I've committed myself to. *Our experiences change who we are.*

What kinds of experiences are we creating for our students? What kinds of experiences are we ourselves open to? What kinds of spaces are available or need to be created if we are to encourage interfaith friendships and co-learning opportunities that are so important for dismantling the deadly stereotypes and hateful caricatures that can so easily emerge in the absence of accurate information or actual encounters with one another?

I want to suggest that this last question about appropriate spaces is crucial if we are hoping to build a sustainable future for interfaith work. There are many ways to create new spaces for this work relevant to the particular contexts where it is taking place. Here I draw three examples from my own context.

The heart of my efforts has gone into creating physical space on the campuses of Andover Newton and Hebrew College—both inside and beyond the classroom. Developing an ethos of interfaith understanding has required new spaces: shared classrooms, space for joint faculty meetings, and space to mark sacred moments in our respective calendars. Once a year we take over the full space of both campuses, and our schools close for the day so that students, staff, faculty, and administration can join in a process of shared learning and relationship-building at our annual "joint community day." More recently we've created CIRCLE House, a physical space on the border of our two campuses for interreligious living, learning, and working. Having a shared physical space designated for this work has changed and expanded the range of possible programming.

Doing this work together changes everything—the questions we ask, the answers we offer, and what we learn about ourselves and one another. For those not blessed by the providence of proximity (though I think changing zoning laws so that all schools for religious leadership are incentivized to co-locate would not be a bad idea), there are other ways to bring new voices into the mix through community partnerships, travel experiences, and even the use of interreligous case studies in the classroom such as those developed by the Pluralism Project at Harvard.

Another "space" that I think is increasingly relevant to and interesting to think about for interfaith work is virtual space. Taking advantage of the internet plays out in my own work in multiple ways. I have taught online courses about interfaith work for years and am a big believer in the possibility of this model for creating constructive online learning communities that bring religiously diverse voices into the classroom. A second example of a growing virtual community is an online site sponsored by CIRCLE called "State of Formation."[6] This blog site for emerging religious and ethical leaders was launched in 2010 (with support from the Luce Foundation) and has grown to include over 150 contributors from a range of religious backgrounds, ethical perspectives, and geographic locations, along with an annual readership of approximately 80,000. A third virtual space is the *Journal of Interreligious Studies* (*JIRS*), housed at CIRCLE. Founded in 2009, *JIRS* is a growing virtual space for diverse scholars interested in and contributing to the field of interreligious studies.

Finally, I have been doing this space-creating work within the academy more broadly. In 2013 the newly approved "Interreligious and Interfaith Studies" group hosted its first set of panels at the AAR meeting in Baltimore. I co-founded this group with a Muslim colleague, Homayra Ziad, and a wonderful steering committee of scholars to create space for new conversations at the AAR.[7] This group is a small space in the vast halls of the academy; each year we are allotted just one panel, which can accommodate up to five papers from scholars. However, interest exceeds our allotment with an average of eighty proposals submitted each year. This has led to creative strategies for increasing our panel allotment; each year we have successfully co-sponsored panels with other groups and petitioned for one additional panel for our own group. Beyond the annual meeting we continue to see an increase in the numbers of majors, minors, concentrations, degree programs, and faculty titles using the terms "interreligious," "interfaith," and "multifaith." Introducing new words in the landscape of academia is itself a powerful way to create new space. My hope is that interreligious studies will continue to emerge as a field that can bridge not only religious divides but also academic divides between practitioners and theorists.

Challenges and Suggestions for
Interreligious Educators

Let me conclude by pointing out three challenges or limits that I see in some of the existing paradigms of interfaith engagement, along with suggestions for overcoming them. First, despite the creative range of models for interfaith engagement, I still find that there is an overemphasis on formal dialogues and interfaith panels, which sometimes adopt a kind of interrogation style of engagement, "How can you defend the treatment of women in your tradition?" "Tell me what you believe about salvation?" These "priest, rabbi, and imam"-styled panels often reflect hierarchical and gender-biased portraits of religious traditions that do not do justice to the diversity

---

[6] To access State of Formation, go to http://www.stateofformation.org.

[7] Founding Steering Committee members include Diana Eck, Paul Knitter, John Makransky, Ravi Gupta, and Or Rose. As some members have rotated off, we have added Rachel Mikva, John Sheveland, and Madhuri Yadlapati.

of perspectives and practices encompassed by any living tradition. In *Nostra Aetate* we are exhorted to both dialogue and *collaboration,* and I would urge that more energy go into creative forms of collaboration as interfaith work expands.

Second, I would suggest that, as practitioners and scholars of interfaith engagement, we need to continue to refine our understanding of and appreciation for the rich complexity of identity categories of which religious identity is a part. Scholars of interfaith work would do well to learn from the work of feminist sociologists and others who have highlighted the complex ways that identity categories intersect and create interrelated systems of discrimination. Bigotry in all its complexity is a major barrier to making, sustaining, and deepening the kinds of interfaith friendships that are so vital and fundamental to the healthy functioning of a religiously diverse democracy.

Finally, I see the tendency to emphasize sameness as the "entrance fee" for solidarity as a limiting factor in this work. We see this in the opening paragraph of *Nostra Aetate*, which focuses "above all" on what people "have in common and what draws them to fellowship" (*Nostra Aetate*, sec. 1). An operative assumption in this document, in many models of interfaith engagement, and in the minds of many of my students is that unity is our goal and recognizing sameness is the path. This assumption is so pervasive that it is almost invisible. A student I had who began class with an almost exclusive focus on the similarities across religious traditions arrived at an unexpected insight by the end of the year. Reflecting on his own transformation he wrote:

> What I had yet to realize was that there is even more need to understand and appreciate each other's differences, and in the process, move beyond tolerance, and beyond simply seeking the familiar. Not everything is a commonality, and that is perfectly okay. In fact, it is necessary. In our difference lies our dimensionality, our depth, our richness.[8]

I would argue that the central quest of interfaith work is not to promote unity but rather to create and sustain healthier and more collaborative relationships between the parts and the whole. And by "the whole," I mean the whole created earth with all its inhabitants—those with particular religious identities and those who identify with no religion, those in the human family and those in the rest of creation. Only a tent this big can wean us from our addiction to polarizing "us/them" rhetoric.

In closing, let me reiterate that my primary context and call is to seminary education. Interfaith engagement has the power to transform the model of how we educate our future religious leaders, both in terms of what we teach and how we teach. My hope is that, in ten years' time, it will be considered insufficient and irresponsible to educate seminarians without attention to the meaning and impli-

---

[8] Unpublished student writing from a yearlong seminar on Jewish and Christian relations, co-taught with Rabbi Or Rose. 2009–10.

cations of living in a religiously diverse democracy. My hope is that we design our seminaries to promote authentic sustained engagement with peers from diverse religious backgrounds. Spaces where coformation experiences can unfold are surprisingly rare. Yet these are the spaces we need if we hope to educate transformative interfaith leaders for the future.

16

Buddhism and Christianity in
a Globalizing and Supplementing World

Sallie B. King

In 1965, with the promulgation of *Nostra Aetate* ("In Our Time"), the Catholic Church declared, "The Catholic Church rejects nothing that is true and holy in these [i.e., non-Christian] religions."[1] This was a visionary and courageous declaration. Buddhists have particularly benefited from the changes ushered in by the church's new openness to other religions represented in this statement. While others might point out that what is considered "true and holy" in other religions could be limited to what is already embraced as true from the church's perspective—that is, this statement might not in fact represent true openness to the other—this has not been the experience of Buddhists.

"The Catholic Church Rejects Nothing
That Is True and Holy in These Religions"

Following the promulgation of *Nostra Aetate*, the church in fact acted on these words of openness to others and on *Nostra Aetate*'s accompanying exhortation to engage in interreligious dialogue and collaboration, founding what would become the Pontifical Council for Interreligious Dialogue and creating the structure of Dialogue Interreligieux Monastique / Inter-Monastic Dialogue (DIMMID).[2] Through these institutions, the church has indeed reached out to other religions in a friendly way and has listened to what others have had to say. This willingness has been quite noticeable in the case of its relations with Buddhism. Thomas Merton, who had long studied Buddhism and yearned to deepen his acquaintance with it, was encouraged by Vatican II and the changes that it represented finally to go on his fateful 1968 trip to Asia, a trip in which he sought out and met with

---

[1] *Declaration on the Relation of the Church to Non-Christian Religions—Nostra Aetate*, proclaimed by Pope Paul VI (Vatican City, 1965), sec. 2, http://www.vatican.va/archive/hist_councils/ii_vatican_council/documents/vat-ii_decl_19651028_nostra-aetate_en.html.

[2] For this history, see the excellent volume by Fabrice Blée, *The Third Desert: The Story of Monastic Interreligious Dialogue* (Collegeville, MN: Liturgical Press, 2004).

many of the most important Buddhist contemplatives of the time. His goals for the trip very much set the tone for the Buddhist-Christian dialogue of which he was a trailblazer. He wrote that he aspired "not only to learn more (quantitatively) about religion and about monastic life, but to become a better and more enlightened monk (qualitatively) myself." He believed that it should be possible to "learn in depth from, say, a Buddhist or Hindu discipline or experience," and went on to say, "I believe that some of us need to do this in order to improve the quality of our own monastic life."[3]

Post–Vatican II and post-Merton, Inter-Monastic Dialogue is dominated by Catholic-Buddhist dialogue. Buddhist monastics and Catholic monastics have lived for months in each other's monasteries, living each other's way of life in all sincerity, open to what they might learn. Catholic monasteries today may have meditation rooms set up entirely in a Zen Buddhist style. In fact, the door is wide open to Catholic monastics who want to learn and practice Buddhist-style meditation. In short, with one or two prominent exceptions (e.g., the negative words about Buddhist spirituality in Pope John Paul II's *Crossing the Threshold of Hope*),[4] it has been Buddhists' experience that the Catholic Church post–Vatican II regards Buddhism's spirituality as not only true and holy but also different from what the church already has and thus worthy of learning "in depth," as Merton said. The Catholic Church has very much taken Buddhist spirituality to heart and has been changed by doing so.[5]

Fifty years later, we can see how prescient *Nostra Aetate* was. The internet, global migration, global travel, and globalization generally have all contributed to the situation in which there is no avoiding one another. Nonetheless, once you have cracked the door open to look beyond your own religion to discover what is true and holy in other religions, people *are* going to walk through that door. Fifty years after *Nostra Aetate*, we can begin to see what some of its implications are and, indeed, just how challenging those implications are.

Today, the religious landscape is much changed from what it was in 1965. In particular, the nature of religious identity is undergoing a sea change in much of the

---

[3] Thomas Merton, *The Asian Journal of Thomas Merton*, ed. Naomi Burton et al. (New York: New Directions, 1968), 313.

[4] His Holiness John Paul II, *Crossing the Threshold of Hope* (New York: Alfred A. Knopf, 1994). For the remarks, see the text below at note 11.

[5] It should be mentioned that Buddhism has also been changed by Christianity, both Catholic and Protestant, in the areas of charitable service and engagement with social, economic, and political issues. An example of Catholic influence on Buddhism is the major Taiwanese Buddhist sect and charitable NGO, Tzu Chi, or "Buddhist Compassion Relief." Tzu Chi has branches in fifty countries and over 10 million volunteers; it is the largest Buddhist charitable organization in the world and the largest NGO in the Chinese-speaking world. It was formed partly as a result of a challenge from visiting Catholic nuns who said to the group of Buddhist nuns, "in the eyes of the world, the Buddhists are but a passive group of people contributing nothing to society." See Yu-ing Ching, *Master of Love and Mercy: Cheng Yen* (Nevada City, CA: Blue Dolphin Publishing, 1995), 66.

world. In some cases, religious identity lines are hardening and becoming sources of anger and enmity, as headlines over the last decades have repeatedly shown. A second group of religious people consists of traditionalists who carry on quietly as they have for centuries with little change in the nature of their religious identity. There is a third group: among significant populations in Europe and North America, the lines of religious identity as traditionally understood are blurring. Without discounting in any way the importance of the other two groups, this essay focuses on those European and North American cases in which the lines of religious identity are blurring. This phenomenon has particular significance for Buddhism and special importance for the Buddhist-Christian dialogue, as this dialogue moves forward "In Our Time."

Widening the focus beyond Catholicism per se, I want to look at some interesting current data on the state of religion in the West. It was thought for some time that religion was dying out in Europe, but this projection has not proved to be the case; instead, religion is changing its form. Manuela Kalsky reports this phenomenon for the Netherlands:

> Nowadays 60 percent of the Dutch citizens say they have no affiliation with a church community. The number of church members is constantly declining. . . . On the other hand nearly 60 percent of the Dutch people still claim to be believers. Only 14 percent call themselves atheists. . . . A lot, namely 40 percent of the people, say that they believe in "iets"—which means "something" in Dutch, so they got the name "ietsisten." These people fall into the category of "unaffiliated spirituals." Many of them are patching together elements from the wisdom sayings of different traditions in an individual way.[6]

She goes on to say that this phenomenon is by no means limited to the Netherlands but applies to Europe in general, and adds, "According to surveys, 75 percent of the Dutch people are convinced that this is the way forward for religion in the future."[7]

At least some of the features noted in Europe also apply in the United States. In a 2009 paper, the Pew Research Center reports that about 18 percent of all American adults say that they are "spiritual but not religious."[8] In a separate study, the Pew Research Center also found that "many Americans mix multiple faiths."

---

[6] Manuela Kalsky, "Looking for a New We," keynote speech, Fryshuset conference, "Tro, Hopp och Fördom," Fryshuset, Stockholm, October 10, 2014, private communication to the author.

[7] Manuela Kalsky, "In Search of a 'New We' Connecting the Differences: A Multimedia Contribution to a Paradigm Shift in Interreligious Dialogue," in *Religions and Dialogue: International Approaches*, ed. Wolfram Weisse, Katajun Amirpur, Anna Körs, and Dörthe Vieregge (Münster: Waxmann, 2014), 151. She cites T. Bernts et al., *God in Nederland: 1996–2006* (Kampen: Ten Have, 2007).

[8] Pew Research Center, "Nones on the Rise: Religion and the Unaffiliated," http://www.pewforum.org/2012/10/09/nones-on-the-rise-religion.

For example: "Though the US is an overwhelmingly Christian country, significant minorities profess belief in a variety of Eastern or New Age beliefs. For instance, 24 percent of the public overall and 22 percent of Christians say they believe in reincarnation—that people will be reborn in this world again and again."[9]

It is important to note that all of these figures suggest that many people no longer need the permission of a religious authority to investigate other religions. Thus Kalsky notes that "the subject is increasingly becoming the final authority in assessing what should and should not be justified in a religious sense. Religious traditions thus become an open inheritance of diverse meanings and values, from which one can borrow freely in order to give meaning and direction to one's life."[10]

Following *Nostra Aetate*, significant numbers of Catholic monastics have engaged in Buddhist contemplative practices. Significantly, many Catholic laypeople are also becoming involved with Buddhism and Buddhist practices, "supplementing" their Catholicism with readings of prominent Buddhist authors such as the Dalai Lama and Thich Nhat Hanh, and/or practicing Buddhist meditation. It is noteworthy that some among the church leadership are clearly more uneasy with laypeople engaging in such practices than with monastics doing so. In his book addressed to a popular audience, *Crossing the Threshold of Hope*, Pope John Paul II, in other respects regarded as an exemplary pro-dialogue pope, infamously (to Buddhists) warned Catholics away from becoming involved with Buddhism, stating flatly, "The doctrines of salvation in Buddhism and Christianity are opposed."[11] Many Buddhists were outraged by what they saw as the caricatured misrepresentation of Buddhist beliefs presented in this book, but many also saw the pope's comments as a clear manifestation of the church's fear of the appeal of Buddhism to Christians in the West.

One comes away from these and some other church leaders' observations with a sense of a profound ambivalence on the part of church leaders regarding Catholics who embrace aspects of Buddhist thought and practice as part of their spiritual life. Should Buddhists conclude that church officials believe that borrowing from Buddhism is encouraged for monastics but discouraged for the laity? On the evidence, this might seem to be the case. For example, the Pontifical Council for Interreligious Dialogue was formed by the Vatican, and DIMMID, the principal body for Catholic monastic interreligious dialogue, reports to that Pontifical Council.[12] Perhaps the officials who approved these institutions and activities believe that monastics can be more trusted to experiment with Buddhist prac-

---

[9] Pew Research Center, "Many Americans Mix Multiple Faiths" [December 9, 2009], http://www.pewforum.org/2009/12/09/many-americans-mix-multiple-faiths.

[10] Manuela Kalsky, "Religious Diversity as a Challenge to Theology: The Research Projects of the Dutch Dominican Study Centre for Theology and Society," http://vu-nl.academia.edu/ManuelaKalsky.

[11] John Paul II, *Crossing the Threshold of Hope*, 85.

[12] Blée, *The Third Desert*, chap. 3, "Autonomy and Assessment," inter alia. See also http://www.dimmid.org.

tices without compromising their fidelity to Catholic doctrine than can the laity. This stance might indeed be reasonable inasmuch as monastics have devoted their lives to God and the church, and have better and deeper training—which might well allow the hierarchy to have confidence that they would not misunderstand or misuse Buddhist thought and practice in relation to their Catholicism. Nevertheless, might not the Catholic laity who embrace Buddhist spirituality do so with the same intention as the monastics, that is, with the intention of deepening their own spirituality?

We should take a moment to consider our judgments about such interreligious borrowing, including what Peter Beyer calls the "bricolage" of putting together one's own religious views by drawing on the many wisdom traditions and associated practices now readily available via the internet or in one's own neighborhood.[13] Two main concerns are often voiced regarding such bricolage with respect to their effect on the individual's spiritual life. (I will consider later two concerns with respect to the effect on religious traditions.)

First is the concern that this behavior is a form of egotism inasmuch as it rejects external authorities and gives all power to the individual to choose and embrace those elements of religion that the individual finds pleasing, from whatever source. There may be something to this concern, but I think there are more things wrong than right with it. Let us first listen to Manuela Kalsky, who points out that "individualization should not be equated simply with individualism. Because, although the individual and their associated personal experience is the prominent authority and source of meaning in life, this does not automatically mean that this individual is egocentric and atomistic." She notes, for example, that many people are working out their personal religious views in the course of their daily lives, which includes their interactions with others.[14] In other words, the mere fact that a person is doing something for himself or herself does not make that act an egotistical behavior.

In addition, I am deeply suspicious of what sounds to me like a Protestant bias in the notion that making what one likes a part of one's spirituality is somehow by definition antithetical to spirituality itself. There are many refugees from angry religion in the United States. Joseph Campbell seems to have liberated a lot of people from a variety of dysfunctional spiritualities by urging them to "follow their bliss." Thich Nhat Hanh tells his followers that a spiritual retreat is a "treat." The Buddha himself said that his Dharma was "good in the beginning, good in the middle, and good in the end," meaning that it should begin immediately to reduce the amount of *duhkha*, or suffering, in one's life, and continue to do so as one progresses with it. So let us not assume that if we are not swallowing bitter pills, our spiritual life is egotistical and self-serving. There are other concepts of how religions function.

A second concern is the problem that if one picks a little of this and a little of that, one's religious life can be quite superficial. Again, it may be, but let us

---

[13] Peter Beyer, "Global Migration, Religious Diversity and Dialogue, in *Religions and Dialogue*, ed. Weisse et al., 55–56.

[14] Kalsky, "In Search of a 'New We,'" in *Religions and Dialogue*, ed. Weisse et al., 158.

think some more before we dismiss this behavior altogether. Why should we not trust and respect that in most cases the nature and seriousness of the intention behind anyone's investigation of Buddhist spirituality, whether lay or monastic, is that they are seriously drawn to deepen their spiritual lives? How can dismissing this likelihood be justified? From a Mahayana Buddhist perspective, this process of being drawn to deepen one's spiritual life—whether on the part of a monastic or a layperson—is the work of the Buddha nature. Some Catholic commentators have said that they see this process (at least among monastics) as the Holy Spirit at work.[15] These, of course, are faith statements—but from within a Buddhist or a Catholic perspective, it is difficult to see how one could justify dismissing them.

From a practical point of view, we may add that it is counterproductive and doomed to failure to try to prevent this investigation, experimentation, and borrowing. In the age of the internet and globalization, it cannot be stopped. It is a part of what the church recognizes as the dialogue of life, and ultimately it is not under anyone's control. Is there a way to embrace it? Is there a way to do for the laity what the church via DIMMID has done for the monastics: to give one's blessing to the journey and then to offer guidance, support, and a context for understanding what laypeople might find in their journeys of discovery in Buddhist spirituality? Such guidance could address elements of egotism and superficiality, as indeed it always has, such phenomena not being, after all, something new in the religious lives of individuals.

A Buddhist Response

What does Buddhism have to say in response to this situation? I focus on two offerings from Buddhism: its notion of what a religion is and its openness to serving as "supplemental" to other religions.

First, it is important here to begin with the most basic question of all: What is a religion and what are its functions? Buddhism has a rather different perspective on this matter than the Abrahamic traditions, and I suggest that the Buddhist view may be rather well suited to make a constructive response to the present situation.

A Buddhist view of what religion is goes something like this: Buddhism portrays itself, and religion in general, metaphorically as a vehicle, a path, or a way for the individual to travel from a condition of *duhkha* (dis-satisfactoriness, ignorance, and suffering) to a condition of enlightenment (fully realized wisdom and compassion). Or again, a religion is a set of tools or methods—including both views and practices—for the individual to use for this purpose, that is, for self-transformation from the condition of *duhkha* to the condition of enlightenment.

What are the implications of this idea of religion for the present situation and for the future of interreligious relations? The Buddhist view makes clear that a reli-

---

[15] See Blée, *Third Desert*, 25, 54, 147, 154ff., 200, 202–3.

gion should be of practical use, both immediately and in the long term. It should rather quickly help people to suffer less and rather quickly help them to grow in wisdom and compassion. We should be able to see concrete results here and now. We should be able to feel the effects of our practice in greater happiness and greater inner peace, and others should be able to see its effects in behavior that is less self-centered and more loving. One should expect to see at least some practitioners who are very advanced in these respects.

With regard to meeting the needs of the present moment, I must say that many Buddhist teachers in the West have been quite skillful at offering those views, practices, and methods out of its vast repertoire that address quite well the particular needs of the present. And why should they not? It was a practice of the Buddha to address his audiences as he found them, to speak to them in a way that they could hear and that would benefit them. The Mahayana developed this practice further with the principle of skillful means: whatever ameliorates or eliminates *duhkha*, whatever promotes and nurtures wisdom and compassion, is moving us in the right direction as sentient beings, and thus is good. Buddhism's skillfulness in speaking to current needs should not be seen cynically as opportunistic but as the continuation of long-standing practice based on compassion for the suffering of all beings and on the view that religion is something practical to be used for the good of all, with principled flexibility.

Second, many Catholic, Protestant, and Jewish people in the West draw on Buddhist practices and ideas and make them a part of their own religious life without feeling any need to leave their religion of birth, if they still identify with it, or to formally become Buddhists. This phenomenon is often called "supplemental Buddhism," that is, Buddhism as a supplement to the religion of one's birth, not a replacement of it. In fact, Buddhism is not drawing large numbers of conversions in the West, though it is drawing many who want to practice its meditations or read its wisdom books.

I don't imagine that anyone planned it this way. For the most part, this arrangement seems to have come about naturally, from the ground up, that is, with Western people feeling that there is nothing wrong with this behavior and much good in it, and so they do. But, for its part, Buddhism is also not only accommodating this practice but, to a considerable degree, encouraging it. For example, the two most popular Buddhist teachers in the West, the Dalai Lama and Thich Nhat Hanh, have perfected the art of removing technical Buddhist terms from their speech and writing when addressing broad Western audiences and replacing such terms with more religion-neutral, "spiritual" language of love and kindness, wisdom and understanding that one does not have to be Buddhist to understand, esteem, or embrace.

Why would Buddhists do this? Or, as I once was asked by Abrahamic dialogue partners, doesn't Buddhism mind, in a sense, being diminished in this way, having bits and pieces of it embraced, without Buddhism in its rich and profound fullness being embraced? But this is the wrong way to think from a Buddhist point of view, for several reasons. First, as discussed, the Buddha believed in meeting people where they are. Before they can understand you, people initially have to hear you, which means that you have to speak their language—both literally and metaphorically—and address the issues and concerns that are important to them. Second, Buddhism's view of human spirituality is developmental. Spirituality is not all or nothing. Each person is in a particular stage of spiritual development and can respond to spiritual teachings only from that level of development. They will accept what they are able to accept. Later, they may be able to respond to more. There is no need to do anything but offer what you have to offer; the response will unfold naturally.

Third, Buddhism offering itself in this way is a manifestation of its understanding of itself as a vehicle, path, or means to a higher end. Because of this self-understanding, some of the more radical Buddhists in recent years have begun quite consciously to think of Buddhism as something that, in a sense, transcends itself, a vehicle that makes available truths, values, and goods that are not the exclusive property of Buddhism itself, though Buddhism expresses them and tries to make them reachable in its own way. For example, Thai Buddhist layman Sulak Sivaraksa says:

> You don't have to profess . . . [a particular] faith, you don't have to worship the Buddha, you don't have to join in any ceremonies. What is important is that you grow in mindfulness, your awareness, and you try to restructure your consciousness, to become more selfless, to be able to relate to other people more meaningfully, so that friendship will be possible and exploitation impossible. To me the essence of Buddhism is this.[16]

The upshot of all this is that Buddhism is proving itself to be quite hospitable to the present zeitgeist. I don't know whether some of this approach might make sense, or be workable, within other religions' perspectives.

"Indeed, she proclaims, and must ever proclaim Christ, 'the way, the truth, and the life' (John 14:6)"

The church is bound to proclaim Christ.[17] May I say from a dialogical Buddhist point of view: Please *do* proclaim Jesus! Of course we want to hear it! But must it be Jesus as "the" one and only way?

Sometimes one hears the complaint that Buddhists are not interested in learning from others in dialogue. This is not really true as a general statement. Buddhists have learned from Christians and taken to heart their message about social engagement and charitable work. But it is true that Buddhists have not

---

[16] Sulak Sivaraksa, *A Socially Engaged Buddhism* (Bangkok: Thai Interreligious Commission for Development, 1988), 186.

[17] The quotation in the subhead is from *Nostra Aetate*, sec. 2.

shown much interest in learning from Christian (or Jewish) *theology*, most likely because there is no God in Buddhism. Buddhists have for two and a half millennia been quite dogged about maintaining this difference from their theistic neighbors, and they are not likely to change now. Are there any other possibilities? Might the Buddhist model of offering itself as a supplement to, not a replacement of, other spiritualities be a model that might make sense for other religions, specifically, for Christianity?

Buddhists, as Buddhists, cannot accept Jesus as Lord; this commitment requires conversion. From a Buddhist perspective, to offer only this Jesus cuts short what Christians can offer the world. But what about Christianity as supplemental? Would Christians be willing to show us a Jesus who could be embraced in a supplemental way? What Jesus would be shown? What Jesus would Buddhists like to have shown to them? What are the obstacles within the church to doing so? Thich Nhat Hanh encourages us to offer others our flower, the best that we have. Can other religions make a decision to offer nonmembers those elements of their traditions that represent the unique, beautiful, and profound best of what their tradition has to offer, in a way that is or could be available to nonmembers? Could this option make sense for other religions? If so, what might it look like? Here are a few suggestions from a Buddhist perspective of what Buddhists might like to hear, and might be able to hear, from Christians, suggestions of what might be possible for Buddhists to consider as supplements to their own spirituality, precious gems from Christianity that do not require a person to become a Christian in order to make them part of one's spiritual life.

Please show us the Jesus whom you love. Make clear to us why you love him so. Please leave aside the heavy theological jargon that keeps Jesus at arm's length from us and bring Jesus to life for us. Tell us many stories of Jesus from the gospels and what they mean to you. Bring Jesus' parables to life for us, such that they take root in our minds and make us wonder, day after day. Show us, make vivid to us the living Christ, the Christ spirit that lives in you and in other Christians—how are your hearts, minds and actions guided by this living Christ? Bring to life for us the Jewish roots of Christianity, perhaps especially the prophets; let us be inspired by their courage, their doggedness, their ability to stand completely alone and do what is right. Help us understand the concept of justice, especially Jesus' justice that is not in an antinomous relationship with love, but is an expression of love.[18] Talk to us of great modern Christians like Mother Teresa and Martin Luther King Jr.; help us understand how their Christianity made them capable of such great deeds. Let us hear about the great Christian mystics and about the spirituality of Christian mysticism in general.

---

[18] See, for example, Johann Baptist Metz, "Facing the World: A Theological and Biographical Inquiry," *Theological Studies* 75, no. 1 (2014): 27; Dorothee Soelle, *The Strength of the Weak: Toward a Christian Feminist Identity* (Philadelphia: Westminster, 1984), 136–38, cited in Dorothee Soelle, *Essential Writings*, ed. Dianne L. Oliver (Maryknoll, NY: Orbis Books, 2006), 54–55.

There is a lot that Buddhists might like to hear from Christians about Christianity if they would leave aside the elements of Christianity that create barriers for non-Christians—the abstruse theology; the insistence on our need for a salvation that we just don't feel we need; and of course, the insistence on Jesus as the "one and only" way. Could you consider the possibility of offering us a Jesus whose path of love we could follow as a supplement to our Buddhism?

Religious Traditions

I quoted Kalsky above as proposing that the future for religious traditions is to be "an open inheritance of diverse meanings and values, from which one can borrow freely in order to give meaning and direction to one's life." This perspective does indeed seem to be the attitude toward religious traditions that a great many people in the West have. But despite all that was said above about the inevitability and respectability of the blurring of the lines of religious identity, it remains crucial for traditions to maintain themselves. In the years ahead, it looks to be a challenge for religious traditions to maintain themselves, among at least those populations who are "spiritual but not religious," and those engaged in spiritual bricolage. These approaches sow the seeds of their own destruction: How can one engage in bricolage, on what will one draw for one's individual spirituality, if the religious traditions with their enormous heritages fall on hard times, with fewer people willing to devote their lives to those traditions and fewer willing to commit to support them financially and otherwise? I see two potential problems for religious traditions in an age of "spiritual but not religious" and bricolage: (1) maintaining the integrity of the tradition and (2) surviving.

From the perspectives of both religious traditions and academia, neither religious borrowing nor, even more, spiritual bricolage is a pretty sight. What will become of the integrity and coherence of religious traditions? What rational sense can it possibly make to force belief in reincarnation into the middle of Christianity (as apparently 22 percent of American Christians do!)? As a scholar and educator in religion, I share this concern![19] Yet there are a few facts to consider in this context.

First, we should not forget that religions as they exist now are already very much the product of assimilating from other traditions. Christianity without Greek philosophy would be unrecognizable. Buddhism in Sri Lanka, Buddhism in Tibet, and Buddhism in Japan are vastly different from each other, due to their absorption of cultural elements from the local geographic region and other religions in the area. This sort of borrowing is a natural process that has always occurred, on both erudite and popular levels.

Second, Buddhism in many parts of Asia, especially East Asia, is very much used to processes of mutual learning and assimilation. China centuries ago devel-

---

[19] The present author is a Buddhist-Christian dual belonger herself, but she tries to make her religious views rationally coherent!

oped the "Three Teachings" (三教 *sanjiao*) syncretism of Buddhism, Daoism, and Confucianism; this syncretism became eminently "normal" there and the religion of the majority of the people. In Japan for centuries most traditional people venerated Buddhas and bodhisattvas from Buddhism, the Shinto deities called "kami," and their ancestors, as taught by Confucianism. This behavior was normative for them.

However, there can be serious problems with this kind of practice. Robert Bellah pointed out that this attitude can degenerate into what he called "overtolerance." "An overtolerant religion," he wrote, "is one that fails to communicate its message to important groups in the society and passively assents in their adherence to heterogeneous and often less developed orientations."[20] An egregious example of such overtolerance is WWII-era Japanese Buddhism, which had absorbed so much of the emperor-worshipping and chauvinistic Shinto-Confucian ethos of the time that its leaders and followers largely did not perceive that there was anything morally questionable from a Buddhist perspective about Japan's effort to build an empire by waging war on its neighbors, and participated in this effort with a sense that it was the moral thing to do.[21]

Religions continue to exist over time by evolving through a dialogical and mutually shaping process with their societies and cultures. A static religion will soon be a dead religion, or a museum piece. Religious traditions absorb from and contribute to their culture's ideas, emotional tenors, enthusiasms, and blind spots, together with other religions in the culture. Mutual sharing is necessary and inevitable. But there is, or should be, a limit to this sharing, as the above example from Japan shows. This limit is especially important in the ethical area.

As for intellectual or conceptual coherence, it is debatable how mutually compatible Greek philosophy and Hebraic thought ever were! The felt tensions of the Greek philosophical elements in Christianity have been serious enough in our own time that coherent proposals have been made in recent years for the replacement in Christianity of Greek thought with Buddhist.[22] So it seems to the present author that it is not a question of *whether* there could or should be borrowing between religions. Not only in our era and the foreseeable future, but also throughout time, there has been mutual borrowing. This exchange is inevitable. The question is *which* ideas should be borrowed. Here there will presumably always be differences between scholars and what is popularly embraced. Scholars will demand and strive to create coherence. Among many on the popular level, however, intellectual consistency will be less of a concern. And, over time, as certain ideas

[20] Robert N. Bellah, "Epilogue: Religion and Progress in Modern Asia," in *Religion and Progress in Modern Asia,* ed. Robert N. Bellah (New York: Free Press, 1965), 191–92.

[21] See Sallie B. King, "The Genesis and Decay of Responsibility in Buddhism," in *Taking Responsibility: Comparative Perspectives,* ed. Winston Davis (Charlottesville: University Press of Virginia, 2001), 173–95.

[22] See Paul Knitter, *Without Buddha I Could Not Be a Christian* (London: Oneworld, 2013); John P. Keenan, *The Meaning of Christ: A Mahayana Theology* (Maryknoll, NY: Orbis Books, 1989).

don't "work" for people—including felt conceptual incompatibility—they will be left behind. This process is natural and age-old.

The greatest concern for the present author is the survival of the religious traditions, the carriers of most of the religious heritage of humankind. Speaking as a Buddhist practitioner, I often reflect on, and feel tremendous gratitude to, the countless individuals who dedicated themselves to the Dharma over the centuries from the time of the Buddha, studying it, practicing it, mastering it to the best of their ability, adapting it, and handing it down. Without that dedication, so much that is so precious would have been lost to us today. Indeed, in our time, quite a few Tibetan Buddhists have risked, and sometimes lost, their lives in the effort to protect the continuity of their traditions into the future. I honor them.

This chain of inheritance applies to all religious traditions but seems especially important in a religion like Buddhism, in which religious mastery is critical. The religious tradition of Buddhism—teachings and teachers, texts, practices, experiences, places, arts, community—nurtures the Buddhist masters, and the masters ensure the ongoing existence and vitality of the tradition. This process cannot continue without the ongoing vitality of both Buddhism as an institutional religion and people who are willing to devote every effort in their lives to plumbing the depths of Buddhism and helping others to do the same. The institution and the mastery are interdependent. Therefore, in the case of Buddhism, it matters greatly that the tradition continue, with its own integrity, an integrity that, though evolving, carries what is most precious from the past into the future. Only a small number of its followers need to be devoted to this degree, but some must be if the institution is to survive as a resource for those who want to engage it to a lesser degree. This is my greatest concern with respect to the era of "spiritual but not religious," a sentiment that is not, and cannot be, self-sustaining.

Inasmuch as we are in a time of rapid change for institutional religion in general, the question of future survival with vitality and integrity applies to all religions. So let us engage in a thought experiment: Let us assume that the trends I have been discussing continue to grow in popularity. How will traditions maintain themselves in a commitment-free age of "spiritual but not religious," of bricolage, and of seemingly endless religious information available for free on the internet? Would there still be some functions for which some among the "spiritual but not religious" and the bricolagers may want to turn to religious institutions? If so, might it be that in such a scenario religious institutions might want to devote more of their resources to these functions, so that they can continue to exist and serve as resources for humankind?

Three particular ongoing functions that religious institutions would need to continue offering into the future, despite the internet and bricolage, come immediately to mind. Despite, or even because of, the fact that individuals would be picking and choosing among a variety of religious teachings, deciding for themselves what makes sense to them and what helps them in their individual lives, and despite the fact that the authority to make all these decisions is rapidly moving from traditional religious authority to the individual, many people might well continue to need and want individual spiritual guidance. It will always be the case that it is one thing to read an inspiring text and quite another to apply it to one's own particular situation and put it into practice. It will always be the case that an individual engaged in serious practice of meditation or contemplative prayer will face challenges. People will always profit from the guidance of those who have themselves deeply explored such territory and are deeply steeped in their tradition's guidance through it. Although acting as a spiritual mentor is a kind of religious authority, and we are presuming a move away from such authority, this authority would clearly not be a commanding or domineering kind, but only the authority of expertise, offered in a loving way. No matter how much spirituality becomes individualized, I believe there will always be a need for spiritual guides who, like Jesus and Buddha, are able to speak "with authority" because of their own wisdom and practice. Of all the ongoing functions for religious institutions in an age of internet and spiritual bricolage, this one seems the most secure.

There is a second ongoing need that religious institutions have always served but that is threatened as we step into the future. How, in an age of internet and spiritual bricolage, can religious institutions provide a home for spiritual/religious sharing and community—for ritual and group celebration, as well as for group practice and discussion of spiritual/religious topics? It seems less certain that religious institutions will be needed for this purpose in the future. The individualization of spirituality is part of the individualization of society that is reaching dysfunctional levels in some societies, notably the United States. Here, according to the Census Bureau, 35 percent of people report moving in a five-year period.[23] Americans go "bowling alone," socialize with friends and family less frequently than had earlier generations, and belong to fewer organizations.[24] Yet we are social animals, and this movement away from the much higher level of human interaction that has been intrinsic to humankind since the beginning of our species takes a very high psychological toll.

Gathering for group ceremony, ritual, celebration, and mourning is a behavior that seems to go back to the dawn of human existence and is found, as far as I know, in all human societies (unless suppressed by tyrannical power). One can only hope that religious institutions will find ways to reshape themselves such that they will better serve the human need for community. Some institutional reshaping is already occurring. From the Buddhist world, there is the example of Soka Gakkai, small group meetings in homes that provide occasions to know others and be known at a deep level, opportunities for profound self-transformation, and strong community. Another new institution can be seen in the Zen, Vipassana, and Tibetan lineages

---

[23] Alison Fields and Robert Kominski, "America: A Nation on the Move," http://blogs.census.gov/2012/12/10/america-a-nation-on-the-move.

[24] Robert D. Putnam, *Bowling Alone: The Collapse and Revival of American Community* (New York: Simon & Schuster, 2000).

of Western Buddhism, which have developed local practice centers for regular gatherings, combined with retreat centers for occasional in-depth practice. These new institutions utilize the expertise of the tradition, amassed over centuries or millennia, but deliver it in a way that suits the present individualistic zeitgeist, thus perhaps preserving the best of both worlds. I observe similar creativity going on in some other religious traditions.

Finally, in our thought experiment, we should consider the possible future role of religious institutions as organizations for engaging in group social action. I am thinking of a site I visited while on a tour with representatives of the Tzu Chi Buddhist movement in Taipei, Taiwan. At the request of the founder of Tzu Chi, Venerable Cheng Yen, a small army of volunteers has taken upon itself responsibility for providing major recycling services in their communities. When we arrived at the recycling center in Taipei, we saw a mountain of empty plastic water bottles with a small group of elderly women sitting on the floor at its edges, deftly sorting the bottles by plastic type. The visual image at first seemed rather distressing, but it transformed before our eyes as we heard it explained. These women were all volunteers. They come every day to sort bottles. They look forward to it. Before they started doing this labor, they sat at home alone all day, their husbands dead, their children gone or at work, and they were lonely and depressed. Now they come to the recycling center, where they not only perform a task that helps both the local community and the world, they also see the friends they have made while sorting and enjoy a much improved social life right then and there. Their lives have meaning, purpose, and pleasure. Their depression has vanished. In this and other ways, Tzu Chi, a new Taiwanese Buddhist sect and charitable organization, has been masterful at creating vital new institutions and bringing together millions of people eager to engage in service as a spiritual practice.

So these are three functions that religious institutions can fulfill—individual spiritual guidance, a home for religious community, and an organization for engaging in group social action—all of which seem viable into the future, spiritually and socially necessary, and not available from the internet. Probably there are other important functions which could be identified. The important point is for the religions to think of what functions they can offer into the future that will allow them to effectively serve humankind and thereby thrive in an age of globalization, "spiritual but not religious" persons, and spiritual bricolage.

17

LEARNING FROM (AND NOT JUST ABOUT) OUR RELIGIOUS NEIGHBORS

Comparative Theology and the Future of Nostra Aetate

John J. Thatamanil

The promise of *Nostra Aetate* is twofold. First, and widely recognized, is *Nostra Aetate*'s new spirit of openness to other religions. On most readings, *Nostra Aetate* moved theology of religious diversity beyond the province of exclusivism to some kind of modest inclusivism.[1] What kind of inclusivism that is has always been a contested matter, a contestation that I will largely leave in the hands of historians. Nonetheless, this move away from exclusivism toward inclusivism is the first major contribution of *Nostra Aetate*.

But a second contribution of *Nostra Aetate* has been insufficiently appreciated: the turn to specificity. *Nostra Aetate* does not speak of "religions" in general but instead points to *specific* teachings and practices of other religions and commends those specificities. *Nostra Aetate* is, therefore, a contribution not only to theology of religious diversity but also to what came later to be called comparative theology.[2]

The work of imagining *Nostra Aetate*'s future requires a commitment to deepen both of these contributions. That deepening requires one critical further step: *Nostra Aetate* calls attention to certain commendable teachings and practices of other traditions, but it does not affirm that the church has anything *to learn* from

---

[1] Briefly, *exclusivism* names the family of positions which holds that salvation, but sometimes also religious truth, is found only in one's home tradition. *Inclusivism* names the family of positions which holds that, although the fullness of salvation and religious truth is found in one's own tradition, partial and fragmentary elements of truth and saving grace can be found elsewhere. God's soteriological efficacy cannot be confined or restricted to one's tradition alone. For a fuller treatment of these models, see Paul Knitter's *Introducing Theology of Religions* (Maryknoll, NY: Orbis Books, 2002) as well as Paul Hedges, *Controversies in Interreligious Dialogue and Theology of Religions* (London: SCM Press, 2010).

[2] Comparative theology is the constructive quest to understand ultimate reality, the human predicament, and world by appeal to the resources of more than one tradition. Comparative theologians regard religious traditions as offering normative resources and not merely as objects of ethnographic or historical curiosity.

those or other teachings and practices. Affirming the possibility and necessity of interreligious learning is the critical next step in advancing the legacy of *Nostra Aetate*. Affirming the possibility of interreligious learning from other traditions would simultaneously be a contribution to both comparative theology and theologies of religious diversity.

The critical limitation of *Nostra Aetate* is that it remains captive to an ethos of religious self-sufficiency. By religious self-sufficiency, I refer to the unarticulated because taken-for-granted tenor and posture of the whole document, the Catholic Church possesses all it needs to know about religious truth in full and hence Christians stand in no positive need of their religious neighbors to move more deeply into the divine life. Rupturing that sense of religious self-sufficiency is a—perhaps the—key next step in interreligious engagement.

Merely affirming the presence of truth or even of salvation outside of one's tradition does not rupture religious self-sufficiency. It is possible, after all, to commend specific features of other traditions or to affirm the presence of the Word and the Holy Spirit outside the walls of the church and still maintain that whatever good might be found in other traditions is but a diminished version of truth found in fuller expression in my own. *Nostra Aetate*, as it stands, affirms both a graded and hierarchical inclusivism. *Nostra Aetate*'s inclusivism is graded because not all religious traditions are placed on equal footing; some religions are granted a higher standing than others. *Nostra Aetate*'s inclusivism is also hierarchical because, although other traditions may have a "ray of the truth" that illumines all people, the church possesses the fullness of that truth in Jesus the Christ. Hierarchical inclusivism is constituted by this part-whole logic.

The church must now make the further affirmation that dedication to the One who is the way and truth compels it to learn from other traditions. An explicit affirmation of learning from religious others would mark a decided shift in the church's posture toward those others. Only when I affirm that I need to and must learn from others do I step away from a posture of asymmetry to a posture of mutuality. When I acknowledge that I do not know all there is to know about religious truth or about God, I can no longer adopt a posture of religious self-sufficiency. I acknowledge then that I stand in need of others to bring me into the fullness of truth. The diversity of religious traditions can then be affirmed as part of the permanent will and providence of God. I no longer operate as though I believe that religious diversity is a historical accident that will, in time, fade away as error is replaced by truth or partial truth is replaced by truth in all its fullness. Therefore, to affirm the possibility and reality of interreligious learning would mark a decisive step beyond current forms of graded and hierarchical inclusivism. At the very least, that step would lead the church to what Paul Griffiths has called an "open inclusivism." However, I believe, with Paul Knitter, that we must call for a posture and position of mutuality.[3]

---

[3] The mutuality position is better known by the term "pluralism." Knitter's term has much to commend it because "mutuality" names and recognizes the need for mutual

I advance this argument in the following stages: first, I quickly take note of the new openness of *Nostra Aetate* toward other religions and commend *Nostra Aetate*'s turn toward specificity. Second, I show that neither of these steps moves the church beyond a posture of religious self-sufficiency. With that retrospective task completed, I then turn to the work of imagining the future of *Nostra Aetate*. I conclude with a few brief paragraphs in which I rewrite *Nostra Aetate* to show just what a revised version might sound like, a new *Nostra Aetate* which embodies the spirit of mutuality that I call for. I will do so particularly by seeking to develop what remains most undeveloped in *Nostra Aetate*—the paragraphs on Hinduism and Buddhism, as well as a restatement of the key paragraph that acknowledges the presence of truth outside of the church.

A Retrospective Assessment

Nostra Aetate begins and ends by setting its reflections within a broader context: the document's theological reflections on religions are meant to be in service to the church's "task of promoting unity and love among men [*sic*]." The document concludes with an explicit rejection of discrimination and issues a call for "fellowship among the nations."[4] These overarching framing goals still remain compelling. It would be a critical omission in any historical assessment of *Nostra Aetate* to ignore the explicit obligations, goals, and virtues for the sake of which the document was written. *Nostra Aetate* makes clear that theological reflection is undertaken for the sake of larger human and social goods. So too, any treatment of the future of *Nostra Aetate*—especially for those who would imagine a revised and improved *Nostra Aetate*—must likewise be explicit about the goals and virtues for which any

---

learning and transformation between traditions. At least some ways of formulating pluralism give the mistaken impression that each tradition is in isolation sufficient unto itself. Even if one holds that various religious traditions grant access to salvific truth—a position that mutualists also affirm—the language and framework of "mutuality" ruptures the sense of self-sufficiency that I challenge in the remainder of this essay. Speaking of mutualists, Knitter writes, "What they want to foster is not just the multiplicity and identity of other religions but also and especially a conversation among them. That's why we are calling this the Mutuality Model rather than its frequently given (and misleading) name, the Pluralist Model. For this model, relationship is more important than plurality." For this very reason, I join Roland Faber and Catherine Keller in using the term "relational pluralism." For Knitter, see *Introducing Theology*, 110. For Roland Faber and Catherine Keller, see their essay, "A Taste for Multiplicity: The Skillful Means of Religious Pluralism," in *Religions in the Making: Whitehead and the Wisdom Traditions of the World*, ed. John B. Cobb Jr. (Eugene, OR: Cascade Books, 2012), 180–207.

[4] *Declaration on the Relation of the Church to Non-Christian Religions—Nostra Aetate*, proclaimed by Pope Paul VI (Vatican City, 1965), sec. 1. http://www.vatican.va/archive/hist_councils/ii_vatican_council/documents/vat-ii_decl_19651028_nostra-aetate_en.html. Future references to this document will be placed in parentheses within the text.

new *Nostra Aetate* might be written. Here, I would like to suggest that the task of promoting unity and love among peoples is likely to remain unmet within any theological framework in which the church does not acknowledge its positive need for the wisdom of other traditions. It is good that the church "rejects nothing that is true and holy in these religions" (sec. 2). Nonetheless, that negative framing is both telling and insufficient. Refusing to reject the true and the holy is, of course, a commendable posture, but nonetheless it is a limited good, particularly when viewed from our historical viewpoint. In terms of an ethico-theological framework, it seems more like a floor than a ceiling. One would expect that any religious community would do at least that, but it hardly seems an exorbitant demand to ask more from the church and other religious communities.

Still better is *Nostra Aetate*'s positive affirmation that the church "regards with sincere reverence those ways of conduct and of life, those precepts and teachings" of other traditions (sec. 2). But this reverence—a strong word connoting profound, even religious, respect—nonetheless remains limited because it is installed within the theological framework of hierarchical inclusivism. The church's reverence is limited because it holds that what is true in other religions is but "a ray of that Truth which enlightens all men [*sic*]" (sec. 2). The church's work remains unchanged: the church "proclaims, and ever must proclaim Christ 'the way, the truth, and the life' (John 14:6), in whom people may find the fullness of religious life, in whom God has reconciled all things to Himself" (sec. 2). But if other religions have only a ray of what Christian tradition holds in full, then, one must ask, What, if anything, would be lost if the rest of the world's religions were lost or erased from history? Would the church itself be diminished and suffer loss? Would the world? And is the evangelical work of the church meant ultimately to replace these religions as the full must complete and replace what is partial?

The very next and crucial paragraph intimates otherwise: "The church, therefore, exhorts her sons [and daughters], that through dialogue and collaboration with the followers of other religions, carried out with prudence and love and in witness to the Christian faith and life, they *recognize*, *preserve* and *promote* the good things, spiritual and moral, as well as the socio-cultural values found among these men [*sic*]" (sec. 2, emphasis added). The three verbs that I have emphasized appear to suggest that the church's goal cannot be one in which the other is replaced. Particularly important is the last of these three verbs, "promote." Recognition and preservation can be done within an antiquarian frame—the way one collects antiquities within a museum, for example, in appreciation for their aesthetic or historical value. On the contrary, one "promotes" only what one takes to have ongoing merit and worth. Spelling out the meaning of this third verb remains an unfinished task in interpreting *Nostra Aetate*.

But I would like to pose a further question: Might a future *Nostra Aetate* add one more verb to this noteworthy list: might the sons and daughters of the church "recognize, preserve, promote, and *receive*" the good things, spiritual and moral, found among these people? It is my sense that the addition of this verb might make all the difference in interrupting the ethos of religious self-sufficiency that *Nostra Aetate* never quite manages to escape. Without the addition of this verb, it is difficult to see just how "dialogue and collaboration" can genuinely be dialogical. What is the point of dialogue if I myself feel that I have nothing to learn and nothing to receive? But if there is wisdom that my tradition and I must receive, then I cannot pretend that my tradition is self-sufficient.

Hence, the call to receive must be added and stressed in order to fulfill what remains at best an implicit promise within *Nostra Aetate* as it now stands. The call to dialogue and collaboration and the call to recognize, preserve, and promote mark an important if not yet decisive break from an exclusivist past. These three verbs, particularly the third, seem a clear indication of a move to inclusivism, albeit an inclusivism that appears to remain hierarchical in nature. Should the verb "receive" be added, *Nostra Aetate*'s theology would move beyond hierarchical inclusivism into, at the very least, open inclusivism. More on this matter later.

Now, let's talk about specificity. *Nostra Aetate* attends to two kinds of specificity. First, and perhaps most obviously, *Nostra Aetate* calls attention to some specific teachings and practices from other religions. Second—and this kind of specificity is so obvious that it escapes our attention—*Nostra Aetate* discusses some religions at length and others only in passing, and it treats those traditions in a telling order. In this connection, the most consequential and concerning slight by *Nostra Aetate* demands special attention: the document makes only passing and somewhat ambiguous reference to the world's various indigenous traditions.[5] *Nostra Aetate* begins its substantive discussion with reference to those "religions . . . that are bound up with an advanced culture." Those traditions that presumably are not "bound up with an advanced culture" merit but a single sentence. Native American traditions, the traditions of Australian aboriginal peoples, and the various traditions of the whole of the African continent are thereby marginalized.

Nostra Aetate's orientation to so-called "world religions" constitutes an impediment that continues to plague the Catholic Church's ongoing relationship with the primordial traditions. The chief blight on Pope Francis's recent visit to the United States rests in Francis's unwillingness to take account of Native American objections to the canonization of Junipero Serra, whose violence toward Native Americans is a matter of historical record. That the Native American demand that the Catholic Church formally renounce the doctrine of discovery also went unheeded suggests that *Nostra Aetate*'s omission of indigenous traditions is indicative not only of a past sin of omission but a current sin of complicity. Any future version of *Nostra Aetate* must remedy this omission of the various religions of the earth, which is particularly

---

[5] "From ancient times down to the present, there is found among various peoples a certain perception of that hidden power which hovers over the course of things and over the events of human history; at times some indeed have come to the recognition of a Supreme Being, or even of a Father. This perception and recognition penetrates their lives with a profound religious sense" (*Nostra Aetate,* sec. 2).

problematic in light of *Laudato Si'* and Pope Francis's repeated calls for care of our common home.[6]

Nostra Aetate articulates a graded inclusivism in which some traditions appear to rank higher than others. The sequence in which religious traditions are discussed suggests a movement from circumference to center, with the various religious traditions receiving more sustained and detailed attention as one moves first from Hinduism and Buddhism and then eventually to Islam and Judaism. *Nostra Aetate* is by no means an exercise in offering a neutral history of religions survey. The document is resolutely theological, and theological judgment is never suspended. In *Nostra Aetate*, the religions are not on par with Christianity, nor are they on equal footing with each other. The amount of attention and textual space accorded to a tradition directly correlates with the degree to which that tradition approximates the truth of Christianity. Hinduism is accorded cursory, albeit respectful, attention—just two sentences. Buddhism, too, is granted two sentences. Then reference is made to a few unspecified "other religions found everywhere," which "try to counter the restlessness of the human heart." By contrast, Muslims are granted an extended discussion of two paragraphs, and Judaism merits a lengthy treatment of eight paragraphs. Historians would remind us that *Nostra Aetate* was meant originally to offer only a treatment of the Catholic Church's relationship to Judaism. Hence, the sustained engagement with Judaism should not surprise. Nonetheless, the impression generated by the document, as it stands, is that some traditions stand on the periphery and others closer to the center, the center being Christianity. Hence my use of the term "graded inclusivism." Even if other traditions contain "truth and holiness," they do not do so to the same degree.

With the work of John Hick, theology of religions moved resolutely into an ethos of theological parity and away from graded inclusivism. Hick, as is famously known, called for a Copernican revolution in religions, one in which Christianity was no longer at the center; rather, "God" or, later in his writings, "ultimate reality" is at the center, and the religions now all orbit around ultimate reality. A curious feature of this Copernican revolution in the religions is the idea that the various religious traditions are in equidistant orbit around ultimate reality. No religious tradition is any nearer to ultimate reality than any other. Hick generated theological parity on Kantian epistemological grounds. Every religious tradition has access only to phenomena and not to the noumenon; what ultimate reality is in itself remains inaccessible to all.

The trouble with the move to an ethos of parity generated by Kantian means is that it is gained at tremendous theological expense. If no tradition's theological claims afford access, even partially and fallibly, to the nature of ultimate reality, then it is hard to see how sustained theological inquiry into those claims could be warranted. The long hard work of comparative theology, which understands itself

---

[6] Pope Francis, *Encyclical Letter—Laudato Si'* (Vatican City, 2015), http://w2.vatican.va/content/francesco/en/encyclicals/documents/papa-francesco_20150524_enciclica-laudato-si.pdf.

to be the quest to learn more about ultimate reality by learning from and with other religious traditions, would appear to be, strictly speaking, impossible. Comparative theology might teach us more about what other traditions hold to be true; it would not, however, grant us any deeper access to theological truth as such.

It follows, then, that any imagined future *Nostra Aetate* demands an alternative formulation that rejects both graded inclusivism, which ranks religions as a whole, as well as regnant Kantian formulations of parity pluralism. I propose that we simply abandon the notion that religions are the sort of entities that admit of either sort of judgment. How does one weigh the merits of religions as a whole? Religions, unlike bowling balls, do not seem to be the sort of entities that can be weighed. Hick's own attempts appear in retrospect to border on the comical. The notion that we could measure religions by how many saints they produce or by their relative merits in generating social goods and avoiding social harm seem flat-footed at best. Why? Because every "religion" is both healing and violating, sometimes at once, and sometimes in its various subcommunities. For much of its history, Christianity was a slaveholding religion. More recently, black Christian communities and abolitionists have sought successfully to save Christianity from its captivity to slaveholding and segregationist ideology, although many forms of white American Christianity still remain oblivious to and complicit with white supremacy. Simply put, religious traditions do not possess the kind of unity and systematicity that would permit "religions" to be weighed against each other so as to merit either summary judgments of superiority or parity. We need a new path into the future beyond both alternatives.

Imagining the Future of *Nostra Aetate* / Imagining a Future *Nostra Aetate*

I contend that there is a tension embedded in *Nostra Aetate* between its general claims about other religions and the specific attention to features thereof. In the subsequent history of Christian theological reflection, that tension has come to define the still contested relationship between two subdisciplines within Christian interreligious engagement: the tension between the so-called theology of religions and comparative theology. Some comparative theologians have argued that the entire project of theology of religions ought to be surrendered, or at least put on hold—hence the call for a moratorium on theology of religions. James Fredericks argued at the beginning of the twenty-first century that no then-available theology of religions was viable.[7] He offered compelling arguments that maintained that all attempts to speak Christianly about the meaning of religious diversity—exclusivism, inclusivism, and pluralism—are not viable. If all extant options in a field fail,

---

[7] See James Fredericks's two books: *Faith among Faiths: Christianity and the Other Religions* (Mahwah, NJ: Paulist Press, 1999) and *Buddhists and Christians: From Comparative Theology to Solidarity* (Maryknoll, NY: Orbis Books, 2004).

then perhaps the questions to which the options are answers are poorly formed or premature from a historical point of view. At any rate, Fredericks believed that a moratorium on theology of religions was in order.

More recently, those who work within theology of religions have argued that there can be no bypassing the task of theology of religions.[8] Every comparative theologian is bound to operate by at least some implicit convictions about the nature, meaning, and validity of religious diversity. Why would one even begin the work of comparative theology if one were convinced from the start that the history of religion is a history of error? Although it is difficult to issue assessments about the relationship between entire subdisciplines, my own judgment is that talk about putting an end to theology of religions for the sake of comparative theology seems to be a thing of the past. Fredericks's call for a moratorium has failed to carry the day. Nonetheless, what seems to abide is a sense that general claims can be made about "religions" as such. There appears to be a tacit understanding that theology of religions can continue to make general claims about the "religions," and that comparative theology can focus on the detailed work of engaging with specific texts, practices, and theologians. But is it meaningful to issue either positive or negative judgments as such about the religions as such or as wholes? If such claims are unsustainable, perhaps the time has come for theology of religions also to take up specificities rather than leaving those to comparative theology alone.

I believe we must work to discover an alternative path between John Hick's parity pluralism and *Nostra Aetate*'s graded inclusivism. That alternative will require rejecting a premise that both share, that it is meaningful to speak about religions as a whole. Whether we seek to rank the religions or charitably classify them all as equal, we assume that such talk about religions is nevertheless meaningful. I hold that this premise stands in need of deep critical interrogation and rejection for multiple reasons:

1. Most of the world's cultures and languages have had neither a word nor a concept for the categories of religion or religions. Even the less reifying notion of "the religious" is challenging insofar as the very idea that some aspects of life are religious and some are not requires the invention of "the secular." As Talal Asad has shown, "the religious" and "the secular" are conceptual Siamese twins; neither can be imagined without the other. To treat a variety of other traditions under the category "religion," thus requires imposing upon other traditions a nonnative category that brings with it enormous complications.[9]

---

[8] One of the strongest of these arguments is Kristin Biese Kiblinger's. See her essay, "Relating Theology of Religions and Comparative Theology," in *The New Comparative Theology: Interreligious Insights from the Next Generation*, ed. Francis X. Clooney, SJ (New York: Bloomsbury T&T Clark, 2010), 21–42.

[9] See Talal Asad, *Genealogies of Religion: Discipline and Reasons of Power in Christianity*

2. Those traditions that we have come to call religions are in every case communities of argumentation and not communities of consensus. To be a Buddhist, Hindu, or a Christian is to be invested in one of these arguments and not the other. If you are interested in whether emptiness can be understood positively as a kind of infinitely open ground of mind and world, or you think that emptiness must be understood negatively as meaning that nothing whatsoever has self-existence or own-being (*svabhava*), you are a Buddhist. If you are involved in an argument about whether Brahman is the transpersonal world-ground and just is one's true Self, or whether you believe Brahman to be the personal object of devotion (*bhakti*) which is the world soul, or whether you happen to believe that Brahman is a personal Lord who is utterly different from the world, you are a Hindu. Given the profound ongoing debates within traditions, it is hard to know how responsible theological conversations about religious traditions can bypass these and other debates and pronounce judgments on religions as a whole.

3. The notion of "religion" seems to bring in its conceptual wake the notion that the religions are neatly distinct and separate from each other, as well as the notion that persons can belong to only one religion at a time. Neither claim is empirically sustainable. Interreligious learning and mutual influence have constituted virtually all of our "religions," and, arguably, singular religious belonging is the exception rather than the rule in the global history of religions.

The upshot of just these observations is that specificity of theological judgment is required not just from comparative theologians but also from theologians of religion. Any future *Nostra Aetate* must find new conceptual and discursive registers that are sensitive to these profound insights from the last fifty years of religious studies scholarship. Attention to contesting and reformulating the category "religion" will require dismissing graded inclusivism that ranks religions as a whole, and it would also require rejecting parity pluralism that maintains religions to be of equal merit. Both kinds of claims presuppose an unsubtle and now obsolete idea about what religion and the religions are. The genuine alternative to both options is a new theology of religious diversity that focuses on specificity and speaks only rarely and cautiously about religions as such or as a whole. In sum, any future *Nostra Aetate* will depend on a new linguistic and theological framework that avoids reifying and essentializing religions. When such a framework is found, we will be closer to addressing the lingering central weakness of *Nostra Aetate*—namely, religious self-sufficiency.

I shall argue that the future of *Nostra Aetate* for Catholic and Christian communities in general rests on a careful integration of *theology of religious diversity*

---

and Islam (Baltimore: Johns Hopkins University Press, 1993) and Talal Asad, *Formations of the Secular: Christianity, Islam, Modernity* (Stanford, CA: Stanford University Press, 2003).

and *comparative theology* for the sake of *constructive Christian theology*. The time is at hand (and now is) for Christians not merely to speak and think positively about religious others but also to learn from them and let that learning enable Christian communities to rearticulate how we understand the meaning of God, world, and the human condition. Without exercises in such learning, even if only incremental, a generalized commendation of openness to other religions will seem half-hearted. Moreover, only interreligious learning can affirm what is most needed in this era, the next step which is, at best implicit, in *Nostra Aetate*: an explicit affirmation that religious diversity is part of the divine providence and is the will of God and not a regrettable error to be remedied by way of Christian mission and evangelization.

Paragraphs for a New *Nostra Aetate*

What might such a new linguistic and theological register sound like? I propose to answer that question by writing, somewhat presumptuously, new language for a new *Nostra Aetate*. What I offer below is not a rewriting of the entire document but only a few key selected paragraphs. I conclude the paper with a brief theoretical explication of what these few paragraphs seek to perform.

1. The Catholic Church reaffirms that it rejects nothing "that is true and holy in [other] religions." The church wishes also to affirm that love of the One who is the Truth compels it to *receive* truth and wisdom from those outside the church, for the Word is also "the light that illumines all people" (Jn 1:9). That saving light has never and can never be extinguished from the lives and the teachings of other traditions.

2. Just as the Apostle Paul and the church with him learned to speak of God as the one in whom "we live and move and have our being" (Acts 17:28) from Greek philosophers (Epimenides), so the church stands prepared to receive with hospitality and gratitude what God has taught and continues to teach to our brothers and sisters of other traditions. The church gratefully acknowledges that it has been and continues to be enriched by the gifts of wisdom and Spirit that God has granted in every age to God's children who are not sons and daughters of the church.

3. The church also confesses in humility that it does not know all there is to know about the Word who has become flesh. We acknowledge that the church can learn more about the Christ from those who have learned to love, follow, and serve him but without entering into full and explicit fellowship in the church. In the maturity and mutuality of fellowship with all those who seek to know God more fully, the church stands prepared not only to teach but also to learn, not only to challenge but also to be challenged.

4. The Catholic Church recognizes the profound depth of the riches of Hindu traditions and their millennia-long struggle to understand the nature of God and of God's relationship to the world. In ways that mirror

conversations within the church, Hindus debate whether the human being is in essence divine (Sankara), whether instead God is the soul of the world and of individual human souls (Ramanuja) and yet distinct from both, or whether the world and God are separate from each other (Madhva).

5. The church recognizes the importance of this debate and looks forward to participating in this conversation with openness and respect. We celebrate the strong affirmation of divine immanence within many Hindu traditions, an affirmation from which the church must continue to learn. The church affirms that God is "nearer to us than we are to ourselves" while maintaining the necessary distinction between creator and creation. The church also acknowledges with special gratitude its indebtedness to Mahatma Gandhi, a Hindu disciple of the Christ, who taught the church to see the Christ afresh as the great *satyagrahi*, one who embodies the virtues and practice of nonviolent resistance.

6. In its further study of Buddhist traditions, the church recognizes and affirms the core Mahayana teaching that all things are empty of a private essence (*svabhava*) because all things are interconnected (*pratityasamutpada*). While the church affirms that God loves and creates all things as precious, distinct, and of singular worth, it, with its Buddhist brothers and sisters, also affirms that we each of us come to be only in and through kinship with all creation. We learn from Buddhist traditions and from reflection on the Trinitarian mystery that to be is to be related. We seek to learn the meaning of our interrelatedness in friendship and deeper collaboration with our Buddhist brothers and sisters.

7. The church acknowledges with a new respect the profound depth of the traditions of the world's First Nations. It recognizes with special reverence the way in which these traditions have long sought to live in intimacy with and care for "our common home." The church acknowledges that these traditions have much to teach it about the Spirit that hovers and broods over the face of the deep, not only at the inception of creation but also in our time. As the church seeks to call the world to care for the imperiled Earth, it seeks to work with indigenous traditions in order to acknowledge, preserve, promote, and to receive the wisdom of First Nations.

A New Pluralism for a New *Nostra Aetate*

I wish now to conclude my reflections by offering an abbreviated explication of these seven paragraphs. As is the case with all conciliar documents, even hypothetical ones, I have taken care to draft these paragraphs in a fashion that walks a fine line between what Paul Griffiths has called "open inclusivism," and an explicit affirmation of pluralism.[10] What these draft paragraphs seek to do, above all, is to

---

[10] See Paul Griffiths, *Problems of Religious Diversity* (Malden, MA: Blackwell, 2001).

puncture the bubble of religious self-sufficiency, which gives the appearance that the church stands in no ongoing need of wisdom from other traditions. On the contrary, I wish to affirm that the church has always needed such wisdom and stands always in permanent need. In so doing, I suggest that religious diversity is part of the permanent will of God.

Virtually every paragraph positions the church as receptive to the work of God in Word and Spirit *extra ecclesiam*. I leave it largely to readers to determine what is entailed by this receptivity. Open inclusivists typically acknowledge that the church has new truth to learn and that some of that truth can be learned from other religious traditions. Open inclusivists, however, typically refuse to argue that other traditions also afford salvation to their adherents. I intimate that other traditions afford not just truth but also salvation.

But I do not affirm that traditions are "equally salvific" to Christian traditions. There is no suggestion herein of parity pluralism. Again, I believe that quantitative claims are misguided and unsustainable. Neither graded inclusivism nor parity pluralism is a credible option. "Religions" cannot be so measured. Is slaveholder Christianity salvific? Can the church's violent subjugation of indigenous traditions and complicity in the extermination of native peoples be considered salvific? Are nationalist Sinhalese Buddhist violence and Hindu casteism salvific? Every human tradition contains both healing and destructive tendencies, and the church and its theologians must engage in theological judgment to sort out what is true and healing from what is false and injurious. Any new *Nostra Aetate* must join the old in exercising careful theological judgment but without falling back into graded inclusivism which rank-orders religions.

Paragraph 2 appeals to Paul's discourse on the Areopagus to name the presence of pagan wisdom in the heart of Christian scripture. Scholars have argued that Saint Paul is quoting the Stoic philosopher Epimenides when he adverts to God as "the one in whom we move and live and have our being." The presence and importance of this verse for the whole of Christian history and its privileged position within scripture testify to the porosity of traditions. I wish here to show that Christian wisdom is, at least in part, constituted by what it has received from alien wisdom traditions. Scripture itself demonstrates that the line between "religions" is hard to draw.

Paragraph 3 is meant to suggest that classical Christian claims to incarnation need not imply that the church can understand the meaning of incarnation apart from the resources and insights of other traditions. Even core Christian affirmations cannot be understood apart from the resources of other traditions. Paragraph 3 prepares for paragraph 5's recognition of the importance of Mahatma Gandhi's novel Christology of Jesus as *satyagrahi*. Taken together, both paragraphs suggest that even a classical high Christology need not imply that God's work in Jesus the Christ means that the church no longer needs its religious neighbors.

Paragraphs 4–6 are meant to illustrate what a new turn to specificity might look like. These paragraphs refuse to speak of Hinduism or Buddhism as a whole.

These paragraphs instead engage specific claims within both families of traditions and explicitly recognize the internal diversity of Hindu traditions. Paragraph 5, in particular, seeks to signal that Christian theologians are also interested in the kinds of debates that are central to Hindu Vedanta traditions. That paragraph signals that Christian theologians will come to these debates with strong antecedent commitments and so will be prepared to challenge and be challenged by other traditions but always in a spirit of hospitality and receptivity. In so doing, I wish to make room for comparative theology in any future *Nostra Aetate*, but comparative theology done for the sake of constructive theological learning. Paragraph 7 takes care to note the importance of indigenous traditions. The paragraph thereby corrects what I take to be a critical oversight of *Nostra Aetate*. The final sentence once more installs the crucial verb "receive" to the three verbs of *Nostra Aetate*.

Finally, let me conclude by reiterating what I take to be the central contention of this essay: a strong affirmation of interreligious learning as integral to the life of Christian communities is necessary to leave behind *Nostra Aetate*'s ethos of religious self-sufficiency. Despite the remarkable new openness found in *Nostra Aetate,* the document as it stands does not explicitly affirm that the church stands in permanent need of other religious traditions. Where such an affirmation is absent, one wonders about the ongoing status and worth of other religious traditions. It is insufficient for the church merely to affirm that truth can be found in other traditions. If every instance of such truth and holiness is already found in exemplary degree within the ark of the church, the church cannot well articulate why its sons and daughters are called to acknowledge, preserve, and promote truth as it is found in other traditions. Only when the church acknowledges that it stands in permanent and holy need of other traditions, even to understand the truth that has been entrusted to it, can the church move toward affirming that religious diversity is part of divine providence.

CONTRIBUTORS

John Borelli is the special assistant for Catholic identity and dialogue to President John J. DeGioia of Georgetown University. In addition, he has served as the US Jesuit Conference's coordinator for interreligious dialogue and relations. Prior to these appointments in 2004, Dr. Borelli assisted the Secretariat for Ecumenical and Interreligious Affairs at the US Conference of Catholic Bishops for more than sixteen years as associate director and as interim director from 2001 to 2002. He managed three ongoing dialogues with Muslims, one with Buddhists, and one with Hindus, as well as other interreligious projects and staffed ecumenical dialogues with Orthodox Christians and with Anglicans. Dr. Borelli was a consultor to the Vatican's Pontifical Council for Interreligious Dialogue for seventeen years. He has coauthored or edited five books and has written three hundred articles in the fields of interreligious and ecumenical relations, theology, and history of religions in the forty years since receiving his doctorate from Fordham University in 1976.

Peter C. Bouteneff is a professor of systematic theology at St. Vladimir's Orthodox Theological Seminary, Yonkers, New York, where he has taught since 2000. He has been active in the ecumenical movement through the World Council of Churches, where he served as executive secretary of faith and order from 1995 to 2000, and through other global and regional interchurch and interfaith bodies. He is the author of *Sweeter than Honey: Orthodox Thinking on Dogma and Truth,* and *Beginnings: Ancient Christian Readings of the Biblical Creation Narratives*, among other works. His most recent book, drawing on his work as a theologian and a musician, is *Arvo Pärt: Out of Silence*, published in 2015.

Charles L. Cohen is the E. Gordon Fox Professor of American Institutions at the University of Wisconsin–Madison. From 2005 to 2016 he served as director of the Lubar Institute for the Study of the Abrahamic Religions. His scholarship has been recognized by, among other awards, the Allan Nevins Prize of the Society of American Historians for his work on the psychology of Puritan religious experience, terms on the councils of both the Omohundro Institute of Early American History and Culture, and the American Society for Church History, and appointment as a distinguished lecturer of the Organization of American Historians. *Gods in America: Religious Pluralism in the United States*, which he coedited with Ronald Numbers, was published by Oxford University Press in 2013. He serves on the editorial board of *Religion and American Culture*, and on the Religious Practices Advisory Committee, Department of Corrections, State of Wisconsin.

Rita M. Gross (1943–2015) was a Buddhist scholar-practitioner who was both a university professor and a dharma teacher. She published widely on Buddhism and gender and recently published the groundbreaking book *Religious Diversity—*

What's the Problem? Buddhist Advice for Flourishing with Religious Diversity. She was authorized as a senior dharma teacher (*acharya* in Sanskrit, *lopon* in Tibetan) by Her Eminence Jetsun Khandro Rinpoche. In that capacity, she taught at Mindrolling Lotus Garden Meditation Center and also throughout North America at Buddhist dharma centers as well as at various colleges and universities. Dr. Gross received her PhD from the University of Chicago in 1975 for the first dissertation on women's studies or feminist methodology in religious studies: "Exclusion and Participation: The Role of Women in Aboriginal Australian Religion." She was a leader of the Women and Religion section of the American Academy of Religion and of the Society for Buddhist-Christian Studies. Her ten books include *Buddhism after Patriarchy: A Feminist History, Analysis, and Reconstruction of Buddhism* (1993), *Feminism and Religion* (1996), and *A Garland of Feminist Reflections, Forty Years of Religious Exploration* (2009). Her forthcoming book is *How Clinging to Gender Identity Subverts Enlightenment.* She published hundreds of journal articles, encyclopedia articles, semipopular writings on Buddhism, and book reviews.

Roger Haight, SJ, was born in northern New Jersey in 1936 and commuted to high school in New York City. In 1954 he joined the Jesuits of the New York Province and spent six years as a student and teacher in the Philippines. After seminary training and a PhD in theology from the University of Chicago, Haight taught successively in Manila, Chicago, Toronto, and Cambridge, Massachusetts. He is currently scholar in residence at Union Theological Seminary in New York City and oversees the Master in Sacred Theology program. He has written on topics related to basic Christian self-understanding such as Christ, church, revelation, faith, grace, and spirituality. He has also engaged issues of liberation and interreligious dialogue. He generally approaches a topic historically and systematically because religious beliefs need constant reinterpretation relative to the cultural situation. Given our new world culture and pluralistic local situations, he believes all religions should acknowledge other faiths in the formulation of their basic beliefs.

Riffat Hassan is professor emerita at the University of Louisville, where she taught for thirty-three years. She is an internationally acclaimed Islamic scholar and activist, articulating a progressive understanding of the religion that influenced Muslims around the world. In the wake of 9/11, Dr. Hassan developed and directed two major international peace-building exchange programs, funded by the US Department of State. Her publications include eight books and almost two hundred book chapters, journal articles, and articles in newspaper special supplements, on such topics as Muhammad Iqbal, women in Islam, and Islam and interreligious dialogue. She has made presentations in settings ranging from local churches to UN conferences in Cairo (1994) and Beijing (1995), where she was a major speaker. She has been particularly involved in interreligious dialogue among Jews, Christians, and Muslims. In 2003, the University of Louisville's College of Arts and Sciences awarded her the Distinguished International Service Award, and in 2012 she was inducted into its Hall of Honor. In March 2012, she won a

Kennedy Center/Stephen Sondheim Inspirational Teacher Award. In May 2013, she received an honorary Doctor of Humane Letters from Meadville Lombard Theological School in Chicago for "outstanding academic achievement and commitment to peacemaking and interreligious dialogue." In May 2013 she also received the Mosaic Award given by the Jewish Family and Career Services for her services to the Louisville community.

Jeannine Hill Fletcher is a professor of theology at Fordham University, Bronx, New York. Her primary area of research in theologies of religious diversity has focused on the intersection with other forms of difference including gender and race, with an interest in the material and political impact of theological projects. Her books include *Monopoly on Salvation? A Feminist Approach to Religious Pluralism* (Continuum, 2005) and *Motherhood as Metaphor: Engendering Interreligious Dialogue* (Fordham University Press, 2013). She serves as the faculty director of service-learning in Fordham's Dorothy Day Center for Service and Justice. Her current work is informed by membership in the Northwest Bronx Community and Clergy Coalition, a multigenerational, multireligious, and multiracial grassroots organization working for social change. Dr. Hill Fletcher's contribution to this volume is part of her new book, *The Sin of White Supremacy: Christianity, Racism, and Religious Diversity in America* (Orbis Books, 2017), which was supported by a grant from the Louisville Institute.

Dwight N. Hopkins is a professor of theology in the University of Chicago Divinity School, and Extraordinary Professor and Research Fellow, Department of Philosophy, Practical and Systematic Theology, University of South Africa. He has created and managed a fourteen-country network focused on global cultures and religions: India (Dalits), Japan (Burakumin), Australia (Aboriginals), Fiji, Hawaii (Native Hawaiians), African Americans, Afro Cubans, Afro Brazilians, Jamaica, Blacks in England, South Africa, Zimbabwe, Botswana, and Ghana. Hopkins explores how to build healthy communities and healthy individuals within communities, how to promote harmony and balance of an individual's internal energy, and how to deal with the wealth of earth, air, and water. He is the author of *Shoes That Fit Our Feet: Sources for a Constructive Black Theology* and *Being Human: Race, Culture, and Religion*; he is the coeditor of *Teaching Global Theologies: Power and Praxis*. Hopkins earned the BA at Harvard University; MDiv, MPhil, and PhD at Union Theological Seminary; and a second PhD at University of Cape Town, South Africa.

Sallie B. King is professor emerita of philosophy and religion at James Madison University and Affiliated Faculty, Professor of Buddhist Studies, Department of Theology, Georgetown University. She works in the areas of Buddhist philosophy and ethics; Engaged Buddhism; Buddhist-Christian dialogue; and the cross-cultural philosophy of religion. She is the author of *Buddha Nature* (SUNY Press, 1991), *Journey in Search of the Way: The Spiritual Autobiography of Satomi Myodo* (SUNY Press, 1993), *Being Benevolence: The Social Ethics of Engaged Buddhism*

(Hawaii, 2005), and *Socially Engaged Buddhism* (Hawaii, 2009). She is coeditor (with Christopher S. Queen) of *Engaged Buddhism: Buddhist Liberation Movements in Asia* (SUNY Press, 1996) and (with Paul O. Ingram) of *The Sound of Liberating Truth: Buddhist-Christian Dialogues in Honor of Frederick J. Streng* (Curzon Press, 1999). She is a former president of the Society for Buddhist-Christian Studies and a member of the Christian and Interfaith Relations Committee of the Religious Society of Friends (Quakers).

Paul F. Knitter is the Emeritus Paul Tillich Professor of Theology, World Religions, and Culture at Union Theological Seminary, New York, as well as Emeritus Professor of Theology at Xavier University in Cincinnati, Ohio. He received a Licentiate in theology from the Pontifical Gregorian University in Rome (1966) and a doctorate from the University of Marburg, Germany (1972). Most of his research and publications have dealt with religious pluralism and interreligious dialogue. Since his ground-breaking 1985 book, *No Other Name?*, he has been exploring how the religious communities of the world can cooperate in promoting human and ecological well-being. More recently, his writing and speaking engagements have focused on what Christians can learn in their dialogue with Buddhists, which is the topic of his 2009 book, *Without Buddha I Could Not Be a Christian*, and of his 2015 book, co-authored with Roger Haight, SJ, *Jesus and Buddha: Friends in Conversation*. Since 1986, he has been serving on the Board of Directors for CRISPAZ (Christians for Peace in El Salvador).

Jerusha Tanner Lamptey is an assistant professor of Islam and Ministry and director of the Islam, Social Justice, and Interreligious Engagement Program (ISJIE) at Union Theological Seminary in the city of New York. Her research focuses on theologies of religious pluralism, comparative theology, and Muslima theology. Dr. Lamptey earned a PhD in theological and religious studies with a focus on religious pluralism at Georgetown University. She also received an MA in Islamic sciences at the Graduate School of Islamic and Social Sciences, and an MA in theological and religious studies at Georgetown University. Before joining the Union faculty in July of 2012, she was a visiting assistant professor in the Department of Theology at Georgetown University. Her first book, *Never Wholly Other: A Muslima Theology of Religious Pluralism* (Oxford University Press, 2014), reinterprets the Qur'anic discourse on religious "otherness" by drawing on feminist theology and semantic methodology. Her current book, *Divine Words, Female Voices: Muslima Explorations in Comparative Feminist Theology* (Oxford University Press, forthcoming), focuses on comparative feminist theology, and argues that comparative engagement is essential to the development of a Muslima theology that moves beyond exegetical and legal reformulation and toward constructive theology.

Rabbi Shira L. Lander is the director of Jewish Studies at Southern Methodist University, where she holds a faculty appointment in Religious Studies. She previously served as the undergraduate adviser and Anna Smith Fine Senior Lecturer for the Program in Jewish Studies at Rice University. Lander earned her doctorate in Judaism and Christianity in Late Antiquity from the University of Pennsylvania and holds a master's degree, rabbinic ordination, and an honorary doctorate from the Hebrew Union College-Jewish Institute of Religion. Previously she taught Jewish and religious studies at the University of Maryland, Baltimore County, St. Mary's Seminary and University, Johns Hopkins University, the University of Delaware, Princeton University, and the Beth Tfiloh Dahan High School, and served as Hillel rabbi to the Baltimore area colleges and universities. Lander was the inaugural Jewish scholar at Baltimore's Institute for Christian and Jewish Studies, where she launched the Jewish Scholars Group on Christians and Christianity that produced the historic document *Dabru Emet*.

Jeffery D. Long is a professor of religion and Asian Studies at Elizabethtown College in Elizabethtown, Pennsylvania, where he has taught since he received his doctoral degree from the University of Chicago Divinity School in 2000. He is the author of *A Vision for Hinduism: Beyond Hindu Nationalism* (IB Tauris, 2007), *Jainism: An Introduction* (IB Tauris, 2009), *The Historical Dictionary of Hinduism* (Scarecrow Press, 2011), and the forthcoming *Indian Philosophy: An Introduction*, a companion reader of primary sources (*Indian Philosophy: The Essential Sources*) (both for IB Tauris), and *Hinduism in America: A Convergence of Worlds* (Bloomsbury Press). He has also published numerous articles and has served as chair of the Dharma Academy of North America (DANAM). An active member of the Hindu community in America, he has served as a consultant for the Hindu American Foundation, and as a member of the board of trustees of his local temple, the Hindu American Religious Institute (HARI). Long is affiliated with the Vedanta Society-Ramakrishna Mission and has recently been invited to hold the Swami Vivekananda visiting professorship at Ramakrishna Vivekananda University at Belur Math, the monastic headquarters of the Ramakrishna Order in West Bengal, India.

John T. Pawlikowski, OSM, has made an extensive study of the Nazi Holocaust, which has enabled him to appreciate the ethical challenges facing the human community as it struggles with greatly enhanced power and extended responsibility for the future of all creation. His scholarly interests include the theological and ethical aspects of the Christian-Jewish relationship and public ethics. A leading figure in the Christian-Jewish dialogue, he was the two-term president and chair of the theology committee of the International Council of Christians and Jews (ICCJ). Pawlikowski also serves on numerous advisory boards and councils, including the board of directors of the Parliament of the World's Religions, and the National Advisory Council of the United States Committee for the World Conference of Religions for Peace. Pawlikowski is the author or editor of more than fifteen books, including *The Challenge of the Holocaust for Christian Theology* and *Christ in the Light of the Christian-Jewish Dialogue*. Pawlikowski also served as editor of *New Theology Review* for seven years.

Jennifer Howe Peace is an associate professor of Interfaith Studies at Andover Newton Theological School, where she co-directs the Center for Interreligious and Communal Leadership Education (CIRCLE), a joint program between ANTS and Hebrew College. Dr. Peace is the founding co-chair of the interreligious and interfaith studies group at the AAR, co-editor of *My Neighbor's Faith: Stories of Interreligious Encounter, Growth, and Transformation* (Orbis Books, 2012) as well as co-publishing editor of the *Journal of Inter-Religious Studies* and "State of Formation" (a blog for emerging religious and ethical leaders). Current projects include a five-year series: *Interreligious Studies in Theory and Practice*, published by Palgrave Macmillan, as well as a new edited volume with Eboo Patel, *Towards a Field of Interfaith Studies*. Dr. Peace's involvement in interfaith organizing beyond the academy includes founding roles with the United Religions Initiative, the Interfaith Youth Core, and the Daughters of Abraham, a movement of book groups for Jewish, Christian, and Muslim women.

Ulrich Rosenhagen is a lecturer in religious studies at University of Wisconsin–Madison and, between 2005 and 2016, was the associate director of the Lubar Institute for the Study of the Abrahamic Religions. He is an ordained pastor, originally in the Evangelische Kirche von Kurhessen-Waldeck and now in the Evangelical Lutheran Church in America. He received his PhD from the University of Heidelberg in 2012. A revised version of his dissertation on religious communication during the American Revolution was published as *Brudermord, Freiheitsdrang, Weltenrichter: Religiöse Kommunikation und Öffentliche Theologie in der Amerikanischen Revolutionsepoche* ("Fratricide, Desire for Freedom, Judge of the World: Religious Communication and Public Theology during the American Revolution," Berlin: Walter de Gruyter, 2015). He was a researcher at the Technical University of Dresden, has held a research fellowship at Boston University, and has published essays on interreligious dialogue, Jewish-Christian Relations, and nineteenth- and twentieth-century Social Protestantism.

Rabbi David Fox Sandmel, a scholar of Jewish-Christian relations and interfaith activist, has served as director of interfaith affairs at the Anti-Defamation League since 2014. From 2003 to 2014, he held the Crown-Ryan Chair in Jewish Studies at the Catholic Theological Union in Chicago. Rabbi Sandmel earned his doctorate in religious studies at the University of Pennsylvania. He received his Rabbinic Ordination and Master's in Hebrew Literature from the Hebrew Union College-Jewish Institute of Religion in Cincinnati. He holds a BA in Jewish studies from Ohio State University. He was the Judaic Scholar at the Institute for Christian & Jewish Studies in Baltimore, where he managed the project that produced "Dabru Emet: A Jewish Statement on Christians and Christianity." He is an editor of *Christianity in Jewish Terms* and *Irreconcilable Differences? A Learning Resource for Jews and Christians*. His commentary on First Thessalonians appears in *The Jewish Annotated New Testament*.

John J. Thatamanil is an associate professor of theology and world religions at Union Theological Seminary in New York. He has taught a wide variety of courses in the areas of comparative theology, theologies of religious diversity, Hindu-Christian dialogue, the theology of Paul Tillich, and process theology. He is the author of *The Immanent Divine: God, Creation, and the Human Predicament: An East-West Conversation* (Fortress Press, 2006). He is currently completing his second book, tentatively titled, *The Promise of Religious Diversity: Comparative Theology and Relational Pluralism* (Fordham University Press). He is the project director of the AAR Summer Seminars on Theologies of Religious Pluralism and Comparative Theology, funded by the Luce Foundation.

Index

Abdullah (Saudi king), 231
Abraham
　Islam's veneration of, 219–20
　as unifying figure, 119n41, 120
Abrahamic faiths, 119n41, 220, 226, 230
Abram, Morris B., 180–81
adoptionism, 152
Ad Gentes (*On the Mission Activity of the Church*; Vatican II), 46, 121
Al-Azhar University, 223n14
Alexi II (Orthodox patriarch), 227
Alliance Israélite Universelle, 183
Al-Thani, Hamad bin Khalifa, 231
American Academy of Religion, 271
American Jewish Committee, 181, 183, 184, 188
Anawati, Georges, 28, 34, 37
Andover Newton Theological School, 267–68, 270
androcentrism, 238, 239, 245–47
anonymous Christianity, 102, 147, 259
Anti-Defamation League of B'nai B'rith, 184
antidiscrimination, 128, 131, 135
antisemitism, 2, 12, 23, 28, 30, 37–38, 41, 116, 154, 180–81, 197
ANTS. *See* Andover Newton Theological School
Apology (Justin Martyr), 147
apophatic theology, 244
Apostles, Jewishness of, 24
Aquinas, Thomas, 98
Arianism, 152–53
Ariarajah, Wesley, 82
Armstrong, Karen, 49, 53–54, 227
arrow parable (Buddhism), 244
Artemon, 152
Asad, Muhammad, 233–34

Asad, Talal, 296
Asian Catholic bishops, 47
atheists, 6n21
atonement, 91, 93
Atonement Christology, 91
Augustine, 77, 97
Aurobindo, Sri, 250n3, 254
Australian Catholic Bishops Conference (2015), 4n16
axial age, 48–50, 52–53
Ayoub, Mahmoud, 69n34

Banki, Judith Hershcopf, 183, 185, 189
Baptist World Alliance, 111n14
Barndt, Joseph, 67n23
Baron, Salo, 187
Barth, Karl, 75, 109, 111, 114, 115, 116, 122–24, 148
Bartholomew (Ecumenical patriarch), 176n58
Bar Yochai, Shimon, 91
Baum, Gregory, 29–30, 33, 79
BCEIA. *See* Bishops Committee for Ecumenical and Interreligious Affairs
Bea, Augustin, 2, 23, 24–25, 30, 31–32, 35, 36, 42, 107, 109n6, 185n35
　explaining *Nostra Aetate*, 40, 41
　influence of, 33
　support for, 37
Beauvoir, Simone de, 247n15
beliefs, attachment to, 240–42
Bellah, Robert, 49–50, 52–53, 285
Benedict XVI, 9, 84, 186–89, 196. *See also* Ratzinger, Joseph
　on Jewish resources for the Christian faith, 83
　on Muslims and Islam, 224–25, 227

Bensahel, Jean-François, 174
Berger, David, 168–70
Bergoglio, Jorge Mario, 56. *See also* Francis
Berkouwer, Gerrit Cornelius, 111
Bernardin, Joseph, 79
Beyer, Peter, 279
Bhagavad Gītā, 256
bin Talal, Ghazi bin Muhammad, 225
bin Talal, Hassan, 231
Bishops Committee on Ecumenical and
    Interreligious Affairs (USCCB), 186,
    191–92
Black Catholic Clergy Caucus, 72n50
Black Christ, 68
black liberation theology, 7
    considering social and economic
        conditions, 128
    diversity in, 141
    emergence of, 128–31
    interreligious dialogue and, 141
    on Jesus' mission, 137–38, 141
    method of, 141
    Nostra Aetate and, 127, 135
    practitioners of, prophetic vocation for,
        139
    worldview of, 141
    on the Yahweh–slave workers covenant,
        136
black theology, 68, 130–31
Black Theology Project (1975), 141
Blakemore, William Barnett, 112n, 120
blood Christologies, 85n25
Blum, Edward, 67–68
Bokser, Ben Zion, 180
Borelli, John, 119n41, 199
Boyarin, Daniel, 89, 90, 91
Boys, Mary, 61–62, 79–80, 165
bricolage, spiritual, 18, 279, 284, 286–87
Bristol Declaration (World Council of
    Churches), 115–16n28
Brown, Raymond, 91
Brown, Robert McAfee, 112n
Buddhism, 48, 69, 70, 119
    four main attachments in, 239–42
    Japanese, 285
    Jesus and, 82
    listening to Christians, 282–84

local practice centers for, 287–88
male/female relationships and, 246
mutual learning and, 284–85
no God in, 283
Nostra Aetate and, 204, 275, 276, 294
practice of, along with other traditions,
    260
on religion, 280–82
religious mastery in, 286
sectarianism in, 239
spirituality in, 18
supplemental, 281–83
traditions of, 286
transcendence of, 282
Buddhist-Catholic dialogue, 276
Buddhist-Christian dialogue, 275–77

Caird, George B., 112n
Campbell, Joseph, 279
Capovilla, Loris, 23, 25
Caspar, Robert, 37
Catechism of the Catholic Church, 223
"Catechism of Trent," 180n9
Catholic-Buddhist dialogue, 276
Catholic Church
    conversations of, with other religions,
        1–2. *See also individual religions*
    ecclesiology of, 145
    evangelization by, and interreligious
        dialogue, 190–94
    on the Jewish Mosaic covenant, 190, 194
    Jewish perceptions of, 185–86
    Orthodox Church and, 143–44
    and the religio-racial project, 64
    reverence of, for other teachings, 292
    superiority of, 7, 10, 50–52
Catholic-Jewish relations, 181–99
Catholic-Muslim dialogue, 203, 211–13,
    223, 225
Catholic-Muslim relations, 224–27
Catholics
    Buddhist practices of, 278–79
    exhorted to dialogue and collaboration
        with other faiths, 2, 39, 46, 50, 272,
        292–93
    Islam's commonalities with, 209–10
    memories of, 182, 186–87, 222–23

Catholic social teaching, 197
Center for Interreligious and Communal Leadership Education, 18, 267, 269, 270
Center for Jewish-Christian Understanding and Cooperation, 160, 172–75, 177
Central Conference of American Rabbis, 186
Central Preparatory Commission (Vatican II), 31, 33
Charter for Compassion, 227
Cheng Yen, 288
Chinese Exclusion Act (US; 1882), 66, 71
Christ. *See also* Jesus
consubstantiality of, with God the Father, 153
decentering of, 15–16
message of, 15–16
superiority of, 122
truth and, 147
whiteness of, 68
Christ Event, 14
Christian-Buddhist dialogue, 275–77
Christian church, connection of, to Israel, 30
Christian-Hindu relations, 251
Christian-Islam Congress, 223n14
Christianity
commonalities of, with Islam, 228
distinct identity for, 80, 81
exclusivist-inclusivist spectrum of, 149
framework for, 94
Jewish roots of, 154
Jewish statements on, 159–78
narrative of, reimagining, 93
post-Holocaust theology of, 160
re-Judaizing of, 83
supremacy of, 55, 68–69
theological foundations of, 55
theological anthropology of, 13
theology of, contradiction inherent in, 54
Christianity in Jewish Terms (Novak and D. Sandmel), 171
"Christianity in Jewish Theology" (French rabbis), 162–64

Christian-Muslim dialogue, 223, 225, 228, 232–33
Christian-Muslim relations, 222
Christians, actions of, toward other religions, 45, 46–47
Christian spirituality, 93–94
Christians and Religious Pluralism (Race), 256
Christian Uniqueness Reconsidered (D'Costa), 151
Christocentrism, 69
cosmic, 119n40
Muslims and, 68
relinquishing, 74
Christology, 152, 232, 300
birth of, 96
blood, 85n25
challenge of, 83
classical options for, 84–85
Incarnational, 84, 85, 88–89
Jesus' Jewishness and, 81–92
Jewish writings on, 89–90
messianic, 85
nonsupersessionist, 85–88
as part of racial project, 67–68
Paul's influence on, 81
pluralism of, 91
problem of, 55
Second Temple Judaism and, 90
as stumbling block for dialogue, 13–14
Church in the Modern World, 38
"Church and Racism, The" (Pontifical Justice and Peace Commission), 197
Church Unity Octave, 24n4
Cicognani, Amleto, 31, 35, 40
CIRCLE. *See* Center for Interreligious and Communal Leadership Education
Cirelli, Anthony, 221–22
civil rights movement, 8, 65
CJCUC. *See* Center for Jewish-Christian Understanding and Cooperation
Clark, Henry, 64–65
Clavairoly, François, 174
Cleage, Albert, 68
Clooney, Francis X., 259
coformation, 268–69
coformational pedagogy, 18–19

Colberg, Kristin, 67
Commission on Doctrine of the Faith and
    Morals, 30n27, 38, 39
Commission on Missions, 28n22
Commission for Religious Relations with
    Muslims, 223n14
Committee on Christian Unity (American
    Baptist Churches), 168
Committee on Doctrine and the BCEIA,
    191
"Common Word between Us and You, A,"
    9, 225–28, 232–33
communities, 132–39
    of argumentation, 297
    of believers, 210
    in the present era, 287
    virtual, 271
comparative theology, 289–90, 294–98,
    301
compassion, axial age and, 49
Complete Works (Vivekananda), 256
Cone, James H., 7, 68, 130–31
Confucianism, 48
Congar, Yves, 38–39, 109n5
Congregation for the Doctrine of the
    Faith, 16, 167, 259
Congregation for the Oriental Church, 27
Consultation of the National Council
    of Synagogues and the Bishops
    Committee for Ecumenical and
    Interreligious Affairs, 186–87,
    190–94
Consultative Panel on Lutheran Jewish
    Relations (Evangelical Lutheran
    Church of America), 168
Coordinating Commission (Vatican II),
    34, 35
Copernican revolution, 150, 151, 250, 294
Council of Centers for Christian-Jewish
    Relations, 160
Council of Constantinople, 152–53
Council for Interreligious Dialogue
    (Vatican), 46, 47
Council of Nicaea, 152–53
Council for Promoting Christian Unity, 196
Courage Project, 19n60
covenants, separation of, 84

creation
    doctrine of, 94–95
    God's power in, 15–16
creation theology, 95, 98, 100
"Criteria for the Evaluation of
    Dramatizations of the Passion"
    (USCCB), 198–99
Crossing the Threshold of Hope (John Paul
    II), 208–11, 276, 278
CRRM. See Commission for Religious
    Relations with Muslims
Cullman, Oscar, 108n, 114–15, 123–24
Cuoq, Josef, 27–28, 34, 37

"Dabru Emet: A Jewish Statement on
    Christians and Christianity" (Jewish
    Scholars' Project), 78, 160, 164–72,
    177–78
Dalai Lama, 278, 281
Dante (Alighieri), 228
Daoism, 48
D'Costa, Gavin, 151
Declaration on Religious Liberty (Dignitatis
    Humanae; Paul VI), 29, 43
"Declaration for the Upcoming Jubilee
    of Brotherhood: A New Jewish
    View of Jewish-Christian Relations"
    (Bensahel et al.), 174–75
declarations, vs. decrees, 35
Decree on Ecumenism (Unitatis
    Redintegratio; Vatican II), 29, 43, 51
deicide, Jews charged with,31, 36, 39, 41,
    113, 174, 180–81
Deloria, Vine, 68
De Smedt, Emiel-Jozef, 41
dialogue. See also individual religions;
    interfaith dialogue; interreligious
    dialogue;
characteristics of, 47n10
    creating conditions for, 267–70, 273
    as engagement, 204
    mission and, 213
    moral action and, 217
    as new way of being church, 47
    religious foundations and, 232
    as theological term, 32
    training for, 214–15

Dialogue Interreligieux Monastique /
    Inter-Monastic Dialogue, 275, 276, 278
Dialogue and Proclamation (Pontifical
    Council for Interreligious Dialogue),
    47, 51
Dibelius, Otto, 107
Dietzfelbinger, Wolfgang, 111n13, 117, 118
DIMMID. *See* Dialogue Interreligieux
    Monastique / Inter-Monastic
    Dialogue
disciples, Jewishness of, 24n4
discrimination, 72–73
    identity categories and, 272
    race and class and, 131
    rejection of, 39
divinity
    humans sharing in, 85–86, 90, 91
    presence of, in all beings, 253, 261
doctrine, spirituality and, 94
*Dogmatic Constitution on the Church. See
    Lumen Gentium*
Doha International Center for Interfaith
    Dialogue, 231
Dominicans, 26
*Dominus Iesus: On the Unicity and Salvific
    Universality of Jesus Christ and
    the Church* (Congregation for the
    Doctrine of the Faith), 51–52, 145,
    167–68, 259
dual covenant theory, 198
dualisms, hierarchical, 238
Duprey, Pierre, 41

earth supremacy, 57–58
Eastern Catholic bishops, 40–41
Eastern church, Judaism and, 80
Ecclesiam Suam (*Pastoral Constitution on
    the Church in the Modern World*; Paul
    VI), 32, 205
ecclesiology, 144–45
Eck, Diana, 53
Eckhardt, Alice, 165
Eckhardt, Roy, 165
ecumenical movement, 1–2
election, concept of, 161
Epimenides, 298, 300
eschatology, 94

ethics, Islamic teaching on, 221
European Lutheran Commission on the
    Church and the Jewish People, 168
Eusebius, 77
Evangelii Gaudium (*The Joy of the Gospel*;
    Francis), 56, 83, 214, 215
evangelization, 251, 258
    interreligious dialogue and, 190–94
    nonconversionary, 190–91
Evrony, Zion, 3n12
exceptionalism, 183
exclusivism, 11–12, 143, 148–50, 154,
    230, 250, 289n1

faith communities, connecting of, 16
Fall, the, 246–47
Felici, Pericle, 31n30, 37–38
fellowship, as central concept in *Nostra
    Aetate*, 204
Fitzgerald, Michael, 223, 224
forgetfulness, strategic, 9
forgiveness, 211–12
Foxman, Abraham H., 188, 189
Francis (pope), 3, 78, 84, 204
    dialogue and, 56–57
    on interreligious dialogue, 214–15
    Islam and Muslims and, 13, 214–17,
        224n21
    on Jewish-Christian bonds, 83
    on religious difference, 12, 214–15
    on salvation for non-Christians, 155
    US visit of, 293
Frankfurter, David, 81
Fredericks, James, 266, 295–96
Fredriksen, Paula, 81
Freud, Sigmund, 246
Frymer-Kensky, Tikva, 164
fulfillment model, 149, 154
"Fundamental Agreement between the
    Holy See and the State of Israel," 197

Gager, John, 80
Gandhi, Mohandas K., 252, 298, 300
Garber, Zev, 90
Gaudium et Spes (*Pastoral Constitution on the
    Church in the Modern World* [*Joy and
    Hope*]; Vatican II), 1, 45, 134–35, 203

Gibson, Mel, 186–87
*Gifts and Calling of God Are Irrevocable,
    The* (Pontifical Commission for
    Religious Relations with the Jews),
    195–96
God
    agency of, 100
    alive in other religions, 46
    articulation of, by religions, 95
    causality of, 99
    Christian idea of, 96
    christomorphic understanding of, 96
    as counterpoint of all human religion,
        123
    creation by, 95
    creative power of, 103–4
    encounters with, 95
    energy and, 95
    finding of, as humans' final goal, 145
    image of, all humans reflecting, 132. See
        also *Imago Dei*
    loving all creation, 95
    mercy of, 233–34
    ninety-nine Names for, 233
    presence of, to religious communities,
        102
    relationship of, to all existence, 95
    religious diversity as will of, 48
    universal fatherhood of, 39
God Is Red (Deloria), 68
"God's Mercy Endures Forever: Guidelines
    on the Presentation of Jews and
    Judaism in Catholic Preaching"
    (USCCB), 199
God as Spirit, 98
Goldberg, Arthur J., 184
Goldmann, Nahum, 184
Good Friday prayer, 187–89
grace, 16, 17, 103, 104
    experience of, 99
    nature and, 15, 97–98
    theology of, 98
    universality of, 97–98
grace-filled natural world, 94, 97–99
Great World Religions argument, 70
Greenberg, Irving, 89
green interreligious dialogue, 57–58

Gregorios, Paulos Mar, 155
Griffiths, Paul, 290, 299
Gross, Rita, 54, 73–74
"Guidelines for Catholic-Jewish Relations"
    (USCCB), 198
*Guidelines and Suggestions for
    Implementing the Conciliar
    Declaration* Nostra Aetate
    (Commission for Religious Relations
    with the Jews), 195, 206–7
guilt, confession of, for treatment of Jews,
    116–17
Gutiérrez, Gustavo, 132n14

Haddad, Philippe, 174
Haight, Roger, 16
ha-Levi, Yehudah, 175, 176
ha-Meiri, Menachem, 169n37
Hanson, Mark, 227
Harrelson, Walter, 111–12n14
Hart-Celler Act (1965), 63
Harvey, Paul, 67–68
Hasidism, incarnational nature of, 90–91
Hasidism Incarnate (Magid), 90
Head of Christ (Sallman), 68
Hebrew College, 267, 268, 270
Heinz, Hanspeter, 171n45
Heldt, Petra, 110n9
Hellwig, Monika, 79
hermeneutical circle, 55
hermeneutics of dialogue, 216
Heschel, Abraham Joshua, 34n38, 36–37,
    113, 184
Hick, John, 49, 55, 150–53, 250, 254, 294,
    296
Hindu-Christian relations, 251
Hinduism, 48, 69, 70, 119
    inclusiveness and, 155
    nonproselytizing nature of, 260
    in *Nostra Aetate*, 39, 204, 294
    Vedanta tradition in, 9, 249, 251
"Hinduism and Shri Ramakrishna"
    (Vivekananda), 249–50
Hindu Pan-Inclusivism, 259
History of Vatican II (Alberigo), 27
Hitler, Adolf, 2
Hoffman, Norbert, 188

Holocaust, the (Shoah), 2, 78, 79, 118, 165, 169, 172, 175, 177, 184, 195, 197
Horton, Douglas, 112n, 113
human rights, dignity and, 133
humans
    dignity of, 7, 128, 132–35, 146n9
    divinity and, 85–86, 91
    fall of, 93
    nature of, moral law and, 33
    origins of, 246
    relationship of, to God, 94
    reliance of, on God, 103
    as social animals, 287
Huntington, Samuel, 229

Ibrahim, Celene, 269
Idel, Moshe, 91
ideology, strongly held, 240–42
idolatry, 169n37
Imago Dei, 141–42, 147
Implementing Vatican II in Your
    Community (Stuber and Nelson),
    114, 116
incarnation
    meaning of, 300
    Muslims' denial of, 211
Incarnational Christology, 14, 84, 85, 88–89, 91
Incarnationalism, 91
Incarnational theology, 90
inclusivism, 10–12, 143, 147–50, 217, 260, 289n1
    balancing act of, 254
    graded, 294, 297, 300
    hierarchical, 290, 292
    Hinduism and, 250–51
    issues in, 154–55
    in Nostra Aetate, 252–54, 257, 290, 294
    open, 283, 290, 299–300
    theological defense of, 154–55
    in Vivekananda, 256
inclusivity, 206
India, independence movement in, 252
indigenous traditions, 6, 293–94
Institute for Christian and Jewish Studies, 164–65nn14–15, 166
interconnectedness, 58, 127, 266

interfaith dialogue, 6, 119, 121, 124–25
    challenges for, 271–73
    lay involvement in, 18
    shortcomings of, 170
    syncretism and, 122
Interfaith Relations Commission of the
    National Council of Churches in
    Christ in the USA, 168
interfaith work, 266–71
International Association for Liberal
    Christianity and Religious Freedom,
    112n
International Council of Christians and
    Jews, 188
International Group of Fathers (Coetus
    Internationalis Patrum), 40
International Jewish Committee for
    Interreligious Consultations, 188
International Scholars' Abrahamic
    Trialogue, 230
International Theological Commission
    (Vatican), 197–98
"Interpretation of the Bible in the
    Church, The" (Pontifical Biblical
    Commission), 198
interreligious borrowing, 279. See also
    religion, borrowing from
interreligious dialogue
    black liberation theology and, 141
    blocking of, 50
    evangelization and, 190–94
    fostering of, 5
    foundation for, 39
    future progress in, 10, 13
    goals of, 17, 19, 75
    green, 57–58
    impetus for, 18
    Jews' advocacy approach to, 183–84
    limits of, 228
    malaise in, 17
    necessity of, 56
    new form of, 57–58
    organizing principle of, 56–58
    Protestant statements on, 3
    religious supremacy as threat to, 53
    skepticism about, 232
    social justice and, 7, 141

interreligious dialogue *(continued)*
  sponsors of, 231
  suggestions for, 19
  theology catching up with, 55
interreligious education, 18–19
interreligious friendship, 46–47
*Interreligious Friendship after Nostra
  Aetate* (ed. Fredericks and Tiemeier),
  266–67
interreligious learning, 290, 297
interreligious relations. *See also individual
  religions*
  divine truth and, 12
  Paul VI's commitment to, 27
  promotion of, 28
Irenaeus, 77
Isaac, Jules, 23, 24, 25, 28, 78, 160, 184, 193
ISAT. *See* International Scholars'
  Abrahamic Trialogue
Islam, 119. *See also* Muslims
  cardinal principle of, 219
  commonalities with Catholicism,
    209–10
  commonalities with Christianity, 228
  demonization of, 225, 226, 228
  interreligious conversation and, 92
  knowledge of, 226
  in *Nostra Aetate*, 204–7, 210, 214,
    216–17, 219–22, 294
  preconciliar preparations and, 27–28
  promoting positive understanding of, 28
  theological anthropology of, 13
  Western interest in, 229
Islamic Revolution (Iran), 229
Islamic Studies, 230
Islamophobia, 230–31
Israel
  meaning of, for the church, 114, 115
  state of, 3n12, 31, 33, 40, 113
  theology of, 124
  Vatican's recognition of, 3n12

James, William, 253
Jaspers, Karl, 48
Jesuits, 26
Jesus. *See also* Christ
  Christians' offering of, 283–84

Christological approaches to, 84–85
humanity of, 85–86, 152
identity of, 13–14, 16
inculturation of, 82
impact of, on spirituality, 94
Islam's veneration of, 220
Jewishness of, 81–82, 84, 91, 198
in Jewish statements on Christianity,
  177–78
Jewish worship of, 169
Jews' acceptance of, 30
message of, refocused, 15
mission of, 136–38
Muslims' view of, 232
as *satyagrahi*, 300
self-presentation of, to the Jewish
  community, 81
shaping Christians' faith in God, 96
significance of, in the West, 93
truth and, 146
uniqueness of, 12, 14, 52, 55
Jesus movement, 80, 96
Jewish-Catholic relations, 181–99
Jewish-Christian relations, reshaping of,
  113–15
Jewish-Christian-Muslim "trialogue,"
  227–30
Jewish covenantal inclusion, 80
*Jewish People and Their Sacred Scripture in
  the Christian Bible, The* (Pontifical
  Biblical Commission), 87–88, 198
Jewish Scholars Group on Christianity, 166
Jewish Scholars' Project, 164
"Jewish Understanding of Christians and
  Christianity, A" (CJCUC), 172–74
*Jewish Understanding of the New
  Testament, A* (S. Sandmel), 161
Jews. *See also* Judaism
  baptism of, 192–93
  biblical critique of, 118
  Christians' relations with, 14, 16
  church's relations with, 4, 9–10, 13, 26
  conversion of, 36, 113
  covenantal inclusion of, 84
  distrusting Christian intentions, 10
  end-times and, 88
  expectations of, for *Nostra Aetate*, 183

Good Friday prayer for, 84, 187–89
historical consciousness of, 9–10
in interreligious dialogue, 183
in the Letter to the Romans, 30
memories of, 9–10, 182, 183–84,
    86–87, 189, 199
messianic expectations of, 14, 87–88
in *Nostra Aetate*, 39, 206–7
prayer for, in Roman Missal, 24
preconciliar preparations and, 25–26, 27
Protestant approach to, renewal of, 114
responding to *Nostra Aetate*, 34, 36,
    180–81
rights for, 183
role of, in human redemption, 85
self-consciousness of, 187
statements of, on Christianity, 159–78
value of, for *Nostra Aetate*, 69
Vatican II and, 25
JIRS. See *Journal of Interreligious Studies*
John XXIII, 2, 23–24, 25, 28, 31–32, 42,
    43, 78, 193
announcing Vatican II, 23–24
changing prayer for the Jews, 24
death of, 26, 32
John Paul II, 13, 47, 84, 190, 196, 204
on Buddhism, 276, 278
on Catholic supremacy, 52
on interreligious dialogue, 212–13
on Jewish-Christian bonds, 82–83
on Muslims and Islam, 208–13, 223–24,
    234
Journal of Interreligious Studies, 271
Judaism. *See also* Jews
bond of, with Christianity, 82–84, 89
Catholic Church's relations with, 77
and the Eastern church, 80
messianic expectations of, 87–88
in *Nostra Aetate*, 153–54, 294
Patristic writers and, 77
seeing Christianity as antisemitic, 78
stereotyping of, 78
theological self-expression of, 89
Justin Martyr, 77, 146, 147, 154

KAICIID. *See* King Abdullah bin
    Abdulaziz International Centre

for Interreligious and Intercultural
    Dialogue
Kalsky, Manuela, 277, 279, 284
Kant, Immanuel, 294
Kasper, Walter, 79, 87, 88, 168
Keeler, William, 186
Ken-sin, Thomas Tien, 26
Kessler, Edward, 168
Khenchen, Thrangu, 244
Khomeini, Ruhollah, 229
Khyentse, Dzongsar, 242
King, Martin Luther, Jr., 7, 68, 132n14,
    137, 138–39, 283
on class relations, 139–40
as influence on black liberation
    theology, 137, 138
leadership of, 138–39
on power, 131–32
theology of, 131
King, Sallie, 74
King Abdullah bin Abdulaziz
    International Centre for Interreligious
    and Intercultural Dialogue, 231
Klein, Naomi, 56
Knitter, Paul F., 148–51, 154, 259, 266,
    290
Koehlinger, Amy, 64nn10–11
König, Franz, 38, 39
Korn, Eugene, 172–73, 175
Korsia, Haim, 174
Kraemer, Hendrik, 148
Krajewski, Stanislaw, 168
Krygier, Rivon, 174
Kühn, Ulrich, 111n13, 118
Küng, Hans, 108, 232

l'Amitié Judéo-Chrétienne de France, 184
Laudato Si' (Francis), 56–57, 294
Levenson, Jon, 170–71
Levinas, Emmanuel, 162
Levine, Amy-Jill, 86, 170
Lewis, Bernard, 228–29
liberation
    Spirit of, 139, 140
    as theological content for US Christian
        churches, 130
liberation theology, 7, 130

Lindbeck, George, 108, 111n13, 121
Long, John, 34n38, 34n40, 37
Lopresti, Matt, 259
Lubar Institute for the Study of the
    Abrahamic Religions, 4–5, 19n60
Luce (Henry) Foundation, 268, 271
Lumen Gentium (*Dogmatic Constitution
    on the Church*; Vatican II), 37, 51, 69,
    145, 205, 210, 214
Luther, Martin, 118
Lutherans, responding to *Nostra Aetate*,
    117–18

MacArthur, Allan, 117, 125
Magid, Shaul, 90–91
Mahayana Buddhists, 281
Maimonides, 175, 176
Malcolm X, 63
manifest destiny, 53
Manuel II Palaeologos, 225
Marans, Noam, 193
Marciano, Raphy, 174
Maron, Gottfried, 109–10n8, 111n13
Mary (mother of Jesus), Islam's veneration
    of, 220–21
Massignon, Louis, 26, 119n41
Maximos IV (Melkite patriarch), 40, 41
Meier, John, 80–81
"Memory and Reconciliation: The
    Church and the Faults of the
    Past" (International Theological
    Commission), 197–98
Merton, Thomas, 17, 234, 275–76
Message to Muslims at the End of Ramadan
    (Francis), 215
Messas, David, 162–63
Messianic Christology, 85, 91
Metaphor of God Incarnate, The (Hick),
    152
Metz, Johann Baptist, 79, 83
Meyer, Albert, 35
Miccoli, Giovanni, 42–43
Middle East, bishops from, 40–41
mission. *See also* evangelization
    connotations of, 36–37
    dialogue as part of, 213
    newly defined, 47

Missionaries of Africa, 26, 27
modernity, 1
Moeller, Charles, 38–39
Moltmann, Jürgen, 79
monastics, 276, 278–79
monotheism, 48, 95
Montini, Giovanni Battista, 26, 119n41.
    See also Paul VI
Moorish Science Temple (New York City),
    66
Moorman, John R. H., 111n14
moral action, dialogue and, 217
morality, transcending identity, 146
Muhammad, portrayals of, 228
Muslim-Catholic dialogue, 203, 211–13,
    223, 225
Muslim-Catholic relations, 4, 9, 13, 28, 37,
    224–27
Muslim-Christian dialogue, 119, 223, 225,
    228, 232–33
Muslim-Christian Liaison Committee,
    223n14
Muslim-Christian relations, 16–17, 222
Muslim Congress, 223n14
Muslims. *See also* Islam
    beliefs of, 7
    commonalities of, with Christians,
        221–22
    cultural colonization of, 231
    interfaith organizations and, 231
    memories of, 222–23
    in *Nostra Aetate*, 39
    promoting interfaith reconciliation, 9
    religious practices of, 208–9, 221–22
    Vatican II and, 26
Muslim World League, 223n14
Mussner, Franz, 84
mutualism, religious, 19
mutuality, 149, 290
Myth of Christian Uniqueness, The (ed.
    Hick and Knitter), 150–51

Nachman of Bratzlav, 90
Nagarjuna, 242
National Committee of Negro
    Churchmen (National Committee of
    Black Churchmen), 128–31, 132n14

National Conference of Catholic Bishops, 168

National Council of Churches, 129

National Council of Synagogues, 186

nationalism, religious, 252

naturalism, grace-filled, 103–4

natural selection, 99–100

nature, grace and, 97–98

NCS. *See* National Council of Synagogues

Nekrutman, David, 172–73

Nelson, Claud D., 112n, 114, 116, 120

Neuner, Josef, 38–39

New Covenant, 69

Nhat Hanh, Thich, 278, 279, 281, 283

Nicholas of Cusa, 45

non-Abrahamic religions, church's relations with, 4. *See also individual religions*

nonduality, 239

Norgren, William A., 111n14, 120

Nostra Aetate (*Declaration on the Relation of the Church to Non-Christian Religions*), 2, 5–8, 46, 232–33

    Ad Gentes in tension with, 121

    American Catholic perspective on, 62–67

    androcentrism of, 245–47

    on antidiscrimination, 8, 128

    anthropology of, 145

    Barth school and, 113–14

    blocking interreligious dialogue, 50

    brevity of, 29

    Buddhists and, 69, 70, 237–48, 275, 276, 294

    as call to dialogue, 121–23

    Catholic-Muslim dialogue and, 203

    central concepts of, 204–5, 228

    central weakness of, 297

    Christian spirituality based on, 14–15

    Christocentrism of, 67–68

    church's actions in, 266

    commemoration of, 3–4, 19

    comparative theology and, 289–90

    contradiction inherent in, 54, 67

    contributions of, 289

    creating possibility of different religio-racial project, 66–67

    crises facing, 29–41

    cultures addressed in, 70

    development of, 23–26, 28–42, 78, 112, 115

    encouraging dialogue, 46–47, 55, 102

    endorsing religious supremacy, 50, 52

    ethics of, 45

    exclusivism and, 10–11, 148

    and the exclusivist-inclusivist spectrum, 155–56

    exhorting followers to interfaith work, 266

    faith statement in, 101

    first public draft of, 28

    in the future, 7, 291–93, 295–301

    grading other religions, 10n29

    heralding new axial age, 48

    Hinduism and, 69, 70, 249–61, 294

    historical assessment of, 291–92

    history and, 9

    implications of, 14, 276–77

    inclusivism of, 10–12, 124, 147–48, 153, 206, 252–54, 257, 289, 290, 294

    on indigenous traditions, 70, 293–94

    interconnectedness in, 124

    interpretations of, 258–59

    Jews and, 69, 78–79, 110n9, 178, 181–85, 206–7, 294

    John Paul II's use of, 208–9

    as living document, 19

    on Muslims and Islam, 204–7, 210, 214, 216–17, 219–22, 294

    novelty of, 61–62

    omitting a statement of guilt, 116–17

    opposition to, from Middle East bishops, 40–42

    optimism of, 63

    ordo for, 39

    Orthodox Christian response to, 143–56

    pluralism and, 150–51

    political ecclesiology of, 67

    prescience of, 127

    promulgation of, 23, 28, 42

    Protestant response to, 109–12

    purpose of, 291

    question underlying, 238

Nostra Aetate (continued)
    rejecting antisemitism, 116, 180–81
    on relationships, 265
    on religious diversity, 7, 205
    relativism and, 102
    religio-racial project and, 62–63, 68
    religious self-sufficiency of, 290, 297, 301
    revolutionary nature of, 45, 47, 55, 61
    social justice assertions in, 127–28, 132
    supremacist theology of, 67–68
    tension in, 295
    theological anthropology of, 67
    theology of, 17, 55, 79, 146
    treating religious others as proximate vs.
        distant, 207
    turn of, toward specificity, 289, 291, 293
    votes on, 39–42
    world religions and, 293–94
"Note on Ambiguities Contained
        in Covenant and Mission, A"
        (Committee on Doctrine and the
        BCEIA), 191–94
Novak, David, 164

Obama, Barack, 227
Ochs, Peter, 164, 172
Oesterreicher, John M., 29–30n25
O'Malley, John, 35
Omi, Michael, 62
On Ecumenism, 32–34. See also *Unitatis
    Redintegratio*
online education, 270–71
"Open Letter to His Holiness, An," 225
Organisation of the Islamic Conference,
    223n14
Orientalists, 228
Origen, 77
original sin, doctrine of, 97
Orthodox Church, 6, 11–12
    Catholic Church and, 143–44
    ecclesiology of, 144–45
    viewing other religions, 144–45
Orthodox Judaism, Jewish-Christian
    relations and, 167, 172–76
Orthodox Union, 186
Osman, Fathi, 220, 232
other

    care for, 74–75
    encounters with, 217
    learning with, 18
    religious agency assigned to, 213
    types of, 207
    valuing of, 68
Ottaviani, Alfredo, 30n27
Outler, Albert C., 109, 112n, 113

Pahlavi, Reza, 229
panentheism, 95, 98, 104
Panikkar, Raimon, 253
parable of the Good Samaritan, 74–75
Paramahansa, Sri Ramakrishna, 249
parity pluralism, 11, 295, 296, 300
Parting of the Ways scholarship, 80–82, 89
Passion of the Christ, The (dir. Gibson),
    186–87
paternalism, 250
Patristic writers, on Judaism, 77
Patterson, W. Morgan, 114
Paul (apostle)
    Jewish context for, 81
    mission of, as Jewish mission, 80
    theological influence of, 81
Paul VI, 2, 26, 36–37, 41, 84, 109n6, 195,
        197, 223, 224
    committed to interreligious relations, 27
    on dialogue as theological term, 32
    instituting changes for Vatican II, 26
    on mission, 36–37
    on Muslims, 234
    Nostra Aetate and, 28, 61
    pushing for statement on relations with
        the Jews, 32, 35
    visiting the Holy Land, 32, 34
Paul of Samosata, 152
Pawley, Bernard, 111n14
Pawlikowski, John, 165
PCID. *See* Pontifical Council for
        Interreligious Dialogue
Pfister, Paul, 38–39
philosophical rationalism, 48
Pius IX, 1n3
pluralism, 11–12, 50, 143, 148, 149–50, 247,
        250, 252, 256, 290–91n3, 299. *See also*
        parity pluralism; religious diversity

Christian spirituality and, 94
Hinduism and, 250–52, 254, 257–58
inevitability of, 102
moral issues in, 153–54
philosophical issues in, 150–51
and realignment of faiths, 151, 153
relational, 291n
repudiation of, 12
theological, 124
theological issues in, 151–53
Pluralism Project (Harvard), 270
Pontifical Biblical Commission, 87–88, 92, 197–98
Pontifical Commission for Religious Relations with the Jews, 195–96
Pontifical Council for Interreligious Dialogue, 223n14, 275, 278
Pontifical Institute for Arabic and Islamic Studies, 216
Pontifical Justice and Peace Commission, 197
Pontifical Theological Commission, 88n34
poverty, 140
prayer, Muslim practices of, 208–9
preferential option for the earth, 57–58
primary causality, 98n18
Protestants
    attitude among, toward Judaism, 78
    calling for interreligious dialogue, 47
    Christology of, 81
    rejecting interreligious dialogue, 6, 124
    theology of, 148
    Vatican II and, 109–12
protology, 94
psilanthropism, 152–53

Qur'an, 13

Rabbinical Assembly of Conservative Judaism, 186, 189
Rabbinical Council of America, 169, 186
Race, Alan, 256
racial justice, 64
racial project, 8, 62
Radhakrishnan, Sarvepalli, 250n3, 254
Rahner, Karl, 97–98, 102n23, 104n29, 108, 119n40, 147, 259

Ramakrishna, Sri, 251, 252, 254, 256, 257
Ramakrishna Mission, 249
Ramakrishna Order, 249, 252
Ratzinger, Joseph, 52, 87, 108, 167. *See also* Benedict XVI
Rausky, Franklin, 174
RCM. *See* "Reflections on Covenant and Mission"
reality, Christian spiritual vision of, 93
rebirth, doctrine of, 13
reconciliation, Catholic-Muslim, 211–12
Redemptoris Missio (*On the Permanent Validity of the Church's Missionary Mandate*; John Paul II), 47, 51
"Reflections on Covenant and Mission" (Consultation of the NCS and Bishops Committee for Ecumenical and Interreligious Affairs), 186, 190–94, 199
refugees, religious diversity and, 266
reincarnation, 278
relationships
    as central concept in *Nostra Aetate*, 204
    interreligious learning and, 268
relativism, 12, 102, 149–50, 169, 170, 250
religion
    addressing ultimate human concerns, 39
    adherence to, 240–42
    assessment of, 295
    borrowing from, 18, 277–80, 284, 286–87
    Buddhism's approach to, 280–82
    categorization of, 296
    changing form of, 277–80
    comparative studies of, 245
    competition and, 94
    Copernican revolution in, 150, 151, 250, 294
    diversity of, 48. *See also* religious diversity
    effectiveness of, 243, 281
    foundations of, 232
    growing awareness of, 49–50
    history of, 48–50
    as human enterprise, 122–23
    imposition of, on others, 241

religion *(continued)*
 learning from, 46–47
 multiple belonging to, 297
 mutual influence among, 297
 mutual sharing of, 285–86
 new framework for, 297
 organized, 18
 overtolerant, 285
 purpose of, 280–81
 self-sufficiency and, 297
 soteriological, 49
 teachings of, meaning of, 244
 theological research on, 119
 truths of, holding lightly, 74
religions, theology of, 46, 237, 295–97
religio-racial project, 62
religiosity, in Islam, 209–10
religious diversity, 205. *See also* pluralism
 affirmation of, 290
 approaches to, 145, 148–49
 as God's will, 298, 300
 inevitability of, 237–39, 247
 interreligious recognition and, 53
 post–Vatican II statements on, 51
 promotion of, 245
 purpose of, 217
 refugees and, 266
 theology of, 52, 297–98
 transformation and, 243
 traditions of, 284, 286
 typology for, 247
Religious Diversity (Gross), 237, 239
religious experience, roots of, 49
religious identity, blurring of, 277
religious language, nature of, 245
religious supremacy, 50, 52–53
 dismantling, 57–58
 religious violence and, 53–54
 threatening interreligious dialogue, 53
 threatening society, 53
Rendtorff, Rolf, 110
*Restating the Catholic Church's Relationship
 with the Jewish People* (Pawlikowski),
 83
Ṛg Veda, 258
Riskin, Shlomo, 172–73, 175
Ritter, Joseph, 34

Roberts, J. Deotis, 130–31
Rolston, Holmes, III, 99–100
Roman Catholic Church. *See* Catholic
 Church
Root, Howard E., 111n14
Rose, Or, 269
Royal Institute for Interfaith Studies, 231
Rudin, A. James, 169
Rumi, Jalal ad-Din, 17, 234

sacred, secular involving into, 99
Said, Edward, 228
Saldarini, Anthony, 80
Sallman, Warner, 68
salvation, 51–52, 93, 97–98, 103, 260
 access to, 167–68
 competing visions of, 63
 human, 86–87
 for Jews, 192–93, 196–97
 for non-Christians, 155
 reincarnation and, 257
 universal, 117, 118
salvation history, 115
Samartha, Stanley J., 48, 121n49
Sanātana Dharma, 257
Sandmel, Samuel, 161–62, 177
Santayana, George, 222
Saraswati, Dayananda, 251
Schillebeeckx, Edward, 99n19
Schleiermacher, Friedrich, 97
Schlink, Edmund, 117, 118, 121–22
Schlink, Ulrich, 111n13
Schmidt, Stjepan, 23
science, Christian faith and, 98–99
"Scripture and Christology" (Pontifical
 Biblical Commission), 198
Scroggs, Robin, 80
Second Sex, The (Beauvoir), 247n15
Second Vatican Council. *See* Vatican II
Secretariat for Non-Christians, 27, 28
Secretariat for Promoting Christian Unity,
 24, 25, 27–31, 36, 38, 39, 41, 107, 108
 influence of, on the council, 42
 support for, 37
 working group on Islam, 37
self-confidence, 133–34, 135
self-esteem, 133–34, 135

self-love, 133–34, 135
Selma (AL), 64
seminary education, 267–68, 272–73
Serra, Junipero, 293
servanthood, 138–39
Shahada (Islamic Creed), 68–69
Sherman, Franklin, 110n9
Shriver, R. Sargent, 229, 230, 232
Shuster, Zachariah, 36
Shutz, Roger, 108n
Signer, Michael, 164, 166
sin, forgiveness of, 93
Sirat, Rene-Samuel, 162–63
Sisters of Saint Joseph, 64
Śiva Mahimna Stotra, 256
Sivaraksa, Sulak, 282
skillful means, principle of, 17, 243–44,
    281
slavery, 71
Smith, Jonathan Z., 207
SNC. *See* Secretariat for Non-Christians,
    27
social action, 195, 207, 211, 288
social justice, 7, 17, 127, 135, 140–41, 222
    antidiscrimination and, 131
    pursuit of, 132
    theologizing, 128
social responsibility, 101
Soka Gakkai, 287
solidarity, religious and racial, 63
Soloveitchik, Joseph, 167n23
Sommer, Benjamin, 89, 91
Soulen, Kendall, 79–80, 86–87
SPCU. *See* Secretariat for Promoting
    Christian Unity
specificity, turn to, 289, 291, 293, 300–301
spirit, as ground for interreligious dialogue,
    17
Spirit of God, 98, 103
spiritual guides, 287
spirituality, 93–94
    Buddhist, 18
    Christian, 14–15
    development of, 282
    individualization of, 287
    personalized, 18
spiritual laws, 255

spiritual but not religious, 277–79, 284,
    286–87
Stangl, Josef, 41
"State of Formation" (blog), 271
Stendahl, Krister, 118n38
Stransky, Thomas F., 23–24n3, 28n21, 29,
    38–39, 42
Stuber, Stanley I., 112n, 114, 116
"Summorum Pontificum" (Benedict XVI),
    187–89
supersessionism, 14, 192, 196, 198
    avoiding, 85–88
    Lutheran adoption of, 118
    rejection of, 110, 124
supplemental Buddhism, 281–83
Swidler, Leonard, 56, 229
Syllabus of Errors" (Pius IX), 1n3
syncretism, 122, 285
Synod of the Evangelical Church of the
    Rhineland, 110

Tabernacle Baptist Church (Selma, AL),
    64
Tanenbaum, Marc, 181–82
Tawhid, 219
Teaching the Historical Jesus (ed. Garber),
    89–90
Teresa of Calcutta, 283
Tertullian, 77
Thatamanil, John, 259
theological anthropology, 13, 67
Theological Commission (Vatican II), 30,
    31
theology. *See also* apophatic theology;
    black liberation theology ; black
    theology; comparative theology;
    creation theology; Incarnational
    theology; liberation theology;
    theology of religions
    clarified by dialogue, 55–56
    discussion of, parameters for, 84
    interreligious dialogue and, 55
    methodology for practicing, 55
    nonnegotiability of, 232–33
    revelation and, 123
theology of religions, 46, 237, 247,
    295–97

theology of religious diversity, 297–98
Thind, Bhagat Singh, 71–72
Third World, politics in, 2
This Changes Everything (Klein), 56
Thomas Aquinas. *See* Aquinas, Thomas
Three Teachings, 285
Tiemeier, Tracy, 266
Tillich, Paul, 102n23, 244
Tisserant, Eugène, 26
"To Do the Will of Our Father in Heaven:
    Toward a Partnership between Jews
    and Christians" (Orthodox rabbis),
    175–76
tolerance, promotion of, 12
Toolan, Thomas Joseph, 64
Touati, Charles, 162, 164
Toynbee, Arnold, 230
transcendent reality, 250
transformation, religious diversity and, 243
trialogue, 227–28
Tridentine Mass, 186
Trungpa, Chögyam, 241
truth
    absolute, 150, 239
    acknowledging of, outside one's
        tradition, 290
    attachment to, 240–42
    outside the Christian church, 148
    claims of, universalized, 241
    conception of, 253
    impartiality of, 147
    Jesus Christ and, 146
    locus of, 251
    presence of, in world religions, 255
    rays of, 13, 51, 125, 128, 204–5, 206,
        209, 253
    Vedas and, 254
tsaddik, 90–91
Tzu Chi (Buddhist Compassion Relief),
    276n5, 288

ultimate reality, conception of, 96
Union of Reform Judaism, 186
Unitatis Redintegratio (*Decree on
    Ecumenism*; Vatican II), 145, 203,
    207
United States

Catholicism in, 63–66
civil rights movement in, 63
discrimination in, 130
divine judgment on, 130
immigration in, 63, 66
Latino population in, 64n
racial ideologies in, 70–71
racial project in, 8
racism in, 64–65, 66n20
religio-racial project of, 62–64, 72,
    75–76
religious diversity in, 53
Vatican II's credibility in, 34
as white Christian nation, 71–72,
    75–76
United Synagogue of Conservative
    Judaism, 186
universal law, 257
US Conference of Catholic Bishops
    (USCCB), 186, 193–94, 198–99

Vajda, Georges, 162
van Buren, Paul, 79, 86, 165
Vatican, dialogue of, with the WCC, 48
Vatican II (Second Vatican Council), 1,
    7, 179
    credibility of, in the US, 34
    as ecumenical council, 24–25
    effects of, on Protestantism, 109
    ensuring attention for separate
        statements, 35
    enthusiasm for, 124
    Jewish observers at, 31, 184–85
    Jews and, 25–26, 27, 33
    John XXIII's announcement of, 23–24
    language of, 35
    media coverage of, 107
    Muslims and, 27–28
    non-Catholic observers at, 107–9
    non-Christian observers at, 27
    Protestant reaction to, 109–12
    role of, 156
    teachings of, on other religions, 45–46
Vedanta tradition (Hinduism), 9, 249,
    252, 253, 254, 261
Vedas, 9, 250–51, 254–55, 257, 256, 259
Velati, Mauro, 30n26

Vingt-Trois, André, 174
Vischer, Lukas, 111n13, 115, 122, 123–24
Visser't Hooft, Willem A., 108n4, 111n13,
   116n, 122, 123–24
Vivekananda, Swami, 9, 249–52
   inclusivism of, 254–57, 259
   pluralism of, 256, 257–58

Wardi, Chaim, 31
WCC. *See* World Council of Churches,
   47–48
Weigel, Gustave, 34n38
We Jews and Jesus (S. Sandmel), 161
We Jews and You Christians (S. Sandmel),
   160, 161–62
whiteness
   Enlightenment project of, 71
   religio-racial project of, 8
white protectionism, 64
white supremacy, 72
WICS. *See* World Islamic Call Society
Willebrands, Johannes, 27n15, 39, 41
Williams, George Huntston, 112n
Williams, Rowan, 227
Winant, Howard, 62

WJC. *See* World Jewish Congress
Wolfson, Elliot, 89, 91
women
   marginalization of, 230
   stories of, in human creation, 246–47
World Alliance of Reformed Churches,
   117
World Conference of Jewish
   Organizations, 184
World Convention of Churches of Christ
   (Disciples), 112n
World Council of Churches, 6, 47–48,
   111n13, 115, 116, 121, 224
World of Grace, A (ed. O'Donovan), 98
World Islamic Call Society, 223n14
World Jewish Congress, 31, 184
World Presbyterian Alliance, 112n
world religions, 6
Wyschogrod, Michael, 166, 171

Yitzhak, Levi, 90

Zaiman, Joel, 186, 187
Ziad, Homayra, 271
Zohar, 91